MUSLIM FAMILY LAW:
A Sourcebook

Muslim Family Law
A Sourcebook

KEITH HODKINSON

CROOM HELM
London & Canberra

© 1984 Keith Hodkinson
Croom Helm Ltd, Provident House, Burrell Row,
Beckenham, Kent BR3 1AT
Croom Helm Australia Pty Ltd, 28 Kembla St,
Fyshwick, ACT 2609, Australia

British Library Cataloguing in Publication Data

Hodkinson, Keith
    Muslim family law.
    1. Family — Law — Islamic countries
    I. Title
    342.6'15'0917671

    ISBN 0-7099-1256-0

Printed and bound in Great Britain by
Biddles Ltd, Guildford and King's Lynn

CONTENTS

Preface

In recent years the focus of the world's attention has been on the Islamic states of the Middle East and their laws. Yet there continues a healthy if small community of learning in the United Kingdom which emphasises the study of Islamic law as it is applied on the Indian subcontinent, a body of law which has gained the label of 'Anglo-Muhammadan law'. This emphasis I believe to be justifiable for a number of reasons. To attempt to teach Islamic law today with reference to the whole of the Islamic world is an enormous task and one which risks an unacceptable degree of superficiality for a one year University under-graduate course. By the same token to look to the law of just one state would be to lose the chance of adopting a comparative approach to the subject and to discuss the social aspects of law. Teaching of Islamic law in the United Kingdom is strongly rooted in the law of India and now of Pakistan by virtue of our historical connections with these countries and has taken on a contemporary relevance with the substantial numbers of U.K. citizens who originate from the sub-continent or are descendants of immigrants from that part of the world. The fact that an English inspired system of courts and legal representation still exists in both countries affords the common lawyer a fascinating comparative view of two entirely different bodies of law in operation in basically similar administrative and legal hierarchies. The fact that the law once applied virtually uniformly by the British in what are now India and Pakistan is being subjected to pressure for change in completely different directions — towards secularism and a uniform civil code in India, towards a 'purer' Islam in Pakistan — offers an interesting comparative study in itself of the way in which courts of law can mould a common body of doctrine to the requirements of the society in which they operate even when dealing with a system which is theoretically immutable.

One of the main difficulties which faces those who study and teach Islamic law is the lack of accessible primary

materials. The need of a source book is keenly felt. Of the
two existing works which may lay claim to fulfilling this
need, A.A.A. Fyzee's "Cases in the Muhammadan Law of India and
Pakistan" dates from 1965 in its last edition, lacks any
statutory material, and emphasises the work of the courts of
British India: of its forty-three case extracts, but four come
from the courts of post Independence India and one from
Pakistan, the centre of the most dramatic upheavals in the
subject in the past twenty-five years. H. Liebesny's "Law in
the Near and Middle East", excellent as it is in many ways,
seeks to cover (at a fairly generalised level) the whole
Muslim world and the subcontinent of India does not by any
means occupy centre stage in the study. Both books attempt to
cover the entire field of Muslim legal material in a very few
pages.

Accordingly, this work, to be followed by a companion
volume dealing with other matters, restricts itself solely to
India and Pakistan, unashamedly throws in its lot with the
modern judicial pronouncements and statutory material which
have wrought such changes in the law and treats only what may
be described as family law, and the sources and applicability
of that law. Some space has been sacrificed to give a concise
summary of the law as it is now applied which seeks to take a
middle path between the intensity of the standard practitioner
works and the generality of the many 'survey works' which the
student has to hand, although the aim of the book is nothing
more than to give a jumping off point for study of Islamic
law. I hope that the book will be useful both as a companion
to the student textbooks normally used in University courses
and in its own right as an independent work. The book is
founded on materials which were available to me up to August
of 1982; the scope of materials included is limited above all
by considerations of space and what follows is some 30 reports
and 180 pages shorter than the first draft. Much critical and
analytical material had to be excised, too, in cutting down
the length of the work but I hope that what is left will be
thought worthwhile and that the bibliography to some extent
compensates for the loss of materials by pointing the reader
in the right direction.

Some very helpful comments have been made by Dr. D. Pearl
of Cambridge University, Dr. I. Edge of the School of Oriental
and African Studies, London, and Dr. N. Calder of Manchester
University. All errors and opinions remain my responsibility.
D.P.S. Computer Services of High Wycombe patiently converted
my almost illegible manuscript into its present form and David
Croom and Melanie Crooks equally patiently restrained me from
further excesses of length and led me through the mysteries of
publication.

I have refrained from meddling with spellings, syntax
etc. in the edited extracts of judgements even where these may

seem disconcerting to the reader and I have left as much relevant material as possible in each extract. The bibliography is not by any means comprehensive and has been confined to English language works, bearing in mind the criteria of readability and accessibility.

Faculty of Law
University of Manchester

Chapter One

INTRODUCTION

The purpose of this chapter is to outline the nature of Muslim law, its principal characteristics and sources. Firstly, though, some terms should be explained. The Arab terms for law are used but rarely by Islamic scholars, who instead tend to use the terms _Shari'a_ and _fiqh_. The _Shari'a_ is the path of the believer, the way which Allah wishes man to pass, and the word is used of the collection of Allah's commands revealed in the Holy Qur'an and in the _Sunna_ or conduct of the Holy Prophet Muhammad. _Fiqh_ is the understanding, explanation and interpretation of the _Shari'a,_ as expounded in the Qur'an and _Sunna_ and the jurists who undertake this task are known as _fuqaha_ (singular _faqih_).

The _Shari'a_ is a divine law. Islam is essentially a religious code of conduct of which law in the western sense occupies but a small part. The _Shari'a_ covers all aspects of a Muslim's life and makes little distinction between moral, ethical and (in a western sense) legal questions. Christianity and the legal systems of peoples adhering to Christianity drew a clear distinction between the religious and the secular, which survives to this day (1). No such distinction is relevant to the _Shari'a_, nor are there any of the distinctions between private and public law which we are used to seeing in western systems of law (it was the triumph of Roman law to make this distinction, not taken by Attic and Semitic systems of law). Because it is a divine law a substantial part of the writings on the _Shari'a_ concerns matters which one would not expect to see in a western legal textbook and treats them in exactly the same manner as the more familiar "legal" topics. Thus many written treatises on the _Shari'a_ begin with a discussion of matters such as ritual, prayer and fasting before passing on to wills, contracts and similar matters. The obverse of this is that the _Shari'a_ pervades the whole of Islam, which is a religion of the law. Whereas western systems of law tend to analyse situations in terms of rights, the _Shari'a_ is couched in terms of duties.

The divine nature of the _Shari'a_ denies the existence of

1

any legislative authority on earth, conceding at most the
capacity of political authorities to make administrative
regulations to procure the implementation of the Shari´a.
(This is the position in Sunni law, which governs the vast
majority of Muslims. The position of the minority Shi´i sects
is somewhat different and is considered separately below.)
Linked to this is the doctrine of the immutability of the
Shari´a. Since the Shari´a is the path dictated by Allah, it
has a timeless and universal validity. If there is a
divergence between the provisions of the Shari´a and the
actual circumstances of society, then it is society not the
Shari´a which must change. Further, the authority of the law
depends not on effective sanctions for disobedience of it on
earth, but on its revealed nature as the word of Allah. This
may partly explain why the Shari´a and the jurists who expound
it have been largely content with acknowledgement of this
theoretical supremacy and have tolerated the rival
jurisdictions of administrative courts and even, to an extent,
of certain customary law (2). Indeed much of the Shari´a is
plainly not intended for enforcement by any human agency, and
even prohibitions central to Islam such as usury, drinking of
alcohol and gambling entail no Qur´anic penalty on earth.
Being a divine law, the Shari´a is extremely idealistic in
outlook. Many of its provisions - particularly (for example)
in the law of divorce, work efficiently and equitably only if
the assumption is made that the parties involved conduct
themselves in accordance with the tenets of Islam (3). The
regulation of contending interests takes second place to the
regulation of man´s relationship with Allah.

The Sources of the Shari´a
    The classical theory of the Shari´a restricts the sources
of understanding (usul al´fiqh) to four: the Qur´an; the
Sunna of the Prophet Muhammad; the ijma or consensus of the
community; and qiyas or process of analogy from the other
three sources. The theory is essentially an attempt to
reconcile the divine and the human elements in the substantive
law and is in modified form the legacy of the work of one
jurist, Shafi´i, a scholar of the 9th to 10th century A.D.,
who is justly known as the father of Islamic jurisprudence.
The significance of Shafi´i, and, through him, the classical
theory, is this: together they ordered on a coherent and
Islamic basis all law that material earlier generations had
handed down (4). This theory of sources is directed less at
the problem of developing new law than at systematising the
existing law and providing a justification for the existing
Islamic legal order. Whatever may be the extent to which the
theory actually corresponds to the historical reality of how
the substantive law was developed before Shafi´i´s time, once
the theory became accepted it dominated all study of the
Shari´a and it is in the light of this theory that later

scholars down to the present day have worked in the exposition of the law(5). It is the triumph of Shafi´i´s work which is the principal cause of the rigidity of the Shari´a and the principal obstacle to its reform. Indeed the Shari´a cannot be understood without reference to the classical theory of sources.

The Qur´an

The Qur´an is the sacred book of the Islamic faith, containing the collection of revelations made by Allah to his Prophet Muhammad in the early part of the 7th century A.D./1st century A.H. It is made up of 114 suras (chapters) which are further divided into verses. It is on this that is founded the Islamic code of conduct both towards Allah and to one´s fellow man. The injunctions of the Qur´an make no distinction between matters which the Christian would categorise as religious, moral, social and legal. The Qur´an is considered the main source of Islamic law. Yet it is by no means a code of law; it lacks any comprehensiveness in this regard. There are no more than 200 verses concerned with what we would term "law" in the western sense. Only the law of succession – which was perhaps the most radical change from the pre-Islamic tribal laws of Arabia imposed by Islam, receives anything like a detailed treatment, and institutions which one would point to as characteristic of Islamic jurisprudence such as waqf (religious endowments of property) are not even mentioned in the Qur´an. The Qur´anic texts deal with specific legal and moral problems put before the Prophet Muhammad ad hoc. There are even verses which appear to contradict each other, revealed at different places and in different circumstances, which have defeated the attempts at reconciliation of even the most ingenious jurists, who have had to fall back on attempts to discover which verse abrogates which. For the Sunni majority at least, the Qur´an provided a limited modification of the existing Arabian customary law rather than an entirely new system of law. (Again, the Shi´i attitude to the pre-Islamic customary law differs, as we shall see later in this chapter.)

The foregoing should not be taken as minimising the importance to be given to the Qur´an as a source of law either in formal or in practical terms. Apart from those verses of a specifically legal character, there are numerous texts relating to purely "moral" and "religious" issues which have been used to provide legal rulings by the process of analogy. Furthermore, of course, the moral and ethical precepts in the Qur´an are the basic criteria by which the scholars of the Shari´a judge alternative interpretations of the law and it was in the light of these precepts that they reviewed existing pre-Islamic customary law in the early days of the Hijra. Thus the influence of the Qur´an permeates the whole of the Shari´a whatever the actual source of a particular rule.

3

The Sunna of the Prophet

The Sunna or practice of the Prophet is a source second only to the Qur´an. This includes the exemplary conduct and speeches of the Prophet Muhammad. As the medium - the human medium - through which the divine law was revealed, he was the one best qualified to explain the meaning the the Qur´an and to decide problems not directly covered by the Qur´anic texts, of which, as has been said, there were many. In the classical theory, the sayings of the Prophet are infallible. But like the Qur´an, these sayings provide nothing like a comprehensive legal regime; like the Qur´an they appear ad hoc to meet specific problems presented to the Prophet for solution.

Sunna cannot exist on its own; to know of it, it has to be communicated in much the same way as decisions of legal tribunals are reported today. This caused particular problems in Islam. With the triumph of the classical theory an earnest search for hadith or reports of the practice of the Prophet was undertaken, and revealed a huge bulk of often contradictory material. The Muslim scholars were acutely aware of the possibilities of fabrication, but since the Sunna of the Prophet was divinely inspired, objective criticism of the content of the hadith was impossible. The only means of challenging the hadith was by challenging the isnad, or line of communication; the criteria for determining the validity of a hadith would be the integrity of the persons relating it, whether it was historically possible for one to have heard it from another, and so on. A separate specialist science grew of collecting and reviewing the hadith, which produced a canon of hadith held authentic (6).

Ijma

Ijma in the classical theory is the agreement of the qualified legal scholars of a given generation, and such agreement is deemed infallible. In a sense ijma is the most important source of law for only those interpretations of the Qur´an and Sunna which are ratified by the ijma are authoritative, and the interpretation put into them by ijma is definitive. A saying of the Prophet is related that "my community will never agree on an error". Once an ijma is reached on a matter it cannot in practical terms be dissented from or changed. Even an agreement to differ among the legal scholars of different schools of thought could be ratified by ijma, and it was ijma which confirmed the broad essentials of the classical theory and held that there was no more room for personal reasoning (ijtihad) in the elaboration of the law, leaving the jurists with scope for activities restricted to taqlid or imitation of their predecessors, glosses, commentaries, compendia and abridgments (7). The great problem with ijma was of course the lack of any method by which to arrive at or prove arrival at agreement. How to secure or prove the agreement of scholars who were scattered far and wide throughout the Islamic empire? This was a problem which has still not been overcome.

Qiyas

Qiyas or reasoning by analogy is the fourth source of law in the classical theory. Qiyas is conceived of as a very subordinate source of law, being the only source dependent on human intellect of a fallible kind. It is accordingly strictly circumscribed. Only when the Qur'an, the Sunna and ijma fail to provide an answer to the legal problem at hand can have one recourse to qiyas.

The Jurists and the Schools of Law

Islamic law was from an early time expounded by private jurists. Unlike many legal systems, in which procedural and substantive law are closely bound up - Roman law, for example, talks of someone having an action against another, rather than a right (8) - the Islamic scholars showed little concern for matters of procedure beyond an idealised and wholly impracticable law of evidence, and even less for the means of enforcing the law. What mattered was the rule, not its enforcement. In so far as the Shari'a was applied, its content was determined exclusively by those scholarly texts recognised as authoritative, which, without any official recognition by the state, had the force of law. Some say that another consequence of the prominent role of private jurists removed from the administration of the law was the tendency to permit the logic of their exposition of the law to triumph over the requirements of practical justice. An oft-cited example is that of the Hanafi school's interpretation of the law of divorce which many regard as a triumph of legal logic over humanity and common sense. Perhaps it was an awareness of this tendency which inspired the huge literature on hiyal by which the Islamic scholars elaborated ingenious (and sometimes ingenuous) ways of circumventing the inconvenient results to which their own logic had led them. Legal devices are characteristic of all jurists' law, but whereas in, for example, Roman law, their use was principally to facilitate the adaption of existing law to meet new requirements for which it was ill suited, they were often necessary in Islam to circumvent an impasse into which the jurists had led themselves by creating an idealised and theoretically immutable system which prohibited activities which proved practically essential.

If the values of the Shari'a are immutable there is no room for a parallel set of principles in mitigation of the hardship they cause: if the Shari'a is divine, there is no room for human legislation - thus the two modes of escape utilised by other systems of law are not available. This explains the great technicality and formality of the law. The

5

hiyal appeared principally in the field of commercial law and enabled the Muslim trader to achieve results at first sight prohibited by the Shari'a which nevertheless complied with it in form if not in substance. Usury and uncertainty in contracts were prohibited by the Qur'an. Many innocent transactions were condemned as gharah (uncertain) by the jurists because of some element of risk, because no-one could tell their value until a later date. Literally hundreds of devices were invented to circumvent such problems, and in particular the prohibition of taking interest on a loan. Not that all jurists approved the use of hiyal, however. There were many, in particular those of the Hanbali and Maliki schools of thought, who opposed them. And it is the existence of schools of law which is a further manifestation of a jurists' law.

It is a natural tendency for scholars to associate more or less formally into groups to discuss and teach. The early scholars of the Shari'a are better described as theologians than lawyers, in so far as the two disciplines can be separated in Islam; their literary output was similar in form and method, and there was and is even a certain symbiosis between the schools of law and theology, although this varied from school to school, and the schools of law seem to have displayed greater coherence and sense of identity than those of theology (9). A large number of schools based on geographical allegiance grew in the early days of Islam but two in particular came into prominence, those in Kufa and Medina. When written treatises by individual scholars began to proliferate the schools developed into followers of individuals rather than expressions of local thought and practice. Kufa followed Abu Hanifa, Medina followed Malik. Although these schools were in no sense formal bodies, the adherence to the doctrine of a particular locality and later to personalities survived even Shafi'i's attempts at unification through a common set of sources (indeed the term madhhab, or school of law, appears only after Shafi'i), and although ijma can be said to have drawn the substantive law of the schools together to some extent it also enshrined the existing differences. Indeed, Shafi'i's writings actually gave birth to a number of new schools of law, though of these only the Hanbali and Shafi'i schools survived alongside the existing Hanafi and Maliki schools. After some initial hostility these four recognised each other's mutual orthodoxy, supported by saying of the Prophet that "Difference of opinion within my community is a sign of the bounty of Allah". The schools settled down to accept spheres of influence, dependent on geographical location, political support and economic factors such as trade links (10).

The characteristics of the different schools and their doctrines broadly reflect their origins, and in some instances differences between them go beyond mere detail to fundamental

principles. The Hanafi and Maliki schools, reflecting their
foundation before the classical era and having roots in local
practice continued to assert certain subsidiary sources of law
rejected by post-Shafi´i schools. Although Shafi´i was
opposed to the idea of schools of thought, a school did in
fact grow out of his supporters, and even they modified
certain of his views on ijma. The Hanbali school represented
an extreme traditionist viewpoint, rejecting even qiyas.
Although Muslim writers in particular are prone to minimise
the differences between the schools, these should not be
underestimated: there are important differences in the
substantive laws of the Sunni schools, particularly with
regard to divorce and custody of children. The mutual
orthodoxy of the schools is reflected in the fact that a
Muslim may join or change his allegiance to any school of law
at any time, even for the sake of convenience where one
school´s legal regime proves more favourable to his purposes
than another´s. The mutual toleration shown by the schools
can be traced back to the times when geographical differences
between Kufan and Medinan law were accepted as both natural
and inevitable. One group of Muslims, however, were never
accepted as being orthodox, and we must now mention this
group: the Shi´a.

Shi´ite Islam

To this point, all discussion has been of Sunni Islam,
that is of the orthodox Islamic community to which perhaps as
many as 90% of Muslims adhere. But there is another group in
Islam set apart from the Sunnis and known as the Shi´a. This
"splinter group" arose out of a political and constitutional
schism over the succession to Caliphate or political
leadership of the Muslim community after the death of
Muhammad. The Shi´a were supporters of Ali, who was fourth
Caliph and husband of Fatima, a daughter of Muhammad. He lost
the Caliphate after a civil war with Mu´awiya who had been
governor of Syria, and was murdered. Whereas the Sunnis held
the right to the Caliphate to depend on membership of the
Quraysh tribe to which Muhammad had belonged, and on election
by the people, the Shi´a maintained that descent from the
Prophet was the criterion. Another minority group, the
Kharijites, rejected all such qualifications relying on
personal piety and ability and depending therefore on
election. But the Shi´a came to accept that descent from the
Prophet conferred a divine right to rule, and that the imam,
their ruler, was divinely inspired and thus both secular and
spiritual leader of Islam. The Shi´a themselves split after
the fourth imam into the Ithna´, ´Ashari and the Ismaili´, of
whom the former believe their last imam to have disappeared
and to be hidden but that he will return and rule again. A
third Shi´ite group, the Zaydi´, rejected the presence of
divine inspiration and require the election of the imam.

Numerically, however, the most significant of these groups are the Ithna-'Ashari and Ismaili of the Shi'a, which, because of the presence (or existence) of a divinely inspired imam, have arrived at a concept of law, indeed a concept of Islam, which is fundamentally different from that of the Sunnis.

The geographical distribution of the Shi'a is roughly as follows: the largest sect, the Ithna-'Ashari, are to be found in Iran and Iraq, with some in India; the Ismaili are centred in India; and the Zaydi in the Yemen. Given the tradition of revolutionary opposition in Shi'ite Islam, it is not altogether surprising that the most violent recent reaction to westernisation should have come in Iran, the centre of Ithna-'Ashari Islam.

The key to Shi'ite Islam is the concept of the imamate. The differences within the Shi'ite movement stem from their divergent views on the nature of the imamate and in legal terms, as well as political, it is the imamate which prevented the Sunni schools from recognising the Shi'a as orthodox. The existence of a divinely inspired imam, with supreme authority on earth removes any possibility of a place for ijma and qiyas; similarly, there is no closing of the gate of ijtihad (11) and no doctrine of taqlid. But most important of all is that, whilst the Sunni schools regard the Qur'an and the sunna of the Prophet as reforming rather than replacing the old customary tribal law, the Shi'a see Islam as a wholly new beginning, invalidating all before it, and in legal terms requiring the jurist to develop an entirely new system of law resting on the authority of the sunna of the Prophet, the Qur'an and the pronouncements of the imam. At the same time it must be admitted that (although the Shi'a deny this) certain distinctive rules of Shi'a law are on the face of it motivated by purely political as opposed to juristic considerations, particularly in the law of inheritance. But the view that political expediency explains the bulk of these differences cannot be maintained. The superficial similarity in the principal sources of law of the Shi'a to those of the Sunnis is misleading, for the relative importance of these sources differs.

The Shi'a claim that their law is a closer and purer reflection of the Qur'an and its spirit; that they have consistently given an objective interpretation of the Qur'an whereas the Sunnis interpreted it in the light of their own vested interest founded in pre-Islamic practice. It is not for us to argue this point. To the western observer the Sunni and Shi'i views represent two equally valid interpretations of Islam. But they are completely different views of Islam and this is frequently reflected in their laws. The most obvious example is in the complex areas of intestate succession, where Sunni law is much more generous to the pre-Islamic agnatic tribal heirs than Shi'i law; and in testate succession, where, for example, in Sunni law there may be no bequest in favour of an heir entitled on intestacy, and no bequest in excess of one-third of the net estate to anyone, without the consent of the heirs after the death of the testator – but where in Shi'i law a bequest may be made in favour of an heir, and bequests in excess of one-third may be consented to before or after the testator's death (12).

But more relevant to this book is the law of marriage, and in this area, the distinctive Shi'ite institution is that of mut'a or temporary marriage. Mut'a literally means enjoyment or use and it is a marriage for a fixed period of time for a payment to the women. The requirements are basically the same as for the lifelong nikah marriage, but although the children of mut'a are legitimate the wife is not entitled to maintenance and there is no limit to four wives such as exists in nikah. Sunni law deems mut'a to be nothing more than a form of prostitution sanctioned by Shi'i jurists. For the Sunnis nikah is the only possible form of marriage, which is lifelong in principle, though of course the ease with which the husband may obtain a dissolution of the union substantially qualifies this assertion in practice (13).

The Originality of the Shari'a

Orthodox Muslim opinion regards the Shari'a as completely original. This has been a matter of considerable controversy. To what extent does the Shari'a owe a debt to other systems of law? Certainly Islam was wholly original in so far as its principal sources are unique: the Qur'an and the practice of Muhammad. It is also true to say that with the expansion of Islam into new, conquered territory, every attempt was made to Islamicise. Again, the maintenance of the personal principle of law assists in the maintenance of a purity in the Shari'a, rendering it less vulnerable to infiltration of ideas not owing their origin to these two principal sources of divine knowledge. But it is hard for the western scholar to accept such opinion without qualification. On the other hand, western scholars have been – in the past at least – guilty of gross exaggeration of the influence of other legal systems, particularly the Roman, on Islamic law. One would not expect acknowledgement of Roman authority for any proposition of law appearing in an Islamic text – such being quite incompatible with an exposition of a legal system whose only authority is the will of Allah (although certain works of philosophy in Islam do acknowledge Greek influences). But this proves nothing as to the question whether or not there was any conscious and direct borrowing by Islamic scholars from the Roman system. There are likenesses and similarities between certain institutions in the systems which appear more than coincidental and seem likely to have been drawn, consciously or not, from Roman and Talmudic law by the Islamic lawyers. Moreover it is simply impossible to ignore, as the classical theory does, the profound influence of local, tribal,

9

customary law which existed in Arabia long before Islam, in a
people for whom tradition, the trodden path, is central to its
civilisation, as well as the customs of contemporary and
earlier civilisations. There seems little doubt that from the
7th century A.D. Islamic thought began to draw from the
Jewish-Christian scholars whose work was so heavily
impregnated with Hellenistic thought and rhetoric and the
Roman tradition; it seems unbelievable that the many converts
to Islam who had been brought up in these traditions should
not impart some of their ideas into the new faith and - since
law was an important part of the education of such people -
into the law. It appears likely that methods of taxation,
waqf and emphyteusis were all derived from foreign sources,
and Schacht gives two examples of alien principles which
enjoyed temporary currency in Islam in the first century of
the Hijra, those of a penalty of twice the value of an object
stolen (from Rome) and the permanent bar to marriage between
persons guilty of adultery (from Christianity) (14).
Ultimately, however, the relationship between the shari´a and
other contemporary legal systems in its formative period is
largely obscure, and many parallels are explicable simply out
of the existence of similar social conditions and
circumstances. To speak of influences in this way is not to
doubt the uniqueness of the system: indeed any similarities
are far outweighed by the differences from any contemporary
law. Even if the basic concepts used by the Islamic scholars
may have been found, consciously or unconsciously, elsewhere,
the system of law they created with them is unique to Islam.

Is the Fiqh a Juristic Discipline?

A few western scholars have argued that fiqh is not a
juristic discipline, not strictly speaking a study of law, but
rather (in the words of Bousquet (15) - one of the more
extreme proponents of this view) a deontology, or catechism,
or even an eschatology. It is argued that the divine nature
of the Shari´a which denies any human legislative authority,
the frequency of sanctions for the commission of prohibited
acts which operate only in the hereafter and not on earth, the
fact that the Shari´a has never been applied in reality in its
entirety and that the administrative rules under siyassa
shariyya and mazalim jurisdiction have in fact had far more
practical importance on the lives of Muslims, and the fact
that the fuqaha have not elaborated any general juristic
theories or principles, together relegate the fiqh to a theory
of ideal conduct.

Needless to say, these arguments have been completely
rejected by the Islamic world, and also it must be said, by
the majority of western scholars. It is true that in theory
the Shari´a depends entirely on the will of Allah, and that
this will is not subject to the control of human logic. But

this theoretical position is an exaggeration of the practical reality, since it omits the great amount of work done by the early Islamic jurists founded on ra´y (independent personal reasoning) and the important contribution made to the development of substantive law by the more disciplined forms of reasoning such as istihsan, istislah, and istishab. More often than not there is some human sanction for conduct not in conformity with the Shari´a. The most that can be said is that in certain areas of human activity the fuqaha felt that conduct could not be viewed from a strictly legal point of view but had to be sanctioned by religious means only or left to moral compulsion. It has always been the case, and remains the case today, that in matters of status, gift and succession the Shari´a governs most Muslims. It is true that outside these areas the doctrine of the Shari´a has often not been applied in practice, but this does not deprive it of the character of law and reduce it to the level of a moral code. The sanctions for breach remain; it merely happens that the political authorities do not enforce it. Nor should one conclude that the rules of the Shari´a on family succession, contracts and the like are not law merely because they are treated in the same manner as and alongside matters such as ritual and prayer, in the texts of the fuqaha. Finally, the argument that Islamic scholars failed to develop a general theory seems to be fallacious in two respects. Firstly, it is an exaggeration, at least so far as modern times are concerned, in which works have appeared couched in terms of general theory, and in the Majalla (the Turkish Code of 1876) one finds a series of 90 maxims setting out general underlying principles of evidence and presumptions of the burden of proof, and some principles of substantive law. Secondly, a failure to develop a general theory of civil obligation or criminal liability does not necessarily indicate a system lacking any juristic character. A similar reluctance to abandon a casuistic mode of reasoning is manifest throughout most of Roman legal history, yet no-one would seek to deny that the ius civile has the status of a legal system, indeed one of the great legal systems. From the Roman point of view this reluctance seems to have been the result of a feeling that abstraction was too dangerous, given that man was unable to forsee all possible events to which the general rule devised might have to be applied. The Muslim scholars saw the additional problem that they might be accused of seeking to decree norms claiming a universality equal to those of the divinely inspired Qur´an and sunna of the Prophet, which would be tantamount to setting up in competition with Allah as a law maker.

Muslim law in India and Pakistan

Muslim law as it is applied in India and Pakistan is sometimes known as Anglo-muhammadan law (16) because of the influence of English law and the administration of justice in the subcontinent, the legacy of which remains clear today. The Muslim law as applied in the subcontinent differs in many important respects from the 'pure' classical law both in substance and in the formal sources relied on. This was not a state of affairs brought about intentionally by the British in India, but an inevitable result of the decision to take over the administration of native law in the normal civil courts rather than to maintain a distinct religious court, and to staff these courts with judges trained in an alien legal system. It was in part, too, a legacy of the administration of justice in the Mughal Empire which had preceded British rule in the subcontinent (17).

Firstly, the literary sources relied on by the courts were themselves not entirely orthodox. The principal authoritative works of the Indian sub-continent, the <u>Fatawa al - Alamgiriyya</u>, and the <u>Hedaya</u>, contained a number of doctrines and legal practices not sanctioned in the classical law of the middle east but accepted by the Indian jurists and it was from these texts that the British courts had to derive their knowledge of the law, through their translations and the advice of local Muslim scholars. In a similar way the advice of the local <u>qadis</u> led to the introduction of much customary law without any truly Islamic basis (18).

Secondly, the judiciary, even in later times when the recruits included Indian Muslims, was trained in the English law and was usually unable to read the original sources. Where his limited knowledge of the Muslim law did not furnish him with a solution to the legal problem before him, the English trained judge quite naturally turned to the English law or analysed Muslim concepts in English terms where there was a superficial similarity, a practice which inevitably led to the exposition of doctrines incompatible with the Muslim law (19). There is an obvious temptation to assume a familiar concept to be identical to one's own.

Thirdly, with a British administration of justice came the doctrine of precedent which meant that incorrect interpretations of the Muslim law came to be perpetuated (20). This had a profound effect on the substantive law. Even the Privy Council, which was not obliged to do so, preferred to apply earlier decisions of the Courts of India.

Fourthly, such misinterpretations were multiplied by the fact that the British courts misunderstood the doctrine of <u>taqlid</u> and felt able in the absence of a binding precedent to propound doctrines for which no authority could be found in the Muslim texts. Allied to this was the influence of the formula "justice equity and good conscience" a term which was identified by Lord Hobhouse to mean "the rules of English law found applicable to Indian society and circumstances" (21). Various enactments invested the courts of British India with the power to give judgement in accordance with this formula

12

(or similar ones) in the absence of a specific direction as to which rule of law to apply (22). This jurisdiction caused the indirect introduction of principles of the common law and equity into a wide range of problems, affecting both substantive rules and principles of interpretation and construction of documents.

As a result of these factors, although the occasions on which the British expressly reformed the Muslim law by statute were relatively few (23), in those areas where the Muslim law continued to be applied the substantive law became markedly different from that of the classical shari'a (24). Evaluations of this hybrid jurisprudence have differed but it is the uniqueness of the law of Islam in the subcontinent that makes it worthy of study in its own right and not merely as a footnote to a study of the classical law of the middle east. In the view of Schacht "Out of this law there has grown a new Anglo-Muhammadan jurisprudence, the aim of which, in contrast with Islamic jurisprudence during the formative period of Islamic law, is not to evaluate a given body of legal raw material from the Islamic angle, but to apply by modern English jurisprudence, autonomous judicial principles to Anglo-Muhammadan law. This law and the jurisprudence based on it is a unique and most successful result of the symbiosis of Islamic and of English legal thought in British India (25)."

Since Independence and Partition one of the major points of interest in the study of Muslim law on the Indian subcontinent has been to observe the paths taken by the Islamic Republic of Pakistan and the secular Republic of India in applying and developing the body of law which they share as a legacy of British rule. This requires some elucidation of the constitutional backgrounds to the two Republics.

Pakistan

Pakistan has had three Constitutions, promulgated in 1956, 1962 and most recently in 1973. The present Constitution of 1973 is in abeyance but was substantially retained by General Zia after his military coup in 1977, though now with significant amendments. The Constitution contains some extremely important provisions for the development of Muslim law.

Chief Martial Law Administrator's Order No.1 of 1981

2. **Certain provisions of Constitution to form part of Order:-**
The following Articles of the Constitution of the Islamic Republic of Pakistan, 1973, which is abeyance, in this Order referred to as the Constitution, shall be deemed to form part of this Order and shall have effect subject to this Order and any Order made by the President or the Chief Martial Law Administrator, namely:-

1, 2, 3, 4, 5(1), 41(1)-(2), 45, 78, 79, 89, 97, 98, 99, 100,
101(1), 102, 118, 119, 128, 137-143, 145-161, 163-181,
183-195, 197, 201, 203B, 203C(1), (2), (5)-(9), 203D, 203J,
204-206, 207(1) and 04-206, 207(1) and (3), 208-212, 227-232,
234, 237, 240-266, 268, 269, 274, 275 and 277-279.
Constitution of the Islamic Republic of Pakistan,1973

Article 2.
Islam shall be the state of religion of Pakistan.

Article 31.
(1) Steps shall be take to enable the Muslims of Pakistan,
individually and collectively, to order their lives in
accordance with the fundamental principles and basic concepts
of Islam and to provide facilities whereby they may be enabled
to understand the meaning of life according to the Holy Qur´an
and Sunnah.

Article 227.
(1) All existing laws shall be brought in conformity with the
Injunctions of Islam as laid down in the Holy Quran and
Sunnah, in this Part referred to as the Injunctions of Islam,
and no law shall be enacted which is repugnant to such
Injunctions.
Explanation: In the application of this clause to the
personal law of any Muslim sect, the expression "Quran and
Sunnah" shall mean the Quran and Sunnah as interpreted by that
sect.
(2) Effect shall be given to the provisions of clause (1)
only in the manner provided in this part.
(3) Nothing in this Part shall effect the personal laws of
non-Muslim citizens or their status as citizens.

Article 228.
(1) There shall be, constituted within a period of ninety
days from the commencing day, a council of Islamic Ideology,
in this part referred to as the Islamic Council.
(2) The Islamic Council shall consist of such members, being
not less than eight and not more than twenty as the President
may appoint from amongst persons having knowledge of the
principles and philosophy of Islam as enunciated in the Holy
Quran and Sunnah, or understanding of the economic, political,
legal or administrative problems of Pakistan.
(3) While appointing members of the Islamic Council, the
President shall ensure that-
      (a)   so far as practicable various schools of thought
           are represented in the Council;
      (b)   not less than two of the members are persons each
           of whom is, or has been a Judge of the Supreme
           Court or of a High Court.
      (c)   not less than four of the members are persons each

> of whom has been engaged for a period of not less than fifteen years, in Islamic research or instruction; and
>
> (d)   at least one member is a woman.

(4)   The President shall appoint one of the members referred to in paragraph (b) of clause (3) to be the Chairman of the Islamic Council.

(5)   Subject to clause (6), a member of the Islamic Council shall hold office for a period of three years.

(6)   A member may, by writing under his hand addressed to the President, resign his office or may be removed by the President upon the passing of a resolution for his removal by a majority of the total membership of the Islamic Council.

Article 229.

The President or the Governor of a Province may, or if two-fifths of its total membership so requires, a House or a Provincial Assembly shall, refer to the Islamic Council for advice any question as to whether a proposed law is or is not repugnant to the Injunctions of Islam.

Article 230.

(1)   The function of the Islamic Council shall be-

> (a)   to make recommendations to Parliament and the Provincial Assemblies as to the ways and means of enabling to encourage the Muslims of Pakistan to order their lives individually and collectively in all respects in accordance with the principles and concepts of Islam as enunciated in the Holy Quran and Sunnah;
>
> (b)   to advise a House, a Provincial Assembly, the President or a Governor on any question referred to the Council as to whether a proposed law is or is not repugnant to the Injunctions of Islam;
>
> (c)   to make recommendations as to the measures for bringing existing laws into conformity with the Injunctions of Islam and the stages by which such measures should be brought into effect; and
>
> (d)   to compile in a suitable form, for the guidance of Parliament and the Provincial Assemblies, such Injunctions of Islam as can be given legislative effect.

(2)   When, under Article 229, a question is referred by a House, a Provincial Assembly, the President or a Governor to the Islamic Council, the Council shall, within fifteen days thereof, inform the House, the Assembly, the President or the Governor, as the case may be, of the period within which the Council expects to be able to furnish that advice.

(3)   Where a House, a Provincial Assembly, the President or the Governor, as the case may be, considers that, in the

public interest, the making of the proposed law in relation to which the question arose should not be postponed until the advice of the Islamic Council is furnished, the law may be made before the advice is furnished:

Provided that, where a law is referred for advice to the Islamic Council and the Council advises that the law is repugnant to the Injunctions of Islam, the House or, as the case may be, the Provincial Assembly, the President or the Governor shall reconsider the law so made.

(4) The Islamic Council shall submit its final report within seven years of its appointment, and shall submit an annual interim report. The report, whether interim or final, shall be laid for discussion before both Houses and each Provincial Assembly within six months of its receipt, and Parliament and the Assembly, after considering the report, shall enact laws in respect thereof within a period of two years of the final report.

Article 231.

The proceedings of the Islamic Council shall be regulated by rules of procedure to be made by the Council with approval of the President.

In addition to these institutions there was founded in 1962, at the same time as the Islamic Council, the Central Institute of Islamic Research whose function was to undertake Islamic research and instruction in Islam for the purpose of assisting in the reconstruction of Islamic society on a truly Islamic basis. The Institute's constitution provided it with four objectives.

(1) To define Islam in terms of its fundamentals in a rational and liberal manner and to emphasise among others the basic Islamic ideals of universal brotherhood, tolerance and social justice.
(2) To interpret the teachings of Islam in such a way as to bring out its dynamic character in the context of intellectual and scientific progress of the modern world.
(3) To carry out research in the contribution of Islam to thought, science and culture with a view to enabling Muslims to recapture an eminent position in these fields
(4) To take appropriate measures for organising and encouraging research in Islamic history, philosophy, law, jurisprudence, etc.

It will be apparent that this constitution has a definite bias in the sense that by its own terms it maps out a certain interpretation and development of Islamic thought, requiring, for example, rational and liberal interpretations, orientated around intellectual and scientific progress of the modern

world. This is quite consistent with the general pattern of
the Islamic bodies of the 1960´s in Pakistan, which were
plainly characterised by a liberal ´modernist´ approach. This
is especially true of the legislature (for example in its
enactment of substantial modernist reforms in the Muslim
Family Laws Ordinance 1961) and of the courts (for example in
the Supreme Court´s decision in the famous Khurshid Bibi case)
(26). It would still be true to say that on balance the
movement of Pakistan since Partition up until the present day
has been towards a modernist stance. The tide does now seem
to be turning, however, although it is too early to say
whether this will be a short term reaction to the past twenty
years or not. The recent strong revival of Islamic
fundamentalism world wide has affected Pakistan and the
Islamicisation process has been accelerated by the Zia
Government, though with a more traditionalist emphasis than
was true of the earlier regimes, albeit that some response to
the pressure for fundamentalist measures may be found even
under the Bhutto regime in 1977. These moves to a ´purer´
Islam are to be found in reforms both in public and private
law as part of a wider range of social and economic reforms
designed to reintroduce a traditional Islamic political,
social and economic order into Pakistan (27). But so far
these reforms have not greatly affected the law of the family
which is the subject of this book, the one major exception
being the reintroduction of Islamic definitions of and
penalties for sexual offences including, in English legal
terms, adultery and fornication (28). More important for
present purposes is the introduction in 1978 of Shariat
Benches attached to each of the Provincial High Courts,
subsequently replaced by one Federal Shariat Court. The
constitution and function of this court is set out below.

Constitution of the Islamic Republic of Pakistan 1973.

Article 203C.
The Federal Shariat Court.
(1) There shall be constituted for the purposes of this
chapter a court to be called the Federal Shariat Court.
(2) The Court shall consist of not more than eight Muslim
members, including the Chairman, to be appointed by the
President.
(3) The Chairman shall be a person who is, or has been or is
qualified to be a Judge of the Supreme Court and a member
shall be a person who is, or has been or is qualified to be a
Judge of a High Court.
(4) The Chairman and a member shall hold office for a period
not exceeding three years, but may be appointed for such
further term or terms as the President may determine:
Provided that a Judge of a High Court shall not be
appointed to be a member for a period exceeding one year

except with his consent and, except where the Judge is himself the Chief Justice, and after consultation by the President with the Chief Justice of the High Court.

(4A) The Chairman, if he is not a Judge of the Supreme Court, and a member who is not a Judge of a High Court, may by writing under his hand addressed to the President, resign his office.

(5) A Judge of a High Court who does not accept appointment as a member shall be deemed to have retired from his office and, on such retirement, shall be entitled to receive a pension calculated on the basis of the length of his service as Judge and total service, if any, in the service of Pakistan.

(6) The Principal seat of the Court shall be at Islamabad, but the Court may from time to time sit in such other places in Pakistan as the Chairman may, with the approval of the President, appoint.

(7) Before entering upon office, the Chairman and a member shall make before the President or a person nominated by him oath in the form set out, in the Third Schedule.

(8) At any time when the Chairman or a member is absent or is unable to perform the functions of his office, the president shall appoint another person qualified for the purpose to act as Chairman or, as the case may be, member.

(9) A Chairman who is not a Judge of the Supreme Court shall be entitled to the same salary, allowances and privileges as are admissable to a Judge of the Supreme Court and a member who is not a Judge of a High Court shall be entitled to the same salary, allowances and privileges as are admissible to a Judge of a High Court.

Article 203D.

Powers, jurisdiction and functions of the Court.

(1) The Court may, on the petition of a citizen of Pakistan or the Federal Government or a Provincial Government, examine and decide the question whether or not any law or provision of law is repugnant to the Injunctions of Islam as laid down in the Holy Quran and Sunnah of the Holy Prophet, hereinafter referred to as the Injunctions of Islam.

(2) If the Court decides that any law or provision of the law is repugnant to the Injunctions of Islam, it shall set out in its decision—

    (a)   the reasons for its holding that opinion; and

    (b)   the extent to which such a law or provision is so repugnant;

and specify the day on which the decision shall take effect.

(3) If any law or provision of law is held by the Court to be repugnant to the Injunctions of Islam—

    (a)   the President in the case of a law with respect to a matter in the Federal Legislative List or the Concurrent Legislative List, or the Governor in

The case of a law with respect to a matter not enumerated in either of those Lists, shall take steps to amend the law so as to bring such law or provision into conformity with the Injunctions of Islam; and

(b) such law or provision shall, to the extent to which it is held to be repugnant, cease to have effect on the day on which the decision of the Court takes effect.

The role of this new Court is considered by the case of Muhammad Riaz (29) considered below (30). The implications of a complete adoption of classical Islamic law where considered in the Supreme Court in Kaikaus v President of Pakistan (31) part of the judgment from which is reproduced below (32).

In addition to all these institutions there was created in 1982 a Federal Council (Majlis - e - Shura) consisting of such persons as the President might determine, to perform such functions as might be specified by the President by order. The functions prescribed for it have turned out to be to help the Government to accelerate the process of the enforcement of Islam; to create conditions congenial for the establishment in the country of Islamic democracy; and to suggest plans of action for the purpose; to benefit the Government with its opinion and wisdom on important national and international matters; and to assist the Government in overcoming economic and social difficulties of the people (33).

Finally it is worth noting the continued suspension of the following two articles of the Constitution. There are well founded fears among the non-Muslims of Pakistan that they are to lose such rights permanently. There exist already proposals for separate assemblies and electorates for the non-Muslim minorities, and some can see in them parallels with proposals in South Africa, which they characterise as tantamount to "religious apartheid".

Article 20.
"Subject to law, public order and morality,-

(a) every citizen shall have the right to profess, practise and propagate his religion, and

(b) every religious denomination and every sect thereof shall have the right to establish, maintain and manage its religious institutions."

Article 36.
"The state shall safeguard the legitimate rights and interests of minorities, including their due representation in the Federal and Provincial services."

It must be admitted, however, that these were not particularly strong provisions in the first place.

India
Constitution of the Republic of India

Art. 372 Continuance in force of existing laws and their adaption

(1)   Notwithstanding the repeal by this Constitution of the enactments referred to in art. 395 (34) but subject to the other provisions of this Constitution all the laws in force in the territory of India immediately before the commencement of this Constitution shall continue in force therein until altered or repealed or amended by a competent legislature or other competent authority.

Art. 13 Laws inconsistent or in derogation of the fundamental rights

(1)   All laws in force in the territory of India immediately before the commencement of this Constitution, insofar as they are inconsistent with the provisions of this Part [on fundamental rights], shall, to the extent of such inconsistency, be void.
(2)   The State shall not make any law which takes away or abridges the rights conferred by this Part and any law made in contravention of this clause shall to the extent of the contravention be void.

Art. 15 Prohibition of discrimination on grounds of religion, race, caste, sex, place of birth or any of them

(1)   The State shall not discriminate against any citizen on grounds only of religion, race, caste, sex, place of birth or any of them.
(2)   Nothing in this article shall prevent the State from making any special provision for women and children.

Art. 25 Freedom of conscience and free profession practice and propagation of religion.

(1)   Subject to public order, morality and health and to the other provisions of this Part, all persons are equally entitled to freedom of conscience and the right freely to profess practise and propagate religion.
(2)   Nothing in this article shall affect the operation of any existing law or prevent the State from making any law—
      (a)   regulating or restricting any economic, financial, political or other secular activity which may be associated with religious practice.....

Art. 26 Freedom to manage religious affairs

Subject to public order, morality and health, every religious denomination or any section thereof shall have the right—
      (a)   to establish and maintain institutions for religious and charitable purposes;

(b)   to manage its own affairs in matters of religion;

(c)   to own and acquire moveable and immoveable property;

(d)   to administer such property in accordance with law.

Art. 44 <u>Uniform civil code for the citizens</u>
The State shall endeavour to secure for the citizens a uniform civil code throughout the territory of India.

These constitutional provisions have raised a number of difficult issues for a Republic in which Muslims are a minority.

Article 372 (1) has been interpreted as establishing that the Muslim personal law continues to be applicable to Muslims in independent India save insofar as superseded or amended by legislation before independence (35). The State retains power to legislate on matters with which the Muslim law is concerned and no provision of the Constitution exempts Muslim law from statutory reform, at least on the majority view of the interpretation to be given to Articles 25 and 26 of the Constitution, which maintains that the personal law is not a matter of religion but merely a secular activity which may be associated with religious practice. This of course would be fervently denied by the bulk of the Muslim (and perhaps Hindu) community in India.
Article 13 has been held by the courts on a number of occasions not to extend to the personal law of the religious communities of India so as to be capable of rendering, for instance, some provision of Muslim law void on the basis that it discriminates against non-Muslims (36). This finding has been subject to severe criticism by academics on the ground that whereas the Muslim law of marriage or divorce as found in the Dissolution of Muslim Marriages Act 1939 is open to challenge Under Art. 13 other parts of that law, not having been reformed or codified, are immune, even thought they may be more "unconstitutional". Nevertheless the judiciary's reading of the Article is maintained, no matter how nonsensical the result may be.
Article 44 has been the subject of the greatest controversy for in it some see an attack on the principles found in Articles 25 and 26, by setting out to abolish the Muslim personal law. The protagonists of the Article point to the interpretation of these earlier Articles adopted by the courts and label the current personal law system a medieval idea which has no place in the modern world. The Article has become entangled in the fundamental conflict between those secularists who see religion as a matter purely of conscience

21

and those who maintain the traditional view of Islam as governing all aspects of life, rejecting any idea of a secular legal code. The controversy is largely political though "theological, social, historical and even philosophical arguments are advanced against the mandate of Article 44" (37). It is unlikely that any government in the foreseeable future would risk sufficient political ill-will in attempting to implement the Article. The Hindu majority is largely indifferent and the Muslim minority almost unanimously opposed to any such uniform code behind which they fear that a Hindu-inspired code would be imposed on them or failing that a code which ignored the religious and cultural demands of Islam. The discussion of article 44 in India has been rather disappointingly unedifying.

If any progress is to be made in this direction it seems more likely to come by way of providing an alternative secular legal regime into which one may opt if one wishes, along the lines of the regime under the Special Marriage Act 1954 (38), while retaining the personal laws for those who wish to keep them. This half way house toward a fused civil code would function as a demonstration model for those who fear that an article 44 code would disregard their religious and cultural interests entirely. Of course, this does not mean that the majority of Muslims would take advantage of this facility if it was offered to them: indeed the evidence, such as it is, from the Special Marriage Act would suggest virtual non-use of its provisions by the Muslim community, though this is largely attributable to a very substantial ignorance of the Act's existence among the Muslim community (39). So long as there is such widespread opposition even to reforms of the Muslim law itself - even where that law is not the classical <u>Shari'a</u> but the Anglo-muhammadan jurisprudence of the 19th century - the prospect of the even more profound changes which would accompany a uniform civil code ever being accepted looks bleak indeed.

The Applicability of Muslim Law Today

India

Muslim Personal Law (Shariat) Application Act 1937

s.1 (1) This Act may be called the Muslim Personal Law (Shariat) Application Act 1937.

(2) It extends to the whole of India except the state of Jammu and Kashmir.

s.2 Notwithstanding any custom or usage to the contrary, in all questions save questions relating to agricultural land regarding intestate succession, special property of females, including special property inherited or obtained under contract or gift or any other provision of personal law,

22

marriage, dissolution of marriage, including talaq, ila, zihar, lian, khula and mubaraat, maintenance, dower, guardianship, gifts, trusts and trust properties, and waqfs other than charities and charitable institutions and charitable and religious endowments, the rule of decision in cases where the parties are Muslims shall be the Muslim Personal Law (Shariat).

s.3 (1) Any person who satisfies the prescribed authority-
   (a)   that he is a Muslim, and
   (b)   that he is competent to contract within the meaning of section 11 of the Indian Contract Act, 1872, and
   (c)   that he is a resident of the territory to which this Act extends
may by declaration in the prescribed form and filed before the prescribed authority declare that he desires to obtain the benefit of the provisions of this section and thereafter the provisions of Section 2 shall apply to the declarant and all his minor children and their descendants as if in addition to the matters enumerated therein adoption, wills and legacies were also specified.

It will be seen that the principal aim of this legislation was to ensure that the ´pure´ Muslim law as interpreted in the subcontinent should prevail over customary laws which had caused considerable social problems insofar as their scope was uncertain and their application deemed detrimental to the interests of women in comparison with the rights afforded them by the Muslim law, particularly in respect of rights of succession, which under the customary laws (based on purely agnatic line) excluded all woman except the widow and daughter, who were themselves restricted to at best a life interest in the estate of the deceased. Note how in respect of most matters, ie. those specified in s.2 of the Act, the Muslim law applies automatically where the parties are both Muslims, but in the case of adoption, wills and legacies a Muslim who desires to be governed by the Muslim law must opt in to the Act. The net effect of the Act was to apply Muslim law to matters which it had not governed in the subcontinent for centuries; but the exemption for agricultural land is of significance. Despite the express direction to apply the Muslim law in these matters these rules will not apply where modified or replaced by statute, as for example in the case of the rules of intestate succession as affected by the Caste Disabilities (Removal) Act 1850 (40).

A number of states have amended the provisions of this central Act, thereby extending the applicability of the Muslim law (41). Furthermore there exist certain Acts which compel courts to apply the Muslim law of succession to specific Muslim communities such as the Cutchi Memons and the Mapillas (42). Consideration of these matters is outside the scope of this book.

Various statutes of general application expressly exempt from their scope Muslim citizens, thereby leaving the courts to apply the Muslim law, important examples being the Dowry Prohibition Act 1961 and the Transfer of Property Act 1882, and the Indian Succession Act 1925.

In the absence of statutory authority for the application of Muslim law, certain rules may be applied on the basis of justice, equity and good conscience: chief among them being the laws of pre-emption which throughout most of India have no express or implied statutory authority and are applied by the courts purely on the basis of this formula (43). In the absence of any custom to the contrary the Muslim law of wills and legacies is applied automatically under the authority of this formula.

Occasionally, just as it is possible to opt into the Muslim law in respect of those matters dealt with into s.3 of the 1937 Act, it is possible to opt out of the Muslim law into a secular regime. Such is the case with the law of marriage, in which it is possible to opt to be governed by the Special Marriage Act (44).

Pakistan

West Pakistan Muslim Personal Law (Shariat) Application Act 1962 (as amended in 1963)

s.1 (1) This Act may be called the West Pakistan Muslim Personal Law (Shariat) Application Act 1962.

(2) It extends to the whole of the province of West Pakistan except the Tribal Areas.

s.2 Notwithstanding any custom or usage, in all questions regarding succession (whether testate or intestate), special property of females, betrothal, marriage, divorce, dower, adoption, guardianship, minority, legitimacy or bastardy, family relations, Waqfs, trust and trust properties, the rule of decision, subject to the provisions of any enactment for the time being in force, shall be the Muslim Personal Law (Shariat) in cases where the parties are Muslims.

s.3 The limited estates in respect of immovable property held by Muslim females under the Customary Law are hereby terminated:

Provided that nothing herein contained shall apply to any such estate saved by any enactment, repealed by this Act, and the estates so excepted shall continue to be governed by that enactment, notwithstanding its repeal by this Act.

s.4 Where a will providing for more than one legatee succeeding to the testator's property one after the other is operative at the commencement of this Act, its further

24

operation shall cease upon the death of the legatee-in-enjoyment.

s.5 The life estate terminated under s.3 or the property in respect of which the further operation of a will has ceased under s.4 shall devolve upon such persons as would have been entitled to succeed under the Muslim Personal Law (Shariat) upon the death of the last full owner or the testator as though he had died intestate; and if any heir has died in the meantime, his share shall devolve in accordance with the Shariat on such persons as would have succeeded him, if he had died immediately after the termination of the life estate or the death of the said legatee:

Provided that the share to which a Muslim female holding limited estate under Customary law would have been entitled under the Muslim Personal Law (Shariat) upon the death of the last full owner shall devolve on her.

s.6 Save as expressly provided by the provisions of sections 3,4 and 5, this Act shall have no retrospective operation.

s.7 (repeals earlier enactments)

The significant differences between this Act and the Indian Act on which it is modelled are firstly that agricultural land is covered by the Act; secondly, that the rules of testate succession apply by force of statute automatically even where there is a customary rule to the contrary; and thirdly, the provisions of ss. 3,4 and 5 on life estates do not appear in the Indian Act.

Neither of these two Acts answers two questions of vital importance. Firstly, who qualifies as a Muslim? Secondly, what law is applicable when one of the parties to a dispute is not a Muslim?

The first question raises particularly difficult issues intimately bound up with questions of faith, but two preliminary points can be made. A person who is born the child of a Muslim father is presumed to be a Muslim; and one who has converted to Islam from another faith or from atheism or agnosticism is deemed as much a Muslim as a person born into the faith. But there is no consensus as the the exact scope of beliefs admitted to the Muslim faith and there is conflicting case law on the matter of proof of adherence to Islam by conversion. The question defeated official enquiries such as the Pakistani Munir Report of 1954, which failed to reach agreement on the correct definition of a Muslim, and what is in many ways an intensely political issue has come before the courts, which, able to deal with pragmatic questions of proof, are perhaps ill suited to decisions on matters of theology. It is likely that in the light of recent events in Pakistan we shall see a divergence between the two countries as to the scope of the term Muslim, insofar as the

Ahmadis have traditionally been regarded as Muslim in India, but are no longer to be considered such in Pakistan.

Pakistan
<u>Chief Martial Law Administrator's Order No. 1 of 1981</u>
s.1A<u>Definitions</u> - In the Constitution and this Order and all enactments and other legal instruments, unless there is anything repugnant in the subject or context,-

> (a) "Muslim" means a person who believes in the unity and oneness of Almighty Allah, in the absolute and unqualified finality of the Prophethood of Muhammad (peace be upon him), the last of the prophets, and does not believe in or recognise as, a prophet or religious reformer, any person who claimed or claims to be a prophet, in any sense of the word or of any description whatsoever, after Muhammad (peace be upon him); and
>
> (b) "non-Muslim" means a person who is not a Muslim and includes a person belonging to the Christian, Hindu, Sikh, Buddhist or Parsi community, a person of the Quadiani group or the Lahori group (who call themselves 'Ahmadis' or by any other name), or a Bahai, and a person belonging to any of the scheduled castes.

In the matter of conversion it can be said that two lines of authority exist: one suggests that an objective test must be adopted, requiring some evidence of actual practice of the faith to which it is claimed that conversion has been made (45). The other imposes a purely subjective test and permits the mere profession of Islam, without more, as proof of the conversion, even if the motives behind the conversion be suspect (46). This second line of authority seems generally to prevail, at least so far as conversion to Islam is concerned (47). The Muslim law, as has been said presumes the child of á Muslim man to be Muslim too: and it seems that this is so strong a presumption that it can even survive the baptism of the child into the Catholic faith in certain cases (48).

The second question unanswered by the Acts, that of the law applicable where only one of the parties is a Muslim, is more difficult. The law has to be deduced from a confusing - and at times conflicting - variety of sources, both statutory and non-statutory, which provide different solutions for different disputes. There are no consistent principles, and detailed consideration of the practical and theoretical problems and their answers are outside the scope of this book (49).

26

Mst KHURSHID JAN (Apellant) v FAZAL DAD (Respondent)
PLD 1964 (W.P.) Lahore 558

[This case required the High Court of Lahore to consider three
questions:
    (i)   What are the sources of Muslim law?
    (ii)   What are the rules of interpretation of Muslim law
         and can Courts differ from the views of Imams and
         other jurisconsults of Muslim law on grounds of
         public policy, justice, equity and good
         conscience?
    (iii) How are the Courts to be guided in case of
         conflict of views among the founders of different
         schools of Muslim law and their disciples, other
         A´imma and Faqihs?]

YAQUB ALI J. - 6. The known sources of Muslim Law are Qur´an,
Sunnah ie. precepts and the conduct of the Holy Prophet (may
peace be upon him), ´Ijama´, Qiyas and Ijtihad.
Qur´an:
    Qur´an consists of divine revelations and is divided into
chapters and verses. It was compiled by Hazrat Abu Bakr and
the first Caliph, within two years of the demise of the Holy
Prophet and completed in its present form by Hazrat Usman the
third Caliph, ten years later. The arrangement is not the
same in which it was revealed but is said to be in accordance
with the plan of the Holy Prophet. The rules of law are
mostly contained in Surat-ul-Baqara, Surat-un-Nisa,
Surat-al-Imran, Surat-ul-Maida, Surat-un-Noor, Surat-ut-Talaq
and Surat-ul-Bano Israel. The Ordinances contained in the
Qur´an were revealed to settle questions which arose for
determination by the Prophet and to repeal the objectionable
customs like unforbidden gambling usury and unlimited polygamy
among Arabs and for effecting social reforms like the raising
of the status of the women, regulating succession and
inheritance on equitable basis, providing protection to minors
and persons suffering from disabilities and to provide
punishment for maintaining law and order. Qur´an is the
absolute word of God, and if there is a clear injunction in
it, that is the rule of decision on the facts of a given case.
There are detailed rules for interpretation of the Qur´an.
Some of them are collected in Chapter IV of Al-Risala by Imam
Al-Shafi under the heading "on the Book of God" eg. general
declarations of the Qur´an intended to be general in which the
particular is included, the explicit general declaration of
the Qur´an in which the general and the particular are
included; the explicit general declaration of the Qur´an
intended to be all particular; category of declaration the

meaning of which is clarified by the context; category of declaration the wording of which indicates the implicit, not the explicit meaning and general declaration which the Sunna specifically indicates is meant to be particular. The following instance is quoted by Imam Al-Shafi´ under the last-named principle which makes its meaning explicit:-

"God, glorious be His praise, said:

And his parents each receive a sixth of what he has left, if he has children, but if he has no children and his heirs are his parents, then his mother receives a third: if, however, he has brothers, his mother receives a sixth (Q.IV 12).

"And He Said:

And half of what your wives leave belongs to you if they have no children; but if they have children, a fourth of what they have belongs to you after any bequests may have been made or debts (have been paid)..... To them belongs a fourth of what you leave, if you have no children; if you have children, an eighth of what you leave belongs to them, after any bequests you may have made or debts (have been paid). If a man or a woman-whose property is inherited has no direct heirs, but has a brother or a sister, each of the two receives a sixth; if they be more than that, they share in a third, after any bequests you may have made or debts (have been paid), without prejudice one to the other; a charge from God; verily God is knowing: gracious (Q.IV 13,15-16).

"Thus God made it plain that fathers and wives are among those He named in various circumstances, the terms being general; but the Sunna of the Prophet indicated that this is intended to mean only some fathers and wives, excluding others, provided that the religion of the fathers, children and wives is the same (ie. Islam) and that each heir is neither a killer nor a slave. And He said:

After any bequests he may have made or debts (have been paid)(Q.IV 15).

"The Prophet made it clear that bequests must not exceed one third (of the deceased´s estate), and the heirs receive the two-thirds; and he (also) made it clear that debts take precedence over bequests and inheritance and that neither the bequest nor the inheritance (should be distributed) until the creditors are (first) paid. Thus if it were not for the evidence of the Sunna and the consensus of the people, there would be no inheritance until after the bequest (was paid) and the bequest would not fail to take precedence over the debt, or be on equal footing with the debt."

Sunnah:

7. But the divine revelations did not cover the facts of every case, the dicta of the Holy Prophet, to whom cases were brought for decision were, therefore, treated as supplements to the Divine Ordinances and accorded the same sanctity. In the beginning there was a controversy as the the authority of Sunnah, for, some believed that if later in point of time it repealed the text of Qur´an. The accepted position, however, is that it is the most authentic source of Islamic Law next to Qur´an. This is based on the doctrine that the holy Prophet, as a recipient of the message of God, was guided by Him in his narrative and action. These both are, thus, the words of God, one expressed in direct form and the other as the interpretation and application of the word of God by His Prophet. There can, thus, be no contradiction between the two of them, and this is the test to judge the authenticity of a Hadith.

8. Much of the important work on Fiqah is contained in the collection of Ahadith in the form of corpus juris as compared to corpus traditionis. Previous to these compilations, Jurists like Imam Abu Hanifa an–Numan ibn Thabit formulated legal theories of speculative character comparable to legal fiction in the modern laws. While he relied on eighteen Ahadith only, Imam Malik (died A.H 179) relied mainly on Ahadith and he gathered them not for their own sake but to use them in law.

9. The earliest and most authentic _musnaf_ is that of Imam Hanbal (died A.H. 240). It contained 30,000 Ahadith narrated by 700 narrators. The first _musnaf_ in which Ahadith are arranged in chapters according to their subject–matter is Sahih by Al-Bokhari (died in A.H. 257). Out of 6,00,000 Ahadith, which were prevalent during his age, he selected only 7,000, including 2,000 repetitions, thus, reducing their number to some 5,000. The principal arrangement in Sahih is legal and affords a basis for a complete system for jurisprudence. The next Sahih is that of Muslim (died in A.H. 261). The two Sahihs are knows as Jamis. There are four other collections:

    (1)   by Ibne Maja (died in A.H. 275),
    (2)   Abu-Daud (died in A.H. 276),
    (3)   Al-Tirmazi (died in A.H. 279), and
    (4)   Al-Nisayee (died in A.H. 303).

By the end of the fifth century of the Hijra, those six compilations came to be regarded the principal and most authentic work on the science of Traditions. Ibne Khaldoon, the great historian of Islam (died A.H. 808), speaks of only five while others speak of seven adding Mauta-i-Imam Malik which contains only 300 Traditions.

10. Even in these authentic compilations of Ahadith there are certain contradictions. How are the Courts to reconcile

them? The answer is two-fold: either the so-called contradiction lies in different rules of decision being laid down for different of facts or that one or more of them are not authentic. There are numerous rules for determining the authenticity of a Tradition. There is a time-limit counted from the death of the Holy Prophet and divided into three periods:

(i) The period of the Companions who were more righteous and had often shared the counsel of the Holy Prophet;

(ii) the successors of the Companions; and

(iii) their successors

The Traditions are classified into three groups:

(i) Those which have received universal publicity and acceptance in each one of the three periods. These are treated with absolute certainty almost as the test of the Qur´an.

(ii) Carrying conviction of genuineness but reported by a limited number of Companions and thereafter in the two successive periods.

(iii) the isolated.

They neither ensure certainty nor carry conviction of genuineness. Some of the Faqihs have not accepted them as having the authority of law. The interpretation of Ahadith is a science in itself and it is not possible to narrate it here. A useful summary of it will be found in Muhammadan Jurisprudence by Dr. Abdur Rahim at pages 77 to 114.

Ijma

11. On the demise of the Holy Prophet (may peace be upon him) in the 12th year of Hijra, the third source of Muslim Law, viz. Ijma´ came into being. An illuminating definition of Ijma is to be found in the following Questions and Answers in Al-Risala of Imam Al-Sharf´i (referred to above):-

"Shafi´i said: Someone has asked me: I have understood your doctrine concerning God´s commands and His Apostle´s orders that he who obeys God obeys His Apostle, (for) God has imposed (on men) the duty of obeying His Apostle, and that the proof for what you held has been established that it would be unlawful for a Muslim who has known the Book (of God) and the Sunna (of the Prophet) to give an opinion at variance with either one, for I know that this (ie. acceptance of the Book and the Sunna) is a duty imposed by God. But what is your proof for accepting the concensus of the public (on matters) concerning which no explicit command of God nor any (Sunna) related on the authority of the Prophet is to be found? Do you assert, with others, that the consensus of the public should always be based on an established Sunna even if it were not related (on the authority of the Prophet)?

Shafi'i replied: That on which the public are agreed and which, as they assert, was related from the Apostle, that is so. As to that which the public do not relate (from the Prophet), which they may or may not relate as a tradition from the Prophet, we cannot consider it as related on the authority of the Prophet - because one may relate only what he has heard for no one is permitted to relate (on the authority of the Prophet) information which may or may not be true. So we accept the decision of the public because we have to obey their authority, and we know that wherever there are Sunnas of the Prophet, the public cannot be ignorant of them, although it is possible that some are, and we know that the public can neither agree on anything contrary to the Sunna of the Prophet nor on an error.

Someone may ask: Is there any evidence of support of what you hold?

(Shafi'i) replied: Sufyan (b. Uyayna) told us from Iabdal-Malik b. Umayr from Abd al-Rahman b. ´Abd-Allah b. Masud from his father, who said: The Apostle said: ´God will grant prosperity to His servant who bears my words, remembers them, guards them and hands them on. Many a transmitter of law is no lawyer himself, and many may transmit law to others who are more versed in the law than they, etc.´

And Sufyan (also) told us from the ´Abd-Allah b. Abi Labid from ´Abd-Allah b. Sulayman b. Yasar from his father, who said ´Umar b. Al-Khattab made a speech at al-Jabiya in which he said:

The Apostle of God stood among us by an order from God as I am now standing among you, and said:

"Believe my Companions, then those who succeed them (the Successors), and after that those who succeed the Successors, but after them untruthfulness will prevail when people will swear, and will testify without having been asked to testify. Only those who seek the pleasure of Paradise will follow the community, for the devil can pursue one person, but stands far away from two. Let no man be alone with a woman, for the devil will be the third man among them. He who is happy with his right (behaviour), or unhappy with his wrong behaviour, is a (true) believer!"

"He asked: What is the meaning of the Prophet´s order to follow the community?

(Shafi'i) replied: There is but one meaning for it."

"He asked: How is it possible that there is only one meaning?

(Shafi'i) replied: When the community spread in the lands (of Islam), nobody was able to follow its members who had been dispersed and mixed with other believers and unbelievers, pious and impious. So it was meaningless to follow the community (as a whole), because it was impossible (to do so) except for what the (entire) community regarded as lawful or unlawful (orders) and (the duty) to obey these (orders).

He who holds what the Muslim community holds shall be regarded as following the community, and he who holds differently shall be regarded as opposing the community he was ordered to follow. So the error comes from separation: but in the community as a whole there is no error concerning the meaning of the Qur'an, the Sunna, and analogy."

12. On the authority of some Traditions, particularly, "Whatever the Muslims hold to be good is good before God"(Taudih p.298 and Kashaful Israr Vol.111,p.258) and certain Quranic texts, Dr.Abdur Rahim has defined Ijma' as agreement of the jurists among the followers of Muhammad (peace be upon him) in a particular age on a question of law. (Taudih p.498; 'Mukhtasar', Vol. II p.29; 'Jam'ul-Jawami', Vol.III p.288), The Qur'anic Texts relied in support of this definition are:-

(i)   'God does not allow the people to go astray after he has shown them the right path.'
(ii)   'Do not be like those who separated and divided after they have received clear proofs.'
(iii) 'Today we have completed your religion.'
(iv)   'What lies outside the truth is an error.'
(v)   'Obey God and obey the Prophet and those amongst you who have authority.'
(vi)   'If you yourself do not know, then question those who do'.
(vii) You are the best of men, and it is your duty to order men to do what is right and to forbid them from practising what is wrong.'
(viii) 'We have made you followers of the middle course so that you may be witnesses (of truth) to others'.
(ix)   'He who breaks away from the Prophet after he has been shown the right path and follows the ways of men other than Muslims, we shall give him what he has chosen and relegate him to hell'.

Besides the traditional and Qur'anic Texts, the Sunni School of Law recognizes the authority of Ijma' on the basis of unanimity of opinion among the Companions. (Bazdawi,p.253; 'Taudih', p.283, 'Mukhtasar' Vol. II, p.30, 'Jam'ul-Jawami', Vol.III, p.308). Imam Abu Hanifa an-Numan Ibn Thabit (born A.H. 80), the first of the four great Imams of the Sunni School, recognized Ijma' of the Companions, the successors of the Companions and their successors and extended it to every age.

13. It was not considered valid by Imam Ibne Hanbal, who is known to have said that any claim of unity is a mere lie

and that the utmost one could claim is that he does not know
of any disagreement on a particular issue. Ibne Hazm
considered only the consensus of opinion among the Companions
as being a sign of early prophetic sanction or approval.
Professor Abu Zahra says:

"The very validity of al-Ijma´ is not a matter of
consensus among Muslims. There are prominent jurists who
have explicitly denied its very existence. There are
others who have admitted its validity, but when an issue
came with a claim of a previous Ijma´, they denied its
very existence".

and concludes:

"It was but for the maintenance of national unity and as
a check against individual deviations, that al-Ijma, was
legalised as an authority after the sacred texts."

In Developments of Muslim Theology, Jurisprudence and
Constitutional Theory (1903 Edition) Duncan B. Mac-Donald,
dealing with Ijma´ as a source of law says:

"Al-Shafi´i is without question one of the greatest
figures in the history of law: perhaps he had not the
originality and keenness of Abu Hanifa, but he had a
balance of mind and temper, a clear vision and full
grasp of means and ends that enabled him to say what
proved to be the last word in the matter. After him
came attempts to tear down, but they failed. The fabric
of the Muslim canon law stood firm. There is a
tradition from the Prophet that he promised that with
the end of every century would come a restoror of the
faith of the people. At the end of the first century
was the pious Khalifa Umar ibn ´Abdal-Aziz, who by some
accident strayed in among the Umayyads. At the end of
the second came al-Shafi´i. His work was to mediate and
systematize and bore especially on the sources from
which rules of law may be drawn."

"But there lay a rock in his course more dangerous than
any mere contradiction in differing traditions. Usages
had grown up and taken fast hold which were in the teeth
of all traditions. These usages were in the individual
life, in the Constitution of the state, and in the rules
and decisions of the law Courts. The pious theologian
and Lawyer might rage against them as he chose; they
were there, firmly rooted, immovable. They were not
arbitrary changes, but had come about in the process of
time through the revolutions of circumstances and
varying conditions. Al-Shafi´i showed his greatness by
recognizing the inevitable and providing a remedy. This
lay in an extension of the principle of agreement and
the erection of it into a formal source. Whatever the
community of Islam has agreed upon at any time, is of
God. We have met this principle before, but never
couched in so absolute and catholic a form. The

33

agreement of the immediate Companions of Muhammad had weight with his first Successors. The agreement of these first Companions and of the next generation after them, had determining weight in the early church. The agreement of al-Madina had weight with Malik Ibn Anas. The agreement of many divines and legists always had weight of a kind. Among lawyers, a principle, to the contrary of which the memory of man ran not, had been determining. But this was wider, and from this time on the unity of Islam was assured."

Majid Khaddurri, in his translation of Risala of Imam Shafi´i (referred to above) at pages 37 and 38 has made the following comments:-

"Shafi´i´s doctrine of consensus, as Schacht rightly points out develops continuously in his writings. It begins as the consensus of a few scholars in a certain locality, following Malik´s method and becomes a concept that includes the entire Muslim community. If the view that the new Risala was written or revised as the last of Shafi´i´s writings is correct, his doctrine of consensus as defined in this work should represent his final formulation. In various parts of Risala, Shafi´i refers to the consensus of the scholars as a method of expounding the law acceptable to contemporary jurists, but in his references to the consensus of the community at large, specially in the chapter on consensus, he undoubtedly tends to invest it with higher authority. Shafi´i ends his chapter on consensus by asserting: ´He who holds what the Muslim community holds shall be regarded as following the community, and he who holds differently shall be regarded as opposing the community he was ordered to follow. So the error comes from separation.....´"

In Reconstruction of Religious Thought in Islam Dr. Iqbal has dealt with the subject of Ijma´ at length and it will be profitable to quote the following:

"But there are one or two questions which must be raised and answered in regard to the Ijma´, Can the Ijma´ repeal the Qur´an? It is unnecessary to raise the question before a Muslim audience; but I consider it necessary to do so in view of a very misleading statement by a European critic in a book called ´Muhammedan Theories of Finance´-published by the Columbia University. The author of this book says, without citing any authority, that according to some Hanafi and Mutazilla writers the Ijma´ can repeal the Qur´an. There is not the slightest justification for such a statement in the legal literature of Islam. Not even a tradition of the Prophet can have any such effect. It seems to me that the author is misled by the Naskh in the writings of our early doctors to whom, as

Imam Shatibi points out in Al-Muwafiqat, Vol. III,p.65, this word, when used in discussions relating to the Ijma´ of the Companions, meant only the power to extend or limit the application of a Qur´anic rule of law, and not the power to repeal or supersede it by another rule of law. And even in the exercise of this power the legal theory, as Amidi-a Shafi´i doctor of law who died about the middle of the seventh century, and whose work is recently published in Egypt-tell us, is that the Companions must have been in possession of a Shariah value (Hukm) entitling them to such a limitation of extension.

"But supposing the Companions have unanimously decided a certain point, the further question is whether later generations are bound by their decision. Shoukani has fully discussed this point, and cited the view held by writers belonging to different schools. I think it necessary in this connection to discriminate between a decision relating to a question of fact and the one relating to a question of law. In the former case, as for instance, when the question arose whether the two small Suras known as ´Muavazatain´ formed part of the Qur´an or not, and the Companions unanimously decided that they did, we are bound by their decision, obviously because the Companions alone were in a position to know the fact. In the latter case the question is one of interpretation only, and I venture to think, on the authority of Karkhi, that later generations are not bound by the decision of the Companions. Says Karkhi: The Sunnah of the Companions is binding in matters which cannot be cleared up by Qiyas, but it is not so in matters which can be established by Qiyas."

14. Ijma´ is now an accepted source of law in Islamic jurisprudence and without it further evolution of laws cannot come into being which is absolutely essential to avoid outmoding of many of the laws in the changed situation and facts of the present age. The all important question, therefore, is how can this source of law-making be utilised in the present day. The answer is fraught with religious and political considerations and we are not in a position to give an authoritative pronouncement on the subject. But on a humbler plane we may point out that Ijma´ is not only a source of Law-making but also bed-rock of unity in Islam. The difficulties in its implementation are, of course, many, particularly the modern trend of a national state which has spread over most of the Muslim countries. Legislation is an important constituent of sovereignty. A national State will therefore, stand in the way of an Ijma ul-Ummat. Indeed, in the dissolution of the office of Khilafat, the possibility was most for ever.

15. That there is need for some uniformity of laws in

Muslim countries goes without saying. In the opening chapter
of his Book "Legal Theory" (II Edition) Mr W Friedman says:
"All systematic thinking about legal theory is linked at
one end with philosophy and, at the other end, with
political theory. Sometimes the starting-point is
philosophy and political ideology plays a secondary part
– as in the theories of the German classical
meta-physicians or the Neo-Kantians. Sometimes the
starting-point is political ideology, as in the legal
theories of Socialism and Fascism. Sometimes theory of
knowledge and political ideology are welded into one
coherent system, where the respective shares of the two
are not easy to disentangle, as in the scholastic system
or in Hegel's philosophic system. But all legal theory
must contain elements of philosophy – man's reflections
on his position in the universe – and gain its colour
and specific content from political theory – the ideas
entertain on the best form of society. For all thinking
about the end of law is based on conceptions of man both
as a thinking individual and as a political being."
A little further it is said:-
"To the further question of the relation of law to
religion ethics, economics and science, no general
answer can be given. These are the sources from which a
particular legal theory may be nourished. Religion
determines the philosophical and political outlook of
the scholastics, ethical principles determine the legal
philosophy of Kant, economics underlies the legal
thought of Marxism, scientific fact study inspires the
functional approach of the realistic movement. The
answer to these questions must therefore be given in
conjunction with any particular legal theory in varying
strength and combination, to form the philosophical and
political valuations from which a legal theory is built
up."

16. The sphere law is much wider in Islam than in any
other jurisprudence. In theory every act of a Muslim is
guided. Our actions are divided into (i) Farz or Wajib; a
duty the omission of which is punished and the doing rewarded;
(ii) Mandub or Mustahab the doing is rewarded but omission is
not punished. (iii) Jaiz or Mubah, that which is permitted,
(iv) Makrooh disapproved by Law but not under penalty and (v)
Haram, forbidden, an action punishable by law. All pious
Muslims are also required to strictly follow the precedent of
the Holy Prophet (may peace be upon him). Religion and law
are thus, inextricably woven into one single Code for Muslims
all over the world. Any radical change in the system of laws
in Muslim countries will, therefore, have the same effect as
differences in religious practices.

17. How is then Ijma´ to be achieved in the present day
conditions? In Reconstruction of Religious Thought in Islam,

Dr. Iqbal has observed:

"One more question may be asked as to the legislative activity of a modern Muslim assembly which must consist, at least for the present day, mostly of men possessing no knowledge of the subtleties of Muhammadan law. Such an assembly may make grave mistakes in their interpretation of law. How can we exclude or at least reduce the possibility of erroneous interpretation?"

He then referred to the ecclesiastical committee of Ulama provided by the Persian Constitution of 1906, conversant with the affairs of the world having power to supervise the legislative activity of the Majlis", and described it as a dangerous arrangement but, perhaps, necessary in view of the national theory of Iran that the King is a mere Custodian of the realm which really belongs to the absent Imam, and the Ulama as representatives of the Imam considered themselves entitled to supervise the whole life of the community and struck a note of warning that the arrangement may be tried if at all only as a temporary measure in Sunni countries. As a remedy, he laid stress on the Ulama forming a vital party of Muslim legislative assemblies helping and guiding free discussion on questions relating to law. Against the possibilities of erroneous interpretations, Dr Iqbal advised reform in the present system of legal education in Muhammadan countries, to extend its sphere, and to combine it with an intelligent study of modern jurisprudence. Two distinct thoughts are visible in these observations. One that the legislative assemblies of the modern States may assume the role of Ijma´ and the other that the sovereignty of the Legislature should not be impaired by subjecting it to the authority of an external organ.

18. The idea of Dr Iqbal seems to underlie the provisions of Article 198 (3) of the 1956 Constitution, which authorised the President to appoint a Commission:-

    (a)   to make recommendations:-

    (i)   as to the measures for bringing the existing law into conformity with the Injunctions of Islam, and

    (ii)   as to the stages by which such measures should be brought into effect; and

    (b)   to compile in a suitable form, for the guidance of the National and Provincial Assemblies such injunctions of Islam as can be given legislative effect.

The present Constitution contains more specific provisions on this subject. The President or the Governor of a Province may refer to the Advisory Council of Islamic Ideology for advice any question that arises as to whether a proposed law disregards or violates, or is otherwise not in accordance with those Principles. The Constitution of the Advisory Council of Islam Ideology is provided for in Articles 199 to 203 of the Constitution. In selecting a person for appointment to the

Council, the President shall have regard to the person's understanding and appreciation of Islam and of the economic, political, legal and administrative problems of Pakistan. The functions of the Council are:-

    (a)   to make recommendations to the Central Government and the Provincial Governments as to means of enabling and encouraging the Muslims of Pakistan to order their lives in all respects in accordance with the principles and concepts of Islam, as set out in the Holy Qur'an and Sunnah; and

    (b)   to advise the National Assembly, a Provincial Assembly, the President or a Governor on any questions referred to the Council under Article 6, that is to say, a question as to whether a proposed law disregards or violates, or is otherwise not in accordance with the Principles of Law-making.

Along with these provisions, Article 207 of the Constitution requires the President to establish an Islamic Research Institute which shall undertake Islamic research and instruction in Islam for the purpose of assisting in the reconstruction of Muslim society, on a truly Islamic basis.

    19. It is only in certain matters, which are regarded as the fundamentals of Islam, such as the saying of five daily prayers, paying the poor-rate, fasting during the month of Ramadan and performing pilgrimage, that laws are established by the Ijma' of the entire body of Muslims (Kashful-Israr, Volume III, page 240). In other matters, the masses are to follow the learned in exposition of laws on the basis of the Qur'anic verse "Obey God and obey the Prophet and those amongst you who are in authority". According to the four Sunni Schools, the words "men in authority" referred to men, who are learned in the laws so as to be considered fit for Ijtihad or Qiyas and not to Rulers or Governors since they themselves are required to conform to the rules of Shariat and to act upon the advice of the learned according to the Qur'anic Text: "That if you yourself do not know them question those who do". The constitutional provisions for the establishment of Advisory Council of Islamic Ideology and Islamic Research Institute, in our opinion, seek to conform to this rule. With due respect to them, the members of our Legislative Assemblies, at present, are not sufficiently learned so as to be considered fit for Ijtihad or Qiyas, the two essential conditions for participating in an Ijma'. This, however, is not a counsel of despair. A remedy against it has been suggested by Dr. Iqbal and we may add that the pre-requisite for every Member of a Legislative Assembly in Pakistan should be a fair amount of knowledge of law-making in Islam. We do not mean that each one of them should be a Faqih or a Mujtahid, but at the same time he should not be wholly unfamiliar with the primary duty of a legislator in an Islamic

38

country.

20. A question may be asked as to what will happen to the unity of Islam so firmly secured by Imam Abu Hanifa and Imam Al-Shafi´i by extending Ijma´ to every age if Legislative Assemblies of Muslim countries are to perform the function of Ijma´ independent of each other. The unity shall, no doubt, be impaired, but we may venture to suggest that the remedy perhaps lies in the setting up of a World Commission of Islamic Ideology and a common Islamic Research Institute, as envisaged in our Constitution of 1962. To begin with, the scope of such a Commission may be restricted to consultation and research, but in due course by mutual consent it may acquire the authority to enforce its views on the member-States as the International Court of Justice at Hague and the United Nations Organization exercise over the States who have subscribed to their Charters. The conclusion to be drawn from the above discussion is that Ijma´ is an important source of law-making in Islam, but in the present conditions it is not feasible to resort to it in an orthodox sense. The Legislative Assemblies are perhaps the only bodies which may perform this function and the duty of the Courts is to interpret and apply the laws to be enacted by them in conformity with the Qur´an and Sunnah.

Qiyas

21. The fourth source of law in Islam is Qiyas which is comparable to legal fiction in western jurisprudence. It is based on Qur´an, Sunnah and Ijma´. Fresh facts and situations arose in the ever-growing Muslim World in the early centuries of Hijra. In many cases neither the dicta of Qur´an nor the Sunnah was applicable in terms. Nor was the rule of decision settled by an Ijma´. Qiyas, or analogical deduction, from these sources was, therefore, the only answer. The Companions had applied Qiyas and so did their successors, but Imam Abu Hanifa was the first to treat it as a formal source of law-making in Islam and he gave great latitude to private opinion and in his formulation relied on eighteen Ahadith only. He is known to have set up a committee of forty learned from among his disciples for the codification of laws, including Yahya ibn Abi Zaid, Hafs ibn Ghiyath, Abu Yusuf, Da´ud at-Tai, Habban, Mandal, Qasim ibn Nu-im and Muhammad. They discussed practical and theoretical questions of law, and their deliberations are sometimes described as Ijma´-i-Abu Hanifa. The entire Code is lost, but we have a small collection of Traditions based on his authority, called ´Musnadu´-i-imam Abu Hanifa´ and a letter which he wrote for the instruction and guidance of his disciple, Abu Yusuf, the Chief Qazi of Bughdad. In the codification of laws Imam Abu Hanifa and his disciples made free use of private judgment and Qiyas.

22. A common place instance of Qiyas is that Qur´an has

39

prohibited only Khumar, that is, a distilled preparation of
dates. The principle underlying the prohibition, however, is
intoxication on account of which one is restrained from
joining a prayer. Every intoxicant which creates such a state
of mind, whether prepared from dates, opium or other drugs,
is, therefore, forbidden by analogy.

23. In literal sense, Qiyas means 'measuring', 'accord'
and 'equality'. It is a process by which the rule of law
embodied in the Qur'an, Sunnah and Ijma' is extended to cases
not covered by their text. The reason of the text on which
analogy is based is 'effective cause' and the legal effect is.
It is to be distinguished from interpretation of Qur'an,
Sunnah and Ijma' though in theory Qiyas is a process of
discovering the Law embodied in them. In Chapter XII of
Al-Risala, Imam Shafi has described Qiyas as follows:

"He asked: On what ground do you hold that (on matters)
concerning which no text is to be found in the Book, nor
a sunnah or consensus, recourse should be had to
analogy? Is there any binding text for analogical
deduction?

(Shafi'i) replied: They are two terms with the same
meaning.

He asked: What is their common (basis)?

(Shafi'i) replied: On all matters which touch the (life
of a) Muslim there is either a binding decision or an
indication as to the right answer. If there is a
decision, it should be followed; if there is no
indication as to the right answer, it should be sought
by ijtihad, and ijtihad is Qiyas (analogy).

He asked: If the scholars apply analogy correctly, will
they arrive at the right answer in the eyes of God? And
will it be permissable for them to disagree (in their
answers) through analogy? Have they been ordered to seek
one or different answers for each question? What is the
proof for the position that they should apply analogy on
the basis of literal rather than the implicit meaning
(of a precedent), and that it is permissible for them to
disagree (in their answers)? Should (analogy) in matters
concerning the scholars themselves be applied
differently from the way it is applied in matters
concerning others? Who is the person qualified to
exercise ijtihad through analogy in matters concerning
himself, not others, and who is the person who can apply
it in matters concerning himself as well as others?

(Shafi'i) replied: (Legal) knowledge is of various
kinds:

The first consists of the right decisions in the literal
and implied senses; the other, of the right answer in
the literal sense only. The right decisions (in the
literal and implied senses are those based (either) on
God's command or on a sunna of the Apostle related by

the public from an (earlier) public. These (God's
commands and the sunnah) are the two sources by virtue
of which the lawful is to be established as lawful and
the unlawful as unlawful. This is (the kind of
knowledge) of which nobody is allowed to be ignorant or
doubtful (as to its certainty).
Secondly, (legal) knowledge of the specialists consists
of traditions related by a few and known only to
scholars, but others (the public) are under no
obligation to be familiar with it. Such knowledge may
either be found among all or a few (of the scholars),
related by a reliable transmitter from the Prophet.
This is the (kind of) knowledge which is binding on
scholars to accept and it constitutes the right decision
in the literal sense such as we accept (the validity of)
the testimony of two witnesses. This is right (only) in
the literal sense, because it is possible that (the
evidence of) the two witnesses might be false.
(Thirdly), (legal) knowledge derived from <u>ijma´</u>
(consensus).
(Finally). (legal) knowledge derived from <u>ijtihad</u>
(personal reasoning) through Qiyas (analogy), by virtue
of which right decisions are sought. Such decisions are
right in the literal sense to the person who applies
analogy, not to the majority of scholars, for nobody
knows what is hidden except God."

24. The substance of this reference perhaps is to
ascertain how far it is permissable for a Qazi and, in the
modern context, for a Court of Law to differ from the Qiyas of
the earlier Imams and Faqihs. In Chapter XV of Al-Risala on
Disagreement (Ikhtilaf)´ Imam Shafi´i has dealt with this
subject as follows:

"He asked: I have found the scholars, in former and
present times, in disagreement on certain (legal)
matters. Is it permissible for them to do so?
(Shafi´i) replied: Disagreement is of two kinds: one of
them is prohibited, but I would not say the same
regarding the other.
He asked: What is prohibited disagreement?
(Shafi´i) replied: On all matters concerning which God
provided clear textual evidence His Book or (a sunna)
uttered by the Prophet's tongue, disagreement among
those to whom these (texts) are known is unlawful. As
to matters that are liable to different interpretations
or derived from analogy, so that he who interprets or
applies analogy arrives at a decision different from
that arrived at by another. I do not hold that
(disagreement) of this kind constitutes such strictness
as that arising from textual (evidence)."

This is followed by instances in which the Companions and
their successors disagreed in their transmission and

concerning which God had provided a textual command and disagreement in the interpretation of Qur´anic communications. For example-

"God said: Divorced women shall wait by themselves for three periods (Q.II,228).
And He said:

As for your women who have despair of (further) menstruation, if you are in doubt, their period shall be three months, and those who have not menstruated as yet. And those who are pregnant, their term is when they are delivered of what they bear (Q.LXV,4).
And He said:

Those of you who die, leaving wives, they shall wait by themselves four months and ten (days) (Q.II,234)."

Some of the Companions of the Apostle said: Concerning divorced women, God prescribed that the period of the ´idda of those who are pregnant should be until they are delivered; but those whose husbands have died should observe an ´idda of four months and ten days. So the ´idda of the widow who is pregnant must be four months and ten days, even if she has been delivered so that she fulfills two ´iddas, since delivery itself does not mean the termination of the prescribed ´idda save in the case of divorce. (Malik, Volume II, page 589: Bukhari, Volume III, page 478; Shawkani; Mayl al-awtar, Volume VI, page 304. They hold, in effect, that delivery is acquittance, while the waiting for four months and ten days is obligatory, and that the widow cannot lawfully remarry until the four months and ten days are completed. (Bulaq, ed., page 79). They believe that she is under obligation in two senses, and that neither one can be waived. It is as if she were subject to the claims of two men, neither one of whom invalidated the other, or if she married (one of them) during the ´idda and had intercourse with him, she would have to fulfill an ´idda before she could marry the other one. Other Companions of the Apostle have held that if she (the widow) has been delivered, it is lawful for her to remarry even if her dead husband is not yet buried. (Malik, Volume II, page 590). Imam Shafi´i said:

"Thus the Qur´anic communication can be interpreted in two ways at the same time, but the most reasonable literal one is that a state of pregnancy puts an end to the ´idda."

At page 139, of Muhammadan Jurisprudence Doctor Abdur Rahim has summed up the subject as follows:

"Rules of law analogically deduced do not rank so high as authority, as those laid down by a text of the Qur´an or Hadith, or by consensus of opinion. The reason is that with respect to analogical deductions one cannot be certain that they are what the Lawgiver intended, such deductions resting as they do upon the application of human reason which is always liable to error. In fact,

it is a maxim of the Sunni Jurisprudence that a jurist
may be right or may be wrong. A Qadi in deciding a case
is not, therefore, bound by a particular rule of
juristic law merely because it has the approval of
certain doctors, but may follow his own view. An
analogical deduction, if agreed upon by the learned as a
body assumes, however, a different legal aspect but that
is because of such agreement and not the strength of the
reasons on which such collective decision may be
founded."

Everyone, however, is not entitled to apply Qiyas. According
to Imam Al-Shafi´i-

"Nobody should apply analogy unless he is competent to
do so through his knowledge of the commands of the Book
of God; its prescribed duties and its ethical
discipline, its abrogating and abrogated
(communications), its general and particular rules, and
its (right) guidance. Its (ambiguous) communications
should be interpreted by the sunna of the Prophet; if no
sunna is found, then by the consensus of the Muslims; if
no consensus is possible, then by analogical deduction.
No one is competent to apply analogy unless he is
conversant with the established sunnah, the opinions of
(his predecessors) the agreement (consensus) and
disagreement of the people, and has (adequate) knowledge
of the Arabic tongue.
Nor is he regarded as competent in analogical
(reasoning) unless he is sound in mind, able to
distinguish between closely parallel precedents and not
hasty in expressing an opinion unless he is certain of
its correctness. Nor shall he refrain from listening to
the opinions of those who may disagree with him, for he
might be warned against (possible) forgetfulness or be
confirmed in his right (judgment). In so doing he must
exert his utmost power not to be misled by personal
(bias), so that he knows on what grounds he has given
one opinion and on what ground he has rejected another.
Nor should he be more preoccupied with the opinion he
has given than with the one with which he disagrees, so
that he knows the merits of what he accepts as compared
with that which he rejects."

25. In the modern extent the place of the Qazi is taken
by the Judges appointed by the authority of the State and the
jurisdiction to interpret and apply Laws is derived from the
Constitution and the Law of the land. The tests laid down by
Imam Al-Shafi´i may not, therefore, be strictly applicable to
the presiding officers of present day Courts. Qiyas is not
the word of God nor Sunnah of the Holy Prophet. It also lacks
the authority of Ijma´. The application of Qiyas cannot,
therefore, be limited to the early doctors nor their opinion,
though entitled to utmost respect, be considered as binding

for all times to come. The fact that the great Imams and
their disciples have differed among themselves on numerous
rules of decision as well as their details also furnishes
further warrant for it. Some recent judgments of our own
Court furnish instances of application of Qiyas by Courts of
law as well as difference of learned Judges with the views of
the learned A´imma and Faqihs.....

Ijtihad

29. While recounting the causes which brought about the
decadence of Muslims, Dr. Sobhi Mahmassani, a learned modern
jurist states-

"After the fall of Baghdad in the 13th century, the
Islamic civilization began to fade, and orthodox or
Sunni jurists agreed that the four well-known Sunni
Schools ie. the Hanafi, Maliki, Shafi and Hanbali were
sufficient. They, thus, agreed upon the closing of the
door of Ijtihad. As a result, new interpretations were
prohibited and, consequently, inconsiderate and slavish
imitation (taqlid) became general."

According to the learned doctor, this resulted in intellectual
stagnation, in the history of Islamic jurisprudence, and to
remedy this evil, it is necessary to reopen the door of
Ijtihad. In support of it, he relies on the view of the
Shieites and the reformists Sunnites, such as Ibn Taimiyya,
Ibn Kayyam Al-Jawziyya Muhammad Ibn Abdul Wahhab, Jamaluddin
Al-Afghani and Sheikh Muhammad Abdullah.

30. In Islamic Law and Constitution, Abdul-ala-Maudood
has defined Ijtihad as an academic research and intellectual
effort which makes the legal system of Islam dynamic and its
development and evolution in the changing circumstances
possible. Ijtihad, however, does not, according to him, mean
completely independent use of one´s opinion. The primary
source of Muslim Law being Qur´an and Sunnah, the legislation
that human-beings may undertake must, therefore, be derived
from this fundamental law, or it should be within the limits
prescribed by it for the use of one´s discretion or the
exercise of one´s opinion. In conclusion, it is observed that
Ijtihad that purports to be independent of the shari´ah can
neither be an Islamic Ijtihad nor there is any room for such
an incursion in the legal system of Islam.

31. Imam Al-Shafi´i includes Ijtihad in Qiyas. In reply
to the question as to what is analogy; is it Ijtihad, or are
the two different; at page 288 of Al-Risala he states that
they are two terms with the same meaning. When asked as to
what is their common basis, he replied that in all matters
touching the life of a Muslim there is either a binding
decision or an indication to the right answer. If there is a
decision, it should be followed and if there is no indication
as to the right answer it should be sought by Ijtihad and
Ijtihad is Qiyas (analogy). Again, while recounting the

various kinds of legal knowledge, the great Imam describes the fourth kind as follows:-

> "Finally, legal knowledge derived from Ijtihad (personal reasoning) through Qiyas (analogy) by virtue of which right decisions are sought. Such decisions are right in the literal sense to the person who applied analogy, not to the majority of scholars, because nobody knows what is hidden except God."

The next question and answer are rather instructive on the subject. The Interlocutor asked. "If legal knowledge is derived through analogy – provided it is rightly applied – should the scholars who apply analogy agree on most of the decisions, although we may find them disagreeing on some? The answer is:

> "Analogy is of two kinds: the first, if the case in question is similar to the original meaning of the precedent, no disagreement on this kind is permitted. The second, if the case in question is similar to several precedents, analogy must be applied to the precedent nearest in resemblance and most appropriate. But those who apply analogy are likely to disagree in their answers."

32. Ijtihad may be in the form of determining the rule of decision in a particular case or class of cases and it attains the status of law by (i) consensus of opinion (Ijma´) of the learned men of the community, (ii) wide popularity of Ijtihad of an individual or a group of individuals and acceptance of their verdict by the people ..... suo motu, such as the four Sunni Schools of the Hanbalite and (iii) adoption by a Muslim Government of a particular form of law, just as Ottoman Government adopted the Hanafi Law. Maulana Maudoodi adds that an institution may be empowered in an Islamic State to legislate and it may enact any particular piece of Ijtihad in the form of law. One may presume that the ´institution´ means a Legislative body, though this momenclature appears to have been purposely avoided by the Maulana.

33. At page 168 of the Muhammadan Jurisprudence, Dr. Abdur Rahim has described Ijtihad and Taqlid as follows:-

> "The word Mujtahid which is a nomen agentis means a person who can make Ijtihad. Ijtihad literally means striving, exerting and as a term of jurisprudence it means the application by a lawyer (faqih) of all his faculties to the consideration of the authorities of the law (that is Qur´an, the Traditions and the Ijma´) with a view to find out what in all probability is the law that is, in a matter which is not covered by the express words of such texts and has not been determined by Ijma´). In other words Ijtihad is the capacity for making deductions in matters of law in cases to which no express text or a rule already determined by Ijma´ is applicable."

45

34. The next question is what are the qualifications of a Mujtahid? As stated by Dr. Abdur Rahim, Sadru´-sh.-Shariat following Fakhru´l Islam says that a jurist should have knowledge of the Qur´an together with its meaning dictionary and legal, and its various divisions, of the traditions including the texts and the authorities thereof, and of the rules relating to analogical deduction. Further, there are different ranks of a Mujtahid. For example, Mujtahidun fi´sh-Shari´ jurists who founded schools of law, such as Abu Hanifa, Imara Malik, Imam Shafi´i and Imam Ibn Hanbal, the founders of the four Sunni Schools; to whom is conceded an absolute and independent power of expounding the law; (2) Mujtahidun fi´l-Madhhab, jurists having authority to expound the law according to a particular School; (3) Mujtahidun-fil-Masa´l jurists who are competent to expound the law on particular questions which have not been settled by jurists of the first and the second ranks; and a <u>fortiori</u> not competent to oppose them on any matter of principle and (4) Mujtahidunu-´l-Muqayyid or Mujtahids with a limited sphere of exposition like those of the last two grades, though of inferior authority as distinguished from Mujtahidunu-´l-Mutlaq. These doctors of inferior authority are divided into three groups, namely:-

(1) Ashabu´t takhrij or those that occupied themselves in drawing inferences and conclusions from the law laid down by higher authorities and in explaining and illustrating what had been left doubtful or general. Abu Bakru´r-Razi was a jurist of this class.

(2) Ashabu´t-tarjih or those who were competent to discriminate between two conflicting opinions held by jurists of a higher rank and to pronounce that "this is better", "this is most correct", "this is agreeable to people", and so on. Qaduri and the author of "Hedaya" have been assigned a place in this rank.

(3) Ashabu´t-tashih or those who have authority to say whether a particular version of the law is strong or weak, namely, whether it is a manifest or rare version of the views of the Mujtahids of his School. The great jurist Sadru´sh-Shariat, the author of Al-Mukhtar, who was rightly called Abu Hanifa the second, is included in this rank.

The last class is of those who cannot decide for themselves whether a particular rule of law is strong or weak in authority and have to accept what the doctors of the above-mentioned classes have laid down, but on questions not dealt with by them, they can proceed upon the analogy of what has been laid down for similar matters, taking into consideration the change in the customs and affairs of men and must adopt a rule which would be most suitable in the circumstances of the case and in accordance with their usage. The author of Durrul-Mukhtar claims to belong to this rank which, according to Dr. Abdur Rahim, corresponds to modern lawyers.

35. Ijtihad is, thus, a very fruitful source of Muslim Law and all modern reformist jurists are agreed that Taqlid should be discarded and the door of Ijtihad thrown open to help in the evolution of laws necessary for meeting new facts and situations as they arise from time to time in different parts of the Muslim world.

Istihsan, Istislah and Istidlal

36. Istihsan and Istislah are doctrines of equity, while Istidlal is a branch of Qiyas applicable to those cases where no analogy is to be found in the Qur´an, Sunnah and Ijma´. Equity, in English sense, claims to override the elder jurisprudence of the country on the strength of an intrinsic ethical superiority. In Roman Law, it was the Law of Nature (Jus Nature), the part of law which natural reason appoints for all mankind. In spite of the fact that the analogy (Qiyas) clearly points to one course but the Legist "considers it better" (Istihsan), he may follow a different course. Under the same conditions, he may choose a free course "for the sake of general benefit to the community" (Istislah). The rule of Istihsan was reduced to definiteness by Imam Abu-Hanifa. He would say "analogy in the case points to such and such rule but under the circumstances I hold it for better to rule such and such". The principle of Istislah enunciated by Imam Malik is when a rule would work general injury it was to be set aside even in the face of valid analogy. It is also called as Musalihul-Mursala Wal-Istislah and has more solid basis than the mere preference of a legist. According to Iam-ul-Jawani, Volume IV, pages 101-102, Imamul-Harmain also held the same view.

37. In literal sense Istidlal means inferring from a thing another thing. The Hanafi jurists used it in this sense in connection with the rules of interpretation, while according to Malikis and Shafi´is it is a distinct method of juristic deduction, not falling within the scope of Qiyas. Istidlal is of three kinds:-

(i) The expression of the connection existing between one proposition and another without any specific effective cause;

(ii) Istishabul-hal or presumption that a state of things, which is not proved to have ceased, still continues; and

(iii) the authority as to the revealed laws previous to Islam.

The first category distinguishes Istidlal from Qiyas because as seen in the earlier discussion on this subject an effective cause is the basis of Qiyas but not so in Istidlal. It may, however, be mentioned that according to Imam Ghazali it is harmful to make a deduction. An instance of the second category is the presumption that a person who has disappeared is alive so that his estate is not distributed among his heirs and according to one School he also inherits from others. The third category of Istidlal is based on the rule of permissibility <u>viz</u>., that which is not forbidden or expressly or impliedly abrogated continues to be rule of decision of general character if it be called for by absolute necessity affecting the Muslims as a body.

38. In the light of the above discussion, a stage has been reached when we may proceed to answer the questions raised in the order of reference.

  I. The first question deals with the sources of Muslim Law;

As seen above, the primary sources of law are Qur´an and Hadith, while Ijma´, Qiyas, Ijtihad and Istidlal are the secondary sources; Istihsan and Istihsab being doctrines of equity and not an independent source.

  II. As to the rules of interpretation of Muslim Law: A clear injunction in Qur´an and Sunnah is binding and no departure is permissible provided that if the effective cause of an injunction has disappeared or an injunction was confined to the facts of a particular case its extension is not warranted.

39. There are, of course, detailed rules for the interpretaion of Qur´an and for testing the genuineness of a Hadith, the two principal subjects of Fiqah. For obvious reasons, it is not possible to set out those rules in this order, but we may take advantage of this opportunity to emphasize that it is of utmost necessity to amend the curriculum of legal studies in Pakistan so as to include Fiqah as a compulsory subject in the examination of Degree of Laws.....

.....41. As every student of Fiqah knows the study of Qur´an and science of its interpretation (tafsir) engaged the best talents among A´imma and Faqihs. Some of the best known commentaries are by Tibri (died A.H. 310), Makhshori (died A. H. 538), Imam Ghazali (died A. H. 504), Wadai (died A. H. 685), Jalal-ud-Din Roomi, Fakhar-ud-Din Razi and Ahmad, commonly known as Mulla Jiwan in the time of Emperor Aurangzeb. Side by side with it, the work on collection of authentic traditions and usages of the Holy Prophet also continued.

42. A reference has earlier been made to the two Sahihs technically called Jamies, the first by Bokhari and the second by Muslim, and the four Sunnah by Ibn Maja (died 303), Abu Daud al-Sajistani (died 275), al-Tirmadhai (died 279) and al-Nasai (died 303). The influence which Bokhari and Muslim had on the evolution of Muslim Laws based on traditions and

48

usages of the Holy Prophet is, indeed, very great. They strengthened the position of the Medinites who upheld the traditions like Shafi'i and Maliki Schools as opposed to the Hanafi or Iraqi School. As mentioned in the earlier part of this order Imam Abu-Hanifa who lived at a time when the precepts and usages of the Holy Prophet were fresh in the memories of the successors of the Companions (Tabacen), relied on only 17 or 18 traditions, but under the influence of Bokhari and Muslim and his followers relied on many more traditions which may be counted by hundreds and thousands.

43. The subject of judging the authenticity of Traditions and usages of the Holy Prophet and their interpretation is indeed very vast and we will content ourselves by quoting from Al-Risala by Imam Shafi'i. Imam Shafi'i said:

> The Sunnah which the Holy Prophet has laid down on matters for which a text is to be found in the Book of God is always in full agreement with that text and clarifying on God's behalf a general text; the Holy Prophet's specification is more explicit than the text. But as for the Sunnah which he laid down on matters for which a text is not found in the Qur'an, the obligation to accept them rests upon us by virtue of the duty imposed by God to obey the Prophet's orders. As to the abrogating and abrogated Sunnas, like the abrogating communications laid down by God to abrogate orders, they are in like manner laid down by the Holy Prophet so that each Sunna may be abrogated by another. As to the contradictory traditions where no indications exist to specify which is the abrogating and the abrogated, they are all in accord with one another and contradiction does not really exist among them. For the Holy Prophet being an Arab by tongue and by country may have laid down as general rule intended to be general and another general rule intended to be particular, or a certain question may have been asked to which he gave a certain concise answer, leading some of the transmitters to relate the tradition in detail and others in brief, rendering the meaning of the tradition partly clear and partly vague, or it may happen that the transmitter of a certain tradition related the answer he heard from the Holy Prophet without knowing what the question had been for had he known the question he would have understood the answer clearly from the reasoning on which the answer was based. The Holy Prophet may have likewise laid down a Sunna covering a particular situation and another covering a different one, but some of those who related that they heard failed to distinguish between the two differing situations for which he had laid down the Sunnas. And he may have laid down a Sunna on a certain matter in conformity with the text of the

49

Qur´an-transmitted by one authority and another in one form in another contradictory to it owing to changes in the circumstances-transmitted by another authority. Hence, the transmission by one authority appeared to many as contradictory to the other, while in reality no contradiction existed at all. He may have also provided a Sunna consisting of an order of permission or prohibition the wording of which was general and he may have provided a second specifying Sunna which made evident that his order of prohibition was not intended to prohibit what he made lawful, nor that his order of permission made lawful what he had prohibited. For all the possibilities of this kind parallel examples exist in the Qur´an. The contradictory Sunna is due either to incomplete transmission rendering it contradictory, although what was lacking can be known from other traditions or it is the product of the transmitter´s imagination. No contradictory tradition from the Prophet was known to Imam Shafi´i for which a possible explanation was lacking or the category to which it belonged was not known."

44. The Imam further said:

"Analogy on the basis of the Sunna falls into two categories, each sub-divided into various forms. God has imposed the obligation of obedience upon men through His Book and His Prophet´s tongue, in accordance with the obligation of obedience set forth in His established judgement that men shall obey His will without challenge to His command. (Qur´an, Surah XIII, verse 41). The Holy Prophet specified the meaning of what God made obligatory or in any narrative transmitted from him so that nothing is left unexplained and the scholars are under obligation to regard this narrative as authentic as other traditions if it expresses the identical meaning. The second category of traditions consists of a general order of permission qualified by a particular order of prohibition. Men should regard all acts under the general order of permission as lawful and the specific act under the particular order of prohibition as unlawful. But in so doing they should not apply analogy to a particular order of prohibition, for the general rule is that an order of permission and analogy must be applied ordinarily on the general, not on the particular rule."

The interlocutor asked Imam Shafi´i if we find in the Qur´an an explicit general meaning which a certain Sunna may either make specific or to which it may give an implicit meaning that is contradictory, did he agree that the Sunna is abrogated by the Qur´an? The Imam replied:

"Since God has imposed on His Prophet the duty to obey His communications to Him, and He testified to his right

50

guidance and imposed on men the duty to obey Him, and since the Arab tongue, as already explained, may give a variety of meanings for each word so that some of the communications of the Book are general and intended to be particular and others particular and intended to be general,and some are general duties which the Apostle specified in the Sunna – a function which the Sunna fulfils in its relation to the Book, the Sunna cannot be contradictory to the Book of God, but will always follow the Book of God, in conformity with His divine communication, and clarify on God´s behalf the meaning intended by God. Thus the Sunna always follows the Book of God."

It is not possible to detail here further rules for judging the authenticity of the precepts and usages of the Holy Prophet and their interpretation, but what the great Imam has said perhaps contains the pith and substance of Ilm-ul-Hadith.

45. As to the competence of Courts to differ from the view of earlier A´imma and Faqihs on the grounds of public policy, justice, equity and good conscience, it may be admitted that this part of the question is not properly framed. As seen above, a Qazi or a Court of Law may differ with the Qiyas of earlier A´imma and Faqihs, but that will be on the basis of interpretation and extension of the rule of decision contained in Qur´anic and Traditional Text or Ijma´ and not on the basis of what appears to be more agreeable to the Judge. A reference has earlier been made to the rules of Istihsan and Istislah, two distinct doctrines of Muslim Jurisprudence. If there is no clear rule of decision in Qur´anic and Traditional text nor an Ijma´ or a binding juristic analogy a Qazi or a Court may resort to private reasoning and, in that, he will undoubtedly be guided by the rules of justice, equity and good conscience or, in terms of Fiqah, by the doctrines of Istihsan and Istislah.

46. The third question referred to the Full Bench likewise needs amendment. It reads:

"In case of conflict of views found in text books on Muslim Law, such as Hedaya, Fatwa-i-Alamgiri, Radd-ul-Muhtar, how are the Courts to determine which of the views is correct?"

In the course of hearing arguments, we found that the more appropriate question which falls for determination under this head is:

"How are the Courts to be guided in case of conflict of views among the founders of different Schools of Muslim Law and their disciples, other A´imma and Faqihs?"

If we are in a position to ascertain with a degree of certainty the opinion of Mujtahidun fish-Shari´ who founded the Schools of Law, such as Imam Abu-Hanifa, Malik, Shafi, and Ibn Hanbal, Mujtahidun fil-Madhahab as Imam Abu Yusuf, Imam Muhammad, Zufar, Hasan Ibn Ziyad and the opinion of Mujtahidun

fish-Shari´ who founded the Schools of Law, such as Imam
Abu-Hanifa, Malik, Shafi, and Ibn Hanbal, Mujtahidun
fil-Madhahab as Imam Abu Yusuf, Imam Muhammad, Zufar, Hasan
Ibn Ziyad and the opinion of Mujtahidun fil-Masa´l as Khassaf,
Tahawi, Sarakhsi, Karkhi, Bazdawi, Halwani and Qadi Khan, who
are called the jurists of the first three ranks, ordinarily
that would be binding on Courts. And if there is a difference
of opinion among them, according to some the Fatwa is that the
view of Imam Abu Hanifa shall weigh even if all his disciples
differ from him. In the absence of any dictum of his, the
decision will be in accordance with the opinion of Abu Yusuf,
then Muhammad, then Zufar and then Hasan Ibn Ziyad. In all
judicial matters and in questions relating to the duties of
the Courts and the Law of Evidence, the Fatwa is based on the
opinion of Abu Yusuf because of his experience as the Chief
Qazi of Baghdad, and in questions relating to the succession
of distant kindred on the opinion of Muhammad. The opinion of
Zufar has been accepted only in seventeen cases, according to
Radd-ul-Muhtar,Volume 1, page 53.

47. The view of Imam Al-Shafi´i on disagreement (of law)
has been reproduced in the earlier part of this order. On all
matters concerning which God provided clear textual evidence
in His Book or a Sunna uttered by the Prophet´s tongue,
disagreement among those to whom these texts are known is
unlawful. As to matters that are liable to different
interpretations or derived from analogy, so that he who
interprets or applies analogy arrived at a decision different
from that arrived at by another, Imam Shafi´i did not hold
that disagreement of this kind constitutes such strictness as
that arising from textual evidence. Lastly, as a doctrine of
juristic preference it is permissible that a Qazi belonging to
one School of Sunni law such as the Hanafi may decide a case
depending on juristic deduction according to Shafi´i law, or
he may make over the case to a Shafi´ Qazi, if there is one
available. In support of this view,Dr.Abdur Rahim has quoted
a number of instances. A Hanafi Qazi,following the views of
other Sunni Schools,may declare that divorce by a drunken
person is not valid, uphold a marriage contracted without two
witnesses being present as valid, set aside the marriage of a
minor contracted by his father in the presence of profligate
witnesses, uphold the sale of a Mudabbar. In Fatawa´ Qazi
Khan, Volume II, pages 451 to 459,and Fatawa´ Alamgiri, Volume
III, pages 439 to 441, the authorities cited in support of
this view are As-Siyaru-l-Kabir, Jamiul Futawa,
Khazanutul-Muftin, Majma´un-Nawazil, Al-Zakhira, Futawa
Rashidud-din, Shaikhul-Islam Abdul Wahabu´sh-Shaibani,
Shaikhul-Islam Ata Ibn Hamza and others. In the modern
context, Courts who have taken the place of Qazis may, with
advantage, apply this rule to mitigate hardship or the rigour
of a particular School of Law to which the parties belong, if
the facts of the case so merit.

52

48. The answer to the third question may be summed up thus:

There can be no disagreement in matters which are provided for in the Quranic and Traditional Text. Similarly, Ijma´ is binding upon all, until changed or modified by another Ijma´. There is, thus, no room for a Court to disagree with it for according to the tradition relied upon by Imam Shafi´i, "whatever the community of Islam may agree upon at any time is of "God". In the case of juristic analogy and Istidlal it is open to Courts to adopt any one of the conflicting views of the earlier A´imma and Faqihs, subject of course to the qualification that they possess the requisite knowledge. Lastly, Ijma´ and Ijtihad in the form of law made by the competent legislative bodies, as envisaged by the modern reformist Jurists will be binding on Courts and it is not permissible for them to differ from those laws on the ground that they conflict with the views of the earlier A´imma and Faqihs.....

WAHIDUDDIN AHMAD, J. - I have had the advantage of reading in advance the well considered and learned judgment proposed by my brother Yaqub Ali, J. I must confess that the problems raised in the questions referred to the Full Bench are too broad and involve most controversial issues. Naturally one must be cautious in dealing with such questions. I am, therefore, most reluctant to answer them in general terms. It is with this object that I would like to record my opinion in as precise terms as possible.

2. The answer to the first question need not detain me. It is accepted by all the Sunni Schools that besides two principal sources of Islamic law namely the Qur´an and Hadis there are two other important distinct sources namely Ijma´ i.e. consensus of opinion and Qiyas i.e. analogical deduction from the above three sources. Istihsan as a source of Law has also achieved considerable importance. It is resorted to in cases where no clear authority is available on a point or where the authorities are of a conflicting nature. In such cases the view is that it is open to jurists to resort to principles of equity for the purpose of deciding the issue before them. In other words Istihsan is juristic preference or equity. Sir Abdur Rahim in his commentary on Muhammadan Jurisprudence on this topic observed at page 163 as under:

"It sometimes happens that a rule of law deduced by the application of analogy to a text is in conflict with what has been expressly laid down by some other text, or by the unanimous opinion of the learned. All the four Sunni Schools of law agree that in such cases the former must give way to the latter. It may happen that the law analogically deduced fails to commend itself to the jurist, owing to its narrowness and inadaptability to the habits and usages of the people and being likely to cause hardships and inconvenience. In that event also according to the Hanafis, a jurist is at liberty to refuse to adopt the law to which analogy points, and to accept instead a rule which in his opinion would better advance the welfare of men and the interests of justice. The doctrine by which a jurist is enabled to get over a deduction of analogy, either because it is opposed to a text or consensus of opinion, or is such that his better judgment does not approve of it, is technically called Istihsan (literally, preferring' or considering a thing to be good) which I have translated juristic preference or equity."

According to Hanafi lawyers it is nothing but hidden analogy. But it cannot be denied that as a source of law it has a much wider scope.

3. The Rules of Istidlal and Ijtihad are more in the nature of further juristic exposition and development of the Muhammadan Law. Therefore, they cannot be treated as independent sources of law. Strictly speaking the principles underlying these rules are outside the domain of Courts of law and prudence demands that the application of these rules should be left to the Legislature of the country, which can usefully adopt them with the aid of leading Theologians and eminent Muslim Jurists.

4. The scope of the second question is very wide. It includes not only the principles on which Qur'an should be interpreted but also the other sources of law. It is, therefore, for consideration whether the Courts of law should put their own construction on the Qur'an. There is lot of controversy on this point. One view is "that nearness to the Prophet, in time and space, implies a greater accuracy in understanding the Quran and that, therefore, we of this generation, being farthest in time, are not best able to understand the Qur'an". Kamal A. Faruqi, a young lawyer, in his recent book on Muslim Jurisprudence at page 108 of the book has forcefully put the other view that "the Qur'an must be approached for the fullest possible understanding, both in the context of early Islamic Arabic of the heroic and classical periods and also in the context of Arabic as a living and developing language". The question, therefore, arises whether Courts of law should solve this controversy. In my judgment this is a path not free from danger and must be avoided. It was for this reason that the Privy Council as early as 1897 disapproved of this tendency and discouraged the Courts of law to put their own construction on Qur'an in opposition to the express ruling of Muhammadan Commentators of great antiquity and high authority. Although much water has flown since then but the view expressed by the Judicial Committee in <u>Agha Muhammad Zafar v. Koolsoom Bibi</u> to the following effect still holds good:-

"But it would be wrong for the Courts on a point of this kind to attempt to put their own construction on the Qur´an in opposition to the express ruling of commentators of such great antiquity and high authority (as the Hedaya and the Fatawai Alamgiri)."

After that decision even late Amir Ali in the fourth edition of his book Muhammadan Law Vol. II in the notes at page 436 had to concede that the enunciation in the Qur´an which was the subject-matter of interpretation, is regarded as a recommendation rather than a rule. This would show that even such eminent jurist could be imperfect in the interpretation of the text of Qur´an. I am, therefore, not inclined to depart from the view taken by the Privy Council. Subject to this in cases arising under Muhammadan Law a clear injunction of Qur´an and Sunnah is binding and no departure is permissible from them. Thus if it is possible to ascertain clear authority from these two primary sources in support of any proposition advanced as a rule it must be followed. But if no clear authority is available resort can be had to other sources referred to above.

5. This brings me to the next point arising out of the second question namely, whether the Courts can differ from the views of Imams and other juris-consults of Muslim law on grounds of public policy, justice, equity and good conscience. Before discussing this aspect of the question it will not be out of place to mention that the history of the development of the Muslim Jurisprudence clearly indicates that the preponderance of the views amongst the Muslim Jurists is that only the qualified jurists of the early days had the faculty of Ijtihad, namely, the right to go back to the original sources for purposes of independent interpretation. They opined that all the jurists since about the end of the Third Hijra are Muqallids, whose duty was only to accept the opinion of their great predecessors without the exercise of private judgment. For this reason the role of the later jurists was mostly confined to resolve the differences of opinion amongst the masters with the object of adopting one or the other view in preference to others, which finds place in the books of Fatawa or legal decisions. The result was that the Judge and juris-consults had no independent capacity and were bound to follow the view of their School in every detail in preference to the views of other Sunni Schools.

6. For this and other historical reasons which need not be mentioned "the gate of Ijtihad" was closed in the third Century. This is the unanimous view of all the Sunni Schools. This rule of law was followed by the Qazis appointed by the secular authorities. It, however, appears that the learned amongst the Muslim refused to accept the office of the Qazi and gradually this office lost confidence of the public because in the administration of justice they began to follow "weak opinion". Consequently about the time of the author of

Durrul Mukhtar the then Sultan of Turkey on the advice of Alama Qasim promulgated an order enjoining upon the Qadi not to follow "weak opinion". In this way the doctrine of Taqlid got firm roots. According to this doctrine jurists have been classified by Muslim Lawyers in order of preference. In one of the Full Bench decisions of the Allahabad High Court <u>Muhammad Yasin v. Rahmat Ilahi</u> (A I R 1947 All.201), Waliullah, J. has summarised the classification as under:-

"According to the recognised doctrine of Taqlid of Muhammadan Jurisprudence, jurists are classified as under:-

(1) Jurists who founded schools of law such as Abu Hanifa, Malik, Shafi´i and Ibn Hanbal, the founders of the four Sunni Schools. To them is conceded an absolute and independent power of expounding the law.

(2) Jurists who are conceded authority to expound the law according to a particular school. They were the disciples of juris-consults of the first rank. Abu Yusuf, Muhammad Zaffar and Hossan Ibn Ziyad are among the most prominent jurists of this class in the Hanafi School.

(3) Jurists who were competent to expound the law on particular questions not settled by jurists of the first and the second ranks. Among the Hanafis Tahawik, Serakhsi, Bazdawi and Qazi Khan attained this position.

(4) Jurists who occupied themselves in drawing inferences and conclusions from the law laid down by jurists of higher ranks and expounding and illustrating what had been left doubtful. Abu Bakrur´r Razi occupies a place in this rank.

(5) Jurists who are generally held competent to discriminate between two conflicting opinions held by jurists of a higher rank. Qaduri and the author of Hedaya have been assigned a place in this rank.

(6) Jurists who have authority to say whether a particular version of the law which has come down from eminent jurists of a particular School is strong or weak. The great jurist Sadrush Shariyat who has been called Abu Hanifa the second, has been given a place in this rank; and lastly

(7) Lawyers who have to accept what the jurists of the above-mentioned classes have laid down. On any question not dealt with by jurists of the higher classes they have to proceed upon the analogy of what has been laid down in similar matters, taking into account the change in the custom, and affairs of men. The author of Durrul Mukhtar belongs to this class".

7. It will thus be noticed that under this doctrine in those cases where difference of opinion is found amongst the three masters the view held by the later doctors about the correctness or otherwise of the opinion is generally followed. In Muhammadan Jurisprudence by Sir Abdur Rahim, the learned author has discussed this topic at page 188, which is as under:

"In such cases accept the view which according to the jurists of the fourth, fifth and sixth degree is correct and has been acted upon. But if in any case the later doctors have not adopted in clear language any one of the conflicting opinions, the law is to be ascertained by proceeding on the view which is most in accord with the habits and affairs of men."

In this connection one of the eminent jurists Sir Shah Sulaiman, C.J. in Anis Begum v.Muhammad Istafa Wali Khan (55 All. 743) observed as under:-

"It would follow that if jurists of the first rank have differed among themselves but the jurists of the second, third and fourth ranks have followed the opinion of one of them, it would not be proper in later times to go behind the opinion of these jurists and prefer the opinion of the majority of the jurists of the first rank which has been discarded by those of subsequent periods. The proper course undoubtedly is to abide by the opinions which have been adhered to in the commentaries which are of recognised authority in India and not to decide the point on any general rule of interpretation based on the majority of votes of the ancient jurists."

It is for consideration whether there is any justification to depart from these principles in interpreting the Muslim Law. Since the time the doctrine of Taqlid was adopted, the position has not considerably changed. I regret to point out that so far as Court of Law is concerned, for obvious reasons it cannot claim with confidence to form independent judgment on intricate questions of Muslim Law. This problem has not arisen for the first time and has received the attention of High Courts in this sub-continent on many occasions. In Aziz Banu v. Muhammad Ibrahim Hussain (A I R 1925 All. 720) Sulaiman, J. as he then was, held that when there is difference of opinion among the jurists the point in dispute cannot be decided by Courts sitting so many centuries afterwards by the examination of traditions only. Reliance must be placed on the opinion of recognised jurists who alone could have undertaken the task of sifting the traditions and, in case of divergence, on their comparative superiority. It will be useful to reproduce the view of the learned Judge at page 723 of the report. He observed:-

"The first difficulty in our way is that all the authorities referred to by the various commentators are not available to us. It is, therefore, impossible to

57

find out exactly how many authorities are one way and how many the other way. Even most of the books which have been made use of by Messrs. Baillie, Shama Charan Sircar and Ameer Ali, have not been laid before us. It is, therefore, not an easy task to say that the conclusion at which these learned authors arrived was necessarily wrong or that it was not supported by authorities other than Sharaya-ul-Islam. Another danger that has to be guarded against was pointed out by their Lordships of the Privy Council in the case of <u>Abdul Fateh Ahmad Ishak v. Russomoye Dhur Chowdhury</u> 22 Cal. 619-22 and the case of <u>Baqar Ali Khan v. Anjuman Ara Begum</u> 25 All. 236. In the last-mentioned case their Lordships remarked:

´That danger is equally great whether reliance be placed upon fresh texts newly brought to light or upon fresh logical inferences newly drawn from old and undisputed texts´.

"It is, therefore, dangerous to depart from the view of the law which has remained unchallenged for at least over half a century and which is to be found in the Sharaya-ul-Islam, the book of the highest authority in India, merely because some other authors have been taken a contrary view."

This problem also came before a Full Bench of Patna High Court in the case of <u>Fazlur Rahman v. Mst. Aisha</u> (A I R 1929 Pat. 81). In that case it was urged by one of the eminent counsels, that the functions of the British Courts in administering the Muhammadan Law are more or less the same as the functions of a Qazi under the Muhammadan rule, and it was contended by him that if we find that a particular form of divorce is not sanctioned by the laws of Qur´an, it is their duty to declare that the divorce pronounced in the bidai form will not be valid. In this connection, Fazal Ali, J. at page 84 of the report observed as under:-

"Now all the commentators are agreed that the words "a third time" should be read after the words "divorces her"´ in verse 230, and the verse means that if the wife has been divorced thrice the divorce is irrevocable and the wife cannot lawfully return to the husband. This is so, because under verse 229 after the divorce is pronounced twice there is an option with the husband to keep or abandon his wife, and in order to complete the divorce he must pronounce it a third time. This is obvious from the use of the word "then" in the aforesaid verse. After the divorce is completed by three pronouncements contemplated by verse 229, it becomes irrevocable under verse 230. The Shias and the Malikis have interpreted the three divorces referred to in these verses to mean divorces pronounced on three different occasions. There is, however, one school of commentators which has taken the view that the language used in the Qur´an is wide enough to include cases in which the divorce has been pronounced thrice on the same occasion. Thus although it may be said that of the two views the one is not so broad and not so well supported by reason as the other, yet when there is a consensus of opinion among a large and influential section of theologians who hold that the words of the Qur´an are capable of the interpretation which sanctions the bidai form of divorce and when we find that the bidai form of divorce has been in vogue among the Hanafi Muhammadans for so many centuries, it is not for us to lay down that the interpretation which does not favour the bidai form must necessarily be preferred to the interpretation which favours it. Nor do "I think we shall be justified in introducing a sudden and drastic change in what has been for generations the accepted law of the Hanafi Muhammadans. I must, therefore, hold that talak-ul-bidat is a valid and binding form of divorce according to the law of the Hanafis and as such is binding upon the parties in this case."

I quite see the force of restoring life to "Ijtihad" as a source of Muslim Law to remove stagnation in the development of Islamic Law. But apart from practical difficulties of having an Ijma of the type recognised by earliest Jurists, the question still remains whether the Court of law should embark on and traverse on this hazardous field. In my judgment nothing has happened since the above decisions were pronounced to justify any departure from the principle of interpretation recognised in them. I would, therefore, hold that it is not open to the Courts of law to differ from the views of Imams and Jurists of Muslim Law if it is in accordance with the consensus or preponderance of authorities of the doctors and Jurists of the later time.

8.   The last question as now formulated is in the following terms:-

"How are the Courts to be guided in case of conflict of views amongst the founders of different Schools of laws and their disciples, other A´imma and Faqihs"?

In the earlier part of the judgment I have fully discussed this aspect of the case. Under the present circumstances, I am firmly of the opinion that the question of differing from the views of A´imma and Faqihs should be resolved according to the doctrine of Taqlid referred to and discussed above. If their interpretation had been accepted as correct by preponderances of authorities of the doctors of the later time it should be accepted without any demur.

9.   In conclusion I would like to point out that most of the difficulties which have arisen in answering the questions referred to the Full Bench can be resolved by proper legislative measures. After the introduction of important

directive principles in this behalf in 1962 Constitution, the responsibility to implement them is on the State and the Legislative Authorities. It is for them to take measures to have an authoritative codification of rules derived from the Shariat. Majalla which is an outstanding achievement of the old Turkish rulers, can be a good basis for meeting the present-day requirement and solving this controversial issue.

ANWARUL HAQ, J. I have read with great care and interest the very learned, illuminating and elaborate opinion proposed to be delivered by Muhammad Yaqub Ali, J. I have also had the benefit of seeing in advance the differing views so ably put forth by my learned brother Wahiduddin Ahmad, J. It is not my intention to embark upon any detailed discussion of the questions referred to the Full Bench but, in view of the far-reaching importance of the issues involved, I deem it necessary to clearly state my own position in the matter.

2. Perhaps, for facility of reference, it would be well to reproduce here the questions which we have been called upon to answer:

(i)   What are the sources of Muslim Law?

(ii)   What are the rules of interpretation of Muslim Law, and can Courts differ from the views of Imams and other juris-consults of Muslim Law on grounds of public policy, justice, equity and good conscience?

(iii) How are the Courts to be guided in case of conflict of views among the founders of different schools of Muslim Law and their disciples, other A´imma and Faqihs? (Question as amended by the Full Bench)?

3. The first question has been answered at great length by Muhammad Yaqub Ali, J. who has, if I may say so with respect, taken pains to bring out the importance and scope of the various accepted and recognised primary and secondary sources of Muslim Law. I have nothing to add to this part of the discussion.

4. As regards the second question, it will be seen that it consists of two parts. The first part aims at stating the rules of interpretation of Muslim Law. I respecfully agree with the answer given to this part of the question by Muhammad Yaqub Ali, J. in paragraphs 39 to 44 of his judgment. These paragraphs furnish an extremely valuable guide for anyone engaged in the task of interpreting and applying Muslim Law.

5. The answer to the second part of the second question, namely, as to the competence of Courts to differ from the views of earlier A´immas and Faqihs on the grounds of public policy, justice, equity and good conscience, is clearly not free from difficulty and controversy. Moreover, there are several aspects to it. In the first place, the question is whether the Courts can put their own interpretation on the

Qur´an. There is no doubt that in the case of <u>Agha Muhammad</u> <u>Jafar v. Kalsum Bibi</u> (24 I A 196) the Judicial Committee of the Privy Council did observe that it would be wrong for the Courts on a point of this kind to attempt to put their own construction on the Qur´an in opposition to the express ruling of commentators of such great antiquity and high authority (as the Hedaya and the Fatawa-i-Alamgiriya) yet this view has not been followed by this Court in recent years. In <u>Mst. Balqis</u> <u>Fatima v. Najm-ul-Ikram Qureshi</u> (P L D 1959 Lah. 566) Kaikaus, J. who delivered the judgment of the Full Bench observed as follows (in paragraph 27 of the judgment on page 584 of the Report):-

"The third reply is that we are really dealing with the interpretation of the Holy Qur´an and on a question of interpretation we are not bound by the opinions of jurists. If we be clear as to what the meaning of a verse in the Qur´an is it will be our duty to give effect to that interpretation irrespective of what has been stated by jurists. ´Atiullah-wa Ati-ur-Rasul´ is the duty cast on the Muslim and it will not be obedience to God or to the Prophet if in a case where our mind is clear as to the order of the Almighty or the Prophet we fail to decide in accordance with it....."

6. This question was also discussed at some length by Muhammad Shafi, J. in <u>Mst. Rashida Begum v. Shahab Din and others</u> (P L D 1960 Lah. 1142). On page 1153 of the Report the learned Judge has expressed himself as under:-

"Thus it is quite clear that reading and understanding the Qur´an is not the privilege or the right of one individual or two. It is revealed in easy and understandable language so that all Muslims if they try may be able to understand and act upon it. It is thus a privilege granted to every Muslim which cannot be taken away from him by anybody, however highly placed or learned he may be, to read and interpret Qur´an. In understanding the Qur´an one can derive valuable assistance from the commentaries written by different learned people of yore, but then that is all. Those commentaries cannot be said to be the last word on the subject. Reading and understanding the Qur´an implies the interpretation of it and the interpretation in its turn includes the application of it which must be in the light of the existing circumstances and the changing needs of the world..... If the interpretation of the Holy Qur´an by the commentators who lived thirteen or twelve hundred years ago is considered as the last word on the subject, then the whole Islamic society will be shut up in an iron cage and not allowed to develop along with the time. It will then cease to be a universal religion and will remain a religion confined to the time and place when and where it was revealed....." .....

61

..... 8. With great humility I venture to submit that it would not be correct to lay it down as a positive rule of law that the present-day Courts in this country should have no power or authority to interpret the Qur´an in a way different from that adopted by the earlier jurists and Imams. The adoption of such a view is likely to endanger the dynamic and universal character of the religion and laws of Islam. At the same time, it is clear that the views of the earlier Imams and jurists are entitled to the utmost respect, and no Court or Commentator would differ from them except for very compelling and sound reasons. I would also like to make it clear at this stage that this difference of interpretation does not, and cannot, mean a departure from a clear injunction of law as contained in the Qur´an or Sunnah, or even Ijma, on any grounds of equity, good conscience or public policy.

9. The next aspect which needs consideration in this behalf is whether the Courts can differ from the views of Imams and other juris-consults of Muslim Law on grounds of equity and public policy. It is clear that this part of the question does not relate to the interpretation of the Qur´an or Sunnah, nor to the interpretation and application of Muslim Law as laid down by Ijma´. It obviously refers to that field of Muslim Law which is covered by Qiyas, Ijtihad, Istihsan, Istislah and Istidlal. Here we are face to face with the doctrine of what is called Taqlid in Muslim Jurisprudence. Relying upon certain decisions of Indian High Courts and an extract from the well-known book on Muhammadan Jurisprudence by Sir Abdur Rahim, my learned brother Wahiduddin Ahmad, J. has expressed the view that "nothing has happened since the above decisions were announced to justify any departure from the principle of interpretation recognised in them. I would, therefore, hold that it is not open to the Courts of Law to differ from the views of Imams and Jurists of Muslim Law if it is in accordance with the consensus or preponderance of authorities of the doctors and jurists of the later time". As against this view, my learned brother Muhammad Yaqub Ali, J. has stated (in Paragraphs 25 and 45 of his judgment) that "a Qazi or a Court of law may differ with the Qiyas of earlier A´imma and Faqihs, but that will be on the basis of interpretation and extension of the rule of decision contained in Qur´anic and Traditional text or Ijma´ and not on the basis of what appears to be more agreeable to the Judge". His Lordship has further expressed the view that "the application of Qiyas cannot, therefore, be limited to the earlier doctors nor their opinion, though entitled to utmost respect, be considered as binding for all times to come. The fact that the great Imams and their disciples have differed among themselves on numerous rules of decision as well as their details also furnishes further warrant for it".

10. It appears to me that before dealing with this aspect of the second question, it would be more appropriate to refer

to the third question before us, as that has a direct bearing on the question as to how far the Courts can differ from the earlier A´imma and Faqihs of Muslim Law. Both my learned brothers (Muhammad Yaqub Ali and Wahiduddin Ahmad, JJ.) have rightly narrated the various categories into which the earlier Muslim Jurists are usually classified by writers on Muslim Jurisprudence. They have also described the rules which obtain in the matter of giving preference to the opinion of one category of jurists as compared to those falling in a lower or a higher category, and I have nothing useful to add to that discussion except to say that I agree with the answer to the third question, as summed up by Muhammad Yaqub Ali, J. in paragraph 48 of his judgment.

11. However, even when the correct view (i.e.the view which should prevail according to the rules laid down by the earlier Muslim jurists) of a particular school of Muslim Law on a given question of law has been ascertained, the question still remains whether the Court which is called upon to decide that case has the power or authority to differ from the view of the earlier jurists. The need for such difference may arise on account of several reasons, such as, for instance, a sincere conviction in the mind of the Court that the rule as laid down by the earlier jurists is not correct according to the Qur´an and Sunnah; or that the rule is no longer appropriate or equitable in the changed circumstances of the present day Muslim society to which the Judge belongs, and that its operation will work undue hardship on one or both the parties before him. It has already been stated that this part of the question does not extend to the law as contained in the Qur´an, Sunnah or Ijma, and, therefore, the question really narrows down to whether we are to adopt the doctrine of Taqlid in all its rigour or whether we are to keep the door of Ijtihad open.

12. I find that even in the cases to which my learned brother Wahiduddin Ahmad, J. has referred, there are clear indications that the Court is not precluded from giving effect to considerations of equity, justice and good conscience. For instance, in _Aziz Banu v. Muhammad Ibrahim Hussain_ (A I R 1925 All. 720), the following observations appear in the judgment of Sulaiman, J. on page 728 of the Report:-

> "Even apart from all these considerations it is the duty of Courts, in cases of divergent opinion, when it seems impossible to ascertain the comparative merits of the authorities, to accept the view which is more in accordance with equity, justice and good conscience. Mr. Ameer Ali in his preface to the third edition at page 7 has referred to the important rule to which attention has been called by Sir William Jones that: "When the great expounders of Musalman Law have enunciated divergent doctrines or expressed different opinions, the Judge administering Musalman Law is to

adopt the one most conformable to equity and the requirements of the times."

Mr. Tyabji also in his book on Muhammadan Law, paragraph 11(a) pointed out;

When Musalman jurists of authority have expressed dissentient opinions on the same question the Islamic Courts presided over by a Qazi have authority to adopt that view which in the opinion of the presiding officer is most in accordance with justice in the particular circumstances."

13. Again, in <u>Anis Begum and others v. Muhammad Istafa Wali Khan</u> (55 I L R 743), Sulaiman, C.J. while observing that "it would not be proper now to go behind such a consensus of opinion and decide a point contrary to such opinion, on the ground that the majority of the three Imams favoured that view in the earlier centuries", went on to say that: "But if in any case the later jurists have not adopted in clear language any one of the conflicting opinions, but have merely stated the conflicting opinions without expressing any preference for either, then it is implied that the conflict of opinion was still continuing without any general concurrence having been attained, and it would then be open to choose whichever of the opinions appears to be the sounder and better adapted to the conditions and the needs of the times".

14. While dealing with the subject of Ijtihad and Taqlid in his book 'The Principles of Muhammadan Jurisprudence', Sir Abdur Rahim has, on page 188, indicated the rule which is to be observed in case of conflict of opinion among the earlier jurists, but the discussion of the subject is, however, not concluded by him on that page, and the observations of the learned author himself are contained on pages 190 to 192 of the Book (1958 Edition). It will be instructive to give here a few extracts from these observations:

"It is to be observed that so far as the administration of justice is concerned it was mainly the appointment of corrupt and incompetent Qazis that led to the formulation of the doctrine of Taqlid in its present form. That the simple remedy of appointing competent men as judges and in other ways securing a proper administration of justice should not have been sought, is apparently due to the fact that the Shari'at or the Islamic Code except during the age of first four Caliphs and for some brief period of time afterwards never had the full support of the heads of the State, who more often that not assumed powers which the law did not concede to them, and in their conduct isolated its vital principles. It is contended that Taqlid introduces the principles of certainty and uniformity in the administration of laws; but it may be doubted whether this advantage is not greatly outweighed by the danger that the rule, if narrowly interpreted, might put obstacles in the way of progress and development of law. Besides it must not be overlooked that Islamic Jurisprudence which accords an absolute authority to Ijma´ or consensus of opinion furnishes by that doctrine a guarantee against such uncertainty in the administration of law as is capable of being avoided. "In support of Taqlid it is further contended that at least since the fifteenth century, it had the implied support of the Sunni Lawyers and would thus be covered by the principle of Ijma´. But the fact supposing it to be so would not, as I have pointed out, bring the rule within the purview of Ijma´..... The lawyers who gave currency to the doctrine, in fact, emphatically lay down, that on questions which have not been clearly pronounced upon by Mujtahids of the first three degrees especially the first and the second, the Mufti and the Qadi, in applying the law must have regard to the change in the circumstances of society, which indeed is in accordance with the vital principles of the system. If this be borne in mind along with the fact that the questions on which Abu Hanifa and his disciples agree are but few, and that they or the later jurists of recognised authority the last of whom lived in the fourteenth century, could not have anticipated most of the questions which now-a-days arise under different combinations of circumstances, and that the doctors who devoted themselves to the task of collecting and sifting the dicta of ancient jurists disagree among themselves as to which of the various conflicting versions of their views is correct, the doctrine of Taqlid should not stand in the way of substantial justice or of the progress of laws in accordance with an advanced society....."

15. My answer, therefore, to the second question referred to the Full Bench is that the rules of interpretation of Muslim Law are as stated by my learned brother Muhammad Yaqub Ali, J.; that the Courts must be given the right to interpret for themselves the Qur´an and Sunnah; and that they may also differ from the views of the earlier juris-consults of Muslim Law on grounds of Istihsan (i.e. equity) or Istislah (i.e. Public good) in matters not governed by a Qur´anic or Traditional Text or Ijma or a binding Qiyas. At the same time, it must be reiterated that the views of the earlier jurists and Imams are entitled to the utmost respect and cannot be lightly disturbed but the right to differ from them must not be denied to the present-day Courts functioning in Pakistan, as such a denial will not only be a negation of the true spirit of Islam but also of the constitutional and legal obligation resting on all Courts to interpret the law they are called upon to administer and apply in cases coming before them.

The majority's view of their role in using the classical sources of Muslim law in Pakistan, subsequently endorsed by the Supreme Court, contrasts starkly with the much more conservative approach taken in the Indian courts, where the Privy Council's decision in <u>Agha Mahomed Jafar v Koolsum Bibi</u> (referred to above) still holds good, and an approach closer to that of Mahiduddin J is maintained.

<u>T.Mahmood, 'The Muslim Law of India', p.13-15</u>

"In India the traditional law of the Muslims is to be accepted as it is found in the books of authority. The courts or the lawyers do not have to locate the principles of law in the Qur'an or the Sunna. Nor have they to look or arrange for <u>Ijma</u> (consensus of the jurists) on any particular issue. As regards other sources mentioned above (<u>Qiyas, etc.</u>) the courts have neither to employ them nor to ask any contemporary jurist to do so in a given case.

Thus each source of law recognised under the classical theory is now, in India, rather dormant. The courts cannot exercise the power of <u>ijtihad</u>; nor do they recognise the authority of any <u>mujtahid</u> of our age. Under the Indian law the courts have to act as <u>muqallids</u> (conformists) in respect of the Sunnis (who agree that the doors of <u>ijtihad</u> are closed) as well as the Shias (who, in theory, believe in the continuing permissibility of <u>ijtihad</u>).

The courts of India have firmly accepted the principle of <u>taqlid</u> by laying down and acting upon the rules stated below.

(i) In administering Muslim law no court should attempt to put its own construction on any Qur'anic text (50).

(ii) No court should examine the conformity of any traditionally settled legal principle with the relevant text of the Qur'an (51).

(iii) No reported Hadis should be taken by the courts literally so as to deduce from it a new rule of law (52).

(iv) The lawyers of the modern age cannot be allowed to introduce new rules of law by claiming that they logically follow from the texts of the Qur'an or Sunna't (53).

(v) No court shall in any way circumvent or deviate from the law as settled by the jurists of the past even if it does not sound "modern", "just" or "logical" (54).

The courts in India have, thus, denied to themselves the role of a mujtahid. Of course, there is nothing either in the

Constitution of India or in any legislative enactment, expressly or impliedly directing the courts to stick to the principle of taqlid. However, the qazis in medieval India too had denied to themselves the power of ijtihad and had acted as convinced muqallids. The modern courts, finding themselves in the position of successors to the qazis, have by tradition accepted and practised the principle of taqlid´ .....
.....The sources actually tapped by the Indian courts for the ascertainment of the provisions of Muslim law applicable in particular cases before them, broadly, are:

(a)   legislative enactments applicable, if any;
(b)   certain books of jurisprudence (fiqh) of the medieval ages, now available in English translation;
(c)   some modern reference books which have in the course of time attained a position of authenticity; and
(d)   judicial precedent.

The courts of India have to apply Muslim law subject to the provisions of all those general legislative enactments, relating to or affecting one or another of the matters in the area of family law and succession, etc., which apply to all Indians alike and do not specifically protect the contrary provisions of Muslim law; they determine the applicability of particular aspects of Muslim law, which is a question different from what are the sources of Muslim law and its application in India.

Numerous legislative enactments and provisions, however, deal in India exclusively with the institutions of Muslim law. While some of them modify substantive provisions of Muslim law, the rest are of a regulatory nature. The courts have to apply the classical Muslim law subject to and in accordance with all this legislation. In no case can a court hold any legislative provision to be ultra vires the classical Muslim law, notwithstanding the contrary position of some theologians. Legislation, thus, constitutes the supreme source of Muslim law in India."

[This last paragraph is of course equally true of Pakistan. Whether it should be so is discussed in the next case extract.]

B.Z. KAIKAUS (Petitioner) v. PRESIDENT OF PAKISTAN (Respondent).
PLD 1980 S.C.160. (Supreme Court - Karam Elahee Chauan J.)

[This challenge to the Constitution of Pakistan by a political pressure group, including a former judge (the named petitioner, who pleaded the case in person), led the Supreme

67

Court to consider the place of Muslim law in British India and the Islamic Republic of Pakistan, the relationship between the Courts and the Executive in pursuing Islamicisation, and the means by which this might be achieved.]

KARAM ELAHEE CHAUHAN, J. The petitioners who claim to be members of a body named by them as a Tanzim-i-Islah-Pakistan, feeling dissatisfied with the legislative, executive and judicial order and system prevalent in the country by or under the 1973 Constitution and other laws continued or made thereunder filed on 7-1-1976 a constitutional petition being W.P. 42 of 1976 in the Lahore High Court under Article 199 of the aforesaid Constitution requesting the said Court to declare that Pakistan being a Muslim Country, it was, as a matter of its own faith as well as the faith of its Muslim population, to be governed by the law of the Holy Qur´an and the Sunnah of the Holy Prophet (may peace and blessings of God be on him) in all spheres of the State viz. legislative, executive and judicial, with the result that the aforesaid organs were bound to regulate their all matters in accordance with the aforesaid law (which was termed by the petitioners as the law of Allah or the Divine Law). This implied, as explained to us by petitioner No. 1, Mr. B.Z. Kaikaus, who personally argued the case on his own as well as on behalf of the other petitioners, both in the High Court as well as in this Court, that if any matter came up before the aforesaid three organs of the state in their respective spheres they should regulate and decide the same according to the Divine Law and ignore any provision of any other law contrary thereto may it be in the Constitution or any statute or anywhere else. It was submitted that the law of the Holy Qur´an and Sunnah being Divine Law, it came into force at once by dint of its own Divine Supremacy and does not depend upon the sanction, order authorization or command of any individual or body for its enforcement. The law of Allah, i.e. the Divine Law, in this way having already become binding upon and applicable to the State as well as the Muslims in this country as a matter of their religious faith whereunder they are bound by that law, therefore, it may be declared formally to be so, so that the various organs of the State and the Muslim population, in particular, which do not in fact and in practice according to him, so feel, may be so guided by a consequent formal declaration of the High Court accordingly, so that they may freely regulate their life and other dealings and matters on those basis. He clarified that as the law of Allah was already in force in this country of Muslims (which was brought into existence with the avowed object of practising and adopting the Islamic Law), therefore, all he wanted was a declaratory recognition of this position and was not seeking a mandamus against anybody to enforce it because according to him it was already in force in the manner above explained by

68

him namely by virtue of the State and the people of Pakistan, possessing a Muslim religion. He emphasized that the Divine Law was the only and sole criterion by which should be judged the public and private conduct of all, rulers and ruled alike, and the chief source of all legislation in the country. He said that political power must be exercised within the framework of the Divine Law, and that it is neither valid nor exerciseable except by and on behalf of the community through the process of mutual consultation (Shoora). The actual reliefs sought by the petitioners in paragraph 46 of their writ petition in their own words were as follows:-

    (1)   A declaration that Pakistan is the sacred Kingdom of Allah and the Holy Prophet Muhammad (peace and blessing of Allah be on him) whose sole sovereign and lawgiver is Allah, whose law is only Allah´s Will to be determined from the Holy Qur´an and Sunnah every word of which is binding, and which together constitute the Sharia, the divine immutable law, that the government of this sacred state is to be carried on only on behalf of Allah, in the name of Allah, and in accordance with the commands of Allah and that every person in authority, in order to decide what action he has to take, puts only one question to himself, what is the Will of Allah? and an injunction in terms of the above declaration to all the respondents to act in accordance with the Holy Qur´an and Sunnah in the slightest degree.

    (2)   A declaration coupled with an appropriate injunction that the Muslims being bound only by the divine law, i.e. the <u>Sharia</u>, the <u>Sharia</u> is the only law in this State, the status of the remaining so called laws including the Constitution being only that of orders whose validity depends on their acceptance as Allah´s will by the judicial <u>ululamr</u> or the judiciary, and that any order or any so-called law including the Constitution, which is in conflict with any part of the Holy Qur´an and Sunnah including the directions relating to justice and righteousness is null and void.....

.....2. A learned Full Bench of the High Court consisting of Sardar Muhammad Iqbal, C.J. and Aftab Hussain and Javid Iqbal, JJ. dismissed the above writ petition by its judgment and order dated 30-4-1976. The salient findings recorded by the High Court were:-

    (i)   that the precise questions raised in the writ petition have already been considered by the High Court in <u>Zia-ur-Rahman v. The State</u> P L D 1974 Note 3 at page 4. (F.B. of five Judges) and by the Supreme Court of Pakistan in the same case in appeal reported in <u>State v. Zia-ur-Rahman</u> P L D 1973 S C 49 wherein it was held that the Constitution was a valid document framed by a validly constituted National Assembly and the Courts of Law could not go outside the Constitution. No doubt a resolution generally known as the "Objectives Resolution" was passed by the then Constituent Assembly on 7-3-1949 laying down the Islamic ideals to be achieved and followed by the country but that document was neither above the Constitution nor was it unalterable or immutable and in any case there was nothing in the Constitution showing that the Resolution had been violated.

(ii) that judiciary can neither declare any of the provisions of the Constitution under which it is created nor the acts validly taken thereunder, as <u>ultra vires</u> and void, because this is not a part of the functions of the judiciary namely the function of the interpretation of laws, to strike down the very Constitution itself or acts taken thereunder. Similarly law is to be made by the relevant Legislature and not by courts whose sole duty is to decide a <u>lis</u> coming before it in accordance with the law with which the Constitution directed it to be decided. For changing one system or pattern of law to give place to another system or pattern the recourse only is political and not the machinery of law Courts, because Courts as already stated simply deal with and perform the function of adjudication and not of enacting or promulgating laws.

(iii) in this way even if there be any limitations on the part of the framers of the Constitution those limitations are only political and not justiciable by judiciary.

(iv) it was submitted by Mr. Kaikaus that the decision of this Court in the <u>State v. Zia-ur-Rehman</u> being against the Divine Law, the High Court should ignore the same (and that this could be done by all and every Judicial Officer or Court at all levels). However, the High Court held that it was not permissible for them to do so because even on the principle of "obey those who are in authority among you", as the Supreme Court was at the apex of the judicial administration, its judgments and decisions were binding on all other Courts in the country.

(v) The petitioner claimed a writ of the type of <u>quo warranto</u> against the entire Legislature, and the executive of the country, questioning their competence to hold their respective offices and positions, on the ground that if they are of the view that the Holy Quran and the Sunnah are not in force in Pakistan in their entirety except to the extent they are enacted as laws, then they are neither true Muslims nor competent to remain in office and power inasmuch as it is a negation of the Divine Law, which the petitioners think is already in force in full in this country and any denial about its operation by the respondents would be sufficient to render them incompetent and unqualified to run the Government in the executive, or legislative spheres, etc. The High Court did not accept this plea on general plane and even otherwise held that the concerned officials and functionaries being Muslims (like and in the same way just as the petitioners were) they were fully qualified to remain in office also from the point of view contained in the objection itself; and

(vi) that the Constitution of Pakistan was not un-Islamic. In this respect the learned Judges referred to the various provisions of the Constitution in detail highlighting its various Islamic features and characteristics in support of their finding, and ultimately in para. 17 held that "it becomes evident from a perusal of these Articles that the 1973 Constitution is neither un-Islamic nor infidel. On the contrary it is the commencement of a sacred project, in which the object or the end is to be attained not through a form but through a process."

3. The petitioners have come up in a petition for special leave to appeal against the aforesaid judgment and order of the High Court dated 30-4-1976 to this Court. We have heard Mr. B.Z. Kaikaus for the petitioners, and the learned Deputy Attorney-General on behalf of the Federal Government and Mr. Akhtar Shabir, learned A.A.-G., on behalf of the Province of the Punjab. Mr. B.Z.Kaikaus has reiterated the same pleas which have been mentioned (in the form of his case) in the beginning of this judgment and which find mention in para. 2 where the findings of the High Court thereon are recorded, and has prayed for the same reliefs which have been reproduced hereinbefore in extenso, laying particular emphasis on reliefs (1) and (2), the rest of the reliefs according to him being consequential and supplementary.....

.....5. It is true that the basic and primary source of all Muslim law is the Holy Qur´an and the Sunnah and the rest are the methods of understanding their meaning, spirit, purpose, guidelines and policy. To say therefore that the law of the Muslims is the Divine Law and that it constitutes the only and

71

sole criterion by which should be judged the public and the private life of all rulers and ruled alike is quite in accord with the spirit of that Law. However, to understand what is the Divine Law on any particular subject or matter, the processes above mentioned have to be resorted to. First you have to look to the original text of the relevant portion of the Holy Qur´an applicable to any precise matter involved in a case. If the matter is covered by the Holy Qur´an, you have to apply the same; failing that you have to look towards Hadis; then to Ijmaa, then resort to Qyas and other methods above mentioned.

6. We may here mention that the purpose of our referring to the sources of Islamic Laws was to show (as the varied nature of those sources themselves indicates) that Islam (or as we may say Islamic Law) in its very nature is not a rigid system of law; and no Muslim can believe that it is an outworn creed incapable of meeting the challenge of the evolutionary forces. Its basic principles of justics and equity; its urge for universal knowledge, its acceptance of life in all its aspects, its world-view, its view of human relations and human destiny, and its demand for an all round and harmonious development stand firmly like a rock in the tempestuous sea of life. Islam is not a priest-dominated theocracy. Its principles are neither hidden nor complicated or involved, and nor impracticable. It is a law which has within it the capacity or capability of being practised, enforced and applied, and adopted at all time and at all places, only if it is understood and interpreted in a true and a proper manner and in its true spirit, keeping in view the environments and the circumstances of the situation at the relevant time.

7. It is well known that Pakistan like India, remained under a foreign rule namely British Rule from the eighteenth century to 1947. In their early days the British for some time carried on the administration of Muslim and Hindu Laws with the help of the Indian Officers, who were called "Advisers to Courts" (original and appellate, civil and criminal) who advised on questions of law. The Muslim officers were known as learned Maulvis, Muftis and Ulemas and the Hindus were known as learned "Pandits". However, it may be mentioned that criminal proceedings in particular were ordered to be governed by the Shariah irrespective of the religion of the offender unless and until the "East India Company´s Government" thought it fit to order otherwise. Being strangers in this field, the British Government, therefore, adopted a policy of compiling or getting compiled English Codes of Muslim Laws as for example Hamilton´s Hedaya (1791); translations of Al-Sirajiyah and commentary thereon called the Sharifiyah, Baillie´s Digest of Muhammadan Law (being translation of Fatawa Alamgiri); Tagor Law Lectures (1891-92) the translation of Mishkat-ul-Masabib, (extracts from Fatawas by Kazee Khan), Muhammadan Jurisprudence (1911) by Abdur

72

Rahim, Principles and Precedents of Muhammadan Law by Macnaghten, etc. With the development of the judicial system following the British pattern through systematized transformation of the educational structure, when lawyers made their appearance this practice had to be abandoned with a further change that in the course of time the Islamic Laws relating to crime, punishments, revenues, land tenancy, proceedings, evidence and partly transfer of property were gradually replaced by enactments of the Legislature. Certain aspects like marriage, dower, divorce, maintenance and guardianship, succession/inheritance, gifts, wills and wakfs, and family matters were still governed by Islamic Law with certain modifications here and there. Customary law was allowed in some places such as a woman could not inherit agricultural land. However, if a particular sect of Muslims had its own rule generally it was followed with respect to that sect, as stated in <u>Raja Deedar Hussain v. Ranee Zahoor-oon-Nisa</u> ((1841) 2 M I A 441). At this place it may be mentioned that, as stated by Sir Abdur Rahim in his Muhammadan Jurisprudence at page 38 "Whatever may have been the demerits of the condemned system, it should, in fairness, be admitted that the <u>fatwas</u> of the Maulvis so far as they can be found in the pages of the old law reports, are a faithful exposition of the Muhammadan Law on the points covered by them." As the store of information accessible to English readers increased, the Judges, both of the Supreme Court and of the "Company's" Courts, began to fall less absolutely dependent on native assistance; and at last, after the extinction of the "Company", and the fusion of the two sets of Appeal Courts in the new High Courts, it was considered that the time had come for dispensing with the latter altogether, at least in the form of Maulvis regularly attached to the Court, and whom the Court was bound to consult (see Act Xl of 1864). The study of Muhammadan Law was not less important and remunerative than before, but in a different way; henceforth it became the business of the Bar to instruct Bench, and the later reports are increasingly full of learned arguments in which untranslated Arabic authorities are freely cited by advocates who combine with this special learning a general legal knowledge to which the Court Maulvis made no pretension. Moreover, the Bench, in its turn, gradually became better qualified to instruct the Bar. All the High Courts have had learned Muslims among their Judges since 1908. Some of the judgments delivered by Mahmood, J., at Allahabad (1887-1893), and by Ameer Ali, J., at Calcutta (1890-1904), are, in fact, exhaustive monographs on difficult points of Muhammadan Law.

8. During the British regime there used to be promulgated laws for this country by means of what are in legal terminology called Charters, Letters Patents, Despatches, Acts, Ordinances, Orders, Regulations, Rules, Bye-laws and other legal instruments of similar nature and

description. When Pakistan was created the Indian Independence Act, and other Acts and Orders, etc. issued at that time, authorised all the existing laws to continue till they were altered or repealed, etc. Same was the theme of the 1956 constitution, 1962 Constitution, and the 1973 Constitution. Since the country was brought into being to enable its Muslim population to order their lives in individual and collective spheres in accordance with the teachings and requirements of Islam, as set out in the Holy Quran and the Sunnah, therefore, obviously, a process had to be resorted to, as it has often been said, for "Islamisation of Laws" because the laws made by the British did not properly or fully (and some comment that in no manner) reflect the Islamic spirit therein and were unsuited to the life and the genius of the people. It is thus clear that it was a legislative measure which had to be adopted for this purpose, and the task aforesaid was obviously of the concerned Legislature, or the Government of the day to finalize that process, and not for the law Courts to enact laws by granting declarations of the kind prayed for in the writ petition from which this petition has arisen and nor could the law Courts of their own forthwith start adjudicating matters in accordance with Islamic Laws or consider the existing legal system as having been repealed and replaced by the Islamic Laws overnight.....

.....13. It cannot be denied, that enforcement of laws - (and we may say so even under Islam) - is the function of the State, which firstly makes known the relevant law to the people by publishing or publicising it so that they may regulate their lives, dealings and conduct, accordingly, and then takes legal steps or actions for its violation. (In fact most of the reliefs contained in the petition are aimed at issuing directions to the State to promulgate and enforce various types of laws mentioned therein); if the Legislature of a country makes no provision for punishing the violation of the laws or does not provide machinery for stopping their violation, obviously the Courts cannot take over that job of enacting laws or prosecuting people at their own will and pass orders in vacuum. That Islamic Law can be introduced by the State and that it is competent to do so or to enforce or declare its enforcement, is clear from the constitutions of the various Islamic countries. As for example in the Syrian Constitution it is laid down in Article 3 (2) that the "Muslim Law is the principal source of legislation". Similarly in the earlier Constitution of Iran it was provided in Article 1 (S C) that the official religion of Iran is Islam. It was further provided in Article 2 that "No act of the National Assembly can be at variance with the sacred principles of Islam". We have no intention to be exhaustive in these illustrations and the purpose of making all these references is that even in Islamic countries, it was the State which had

74

to provide, that law in force there shall be Islam, so that the people become aware of it. This will all the more be necessary where even non-Muslims in any matter are also to be treated in accordance with Islamic Law wherever so provided by that law itself (e.g. criminal matters). In our country also where there is a written constitution obviously any provision for making Shariah as the basic or principal source of all law shall have to be provided for by the declaration of the appropriate, Legislature, i.e. the state, and not by a Court-declaration, because, as already above mentioned, Courts cannot enact laws.

14. Another thing to be taken note of is that in the matter of doing Ijtehad, i.e. applying legal process for the construction and interpretation of Islamic Laws (or if we can say even for Islamisation of laws) there are two well-known schools of lawyers (if we can use this term in general). One is the school of what has been termed by jurists as "traditionalists" (or orthodox schools) and the other is school of "modernists". The traditionalist school denies the right of Ijtehad to later generations. A good deal of energy was devoted to this controversy, but it appears that it died out in Near East, or majority of Middle East countries – (as put by Schacht, Chapter 15, at page 102) – where many Islamic Schools of traditional background "without necessarily sharing all the opinions of the Modernists, recognize that effort as legitimate and act, in a way as their advisers; the uncompromising demand of taqlid, the unquestioning acceptance of the traditional doctrine of one school of law, in particular, have lost much ground and legislation of Islamic Laws by enactments became in vogue in many Islamic countries like Turkey, Syria, Egypt, Iran, Jordan, Libya, Morocco, Algeria, and Sudan, etc. most of which have the written constitutions and various written and codified laws. (At the moment there are 47 Islamic States in the world). It may, however, be mentioned that the interest and importance of the orthodox/traditional Islamic Law, which has existed for more than a thousand years and is still eagerly studied all over the Islamic world, is not affected by these changes. It still casts its spell over the laws of contemporary Islamic States : in the States of traditional orientation, such as Saudi Arabia, as the law of the land and in the States of modernists' orientation as an ideal, influencing and even inspiring their secular legislation. Now which school of thought is to be followed in and by Pakistan and to what extent and in which matters in the process of "Islamisation of Laws" is the job of the concerned Legislature to decide, though it may be pointed out that according to the trend of the case law, so far developed in Pakistan, opinions have been expressed that it is not necessary to stick to the views of the traditionalists, if the context of the Holy Qur'an and the Sunnah is clearly to the contrary on any particular point.

15. Reference here may be made to <u>Mst. Balqis Fatima v.
Najm-ul-Ikram Qureshi</u> (P L D 1959 Lah. 56) (judgment by B. Z.
Kaikaus, J., as then he was) where at page 584 in para. 27, he
held that "the third reply is that we are really dealing with
the interpretation of the Holy Qur'an and on a question of
interpretation irrespective of what has been stated by
jurists, "Atiullah-wa-Ati-ul-Rasul" is the duty cast on the
Muslims and it will not be obedience to God or to the Prophet
if in a case where our mind is clear as to the order of the
Almightly or the Prophet we fail to decide in accordance with
it. We are concerned here with the interpretation of the
verse relating to <u>Khula</u> and as I have already stated its
interpretation must be that the Court or the State has
authority to direct a <u>Khula</u>. Similar considerations apply to
the interpretation of the traditions of the Prophet.".....
[The learned judge then summarised the views expressed in Mst.
Khurshid Jan's case (above)]
.....19. The matter came up for examination before this Court
as well in <u>Mst. Khurshid Bibi v. Baboo Muhammad Amin</u> (P L D
1967 S C 97) (S. A. Rahman, Fazle Akbar, Hamoodur Rahman,
Muhammad Yaqub Ali, and S. A. Mahmood, JJ). On page 113, S.
A. Rahman, J. who wrote the leading judgment for the Court,
held that "the fundamental laws of Islam are contained in the
Qur'an and this is, by common consent, the primary source of
law for Muslims. Hanafi Muslim jurisprudence also recognises
hadith, <u>ijtehad</u> and Ijma' as the three other secondary sources
of law. The last two really fall under a single category of
subsidiary reasoning, <u>ijtehad</u> being by individual scholars
and <u>ijma</u> being the consensus of scholars who have resorted to
<u>ijtehad</u> in any one age. That this is the order of priority,
in their importance, is clear from the well-known hadith,
relating to Muadh-Ibne-Jabal who was sent by the Prophet as
Governor and Qazi of Yemen. The Prophet asked him how he
would adjudicate cases; "By the Book of God", he replied.
"But if you find nothing in the Book of God, how?" "Then by
the precedent of the Prophet". "But if there be no
precedent?" "Then I will diligently try to form my own
judgment." On this, the Prophet is reported to have said,
"Praise be to God Who hath fulfilled in the messenger sent
forth by His apostle that which is well pleasing to the
apostle of Allah." The four orthodox schools of Sunni Fiqh
were headed by Imam Abu Hanifa, Imam Malik, Imam Shafe'i and
Imam Ahmad-bin-Hanbil. The learned Imams never claimed
finality for their opinions, but due to various historical
causes, their followers in subsequent ages, invented the
doctrine of <u>taqlid</u>, under which a Sunni Muslim must follow the
opinions of only one of their Imams, exclusively, irrespective
of whether reason be in favour of another opinion. There is
no warrant for this doctrinaire fossilization, in the Qur'an
or authentic Ahadith. In the Almital-wan-Nibal (page 39), it
is stated that the great Abu Hanifa used to say "This is my

opinion and I consider it to be the best. If someone regards another person´s opinion to be better, he is welcome to it for him is his opinion and for us ours".

20. Now that we have quoted the view of Ex-Chief Justice of Pakistan S. A. Rahman, in the above case, we may refer to his book on "Punishment of Apostasy in Islam", where he has shown by making Ijtehad that the punishment of an apostate by stoning him to death is not justified in Islam except where apostacy amounts to a treason against the State. A similar Ijtehad was made by Sir Abdur Rashid, the first Chief Justice of Pakistan, in certain spheres of Muslim family laws while heading a commission on that subject. Another example can be cited of the Dissolution of Muslim Marriages Act VIII of 1939 which was promulgated after obtaining views or Fatwas of a large number of "Ulemas" of the undivided India, and was based on the principle that if any matter is not provided for in any school but is provided for in another school or schools, then the view of the schools where it is so provided can be followed and adopted as a law. See Gazette of India (1936) part 5, page 154.

21. This is now the proper place to attend to the plea of Mr. B.Z. Kaikaus that Islamic Law does not need "legislation" or that "legislation" in Islam is not permissible in the modern sense of that term for law is already contained in the text (viz. the Holy Qur´an and the Sunnah). This is quite true, but all it means is that according to Islamic Law no such law can be made which overrides that law inasmuch as Islamic Law is comprehensive by itself, permanent and applicable at all time and place. Again this is only one aspect of the matter, because, existence of law is one thing and its enforcement by legislative steps and extension by means of Ijtehad is another thing. For that purpose there are again two methods (and without trying to be exhaustive there may be more); One is as suggested by Mr. Kaikaus just to declare (the declaration is of course to be made by an enactment by the State) that in all matters pertaining to the Muslim population of this country the law shall be as contained in the Holy Qur´an and the Sunnah and stop at that, leaving the people to find out for themselves, as to what that law is on any and every matter with which they may have to deal at any particular time or in general, and regulate their individual and public life accordingly. Similarly and in the same way leave the Courts also at that, so that, wherever any matter comes before them they may find out the law for themselves and should be free to make a research or ijtehad of their own with the help of the lawyers and the commentaries, codes, and other legal material now in abundance in Pakistan. The other method is to codify the laws on various subjects by enactments etc. for easy understanding and consumption. This method, in order to adopt and mould the existing laws in conformity with the "Primary text", may include the process of

doing Ijtehad on various subjects and in various fields within the framework and the limits permissible under the "sources of Islamic Laws". The advantages of codification will be (a) cognoscibility of law; (b) to remove uncertainty of law; (c) check the introduction of the technical rules of the English Law, e.g. the western concept of the maxim of justice, equity and good conscience; (d) to avoid, as they are sometimes called by some as, evils of judicial legislation; (e) to preserve the customs suited to the people of the country; and (f) the unifying influence of Codes. However, objections against this method generally advanced are (1) inherent incompleteness of codes, though its remedy would be time to time Revision and Ijtehad, etc. (2) stereotyping of law by codification and judge-made law (3) alleged inadaptability of Islamic Law to codification; (4) alleged failure of existing codes; (5) the difficulty to satisfy members of each community who may insist that their own personal law be applied to them; and (6) the belief that it will amount to encroachment upon religion whereunder God alone is the legislator in Islam – an objection shared by Mr. Kaikaus herein.

22. The High Court in <u>Mst. Khurshid Jan v. Fazal Dad</u> (P L D 1964 Lah. 558) also made some suggestions for Islamisation of Laws which may be noted by any reader interested in the subject.

23. Mr. A. K. Brobi in his inaugural speech on 10-4-1970 before the participants of a Conference on "Islamisation of Laws" at Karachi (contained at pages 193 to 211 of his book "Islam in the Modern World") (1975 Edition) advocates the method of codified legislation, observing in his usual analytical style that "it is precisely in this sense that the Qur'an is a universal book of Man's guidance : its universality lies in its being a never failing source of basic law for the Moslems down the ages. But, then, basic law itself hands over to the Moslem community the authority to frame, what may be considered, appropriate bye-laws for regulating the conduct of the members of the community. It is in this sense that Qur'an is to be regarded as a Book of guidance which is valid for all times. It is basic law and also a charter for the Moslem community to make laws within the limits prescribed therein. Guidance is to be contradistinguished from the concept of religious law which prescribes, as does for example the law of Moses, the ten commandments. In pre-Islamic religions, religious law was no more than an unconditional imperative. In those days the law was in the form of a command, if only because the condition of human evolution was such that law could be useful only if it was confined within the narrow precincts of the imperative theory of law, that is to say, as representing a command. With Islam, the primary concept of law is that it is a system of guidance, the law-Giver who was Quaidr has primarily become a Hadi, a Guide. The Quran therefore provides a sort of

78

normative jurisprudence and within the framework of the limits imposed by the basic law gives freedom to the Moslem community to frame bye-laws for organising their institutions, be they economic, political, social, etc. with a view to carrying into effect the specific purposes incidental to and in confirmity with the Qur´an, which is also for that reason termed Furquan; that is to say, it shows how man is to discriminate between good and evil". Dr. Tanzilur Rahman in this respect in his book "A Code of Muslim Personal Law" at page 9 opines under the head "In Pakistan Constitution" that "The Qur´an and Sunnah are the two pillars of the Islamic Shariah which have been recognized as such in all the Constitutions of Pakistan. It has been guaranteed in our Constitution that no law shall be made repugnant to the injunctions of Islam as enshrined in the Qur´an and the Sunnah. What we require today is to derive norms from the Hadith and Sunnah literature for the purpose of re-statement and codification of Islamic laws, to infuse the corpus juris of Pakistan with them, to keep the living and organic relationship between the two as an active force for our socio-religious fabric of spiritual and worldly life, to provide the general direction for authentic practice and ultimately to develop into a formal discipline to impart stability and consistency to our reorientation and social reorganisation on purely Islamic pattern." Similar is the suggestion by Fyzee in his book above-mentioned.

24. As regards the 1973 Constitution, as pointed out by the learned counsel for the respondents, it also contains a scheme and procedure for Islamisation of the laws and lays down the guiding principles and the method to be adopted in that respect. Reference may be made to the Preamble of the Constitution and Articles 1 to 5, 8 to 40 and 227 to 230. In pursuance of these provisions the State has promulgated Offence of Zina (Enforcement of Hadood) Ordinance VII of 1979 ; Offence of "Qazf" (Enforcement of Hadd) Ordinance VIII of 1979 ; and Zakat and Usher (Organization) Ordinance XXIX of 1979. It has set up a Shariat Bench in each High Court of a Province and an Appellate Shariat Bench in the Supreme Court giving them power to strike down any relevant law which may be in conflict with or against the Sharia. See Articles 203-A to 203-E of the Constitution as added by the President´s Order No. 3 of 1979 which should be read with the relevant rules which authorise the superior Courts to avail of the services, suggestions, and the views of "the learned" in the Islamic Law, on any relevant point coming up before them. By the time this judgment has been completed, the pattern has further been changed; now there will be a Federal Shariat Court instead of a Shariat Bench in each High Court. Similarly the Islamic Ideology Council has been directed to finalize their recommendations for Islamisation of laws as quickly as possible. The said Council in its own turn has availed of the services of the foreign Islamic experts for guidance and

advice, and this way the work is gradually proceeding ahead. Mr. B.Z. Kaikaus submitted that this was not enough and that something more and quickly should be done in this respect and that it was due to the slow speed of the concerned authorities that the petitioners were constrained to file this petition. On his part he was of the view that this was not a difficult task and could be done overnight by just issuing a simple declaration of the kind contained in his relief No.(1). Be that as it may, the point which we want to emphasize is that the job above-mentioned in its very nature, is of a legislative and political character to be performed by the State by enacting the necessary laws for Islamisation of the existing laws or even to promulgate new laws on that pattern but within the hemisphere of the Holy Qur´an and the Sunnah.

25. Before parting with this case, we may here state something about judicial and legislative functions. Basu in his commentary on the Constitution of India (4th Edn.) (Vol. 2) at page 331 states that "the distinction between a judicial and a legislative act is well-defined. The one determines what the law is, and what rights the parties have with reference to transactions already had : the other prescribes what the law shall be in future cases arising under it" (Field, J. in Sinking Fund Cases (1878) 92 U S 700). "A judicial enquiry investigates, declares and enforces liabilities as they stand on present or past facts and under laws supposed already to exist. That is its purpose and end. Legislation, on the other hand, looks to the future, and changes existing conditions by making a new rule to be applied thereafter to all or some part of those subject to its power." (Prentis v. Atlantic Coast Co. (1908) 211 U S 210). "To declare what the law is or has been is a judicial power ; to declare what the law shall be is legislative." (Ogden v. Blackledge 2 Cr. 276 ; Dash v. Van Kleeck (1811) 7 Johns. 498). "It is not for the Judges to alter the law, even though they have reasons to doubt the wisdom or justice of any provision or to find that the Legislature has made a mistake or was even deceived Labrador v. The Queen 1893 A C 104. The same jurist in his commentary under Article 122 states that a writ would not lie against a Legislature to prevent it from passing a Bill on the ground that the Bill, if passed, would contravene some Fundamantal Right". (Chhoteylal v. The State of U.P. A I R 1951 All.228). "The Court would have jurisdiction to declare the Act void after it is passed and a proper proceeding is brought by a person who is affected by the Act. (Mason´s Manual of Legislative Procedure (1953) p.35)." Similar view is expressed by A. K. Brohi in his "Fundamental Law of Pakistan" at pages 160/333 and 469. He states with reference to 1956 Constitution that "Article 4 also prohibits the State from enacting any law, "which takes away or abridges rights conferred by this part", and declares that "any law in contravention of this clause shall, to the

extent of such contravention, be void". (See Article 4, clause (2)). Despite the fact that the Constitution contains an express prohibition directed against the legislative organs thereby preventing them from making any law which takes away or abridges the rights conferred by this Part, there is no known method whereby the Legislature can be prevented from enacting laws, which are inconsistent with the fundamental rights guaranteed under the Constitution. No mandamus can lie to compel the Legislature to do or refrain from doing any act. (For an unsuccessful attempt to obtain prohibition against a legislative body see <u>Rex v. Legislative Committee of the Church Assembly Ex parte Haynes Smith</u> ((1928) 1 K B 411). Besides, when the Bill is introduced in the House it does not become an Act of the Legislature until it has actually been taken through the various stages of law-making and has received the assent of the Governor, if it is a Provincial law, and of the President, if it is a Federal law. It is thus only the completed act of the Legislature which can be prohibited, and when the Act is actually passed it is no use prohibiting it as it can be declared void by Courts. Thus it is not the mere projected adventure by the Legislative Assembly which is calculated to result in the consummation of a law which purports to take away fundamental rights of the citizens that can be prohibited by courts. Every Bill that is moved in the State Legislature can be opposed by any one of its members, and even if its principle is accepted it can be amended and drastically modified. It would thus be worse than useless for any Court, assuming it had the jurisdiction to issue mandamus to legislative bodies, to interfere with legislative process when the act of the Legislature is not complete. If the Act, as "finally emerges is in conflict with the fundamental rights, it would <u>ipso facto</u> be void and can be declared as such by our Courts." See also <u>Narainder Chand v. U. T. H. P.</u> (A I R 1971 S C 2399) it was observed that "no Court can issue a mandate to a Legislature to enact a particular law. Similarly no Court can direct a subordinate legislative body to enact or not to enact. The relief as framed by the appellant in his writ petition does not bring out the real issue calling for determination. In reality he wants this Court to direct the Government to delete the entry in question from Schedule A and include the same in Schedule B. "See also <u>Umayal Achi v. Lakshmi Achi</u> (A I R 1945 F C 25) for the same view.

26. Examining the reliefs claimed by the present petitioners in their writ petition, as reproduced above, and as reiterated before us, it will be noticed, that though drafted very strategically in the form of claiming declarations as to what the law of this country is, in pith and substance, they purport to achieve and are aimed at getting declarations as to what the law should be in general or with regard to various specific matters mentioned there in

particular. The frame of the writ petition and its potentials clearly indicate that the petitioners were desiring an overhauling or Islamisation of the entire legal framework of this country.

27. The High Court in the circumstances was justified to dismiss the writ petition for want of jurisdiction to grant the reliefs claimed therein. The view of the High Court in this respect is not open to any exception and none was successfully pointed out to us, particularly when it was in confirmity with the law already declared by this Court in The State v. Zia-ur-Rahman and others (P L D 1973 S C 49) which still holds the field and extracts and passages whereof were correctly relied upon by the High Court.

28. The result is that the petitioners have made out no case for interference in the High Court judgment. The petition is consequently dismissed.

MUHAMMAD RIAZ (Appellant) v. FEDERAL GOVT. (Respondent) PLD 1980 F.S.C. 1. (Federal Shariat Court)

[This decision considers the role and approach of the Federal Shariat Court in determining the validity of any law challenged as repugnant to Islam under Article 203 of the 1973 Constitution (as amended).]

AFTAB HUSSAIN, J. - 8. Article 203-D of the Constitution provides that if the Federal Shariat Court finds that any provision of law is repugnant to the Injunctions of Islam it shall state the extent to which such law or any of its provisions is so repugnant. It further provides that if any law or provision of law is found by the Court to be so repugnant the President with respect to a matter in the Federal or Concurrent Legislative List, or the Provincial Government in the case of law with respect to a matter not enumerated in any of these lists shall take steps to amend the law so as to bring it in conformity with the provision of Islam and such law or its provisions as are held to be repugnant shall cease to have effect on the day on which the judgment of the Court takes effect. Similar were the powers of the Shariat Benches of the High Courts.

9. The above Constitutional provision contemplates that when a law can be rendered ineffective without leaving a vacuum it shall cease to have effect after the expiry of the time fixed by the Court. But in case the law requires amendment, the judgment can become effective only after the amendment as ordered by the Court is made by the relevant Legislature.....

.....12. Before proceeding to consider the questions raised in this petition I would like to deal with the extent of jurisdiction of this Court. Article 227 of the Constitution provides that existing laws shall be brought in conformity with the injunctions as laid down in the Holy Qur´an and Sunnah of the Prophet (peace be upon him) and no law in future shall be made which is repugnant to the Holy Qur´an and Sunnah. The jurisdiction of this Court under Article 203-D is, therefore, limited to discovering the repugnance of a law or provision of law to the holy Qur´an and Sunnah.

13. The principle under which the repugnance of a particular law to the Injunctions of Islam has to be judged is thus limited to the consideration of the question whether the laws sought to be challenged before this Court are in conformity with the Injunctions of Islam as laid down in the Holy Qur´an and Sunnah of the Prophet (peace be upon him). It would, therefore, be clear that the language of the Constitution does not warrant any attempts at harmonizing the laws with any particular jurisprudence (Fiqh) or jurisprudence of any particular school of thought or sect. On the other hand it appears that reference to any particular doctrinal approach (fiqh) has been eliminated deliberately so as to enable the Courts to test the validity of a law only on the criteria of commendments laid down in the holy Qur´an or the Sunnah of the Prophet (peace be upon him).

14. Looked in this context it would be clear that though doctrinal approach (fiqh) of different schools of thought may have a persuasive value which it undoubtedly has and in many cases full assistance may be obtained from it in the interpretation of the texts of the holy Qur´an on traditions yet this Court cannot blindly follow the doctrines (fiqh) of a particular sect. If the intention of the Constitution had been to apply a sectarian doctrine to matters of public law (as distinguished from personal law) all the difficulty would have been obviated by replacing the present public law by Fatawa Alamgiri. But clearly this is not the object of the Constitution to which it appears abhorrent to demolish the existing legal structure in order to raise a new structure of public law. The constitutional intent is only to repair the existing structure by eliminating from it what is repugnant to the divine law comprised in the holy Qur´an and the Sunnah of the Prophet (peace be upon him) and amending the law to make it conform to the said divine law.

15. Interpretations of the divine law is a matter which would require the facility of consulting opinions of all our renowned jurists. The possibility cannot be ruled out that the interpretation on a particular point by a jurist belonging to school of thought different from the one to which I belong may commend itself to me as being more in line with the requirements of the modern Muslim Society in the country. In view of the compatibility of such view with the requirements of our society it will be logically realistic to adopt it as affording guidance in the task assigned to this Court. Some

problems faced by this country may, however, be absolutely new problems for which no jurisprudence may provide any guidance. It is also possible that while differing on a point our old jurists might have taken into consideration different alternative but might have either ignored some alternative or the requirements of the modern society may produce or generate a new option. It may not be possible in such cases to rely upon their view. The elimination from the text of the Constitution of reliance upon a particular sectarian doctrine is not, therefore, without reason.

16. In my view the methodology to remove from our laws any incongruity with the holy Qur´an and Sunnah should be as follows:-

(1) To find in the first instance the relevant verse or verses in the holy Qur´an regarding the question in issue;

(2) To find out the relevant Hadis (Tradition), of the Holy Prophet (peace be upon him);

(3) To discover the intent of the Qur´anic verse from the Traditions of the holy Prophet (peace be upon him);

(4) To ascertain the opinions of and views adopted by all jurists of renown on that matter and to examine their reasoning in order to determine their harmony with the present day requirements, or if possible to modulate them to the demand of the modern age; and

(5) To discover and apply as a last resort any other option which should no doubt be in harmony with the holy Qur´an and Sunnah.

17. It may be worthwhile mentioning that more or less the same principles are adopted by the Council of Islamic Ideology, as would be clear from pages 18 and 19 of ´Majmua Qawaneen-e-Islam, Vol.I by Dr. Tanzil-ur-Rehman (now Justice). Principles followed by the Council are:-

(1) To discover the text of the Holy Qur´an and to refer to it.

(2) If the Injunction in the holy Qur´an is clear and does not require any further elucidation or warrant any difference of opinion, to accept it without any hesitation.

(3) If there be any difference of opinion on the interpretation of the Injunctions in the holy Qur´an, to find out the relevant Hadis.

(4) If there be different Traditions and if it be difficult to harmonise them, to find out the correct Hadis on the principles laid down for discovery of such Hadis.

(5) If there be no Injunction either in the Holy Qur´an or in the Tradition but there be ´Isma among the Caliph or different Imams to adopt the

same.

(6)   In case of difference of opinion between different
       Imams to find out the version which has so far
       been preferred and to adopt it only in case it is
       in accordance with the requirement of the present
       era.

(7)   In case it cannot be adjusted to modern
       conditions, to adopt any of the several views of
       the jurists.

(8)   In case there be no guidance in the Holy Qur´an
       and Sunnah and the opinions of different schools
       of thoughts also be not acceptable, to resort to
       Ijtihad.

18. Thus the Council also accepts the principle of
choosing from the opinions of our renowned jurists and as a
last resort of embarking upon Ijtihad, the object in either
case being to reconcile the requirement of the present era
with the teaching of the Qur´an and the Sunnah.   19. Now
while venturing upon the function constitutionally assigned to
this Court it is necessary to remove a serious
misunderstanding and also to reiterate the established
principles of interpretation of law of the Qur´an. The general
view which is not based upon any comparative study, is that
our statute law and the law of the Qur´an are poles as under
and the twain shall never meet. The view is obviously
fallacious. The shariah has impliedly and sometimes expressly
approved the customs and usages of the Arab society save to
the extent of their incongruity to the tenets laid down by the
Qur´an and the Sunnah particularly what is declared as
unlawful or lawful. In this respect the view of Shah
Waliullah has been summed up as follows by Dr. Muhammad Iqbal
in his lecture ´The Principle of Movement in the Structure of
Islam´:

       "Shah Waliullah has a very illuminating discussion on
       the point. I reproduce here the substance of his view.
       The prophetic method of teaching, according to Shah
       Waliullah, is that, generally speaking, the law revealed
       by a Prophet takes especial notice of the habits, ways,
       and peculiarities of the people to whom he is
       specifically sent. The prophet who aims at all
       embracing principles, however, can neither reveal
       different principles for different peoples, nor leave
       them to work out their own rules of conduct. His method
       is to train one particular people, and to use them as a
       nucleus for the building up of a universal shariat. In
       doing so he accentuates the principles underlying the
       social life of all mankind, and applies them to concrete
       cases in the light of the specific Hadis of the people
       immediately before him."

20. Islam thus recognised that not all customs and usages
of the Arabs were repugnant to Shariah ; and maintained most

85

of them as good law. Our statute laws whether inherited from the British Government or enacted after Independence are based upon the principle of common good and justice, equity and good conscience which is the same as the principles of public good (Masaleh Mursila) of Imam Malik and principle of Istihsan of Imam Abu Hanifa. A fortiori these laws must be more in harmony with Shariah. In some respects the statute law may not fulfil the standard of the law of the Qur´an and may also be repugnant to it but such instances are few.

21. Consequently the first principle to be invoked is to test these laws on the principles of' Halal (lawfulness) and Haram (unlawfulness) as laid down in the divine law.

22. The holy Qur´an has expressly stated what is unlawful and prohibited. The Prophet of God has made additions to this category, but it cannot be doubted that the authority to declare something unlawful or prohibited lies with the Almighty or His Holy Prophet (peace be upon him) and it is not lawful for any person to render unlawful what is lawful (see 66 : 1).

"O Prophet why bannest thou that which Allah hath made lawful for thee."

In 10 : 60 rebuke is administered for this: "Have you considered what provision Allah hath sent down for you, how have you made of it lawful and unlawful."

23. Allama Shabir Ahmad Usmani has repeated and developed this principle in his commentary of the Holy Qur´an at various places see pages 33, 138, 157, 159 and 363. Any silence about lawfulness or prohibitions about any matter makes it pardonable which means that it cannot be categorised as unlawful. Elam-ul-Mowaqieen by Hafiz Ibne Qayyum, Vol. II, pages 215, 225, 226, 229, 322, 325, 358 and 661 (printed by Ahle Hadis Acadamy, Lahore).

24. The second principle is that by the change of customs and usage the doctrinal opinion may also change. (See Elamul Maqqieen by Hafiz Ibne Qayyum, Vol. II, pages 822 and 843). This principle highlights the importance only of change of custom but also change of era and change in society in the context of evolution and dynamism in the field of law, which is taken care of by the principle of Ijtihad.

25. The third principle is that concessions and rights if misused by the people can be suspended or withdrawn as was done by the Second Caliph by treating three divorces uttered at the same time as three and irrevocable, contrary to Sunnah of the Prophet (peace be upon him) which treated any number of simultaneous divorces as one. Hazrat Umar introduced this law when he found that the facility or concession was being generally misused.

26. A fourth principle is that it is better not to ward off a transgression if its stoppage leads to the spread of more malignant vices (Elam-ul-Mowaq-qieen, Vol. II, page 772).....

ZAKAULLAH LODHI, J. - We are required to construe the Injunctions of the Holy Qur'an and the Sunnah in the light of such conditions as were prevalent at a particular juncture of time in the society in which Islam was practised first in its true spirit and not to try to apply it by rigidly adhering to the grammatical meanings of a particular verse and by divorcing the impact and bearing of the general scheme and spirit of Qur'an as well as the goal in view of the Holy Prophet (peace be upon him). The greatest of exponents of Islamic Laws always adopted this course in their own times and provided a guideline for us. Such other questions, as the examination of the historical background of our people, their temperament and the place and position that they occupy in the present day civilisation are other considerations which shall have to be kept in mind.....

———

Chapter Two

VALIDITY OF MARRIAGE

The institution of marriage is at the centre of Muslim personal law. The validity of a marriage may determine legitimacy, rights to inheritance, criminal liability for certain sexual acts, as well as the obligations of maintenance etc., which attach to the status of marriage. It is generally held that Muslim marriage is not as in Christian theology a holy sacrament but a civil contract. However, there has been much criticism of this attitude:

Tanzil-ur-Rahman, "A Code of Muslim Personal Law" Vol. I, p.18

"So far as the nature of the marriage contract is concerned the High Courts of Indo-Pak subcontinent and the Privy Council of the United Kingdom are all of the view that Nikah, like other contracts, is a civil contract. Justice Syed Mahmud, an eminent judge of undivided India, in the case of Abdul Kadir vs. Salima Bibi I.L.R. (1886) 8 All. 149, discussing nearly ninety years ago the features of Nikah under Muslim Law, subscribed to the view that Nikah amongst Muslims is not a sacrament, rather it is purely a civil contract. This concept, in fact, is in conformity with the view of Shama Charan Sarkar (Tagore Law Lectures 1875). For Muslims, marriage contracts, unlike those of the Hindus, require no religious rites and ceremonies. Almost all the courts of Indo-Pak subcontinent, accepting Justice Mahmud's view, have held Nikah to be purely a civil contract. This view has been so much stressed that other aspects of Nikah have receded into the background. The latest pronouncement of the highest judicial authority in Pakistan i.e. the Supreme Court, in Khurshid Bibi's case P.L.D. 1967 S.C. 97, on this point, is of vital importance.
Mr. Justice S.A. Rahman who wrote the judgement says that 'marriage among Muslims is not a sacrament, but is in the nature of civil contract. Such a contract undoubtedly has spiritual and moral overtones but legally, in essence, it remains a contract between the parties.....' This judgement

does not say that marriage is purely a civil contract, or, for that matter, a civil contract. It merely regards it to be in the nature of a civil contract. Justice Qadir al-Din Ahmad, in a Karachi case, <u>Muhd. Yasin vs. Khushnuma Khatoon</u> 2 Kar. W.L.R. 29 (1960), discussing the characteristics of marriage contract had earlier observed that ´if religious ritual is not an essential part of the transaction it does not mean that it has no sacred and no higher religious purpose enjoying the sanctity of religion and pleasure of God. There is a sanctity attached to it from the beginning to the end by conceptions of rights and obligations which, if treat´ed without the holiness which they possess in their nature, would be profane and cease to be Islamic in character.´

The view point of Justice Qadir al-Din Ahmad that <u>Nikah</u> in Islamic <u>Shari´ah</u> is not merely a civil contract, it has attached to it a religious sanctity as well, has a sound basis. <u>Nikah</u> to Muslims does not only bring legal and social advantages; it also confers on them innumerable religious and spiritual benefits.

It, however, appears that generally the courts while holding a Muslim marriage to be a purely civil contract were anxious to distinguish it from the Hindu and Christian concepts of marriage wherein it is regarded as a sacrament. Although marriage contract in Islam has a certain resemblance with a civil contract, it would be absolutely wrong to say that it is a purely civil contract. The following considerations that flow from a marriage contract shall make clear the distinction between the two:

1. Constitution and performance of a civil contract is governed by the law of contract while the constitution and performance of a marriage contract is governed by Islamic <u>Shari´ah</u>.

2. In a civil contract, the parties may not be Muslim individuals alone. They may even be firms, companies, or corporations or the governments. A Muslim marriage contract can only be made between Muslims or a Muslim male and a <u>Kitabiyyah</u> female, where no legal prohibition exists.

3. In civil contracts the rights and obligations of the parties concerned are determined by the contract itself, subject to the law of the land, whereas the rights and obligations of the married couple get determined automatically in accordance with the injunctions of Islam. Parties may, however, have the right to vary or modify some of the terms, but not so as to nullify the essential characteristics of a marriage contract under the <u>Shari´ah</u>.

4. Ordinarily a civil contract is terminable by either party, subject to the liability of paying compensation, whereas there are checks on the termination or dissolution of a marriage contract, specially on the part of the wife.

5. In a civil contract presence of witnesses is not essential, whereas in a marriage contract the presence of

witnesses at the time of Nikah is an essentiality according to all Sunni schools of fiqh. The Maliki school of fiqh lays great stress on the publicity (i´lan) of Nikah which is equally distinct from a civil contract.

In substance a Muslim marriage contract is a sanctified religious contract. The rights and obligations between husband and wife arising therefrom are, however, of civil nature and they may be enforced through courts as such. But Nikah, merely on account of rights and obligations between husband and wife arising therefrom being of civil nature, cannot be called merely a civil or social contract.

The rights arising out of an Islamic marriage contract are not the gift of any legislative body of a country; they emanate from the proposal and acceptance of the parties made at marriage time. The rights and obligations arising thus are a cohesive whole based on the biddings of God and traditions of the Prophet. Hence Muslim jurists regard Nikah to be both temporal and religious at the same time.

Nikah - A Religious Injunction:

Nikah has been denominated by the Prophet as his Sunnah. Hence, Nikah, in certain circumstances, is an obligatory Sunnah (muwakkadah). If one is apprehensive of his committing adultery, in spite of his being capable of providing maintenance and paying dower to a woman, Nikah, for him, is obligatory (Wajib). He will be committing a sin if he does not contract marriage. One is apprehensive of transgressing the limits of God (hudud Allah) in marriage, Nikah for him is abominable (makruh). According to the sayings of the Companions of the Prophet, Nikah has a preference over superogatory ritual i.e. nafl prayers.

Islamic law, therefore, holds that the institution of marriage is comprised of both the ´ibadat (worships) and the mu´amalat (worldly affairs). In its constitution it is a civil contract in which the free consent of both the parties is essential; on the accomplishment of it, however, the relationship of both the contracting parties is not determined as of a pure civil contract, but is determined in combination with its religious connotation."

————————

The essence of nikah is its permanence: subject to divorce it is a lifelong institution and any term to the contrary is void. However, the Shi´a have admitted the concept of a marriage expressly limited in duration, on the basis of pre-Islamic practice tolerated by the Holy Prophet Muhammad but subsequently suppressed by the Caliph Umar: the mut´a marriage. This is considered later (2).

The traditional scheme of discussion adopted by Muslim jurists in determining the validity of a marriage is to consider four conditions (<u>shurut</u>), to which modern Muslim jurists have added a fifth to meet modern developments in some Muslim states. The conditions are: <u>shurut al-in´ iqad</u> (conclusion of the marriage); <u>shurut al-sihha</u> (concerning impediments to the marriage); <u>shurut al-nufudh</u> (the effectiveness of the marriage, e.g. capacity of the parties); <u>shurut al-luzum</u> (the bindingness of the marriage, e.g. the doctrines of <u>kafa´a</u> and <u>khiyar al-bulugh</u>); <u>shurut al-sijill</u> (requirements of registration etc., imposed by modern legislation). However, an approach more familiar to students of western legal systems will be adopted here, dealing with capacity, formality and the consequences of failure to comply with these requirements.

To have full capacity to marry in Hanafi law the parties must be of opposite sex, of sound mind and have attained puberty. The Hanafi school is unique among the Sunni schools of law in granting full capacity in marriage even to the virgin adult woman. Puberty for both girls and boys is presumed in the subcontinent at fifteen (3) years in the absence of evidence to the contrary but puberty may be shown earlier, the minimum acceptable ages being nine (4) and twelve (5) years respectively. Marriages by persons below this age are however quite possible. Firstly, a marriage contracted personally by a minor who has reached the ´age of discretion´ is valid but suspended until the minor´s marriage guardian gives his consent (6). Secondly, the minor´s marriage guardian may contract the minor in marriage on his or her behalf at any time before puberty and this will be fully effective subject to the qualification that the minor may in certain circumstances exercise an option to repudiate the marriage on attaining puberty, the <u>khiyar al-bulugh</u>. This is considered later. Nevertheless the <u>jabr</u> or power of imposing a marriage on a minor in this way has no Qur´anic endorsement and the perceived evil of child marriages has led to legislation which seeks to restrain it by means of criminal sanctions: by the Child Marriage Restraint Act 1929, as amended in India by the Child Marriage Restraint (Amendment) Act 1978 and in Pakistan by the Muslim Family Laws Ordinance 1961. Nevertheless, despite the criminal sanctions it will be seen that the marriage itself is valid and there is a short time limit on prosecutions:

Child Marriage Restraint Act 1929 (as amended)

.....2.   In this Act, unless there is anything repugnant in the subject or context, -
- (a) "child" means a person who, if a male, is under eighteen years of age, and if a female, is under fourteen years of age;
- (b) "child marriage" means a marriage to which either of the contracting parties is a child;

(c) "contracting party" to a marriage means either of the parties whose marriage is or is about to be thereby solemnised; and

(d) "minor" means a person of either sex who is under eighteen years of age.

3. Whoever, being a male above eighteen years of age and below twenty-one, contracts a child marriage shall be punishable with fine which may extend to one thousand rupees.

4. Whoever, being a male above twenty-one years of age, contracts a child marriage shall be punishable with simple imprisonment which may extend to one month, or with fine which may extend to one thousand rupees, or with both.

5. Whoever performs, conducts or directs any child marriage shall be punishable with simple imprisonment which may extend to one month, or with fine which may extend to one thousand rupees, or with both, unless he proves that he had reason to believe that the marriage was not a child marriage.

6. (1) Where a minor contracts a child marriage, any person having charge of the minor, whether as parent or guardian or in any other capacity, lawful or unlawful, who does any act to promote the marriage or permits it to be solemnised, or negligently fails to prevent it from being solemnised, shall be punishable with simple imprisonment which may extend to one month, or with fine which may extend to one thousand rupees, or with both:

Provided that no woman shall be punishable with imprisonment.

(2) For the purposes of this section, it shall be presumed, unless and until the contrary is proved, that where a minor has contracted a child marriage, the person having charge of such minor has negligently failed to prevent the marriage from being solemnised.....

.....9. No Court shall take cognizance of any offence under this Act after the expiry of one year from the date on which the offence is alleged to have been committed......

.....12. (1) Notwithstanding anything to the contrary contained in this Act, the Court may, if satisfied from information laid before it through a complaint or otherwise that a child marriage in contravention of this Act has been arranged or is about to be solemnised, issue an injunction against any of the persons mentioned in sections 3, 4, 5, and 6 of this Act prohibiting such marriage.

(2) No injunction under sub-section (1) shall be issued against any person unless the Court has previously given notice to such person, and has afforded him an oportunity to show cause against

the issue of the injunction.

(3) The Court may either on its own motion or on the application of any person aggrieved rescind or alter any order made under sub-section (1).

(4) Where such an application is received, the Court shall afford the applicant an early opportunity of appearing before it either in person or by pleader; and if the Court rejects the application wholly or in part, it shall record in writing its reasons for so doing.

(5) Whoever knowing that an injunction has been issued against him under sub-section (1) of this section disobeys such injunction shall be punished with imprisonment of either description for a term which may extend to three months, or with fine which may extend to one thousand rupees, or with both:

Provided that no woman shall be punishable with imprisonment.

––––––––––

Note: In India, by the Child Marriage Restraint (Amendment) Act 1978 the relevant ages are 18 for a girl and 21 for a boy. In Pakistan, by the Muslim Family Laws Ordinance 1961 s12(1)(c) the relevant ages are 16 for a girl and 21 for a boy. There are also other changes: the Indian Act applies the same age requirements to the Christian Marriage Act 1872 and to the Hindu Marriage Act 1955.

Child Marriage Restraint (Amendment) Act 1978

s.2   Amendment of section 2 - In section 2 of the Child Marriage Restraint Act, 1929 (19 of 1929) (hereinafter referred to as the principal Act), the following section shall be inserted, namely:-

   ´(a) "child" means a person who, if a male, has not completed twenty-one years of age, and if a female, has not completed eighteen years of age;´

Muslim Family Laws Ordinance 1961

s.12   In the Child Marriage Restraint Act 1929 (XIX of 1929),

   (1)   in section two, -

   (a) in clause (a), for the word ´fourteen´ the word ´sixteen´ shall be substituted;

   (b) in clause (c), the word ´and´ shall be omitted; and

   (c) in clause (d), for the full stop at the end a comma shall be substituted, and thereafter the following new clause (e) shall be added, namely:-

"(e) "Union Council" means the Union Council or the Town or Union Committee constituted under the Basic Democracies Order, 1959, (P.O.No.18 of 1959) within whose jurisdiction a child marriage is or os about to be solemnised";

(2) section three shall be omitted;

(3) in section four, for the words ´twenty one´ the word ´eighteen´ shall be substituted;

(4) in section nine, after the words "under this Act", the words "except on a complaint made by the Union Council, or if there is no Union Council in the area, by such authority as the Provincial Government may in this behalf prescribe, and such cognizance shall in no case be taken" shall be inserted; and

(5) section eleven shall be omitted.

[The Union Councils no longer exist: their role is usually performed by a civil judge.]

————————

A Muslim woman may be married only to one husband at any given time (7). A Muslim man, however, may be married to a maximum of four women (8). This right to contract polygamous unions is not unqualified even in the classical law of Islam and there are a number of ways of further restricting the right which have been used in recent times. The Qur´an imposes a moral requirement that the husband should be able to treat his wives equally, in an objective sense according to the interpretation of most jurists, but without any enforceable restraint on marriage to more than one woman if he cannot. It being admitted that equal affection is impossible for ordinary mortals (though the Prophet Muhammad himself was a polygamist) Muslim states have reinterpreted the Qur´anic injunction in subjective terms and have placed restrictions on polygamy, more or less ineffective. In India there has been no such reform for marriage between Muslims but in Pakistan there has been some attempt to regulate the practice, in the Muslim Family Laws Ordinance 1961: it will be seen that despite the criminal penalties and financial consequences for the husband who ignores these procedures the marriage is still valid, though it cannot be registered and the first wife has the ability to obtain a divorce on the basis of the contravention. The relevant provisions are s.6 of the 1961 Ordinance and Rule 14 of the West Pakistan Rules under the 1961 Ordinance. For convenience the whole of the Ordinance, in so far as it relates to validity of marriage, is reproduced below. Note in particular S.1(2) on the extent and application of the Ordinance.

95

Muslim Family Laws Ordinance 1961 (as amended)

1. **Short title, extent, application and commencement** –
(1) This Ordinance may be called the Muslim Family Laws Ordinance, 1961.
(2) It extends to the whole of Pakistan, and applies to all Muslim citizens of Pakistan, wherever they may be.
(3) It shall come into force on such date as the Central Government may, by notification in the official Gazette, appoint in this behalf.

2. **Definitions** – In this Ordinance, unless there is anything repugnant in the subject or context –
(a) "Arbitration Council" means a body consisting of the Chairman and a representative of each of the parties to a matter dealt with in this Ordinance:
> Provided that where any party fails to nominate a representative within the prescribed time, the body formed without such representative shall be the Arbitration Council:

(b) "Chairman" means the Chairman of the Union Council or a person appointed by the Central or a Provincial Government, or by an officer authorized in that behalf by any such Government, to discharge the functions of Chairman under this Ordinance:
> Provided that where the Chairman of the Union Council is a non-Muslim, or he himself wishes to make an application to the Arbitration Council, or is, owing to illness or any other reason, unable to discharge the functions of Chairman, the Council shall elect one of its Muslim members as Chairman for the purposes of this Ordinance:

(c) "Prescribed" means prescribed by rules made under section 11;
(d) "Union Council" means the Union Council or the Town or Union Committee constituted under the Basic Democracies Order, 1959 (P.O. No. 18 of 1959), having in the matter jurisdiction prescribed:
(e) "Ward" means a ward within a Union or Town as defined in the aforesaid Order.

3. **Ordinance to override other laws, etc.** –
(1) The provisions of this Ordinance shall have effect notwithstanding any law, custom or usage, and the registration of Muslim marriages shall take place only in accordance with those provisions.
(2) For the removal of doubt, it is hereby declared that the provisions of the Arbitration Act, 1940 (X of 1940), the Code of Civil Procedure, 1908 (Act V of 1908), and any other law regulating the procedure of courts, shall not apply to any Arbitration Council.....

.....5. **Registration of marriages** –

(1) Every marriage solemnized under Muslim law shall be registered in accordance with the provisions of this Ordinance.

(2) For the purpose of registration of marriages under this Ordinance, the Union Council shall grant licences to one or more persons, to be called Nikah Registrars, but in no case shall more than one Nikah Registrar be licensed for any one Ward.

(3) Every marriage not solemnized by the Nikah Registrar shall, for the purpose of registration under this Ordinance, be reported to him by the person who has solemnized such marriage.

(4) Whoever contravenes the provisions of sub-section (3) shall be punishable with simple imprisonment for a term which may extend to three months, or with fine which may extend to one thousand rupees, or with both.

(5) The form of _nikah nama_, the registers to be maintained by Nikah Registrars, the records to be preserved by Union Councils, the manner in which marriages shall be registered and copies of _nikah nama_ shall be supplied to the parties, and the fees to be charged therefor, shall be such as may be prescribed.

(6) Any person may, on payment of the prescribed fee, if any, inspect at the office of the Union Council the record preserved under sub-section (5), or obtain a copy of any entry therein.

6. _Polygamy_ –

(1) No man, during the subsistence of an existing marriage, shall, except with the previous permission in writing of the Arbitration Council, contract another marriage, nor shall any such marriage contracted without such permission be registered under this Ordinance.

(2) An application for permission under sub-section (1) shall be submitted to the Chairman in the prescribed manner, together with the prescribed fee, and shall state the reasons for the proposed marriage, and whether the consent of the existing wife or wives has been obtained thereto.

(3) On receipt of the application under sub-section (2), the Chairman shall ask the applicant and his existing wife or wives each to nominate a representative, and the Arbitration Council so constituted may, if satisfied that the proposed marriage is necessary and just, grant, subject to such conditions, if any, as may be deemed fit, the permission applied for.

(4) In deciding the application the Arbitration Council shall record its reasons for the decision, and any party may, in the prescribed manner, within the prescribed period, and on payment of the prescribed fee, prefer an application for revision, in the case of West Pakistan,

to the Collector and, in the case of East Pakistan, to the Sub-Divisional Officer concerned and his decision shall be final and shall not be called in question in any court.

(5) Any man who contracts another marriage without the permission of the Arbitration Council shall –

(a) pay immediately the entire amount of the dower, whether prompt or deferred, due to the existing wife or wives, which amount, if not so paid, shall be recoverable as arrears of land revenue; and

(b) on conviction upon complaint be punishable with simple imprisonment which may extend to one year, or with fine which may extend to five thousand rupees, or with both.....

.....10. <u>Dower</u> – Where no details about the mode of payment of dower are specified in the <u>nikah nama</u>, or the marriage contract, the entire amount of the dower shall be presumed to be payable on demand.

11. <u>Power to make rules</u> –

(1) The Provincial Government may make rules to carry into effect the purposes of this Ordinance.

(2) In making rules under this section, the Provincial Government may provide that a breach of any of the rules shall be punishable with simple imprisonment which may extend to one month, or with fine which may extend to two hundred rupees, or with both.

(3) Rules made under this section shall be published in the official Gazette, and shall thereupon have effect as if enacted in this Ordinance.....

West Pakistan Rules Under The Muslim Family Laws Ordinance 1961

1. These rules may be called the West Pakistan Rules under the Muslim Family Laws Ordinance, 1961.

2. In these rules, unless there is anything repugnant in the subject or context –

(a) "Form" means a form appended to these rules;

(b) "Ordinance" means the Muslim Family Laws Ordinance, 1961 (VIII of 1961);

(c) "Register" means a register of <u>nikahnamas</u> prescribed under Rule 8; and

(d) "Section" means a section of the Ordinance.

Arbitration Council

3. The Union Council which shall have jurisdiction in the matter for the purpose of clause (d) of section 2 shall be as follows, namely:

(a) In the case of an application for permission to contract another marriage under sub-section (2) of section 6, it shall be the Union Council of the Union or

Town where the existing wife of the applicant, or where he has more wives than one, the wife with whom the applicant was married last, is residing at the time of his making the application:

> Provided that if at the time of making the application, such wife is not residing in any part of West Pakistan, the Union Council that shall have jurisdiction shall be –
> (i) in case such wife was at any time residing with the applicant in any part of West Pakistan, the Union Council of the Union or Town where such wife so last resided with the applicant; and
> (ii) in any other case, the Union Council of the Union or Town where the applicant is permanently residing in West Pakistan;.....

4. Where a non-Muslim has been elected as Chairman of a Union Council, the Council shall, as soon as may be, elect one of its Muslim members as Chairman for the Purposes of the Ordinance, in the manner prescribed for the election of a Chairman of a Union Council.

5. (1) All proceedings before an Arbitration Council shall be held <u>in camera</u> unless the Chairman otherwise directs with the consent of all the parties.
(2) The Chairman shall conduct the proceedings of an Arbitrator Council as expeditiously as possible.
(3) Subject to the provisions of sub-rule (4), such proceedings shall not be vitiated by reason of a vacancy in the Arbitration Council, whether on account of failure of any person to nominate a representative or otherwise.
(4) Where a vacancy arises otherwise than through failure to make a nomination, the Chairman shall require a fresh nomination.
(5) No party to proceedings before an Arbitration Council shall be a member of the Arbitration Council.
(6) All decisions of the Arbitration Council shall be taken by majority, and where no decision can be so taken, the decision of the Chairman shall be the decision of the Arbitration Council.
(7) A copy of the decision of the Arbitration Council, duly attested by the Chairman, shall be furnished free of cost to each of the parties to the proceeding.

6. (1) Within seven days of receiving an application under sub-section (2) of section 6 or under sub-section (1) of section 9, or a notice under sub-section (1) of section 7, the Chairman shall, by order in writing, call upon each of the parties to nominate his or her representative, and each such party shall, within seven days of receiving the order, nominate in writing a representative and deliver the nomination to the

Chairman or send it to him by registered post.

(2) Where a representative nominated by a party is, by reason of illness or otherwise, unable to attend the meetings of the Arbitration Council, or wilfully absents himself from such meeting, or has lost the confidence of the party, the party may, with the previous permission in writing of the Chairman, revoke the nomination and make, within such time as the Chairman may allow, a fresh nomination.

> "Provided that where a party on whom the order is to be served is residing outside Pakistan, the order may be served on such party through the Consular Officer of Pakistan in or for the country where such party is residing."

(3) Where a fresh nomination is made under sub-rule (2), it shall not be necessary to commence the proceedings before the Arbitration Council de novo, unless the Chairman, for reasons to be recorded in writing, directs otherwise.

6A. (1) Wherever, it is made to appear to the Collector, whether on the application of a party to the proceedings or on his own information, that the Chairman is interested in favour of a party to any proceedings before the Arbitration Council or is prejudiced against any such party, or that the Chairman is misconducting himself in any such proceedings, the Collector may, after giving notice to all the parties to the proceedings, appoint any other member of the Union Council as the Chairman for purposes of this Ordinance, and pending the passing of such order may stay the proceedings before the Arbitration Council.

(2) A Collector passing an order under this rule shall record in writing his reasons for the same.

Registration of Marriages

7. (1) Any person competent to solemnise a marriage under Muslim Law may apply to the Union Council for the grant of a licence to act as Nikah Registrar under section 5.

(2) If the Union Council, after making such inquiries as it may consider necessary, is satisfied that the applicant is a fit and proper person for the grant of a licence, it may, subject to the conditions specified therein, grant a licence to him in Form I.

(3) A licence granted under this rule shall be permanent and shall be revocable only for the contravention of any of the conditions of a licence granted under this rule.

(4) If any person to whom a licence has been granted under this rule contravenes any of the conditions of such licence, he shall be punishable with simple

imprisonment for a term, which may extend to one month, or with fine which may extend to two hundred rupees, or with both.

8. (1)   The Union Council, shall, on payment of such cost as may be determined by the Provincial Government, supply to every Nikah Registrar a bound register of nikahnamas in Form II, and seal bearing the inscription. "The seal of Nikah Registrar of Ward (x).....(y)....."

(2)   Each Register shall contain fifty leaves, consecutively numbered, each leaf having a nikahnama, in quadruplicate, and the number of leaves shall be certified by the Chairman.

(3)   Notwithstanding the payment of cost under sub-rule (1), the register and the seal remain the property of the Union Council.

9. (1)   For the registration of a marriage registered under section 5, the Nikah Registrar shall be paid by the bridegroom or his representative a registration fee of two rupees, or when the dower exceeds two thousand rupees, a fee calculated at the rate of one rupee for every thousand or part of the thousand rupees of such dower, subject to a maximum fee of twenty rupees.

(2)   Of the fees received under sub-rule (1), the Nikah Registrar shall retain for himself eighty per cent and shall pay the remaining twenty per cent to the Union Council.

(3)   Where dower consists of property other than money, or partly of such property and partly of money, the valuation of the property shall, for purposes of fees under sub-rule (1), be the valuation as settled between the parties to the marriage.

10. (1)   The Nikah Registrar shall, in the case of a marriage solemnized by him, fill in Form II, in quadruplicate, in the register, the persons, whose signatures are required in the Form shall then sign, and the Nikah Registrar shall then affix his signature and seal thereto, and keep the original intact in the register.

(2)   The duplicate and triplicate of the nikahnama filled in as aforesaid, shall be supplied to the bride and the bridegroom, respectively, on payment of fifty paisa each, and the quadruplicate shall be forwarded to the Union Council.

(3)   If any person required by this rule to sign the register refuses so to sign, he shall be punishable with simple imprisonment for a term which may extend to one month, or with fine which may extend to two hundred rupees or with both.

11. (1)   Where a marriage is solemnised in Pakistan by a person other than the Nikah Registrar, such person shall fill in Form II, to be had loose on payment of such

101

price as may be determined by the Provincial Government, the persons whose signatures are required in the Form shall then sign, and the person solemnizing the marriage shall then affix his signatures to the Form and ensure delivery, as expeditiously as possible, of the same together with the registratin fee to the Nikah Registrar of the Ward where the marriage is solemnized.

(2) If any person required by this rule to sign the Form refuses so to sign he shall be punishable with simple imprisonment for a term which may extend to one month, or with fine which may extend to two hundred rupees, or with both.

12. (1) In the case of a marriage solemnized outside Pakistan by a person who is a citizen of Pakistan, such person shall ensure delivery of Form II, filled in, in accordance with the provisions of Rule II, together with the registration fee, to the consular officer of Pakistan in or for the country in which the marriage is solemnized, for onward transmission to the Nikah Registrar of the Ward of which the bride is a permanent resident, and in case the bride is not a citizen of Pakistan, the Nikah Registrar of the Ward of which the bridegroom is such resident.

(2) In the case of a marriage solemnized outside Pakistan by a person who is not a citizen of Pakistan, the bridegroom, and where only the bride is such citizen, the bride, shall for purposes of filling in, as far as may be, Form II, be deemed to be the person who has solemnized the marriage under sub-rule (1).

13. On receipt of Form II under Rule 11 or Rule 12, the Nikah Registrar shall proceed in the manner provided in Rule 10 as if the marriage had been solemnized by him:

Provided that, except where the marriage has been solemnized within his jurisdiction, it shall not be necessary for the Nikah Registrar to obtain the signatures of the necessary persons.

Polygamy

14. In considering whether another proposed marriage is just and necessary during the continuance of an existing marriage, the Arbitration Council may, without prejudice to its general powers to consider what is just and necessary, have regard to such circumstances, as the following amongst others:-

Sterility, physical infirmity, physical unfitness for the conjugal relation, wilful avoidance of a decree for restitution of conjugal rights, or insanity on the part of an existing wife.

15. An application under sub-section (1) of section 6 for permission to contract another marriage during the subsistence of an existing marriage shall be in writing, shall

state whether the consent of the existing wife or wives has been obtained thereto, shall contain a brief statement of the grounds on which the new marriage is alleged to be just and necessary, shall bear the signature of the applicant, and shall be accompanied by a fee of one hundred rupees.

Revision

16. (1) An application for the revision of a decision of an Arbitration Council, under sub-section (4) of section 6, or of a certificate under sub-section (2) of section 9, shall be preferred within thirty days of the decision or of the issue of the certificate, as the case may be, and shall be accompanied by a fee of two rupees.
(2) The application shall be in writing, set out the grounds on which the applicant seeks to have the decision or the certificate revised, and shall bear the signature of the applicant.

Records and their inspection, etc.

17. As soon as may be after the Arbitration Council has given its decision under Rule 6, the record of the proceedings before it in which such decision has been given shall be forwarded by the Chairman to the office of the Union Council, where it shall be preserved for a period of five years from the date of the decision.

18. (1) The quadruplicate of the nikahnama forwarded by the Nikah Registrar under sub-rule (2) of Rule 10 shall be preserved in the office of the Union Council until such time as the register containing the originals is, on being completed, deposited by the Nikah Registrar in such office.
(2) The completed register so received shall be preserved permanently.
(3) In the office of the Union Council there shall be prepared and maintained an index of the contents of every register, and every entry in such index shall be made, so far as practicable, immediately after the Nikah Registrar has made an entry in the register.
(4) The aforesaid index shall contain the name, place of residence and father's name of each party to every marriage registered within the Union or Town, as the case may be, and the dates of the marriage and registration.

19. (1) Subject to the previous payment of the fees prescribed in sub-rules (2) and (3), the index and the register shall, at all reasonable times, be open to inspection at the office of the Union Council by any person applying to inspect the same and copies of entries in the index and the register, duly signed and sealed by the Chairman, shall be given to all persons applying for such copies.　　　　103

(2) The fee for the inspection of an index or register shall be fifty paisa.

(3) The fee for a certified copy of all or any of the entries relating to a marriage shall be:-

(a) for those in an index .. Fifty paisa
(b) for those in a register .. Two rupees

(4) Fees payable under this rule shall be credited to the Union Council.

Payment of fees

20. Except fees payable to the Nikah Registrar, [or the Union Council under the provisions of Rules, 9, 10, 15 and 19] which shall be paid in cash, all fees payable under these rules shall be paid in non-judicial stamps.

Complaints

21. No Court shall take cognizance of any offence under the Ordinance or these rules save on a complaint in writing by the aggrieved party, stating the fact constituting the offence.

FORM I

Licence granted in pursuance of section 5 (2) of the Muslim Family Laws Ordinance, 1961 (VIII of 1961)

In pursuance of sub-section (2) of section 5 of the Muslim Family Laws Ordinance, 1961 (VIII of 1961), the Union Council/Union Committee/Town Committee of................in the district of................hereby grants this................day of................19................to Mr................son of................resident of................this licence to be from the said date the Nikah Registrar for the following Ward/Wards.

(1) Ward..........
(2) Ward..........
(3) Ward..........
(4) Ward..........
Seal.   Signature of Chairman

CONDITIONS

1. This licence is not transferable.

2. This licence is revocable for breach of any of the provisions of the Muslim Family Laws Ordinance, 1961 (VIII of 1961), or the rules made thereunder or any condition of this licence.

3. The registers and seal supplied to the Nikah Registrar shall be returnable to the Union Council, without refund of cost, when this licence expires or is revoked.

4. The Nikah Registrar shall not put the seal supplied to him to any improper use.

5. Such other conditions, if any, as may be specified by

the Provincial Government.

FORM II
Form of Nikahnama

    (1)   Name of Ward...............Town/Union...............
Tehsil/Thana ....and District...............in
which the marriage took place.

    (2) Name of the bridegroom and his father, with their
respective residences....................................

    (3) Age of bridegroom...............

    (4) The names of the bride and her father, with their
respective residences....................................

    (5) Whether the bride is a maiden, a widow or a
divorcee................

    (6) Age of the bride...............

    (7) Name of Vakil, if any appointed by the bride,
father's name and his residence:
        ....

    (8) The name of the witnesses to the appointment of the
bride's Vakil with their fathers' names, their residence and
their relationship with the bride:
        (1)...
        (2)...

    (9) Name of the Vakil, if any appointed by the
bridegroom, his father's name and his residence:
        ....

    (10) The names of the witness to the appointment of the
bridegroom's Vakil, with their father's names and their
residences:
        (1)...
        (2)...

    (11) Name of the witnesses to the marriage, their
father's names and their residences:
        (1)...
        (2)...

    (12) Date on which the marriage was
contracted...............

    (13) Amount of dower...............

    (14) How much of the dower is mu'wajjal (prompt) and how
much ghair mu'wajjal (deferred).

    (15) Whether any portion of the dower was paid at the
time of marriage. If so, how much:
    ....

    (16) Whether any property was given in lieu of the whole
or any portion of the dower with specification of the same and
its valuation agreed to between the parties:
    ....

    (17) Special conditions, if any:
    ....

(18) Whether the husband has delegated the power of divorce to the wife, if so, under what conditions:
....

(19) Whether the husband's right of divorce is in any way curtailed:
....

(20) Whether any document was drawn up at the time of marriage relating to dower, maintenance, etc. If so, contents thereof in brief:
....

(21) Whether the bridegroom has any existing wife, and, if so, whether he has secured the permission of the Arbitration Council under the Muslim Family Laws Ordinance, 1961, to contract another marriage:
....

(22) Number and date of the communication conveying to the bridegroom the permission of the Arbitration Council to contract another marriage
....

(23) Name and address of the person by whom the marriage was solemnized and his father
....

(24) Date of registration of marriage.

(25) Registration fee paid:

Signature of the bride-
groom or his Vakil:

Signature of the witness to
be appointed of bride-
groom's Vakil:

....

Signature of the
bride

Signature of
the Vakil of
the bride

Signature of the
witness to be
appointed of the
bride's Vakil

....

....

....

Signature of the
witnesses to the
marriage

Signature of the
person who
solemnized the
marriage:

(1)...............

....

(2)...............

....

Signature and seal of
the Nikah Registrar.

....

Seal

Although the practice of polygamy is in decline throughout the Muslim world as a result of both social and economic factors, the arguments for and against its legality and morality continue unabated. At various times and in various countries a bewildering array of defences of polygamy have been raised. But the four most commonly and most seriously advanced have been, firstly, that polygamy is endowed with Divine authority since the Qur'an gives express discretion to a man to have more than one wife. This defence has been taken up on two levels. At the more specific level it is argued in India that the right of polygamy is a religious matter which by virtue of the Constitution the Indian Parliament has no right to interfere with. This resolves itself into the question whether polygamy is a matter of religion and therefore within the scope of Article 25(1) or whether it is a secular practice associated with religion and therefore within the scope of Article 25(2)(a)(9). At a more general level the nature of the Qur'anic authority for polygamy has been disputed and in Tunisia legislation has effectively prohibited polygamy on the basis of an argument that polygamy is permitted by the Qur'an only if the husband is able to treat his wives equally (10): whereas orthodox traditional interpretation of this condition has held that objective indicia of equal treatment, e.g. in terms of maintenance, time spent with each wife etc., alone is intended, the Tunisian legislators argued for a subjective interpretation, requiring equal love and affection etc. to be given to all the wives. Whereas the Prophet might be capable of this, he was exceptional and these requirements were beyond ordinary men and accordingly polygamy was forbidden to them.

Secondly, it has been argued that polygamy will often be justified because the wife is barren or unwell and from the husband's point of view polygamy will enable him to have children without doing his barren or sickly wife the disfavour of divorce which might leave her ill provided for and which is condemned by the Prophet as the most hateful of permitted things.

Thirdly, it is argued that polygamy helps to prevent immorality. Islamic orthodox leaders look to the West and point to prostitution, rape and fornication, and adultery and the high divorce rates as products of a monogamous society. They argue that for some men one sexual relationship is not enough and that it is better to contain this libido within a legal framework of marriage than to let it run unbridled as an extra-legal activity. They argue that the Western practice of remarriage after divorce is 'successive polygamy', morally little different, if not worse than, Muslim polygamy. However, immorality and divorce are hardly infrequent in the Indian sub-continent in polygamous communities and at least some Muslims argue that the answer lies in stricter

107

prohibitions on illicit sex and the reintroduction of Islamic criminal penalties for <u>zina</u> such as have been enacted in Pakistan, rather than in extending the capacity to marry.

Fourthly, polygamy is defended as protective of widows and orphans and of catering for the possibility of a great excess of women over men in time of war by providing them with greater opportunities of marriage and therefore maintenance and care than they would otherwise enjoy. The critics of polygamy concede this possibility but claim that such care for widows and orphans, if not adequately provided for by the husband's estate or by the <u>wasi</u> (guardian) is more properly the responsibility of the whole nation in a modern state. The general thrust of anti-polygamy tracts, however, is that the Qur'anic provisions themselves speak against polygamy in the sense that they reformed the pre-Islamic practice of unlimited polygamy; that a reformer such as Muhammad can only go so far in changing society within a short time span; and that whereas universal monogamy was the desired end, limited polygamy was a compromise to meet the needs of the day. Since then, argue the opponents of polygamy, society has progressed both socially and economically, and the justifications which may have existed for limited polygamy have long ago disappeared and polygamy is now no longer consonant with civilised values. Given the actual incidence of polygamy in India and Pakistan today, the question is one of theoretical rather than practical importance for the majority of the Muslim population (11).

A Muslim does not enjoy a complete freedom of choice as to his or her marriage partner. A Muslim man may marry a woman who is Muslim or a <u>kitabiyya</u>, that is a woman who adheres to one of the revealed religions. He may not marry an idolatress or atheist under any circumstances (12). The Muslim woman has not even this choice. She may marry only a Muslim man. The reasoning for this is clear; the child of such a union will take on the religion of its father according to the Muslim law, and thus any mixed marriage involving a non-Muslim man and a Muslim woman would deprive Islam of the children.

In the Indian subcontinent statute has to a considerable extent intervened in this area of law.

The Christian Marriage Act 1872

s.4 Every marriage between persons, one or both of whom is or are a Christian or Christians, shall be solemnized in accordance with the provisions of [section 5]; and any such marriage solemnized otherwise than in accordance with such provisions shall be void.

It will be seen that the Act, which provides for a Christian marriage ceremony and which still applies in both India and Pakistan, will govern any marriage of a Muslim man with a Christian woman and any marriage ceremony which did not comply with its requirements would be void, at least on a straightforward reading of the Act, which also provides (in s.88) that a marriage between a Christian man and a Muslim woman cannot be solemnised under the Act. The consequences of marrying under this regime would appear to be that the marriage can be dissolved only under the Indian Divorce Act 1869. However, in the Supreme Court of Pakistan in <u>Jatoi v. Jatoi</u> (13) a somewhat different view of the Act was taken and it was held that after the enactment of the Muslim Family Laws Ordinance 1961, so far as Pakistan was concerned, the Muslim man had a right to divorce his wife in accordance with the Muslim personal law as amended by the 1961 Ordinance even if they had married under the 1872 Act.

Moreover, the favoured view in Pakistan now seems to be that a marriage under Muslim rites will be recognised by the courts notwithstanding s.4, even where one of the parties is a Christian, on the basis that the Act should be read in such a way as to apply only to marriages between Christians and Muslims which purport to be Christian ceremonies: a view once argued but rejected by the superior courts of British India has now succeeded before the superior courts of Pakistan (14).

A further possibility in some circumstances is to register a Muslim marriage under one of the Special Marriage Acts, though this has the rather dramatic effect of replacing the Muslim matrimonial regime with an entirely statutory and secular regime which renders it unattractive to many quite apart from the necessity, if one is to take advantage of it in Pakistan, of making a statutory declaration that the parties do not adhere to any faith dealt with in the Acts. Because of various amendments the Act now differs markedly in India and Pakistan from the original Act. The present position is summarised below:

Pakistan

The Special Marriage Act 1872 provides that a secular form of marriage is available for (a) persons, neither of whom profess the Christian or Jewish or Hindu or Mohammedan or Parsi or Buddhist or Sikh or Jaina faiths (b) for persons both of whom profess Hindu, Buddhist, Sikh or Jaina faiths. Where the parties marry under this Act the union is monogamous and divorce may only be effected under the Indian Divorce Act 1869, regardless of subsequent conversions. (15).

India

The Special Marriage Act 1954 (as amended in 1976 – s.21A) provides that <u>whoever</u> marries, or registers their existing marriage, under this Act, is governed by the secular regime which it applies, and can divorce only under the provision of this Act, whatever subsequent changes of faith etc. the parties may undertake. Furthermore the law of succession applicable to the estates of the parties to such a union is that of the Indian Succession Act 1925, if one of them is Muslim (since 1976, this does not apply to members of certain other faiths, where both spouses are of the same faith).

The Pakistani Act, to be of any use to Muslims, does of course require them in effect to renounce Islam, and it has been held (16) that a marriage solemnised under that Act was null and void where the parties who at the time had made declarations to the effect that they belonged to none of the named religions subsequently denied ever having renounced their faiths. On the other hand Indian decisions on the 1872 Act maintain that the genuineness of the parties´ beliefs is irrelevant once a declaration has been made, which is conclusive (17).

Assuming that the chosen partner is of an acceptable faith, the Muslim law raises bars to marriage between certain persons related by marriage (affinity) blood tie (consanguinity) and fosterage. So far as consanguinity is concerned a man may not marry any of his ascendants or descendants, his sister or descendants of his brothers and sisters. He may marry his cousin and such marriages are indeed common. The bar of affinity arises between a man and any ascendant or descendant of his wife and any former wife of any of his ascendants or descendants, except that in Hanafi law a marriage with a descendant of his wife would be permissible if he had not consummated the earlier marriage. Fosterage is a relationship which arises out of the breast feeding of a child by a woman not the child´s mother: it creates a bar between the child and the woman who breast fed him, her own child or his foster sister. He can marry a foster sister of one of his natural brothers or sisters. There are certain other hypothetical but unlikely relationships which are barred by fosterage, but this is such a rare phenomenon now anyway as to be unimportant for our purposes (18).

A further bar which arises between certain persons is created by the commission of _zina_ (unlawful sexual intercourse). A man who has committed _zina_ with a woman may marry the woman in question but he becomes barred from marrying those relatives whom the bar of affinity would have prevented him marrying had he married the woman with whom he committed _zina_.

Yet another bar based on relationship is that of unlawful conjunction (_jam´_) which prohibits the marriage of a man to a woman who is related to his existing wife so closely by consanguinity, affinity or fosterage that had the two women been of different sexes they could not have married each other

110

(19). The most obvious practical application of this is that a man cannot marry two sisters or a niece and an aunt, though it is still an open question whether his divorcing the first enables him to marry the second (20).

The next bar to be mentioned arises out of attempts by the Prophet to restrict the abuse by men of their unqualified right of repudiating, i.e. divorcing their wives. A man who has divorced his wife three times may not remarry her until she has gone through an intervening marriage with another man which has been consummated and then dissolved.

The final bar to be considered is that between a man and a woman undergoing ʿidda. The Qurʾanic basis of ʿidda is well established and it applies equally to kitabiyya women as to Muslims. ʿIdda is a period of time which a divorced or widowed wife must pass at the end of her marriage before she may remarry, where that recently ended marriage had been consummated or a presumption of consummation arose. The duration of ʿidda varies with the circumstances but generally it is three menstrual cycles (three months if the woman does not menstruate or does so highly irregularly) after a divorce, four months and ten days after the death of the husband brings the marriage to an end. The principal purpose of ʿidda is to ensure that the paternity of any child born soon after the dissolution of the marriage is certain by giving adequate time for a pregnancy to become apparent. In this context the concept of valid retirement (khalwat) becomes relevant. An irrebuttable presumption of consummation arises where the husband and wife are alone together in a place to which no one else may have access without their consent or where no one can observe them, and where there is no physical or legal impediment to their having sexual intercourse. Where valid retirement takes place it has the same effect as actual consummation for the purposes of dower, paternity, ʿidda, maintenance and the rule against unlawful conjunction, but not for the rules requiring an intervening consummated union before a man may remarry his triply divorced wife.

Whereas minors must be contracted in marriage by their marriage guardian if the marriage is to be fully effective, even the adult and sane may if they wish use an agent for the purposes of marriage, which may be of particular use where, for example, the marriage is an arranged one in which the parties themselves are a considerable distance apart (21). The agent must have attained puberty and be of sound mind though some Hanafi jurists maintained that an agent need be only of the age of discretion. The consent of all those from whom consent is required must not be obtained through duress or some trick: such an invalid consent will render the marriage fasid, irregular, unless it is later ratified by the victim of the duress or fraud (22). Express consent is required except in the case of the virgin girl, where the Muslim jurists do accept the possibility of implied consent

111

through conduct.

The formal requirements of the marriage are relatively simple. The marriage is effected simply by an offer by or on behalf of one of the parties and an acceptance by or on behalf of the other, made at the same meeting and in the presence of two male witnesses or one male and two female witnesses (23). The concept of a meeting and its duration is strictly regulated. The terms of the offer and acceptance must conform and there are certain rules as to the tenses in which they must be made, such that one at least must be in the past tense; e.g. imperative (offer) plus past (acceptance), or past (offer) plus past (acceptance): this is because it is not possible to contract a future marriage. The witnesses must be adult, sane and Muslim and hear the entire proceedings, except perhaps when the bride is a kitabiyya, a non-Muslim woman of a revealed religion, in which case the witnesses may be non-Muslims in the view of Abu Hanifa and Abu Yusuf.

The classical law does, however, admit of a presumption of marriage out of prolonged and continuous cohabitation as man and wife by the parties and out of the acknowledgement by the man of the woman as his wife or of their child as his legitimate offspring. Such a presumption cannot arise where the woman concerned was an acknowledged prostitute or, of course, where she was one whom the man could not marry lawfully. The presumption still applies in the sub-continent (24). Clearly the lack of formal requirements may make proof, or rather disproof, of it extremely hazardous and in both India and Pakistan some limited steps have been taken to encourage registration.

The stronger moves have been made in Pakistan where the Muslim Family Laws Ordinance 1961 s.5 provides that every marriage solemnised under Muslim law shall be registered in accordance with the provisions of the Ordinance in a register held by a Nikah Registrar: every marriage not solemnised by the Nikah Registrar must be reported to him, for registration, by the person who has solemnised the marriage, failure to do so attracting criminal penalties. Nevertheless, failure to register the marriage does not invalidate it and it may still be proved by other means though the court will be reluctant to receive such evidence (25).

There are in India no compulsory procedures for the registration of a Muslim marriage though in some states a voluntary registration is possible under statutory schemes (26). Such registration cannot, any more than it can under the compulsory Pakistan legislation, validate an otherwise invalid marriage. A similar attitude to registration has been adopted in the same Acts in respect of talaq, khul´ and talaq tafwid concerning dissolutions of marriage in respect of which separate registers are maintained for voluntary registration. However, it seems that in practice "These Acts do not serve any useful purpose in any of the four States where they apply,

112

since registration of marriages and divorces is left by their provisions entirely to the sweet will of the parties to such transactions: and they hardly care to do so." (27) All attempts to introduce compulsory registration in India have met with political opposition.

Failure to comply with the conditions of validity of marriage already considered does not have the same result in every case, for in the Indian subcontinent the Hanafi jurists have come to accept a complicated threefold classification of marriages, which is a curious mutation of and compromise between conflicting views of Abu Hanifa, his two "companions" and other medieval Hanafi jurists, in effect adopting the reasoning of the companions but the terminology of Abu Hanifa (28). The classification distinguishes between the <u>sahih</u> marriage, which in all respects complies with the conditions laid down by the Shari´a; the <u>fasid</u> marriage, which though good in itself because the parties to it are capable of fulfilling the purposes of the contract is for some extraneous reason irregular; and the <u>batil</u> marriage, which is no marriage at all being bad in itself and wholly void. The <u>sahih</u> marriage is fully effective; the <u>fasid</u> marriage has some limited effects if consummated; and the <u>batil</u> marriage has no effects though it may render the parties liable to criminal penalties for <u>zina</u> (unlawful sexual intercourse). However, this distinction is far from clear in the traditional texts and in practice some unions which one might expect to be <u>fasid</u> are <u>batil</u> and vice versa and some jurists use the terms indiscriminately or disagree on the correct classification. The position is further complicated by the doctrine of ´semblance´ accepted by other schools and even by some Hanafi jurists either in addition to or in place of this threefold classification by which doubts or ambiguities as to the parties´ status mitigate the consequences of the marriage and which then treats <u>batil</u> marriages in the same way as <u>fasid</u> marriages are treated by those accepting the threefold classification, while maintaining (formally) a simple distinction between fully valid and fully invalid marriages. Clearly in former times much of this confusion was generated out of a desire to avoid the mandatory and inflexible penalties for <u>zina</u> wherever possible. What follows is thus not entirely free from dispute.

On discovery of the fact that their union is <u>fasid</u> the parties must at once separate, but their union is not wholly without effect. If it has been consummated the man must pay the woman a dower, the specified dower or her proper dower, whichever be less, and the woman must observe an ´idda period before she can marry. The bar of affinity is raised between relations of the parties in the same way as if the union had been <u>sahih</u>. Any children of the union are legitimate and maintenance of them is obligatory on the father. There are, however, no rights of inheritance between the spouses themselves. The following unions have commonly been held to be _fasid_: a marriage without the appropriate number of witnesses (29); marriage to a woman still undergoing ´idda (30); marriage between a woman and a man who already has four wives (31); marriage contrary to the prohibition on unlawful conjunction (32).

The _batil_ marriage is, as has been said, wholly without effect. The following unions have commonly been held to be _batil_: "unions" where there was no valid offer and acceptance (33); marriages between a man and a woman related within the forbidden degrees on account of consanguinity affinity or fosterage (34); between a man and a woman whom he has divorced three times unless there has been an intervening marriage between her and another man which has been consummated and dissolved (35); between a man and a pregnant woman unless the man is the father of the embryo (36); between a man and a woman who already has a husband (37).

It is far from certain whether the courts of the Indian subcontinent will consider a marriage between a Muslim man and a non-_kitabiyya_ or a Muslim woman and a non-Muslim man to be _fasid_ or _batil_, partly, it would seem, through confusion as to the rationale of the _sahih-fasid-batil_ classification. Ameer Ali, one of the most influential jurists of British India, took the view that the true distinction between _batil_ and _fasid_ unions is that between bars which are perpetual and bars which are temporary or removeable. Because a non-Muslim could convert to an acceptable faith and thereby render the union permissible in Muslim law, Ameer Ali regarded the marriage in contravention of the religious bars as being merely _fasid_ (38). This view was rejected by the majority of jurists who preferred the traditional view that such a union was bad in itself and _batil_ and the majority view has until now been accepted by the courts (39).

Shi´a Marriage Law

The Shi´a law of marriage differs markedly from that of the Sunnis, for example in its rule that no witnesses are necessary to the procedure of offer and acceptance, but most notably in its recognition of the _mut´a_. The _mut´a_ is a marriage limited to a set period of duration agreed by the parties, which may be as little as a day, and which is dissolved automatically on the expiry of that period. Most of the rules applicable to _nikah_ apply equally to _mut´a_ but there is no restriction on the number of wives a man may contract _mut´a_ with, whether or not he also has a wife or wives by a _nikah_ marriage. During the existence of the _mut´a_ the husband may not divorce his wife but he may without her consent make a gift to her of the remainder of the term, thereby bringing the contract to a premature end. The wife receives not a dower (_mehr_) as in _nikah_ but an _ijra_ or reward which is essential to

114

the contract of marriage, and if the wife abandons the husband
before the expiry of the period agreed the husband may deduct
a proportionate part of the ijra. The offspring of such a
union are legitimate, with all that that implies, but the wife
has no right to maintenance unlike the wife of a nikah, and
neither spouse acquires any right of inheritance from the
other by virtue of the mut´a.

The mut´a is extremely controversial, fiercely criticised
by the Sunnis and equally staunchly defended by the Shi´a
(40), though in practical terms it is extremely rare and
geographically limited so that the debate is in large measure
one of principle (41). Sunni law deems mut´a to be nothing
more than a form of prostitution sanctioned by Shi´i jurists.
For the Sunnis nikah is the only form of marriage, which is
lifelong in principle, though of course the ease with which
the husband may obtain a dissolution of the union
substantially qualifies this assertion in practice.

As a matter of history, it seems that mut´a was extremely
common in Arabia before Islam, indeed tolerated by the Prophet
and at least according to Shi´i histories practised by
companions of the Prophet. The practice after the death of
the Prophet and was banned only by the second caliph, since
when the Sunni´s considered mut´a unlawful. They consider
that the Shi´a´s insistence on the validity of mut´a is purely
politically motivated. The Shi´a argue that at the time the
Qur´anic verses XXIII 5 - 7 and LXX 29 - 31 were revealed in
Mecca, concerning intercourse, mut´a was a well known practice
and if mut´a had not been a true marriage it would clearly
have been forbidden. Since it was not forbidden by the
Prophet it must be a legitimate marriage. Verse IV:24 which
the Shi´a claim supports mut´a is said to be abrogated by
later verses, according to the Sunnis. Moreover, say the
Shi´a, the fact that mut´a was still practised until the time
of the second caliph and that the caliph forbade it indicates
that until that time it was legitimate. Of course, the
legislative authority of the caliphs is not recognised by the
Shi´a, whose imams permit mut´a. The Shi´a also justify mut´a
on grounds of public interest. The permanent union clearly
does not satisfy the sexual desire of certain men, and yet
adultery and fornication are sins of the highest order.
Islam, say the Shi´a, has authorised temporary marriage under
certain conditions to separate it from adultery and
fornication, including the requirement that the women be
single and married to one man at a time and to keep ´idda
(half the time of a permanent marriage), and in doing so
channels the sexual desires of these men in a way which
minimises the threat to morality: better to control an
undesirable practice within the framework of the law than to
allow it to go uncontrolled outside the law.

Mt. GHULAM KUBRA BIBI (Appellant) v. MOHD. SHAFI (Respondent)
A.I.R. 1940 Peshawar 2. (Mir Ahmad J.)

Judgement: Mohammad Shafi sued Mt. Ghulam Kubra for restitution of conjugal rights. He also impleaded her parents and asked that an injunction should be issued against them to restrain them from interfering in his marital relations with his wife. The defence taken by Mt. Ghulam Kubra was that she was never married to Mohammad Shafi. There was also a question whether the woman was of age at the time when she was married. Evidence was led by the other side. The mullah appeared and he said that he read the nikah at the instance of the grandfather of the girl. He categorically denied that anyone was sent to the girl to enquire from her whether she agreed to the marriage. One Mistri Abdul Karim, on the other hand, vaguely deposed that there were two witnesses of the nikah.....

.....According to Mahomedan law, it is absolutely necessary that the man or someone on his behalf and the woman or someone on her behalf should agree to the marriage at one meeting, and the agreement should be witnessed by two adult witnesses. As women are in pardah in this part of the country it is customary to send a relation of the woman to her inside the house accompanied by two witnesses. The relation asks the girl within the hearing of the witnesses whether she authorises him to agree to the marriage on her behalf for the dower money offered by the husband. He explains to her the detail of the dower proposed. When the girl says "yes" or signifies her consent by some other method, the three persons come out. The future husband and those three persons are then placed before the Mullah. The Mullah asks the boy whether he offers to marry the girl on payment of the specified dower. He says "yes". Then the relation, who had gone inside, tells the Mullah that he is the agent of the girl. The Mullah asks him whether he agrees to the marriage on payment of the specified dower. The relation says "yes". The witnesses are present there so that if the Mullah has any doubt he should question them as to whether the relation is a duly authorized agent of the girl. Directly both sides have said "yes" the Mullah reads the scriptures and the marriage is complete.

I have been at pains to describe the method which is usually adopted in this part of the country for effecting a marriage in order to show that the vague allegation that there were two witnesses of the nikah has no value and that it should be proved that the whole procedure has been gone through: in particular when the man who read the nikah is positive that no one was sent to the girl to enquire from her whether she was a willing party. It is on the record that the girl was 17 years of age when her marriage was solemnized. It appears that the parties did not know then that according to

116

Mahomedan law a girl becomes major for the purposes of marriage when she reaches the age of puberty, which is presumed to be the age of 15 years. I think they were under the impression that she could not be major up to 18 years of age, as is the general law, and I guess that the girl was, therefore, given away by the grandfather and not personally consulted. For when a girl is minor it is permissible in Mahomedan law that her father or grandfather or other paternal relations should give her away. The marriage is valid and called a nikah all the same.

It is interesting to point out that such nikah also requires two adult witnesses. The witnesses produced in this case have only said that they were the witnesses of the nikah. Who knows whether they were not witnesses of the giving away of the girl by the grandfather. For the reasons given above I hold that no valid marriage has taken place in this case.....

HABIB v. THE STATE
P.L.D. 1980 Lah. 791 (Muhd. Sarwar J.)

Judgement.....Learned counsel for the petitioner has stressed that since the nikah was not registered according to the provisions of the Muslim Family Laws Ordinance therefore, a presumption should be raised that there was no nikah.....
.....Without prejudice to the case of either party, I may straightaway observe that under Islamic law, nikah can be performed orally and such a nikah is not invalidated merely because it is not registered according to the provisions of the Muslim Family Laws Ordinance 1961. However, that Ordinance provides a punishment if one contravenes the provisions regarding the registration of nikah.....

NASIM AKHTAR v. THE STATE
P.L.D. 1968 Lah. 841 (Shaukat Ali J.)

[The appellant had been convicted of murder of a man with whom she lived. She pleaded self defence to an attempted rape of her by the deceased man. This defence was not, of course, available to her if, as the prosecution alleged, she had been lawfully married to the man.]

Judgement.....It must not be forgotten that at the relevant time Muslim Family Laws Ordinance were in force and every marriage was to be recorded in a register maintained by the Registrar of Marriages. The fact, that this marriage was not entered in the office of the Union Council coupled with the discrepant evidence on this point, we are of the view that the claim of the prosecution that Muhd. Ashiq deceased was the husband of Mst. Nasim Akhtar, was incorrect and that there was

117

no matrimonial string between the two. It may be that it was a clandestine marriage or that Mst. Nasim Akhtar had illicit intimacy with the deceased.

———————

MOHD. MUSTAFIZUR RAHMAN KHAN (petitioner) v. MRS. RINA KHAN (respondent)
P.L.D. 1967 Dacca 652. (Abdulla, J.)

Judgement.....the petitioner claims that the marriage was celebrated under the Special Marriage Act 1872, Act III of 1872, the essentials of such a marriage is set out in s.2 of the Act, which reads as follows:

"2. Marriages may be celebrated under this Act between persons neither of whom professes the Christian or the Jewish, or the Hindu or the Muhammadan, or the Parsi or the Buddhist or the Sikh or the Jaina religion, (or between persons each of whom professes one or other of the following religions, that is to say, the Hindu, Buddhist, Sikh or Jaina religion)".....

It is obvious, therefore, that neither Christian nor a Muhammadan can marry under the provisions of this Act. So far as the petitioner is concerned he has himself said that he did not like the idea of a marriage under this Act as it meant renunciation of his religion. He has signed the declaration form saying that he does not profess any religion but when the Court asked him whether he had made any subsequent changes in his official records he answered ´No´. In the affidavit which he has sworn he has described himself as a Muslim. Therefore, it remains a fact that before his declaration he was a Muslim and after his declaration he continued to be a Muslim. For a Muslim to say that he is not a Muslim it is apostasy. The provisions of the Act itself makes any false declaration punishable. If the petitioner has not in fact renounced his religion he has made a false declaration. So far as the respondent No. 1 is concerned she has categorically stated that she is a Christian, Roman Catholic and she never renounced her faith and, therefore, she in fact has given a false declaration in the declaration form Exh. 2. In the case of Dr. Niranjan Das Mohan v. Mrs. Ena Mohan and others (A I R 1943 Cal. 146 (150) it has been laid down that what the parties were or not at heart is as irrelevant for the purposes of this section as it would be difficult to ascertain, the criterion is that they professed or did not profess according to their declarations made at the time. Facts of the case were that the actual declaration form was not available and the contention was raised that the declaration made by the parties before the Registrar was defective. The respondent said that while she herself declared that she professed no religion, the petitioner declared that he was a Hindu. The petitioner in Court further said that he too declared that he
118

professed no religion. Their Lordships concluded that as the actual declaration was not available it was difficult to say what happened. Had there been any such irregularity or discrepancy as the respondent stated then the Registrar would not have solemnised the marriage. Then the question was raised that even if the declaration had been made, it was in fact false, since the respondent, according to her evidence of the trial was, was always a Christian at heart and yet she declared before the Registrar that she professed no religion. Therefore, their Lordships were pleased to hold that even then the marriage could not be avoided whatever penalty she might incur for making a false declaration under section 21 of the Act and their Lordships gave their reasons which I have stated already. But the obvious lacuna in the reasoning is that the Act applies only to those persons who do not profess the specified religions or both of whom do not profess the specified religions. Unless one is not a Christian or not a Muslim, so far as this case is concerned, one cannot contract a marriage under this Act. Therefore, I hold that on the evidence of Rina Ghosh herself and on the admission of the petitioner neither of them were competent to contract a marriage under the Special Marriage Act and as such the whole proceedings before the Marriage Registrar, Jessore, was void.....

SHAHZADA BEGUM (Appellant) v. Sh. ABDUL HAMID (Respondent)
PLD 1950 Lahore 504. (S.A. Rahman J.)

Judgement.....The appellant's marriage was sought to be avoided by the appellant on several grounds in the Courts below, but her learned counsel has confined his arguments before me to two grounds only. In the first place, he contends that the marriage of the parties was a clandestine affair and as due publicity required by Muslim Law was not given to the nikah, the marriage was invalid. Secondly, he alleges that this was a marriage between unequals,for the two-fold reason that the respondent was very much older than the appellant and had several children from his first two wives I need not, therefore, discuss the other grounds which are not pressed before me.

On the question of publicity for the nikah, learned counsel for the appellant referred me to several Ahadis quoted in section 9 of the Mishat-ul-Masabih Book II translated by Al-Haj Maulana Fazl-ul-Karim. It is no doubt mentioned in these Ahadis that the Prophet directed that the marriage be proclaimed in the public and in one of these Ahadis it was even stated that the demarcation between lawful and unlawful things in marriage is proclamation and daf (small hand drum). But I do not find in these Ahadis any reference to the quantum of publicity required to validate a marriage. All that one

119

can say, therefore, is that publicity would be desirable for the marriage and a public proclamation by means of a beating of drum may even be preferable, but it does not seem to follow that if no drums are beaten or "public" proclamation is made, the marriage would become void.

Learned counsel also referred to "Religion of Islam" by Maulana Muhammad Ali, page 625, as authority for the view that proclamation of the marriage is necessary. Here again, there is no pronouncement by the author that a marriage performed in the presence of two male adult witnesses by a nikahkhan, would be invalid if no further publicity were given to the fact of marriage. It is undoubtedly true that in the present case, as the evidence shows, the parents of the plaintiff were kept out of knowledge of the marriage mainly at her own request as she wanted to inform them of the nikah in her own way and at an appropriate time. But it was not a secret marriage in the sense contended for by the learned counsel for the appellant, as is clear from the fact that in July 1943, the appellant in a petition submitted to the Inspectress of Schools, Lahore, signed herself as the wife of the respondent. Learned counsel for the appellant frankly concedes that he can quote no authority, judicial or otherwise, to the effect that a marriage performed in the circumstances of the present case would be invalid on the ground that no public proclamation was made.

According to the various text books on Muslim law, even the absence of witnesses at the nikah would merely make the marriage irregular and not void. Reference in this connection may be made to para. 197 of Mulla's Muhammadan Law, 11th Edition, and pages 101 and 114 of Wilson's Anglo Muhammadan Law, 6th Edition. There is also a Single Bench authority of the Allahabad High Court in Mst. Bashirunnisa and another v. Bunvad Ali and another 50 I C 677 (1919) in support of the view that a marriage contracted without witness is not illegal, but merely irregular and irregularity would be curable by consummation of the marriage. The late Syed Amir Ali adopted a similar view in Volume II of Muhammadan Law, 5th Edition, page 312, and it would seem to follow that a marriage duly performed in the presence of two persons could not be described as invalid in any sense. I, therefore, repel the contention raised by learned counsel for the appellant on the first ground.

The argument based on the alleged inequality between the parties is, in my opinion, not acceptable in the circumstances of this case. Learned counsel referred to various authorities in support of the proposition that in the case of misalliance, the guardian or parents of a major girl have the right to object to the marriage and have it cancelled. Amir Ali's Muhammadan Law, Volume II at pages 364 and 368, was quoted and similar references are to be found in Sir Abdur Rahim's Muslim Jurisprudence at the pages 332 and 240. Reliance was also placed on the <u>Fatawai Alimgiri</u>, Amir Ali´s Urdu translation, pages 177, Hamilton´s <u>Hedaya</u>, page 34 (Grady´s Edition) and <u>Fatawai</u> Qazi Khan pages 35, 76 and 77 (Muhammad Yusaf Khan´s translation). The principle may be admitted that the guardian or other relatives of an adult Muslim girl may have the right to object to an ill-assorted union on the ground that it brings the family into disrepute, etc. Learned counsel, however, agrees that there is no recorded case either in the judicial authorities or in the books referred to of a union having been dissolved on the mere ground of disparity of ages between the husband and the wife. I do not think that the fact of the respondent, having another wife and children could offend against the principle underlying the doctrine of <u>Kafat</u>. Learned counsel argues that the instances quoted by the various authors are only illustrative and do not exhaust the circumstances under which the unequal marriage contracted by a female who is <u>sui juris</u> could be objected to. Learned counsel for the respondent on the contrary, has challenged the competency of the appellant to raise this question in second appeal on the ground that this point was not taken in the Courts below. It involves the question of fact as to the relevant ages of the parties. Even if, however, the ages of the parties as disclosed by them in their own statements be accepted as correct, it would appear that the difference between the ages of the husband and wife was about 15 years or even less at the time of the marriage. In my opinion therefore the principle invoked does not cover the present case in any event as the disparity between the ages of the two spouses is not so glaring as could lead to the <u>prima facie</u> inference that it was an unconscionable match. We must also keep in mind the fact that the appellant was an educated woman of mature age when she entered into this marriage with the resondent. In my opinion this ground also fails and the marriage cannot be annulled.

No other point was argued before me in this appeal which fails and is hereby dismissed. It appears to me that the wife is very reluctant to go back to the husband, but the latter, though he has another wife, is unwilling to release her from the marital bond. Both the Courts below put to the respondent whether he was prepared to divorce his wife who was no longer desirous of continuing the marital connection. The respondent was adamant in his refusal. In view of this fact, I leave the parties to bear their own costs throughout. The decision will be communicated to the parties or their counsel.

[On the doctrine of Kafa´a, see Chapter 4 below].

TAJBI (Appellant) v. MOWLA KHAN (Respondent)
1917 I.L.R. 41 Bombay 485. (Beaman J.)

Judgement.....The only question we have to answer is whether
Tajbi is, under the Mahomedan Law, the legitimate daughter of
Hussankhan.

The admitted facts are that he first married Amabi, and
subsequently her sister Sadabi, who is the mother of Tajbi.
The later marriage took place during the subsistence of the
marriage with Amabi, and both sisters appear to have survived
him.

The same question arose in the case of Aizunnissa Khatoon
v. Karimunnissa Khatoon ((1895) 23 Cal. 130). The Calcutta
High Court held that the issue of a sister of the husband's
first wife, if the second marriage was contracted or
consummated during the continuance of the first, that is
before the sister first married had died or been divorced, was
illegitimate.

We are unable to agree with that view of the Mahomedan
Law. There is nothing in the reasons to be found in the
judgment, there is nothing in the mass of material upon which
the judgment is based, which, in our opinion, would warrant a
Court in over-riding so high and so clear an authority as the
Fatwa-i-Alamgiri.

Briefly the reasoning of the learned Judges in the case
of Aizunnissa Khatoon v. Karimunnissa Khatoon ((1895) 23 Cal.
130) may be thus summarized:-

(1) No distinction can be drawn from the language of the
original text in the Quran between the prohibited women
mentioned in it.

The words used suggest no such distinction or any
intention to make it.

It cannot be maintained on grounds of law, or reason, or
even when looked at in the light of common sense.

(2) The weight of authority (contained in the writings of
accredited authorities on the tradition, and the law) is
against the law laid down in the Fatwa-i-Alamgiri.

(3) The reasoned conclusions of Baillie upon the point,
set forth in Chapter VIII, Bk. I, are his own, and are not
drawn direct from his chief authority, the Fatwa-i-Alamgiri.
They are, therefore, entitled to no more weight than the
opinions of any other modern writer on the Mahomedan Law.
Similarly, Ameer Ali, in summing up this topic, is not clear,
and even if his considered opinion is the same as Baillie's,
it is certainly of no higher authority.

(4) Doubt has been thrown upon the authority of the
Fatwa-i-Alamgiri by later Mahomedan lawyers such as the author
of the Rudd-ul-Muhtar; and

(5) The text directly in point professes to be based upon
the authority of the Muhit of Sarakhshi (1096), the original

122

of which was not before the Court.

The learned Judges of the Calcutta Court recognized, and accepted the classification of marriages with prohibited women in two categories. (1) Those which were "batil" or absolutely void, and (2) Those which were "fasid" or only invalid (or irregular). Also they recognized and accepted the general rule regulating the resultant legal consequences of marriages falling within the one or the other category. Void marriages could have no legal effects, invalid marriages, if consummated, could. Last, they also appear to have accepted the criterion in general use for determining whether a marriage with a prohibited woman should be classed in the category of void, or of invalid marriages. This criterion is to be sought in the nature of the prohibition; if that be permanent, then the marriage is void, if temporary, then the marriage is invalid. Adopting the classification, its legal consequences, and the test, the Judges held that a marriage with a sister during the subsistence of a prior marriage with her sister was void, and whether consummated or not, had no legal consequences, and that this was so because the prohibition against marrying two sisters together was a permanent prohibition, and brought a wife's sister within the "moharrim" or (in effect) the pale of incestuous adultery. It will thus be seen that the true foundation of the judgment was the very strong opinion the learned Judges held upon the true and intended meaning of the passage in the Quran. There is now a general consensus among the best modern text-book writers on Mahomedan Law, that the case of <u>Aizunnissa Khatoon</u> <u>v. Karimunissa Khatoon</u> ((1895) 23 Cal. 130) was wrongly decided. Whether Ameer Ali was clear upon the point in his book then before the Court or not, he has made his own view unmistakably clear in later editions.

In dealing with a point of this kind it is well to remember that where the origin of law lies in Revelation, Divine or semi-Divine communication, or inspiration, the form of expression is almost certain to be extremely compendious. For all purposes of modern jurisprudence and applied law, derived from such sources, Courts have almost invariably to draw upon the amplification of the first Revelation, taking the form of Treatises, themselves some times sacro-sanct, and later of mere commentaries of admittedly human origin. In administering the Hindu Law, English Courts rarely, if ever, have recourse to the Shrutis. The Smritis of Manu and Yajnavalkya, e.g., being, if not actually, Divine, sacro-sanct, are, wherever expressly applicable, of paramount authority. But in practice the Courts of India rely far more upon the critical commentaries, such as the Mitakshara, the Mayukha, and in Bengal, the Dayabhaga.

In interpreting a highly condensed text such as that in the Quran, prohibiting certain women, supposing the actual words to leave any material point ambiguous, the Courts must

look to the way in which the most authoritative exponents of
the law thus enjoined have understood it, and to what extent
traditions thus legitimately moulded have gradually come to be
established, and accepted as integral parts of the Mahomedan
Law, as long as that law was administered by Mahomedan lawyers
in Mahomedan Courts. The Fatwa-i-Alamgiri stands in much the
same relation to the Mahomedan Law, first revealed it is true,
but later going through a long process of traditional
interpretation and resultant moulding in the hands of sages
and learned lawyers, as the Institutes of Justinian stood to
the Roman Law which had preceded them. The Fatwa-i-Alamgiri
was an authoritative exposition of what the Mahomedan Law was,
at a time when Mahommedanism was at the height of its power in
this country.

By the time of Aurungzeb, Mahomedanism, as a temporal
power, had perhaps passed its zenith, but through the
centuries which separated Mahommed, from the leading lawyers
of Aurungzeb's Empire, Mahomedanism had absorbed and
represented in more than one important sphere the highest
mental culture. The codification of the Mahomedan Law, as it
had, in the meanwhile, been shaped by its leading exponents,
was the work of men, whose minds may be allowed to have been
strictly trained, to systematize, and reduce to coherent and
practically applicable principles, much that had been matter
of dispute, uncertainty and controversy. And where the
authors of the Fatwa-i-Alamgiri announce without doubt or
qualification the legal limits and proper mode of
administering the law the prophet had in mind, in such a
connection as this, we do not see where Courts can look for
better authority, or why they should set themselves to
interpret over again what was thus declared in the plainest
and simplest language. In this connection reference may be
made to the observations of the Privy Council in Aga Mahomed
Jaffer Bindanim v. Koolsom Beebee ((1897) 25 Cal. 9 at p.18).
Their Lordships say that "they do not care to speculate on the
mode in which the text quoted from the Quran, which is to be
found Sura II, vv. 241-2, is to be reconciled with the law as
laid down' in the Hedaya and by the author of the passage
quoted from Baillie's Imamia. But it would be wrong for the
Court on a point of this kind to attempt to put their own
construction on the Quran in opposition to the express ruling
of commentators of such great antiquity and high authority."

Abating the authority of such a passage as that upon
which we are commenting from the Fatwa-i-Alamgiri, by pointing
out that it is expressly based upon an earlier work, the Muhit
of Sarakhshi, which the learned Judges would have wished to
see for themselves, appears to us to miss the point. In the
first place it is, to say the least of it, unlikely, that any
two English Judges would have been more competent to give a
text from the Muhit its real meaning than the compilers of the
Fatwa-i-Alamgiri. In the second place the citation of

124

authority in such a book as the Fatwa-i-Alamgiri, whether or not its meaning may be capable of other interpretations, need be taken no further than this, that what is expressed upon it is what, in the considered opinion of the Authors of the Fatwa-i-Alamgiri, is the right law. That, and that alone, appears to us to be what Courts are first to consider in valuing the authority of the Fatwa-i-Alamgiri. Thirdly, whatever may now seem to be the literal face meaning of a passage in the Quran, Courts cannot forget that the law flowing from that Revelation had by the time the Fatwa-i-Alamgiri was published, been administered in Mahomedan Courts under the rule of Mahomedan Sultans and Emperors for ten centuries, and therefore that the exposition of it at that time by the highest available legal talent, by all the best jurists in the service of Aurungzeb ought to be highly respected. Last, we cannot admit that such a work as the Rudd-ul-Muhtar, written as late as 1817 A.D., can be or ought to be weighed, as authority, against the Fatwa-i-Alamgiri. The Mahomedan Empire of India had long been extinct. The author (from whom immensely long and often highly confused and sometimes altogether irrelevant excerpts have been made in the Appendix to the judgment of the Calcutta High Court), is extremely dogmatic, and gives many indications of the high opinion he entertains of himself. But it is safe to say that no Mahomedan would put him upon the same level, or anywhere near the same level, as the compilers of the Fatwa-i-Alamgiri. We have no right to discredit the latter because the Rudd-ul-Muhtar throws doubt upon its authority.

Before considering the text in the Quran, these propositions may be stated. We do not think any one of them will be seriously disputed.

(1) The prohibited women fall into three classes: (a) those who are prohibited for consanguinity; (b) for affinity; (c) for unlawful conjunction.

(2) The ground of permanent prohibition is that marriage with a woman so permanently prohibited would be incestuous at any time by reason of consanguinity, or at any time after the bar had been established by affinity.

(3) The grounds of temporary prohibitions are various. But the notion of incest certainly underlies the particular prohibition now under discussion. But the ground of the prohibition, confined to that notion, is clearly not permanent. It is incestuous to have two sisters in marriage together; but it is not incestuous to marry a wife's sister after the wife has been divorced or died. It at once becomes clear that, unlike the cases of permanent prohibition for affinity (although this too is referable to affinity for its substantial reason) the prohibition will not survive the removal of the person by death or divorce, marriage with whom has first set up the bar of affinity. No one has yet contended that a Mahomedan may not marry his wife's sister,

125

merely because she was his wife's sister. Here then is a case of continuing condition, or obstacle, which ceasing to exist, the disability disappears. Otherwise, in all cases of permanent prohibitions for consanguinity or affinity. The distinction is quite simple and plain. On the ground of affinity a man is permanently prohibited from marrying his mother-in-law or his step-daughter. He could not marry them after the death of his wife. But a man is not permanently prohibited, on the ground of affinity or any other ground, from marrying his wife's sister. After his wife's death, he may of course marry her sister. It seemed to the learned Judges of the Calcutta High Court that no reason could be given for such a distinction, and when they looked at the matter in the light of common sense, they were equally at a loss. Even were that so, Courts must not be too exacting in getting at sound reason for all the rules laid down in Oriental, archaic, often very arbitrary, systems of law.

(4) Marriage with a permanently prohibited woman is void, and has no legal consequences. Marriage with a temporarily prohibited woman, if consummated, may have legal consequences.

(5) Three principal consequences are: Right to dower, Obligation to perform _iddat_, Legitimacy of issue, "the establishment of _nasab_, or paternity."

To be clear whether a marriage is absolutely void, or only invalid, or irregular, or illegal (the latter word appears to be used loosely, and applied to both classes of marriage) it is necessary to enquire whether one or more of these legal consequences flow from the marriage under any conditions. If they do, then the marriage cannot have been void.

Next we will state what we think to be the only principle upon which our Courts can hope to regularize the administration of the Mahomedan Law upon the point. It needs to be systematized, and placed upon a solid ground of intelligible and virtually universal principle, if we are ever to be freed from the chaos of texts, glosses, definitions, illustrations, distinctions and exceptions which most of the Doctors of the Mahomedan Law abound.

Confined to the question we have to answer, and leaving aside for the moment express authority where the legitimacy of the issue of a marriage is disputed, it must be first found whether the marriage was absolutely void, or only invalid. The test is whether the woman married was permanently, or only temporarily, prohibited. If it be found that she was only temporarily prohibited, although the contract made while that prohibition persisted, was a void contract, if followed by sexual intercourse, the woman will be entitled to dower, will be under obligation to perform _iddat_, and the issue if born after six months will be legitimate.

We will now deal with the text in the Quran. It runs as follows in Sale's translation (pages 62, 63). "Ye are forbidden to marry your mothers, and your daughters, and your sisters, and your aunts both on the father's and on the mother's side, and your brother's daughters, and your sister's daughters, and your mothers who have given you suck, and your foster sisters, and your wives' mothers, and your daughters-in-law (step daughters?) which are under your tuition, born of your wives unto whom ye have gone in (but if ye have not gone in unto them, it shall be no sin in you to marry them), and the wives of your sons who proceed out of your loins; and ye are also forbidden to take to wife two sisters, except what is already passed: for God is gracious and merciful."

The literal translation is "made unlawful upon you, your mothers and your daughters and your sisters etc., etc., and to join together two sisters, etc."

This makes it clear beyond doubt that what was forbidden was not marriage with a wife's sister, but "joining together two sisters," in other words, this prohibition is against unlawful conjunction, and from its very nature temporary. Had the text borne the meaning put upon it by the Calcutta High Court, the wife's sister would have been expressly prohibited, as all the other women are. This strikes at the root of most of the reasoning in the judgments of the Calcutta High Court, and deprives it of much of its force. It might be argued that although a marriage is temporarily and not permanently prohibited, yet, if it takes place in fact while the temporary prohibition is in force, it is as void as though it had been permanently forbidden. If that were really so, it would destroy one of the principles upon which the sound and systematic administration of this part of the Mahomedan Law in our Courts must rest.

But we doubt whether it is. Rigorously analyzed the ground of the doctrine, that a marriage with a woman permanently prohibited is absolutely void, is simply that from the moment that prohibition takes effect, any sexual connection with her must always be incestuous. And no issue of necessarily incestuous intercourse can ever be legitimate. But even on the confused dicta of the Mahomedan lawyers, it would not be contended that where a man simultaneously married two sisters, and had intercourse with them both, but could not remember with which first, and both had issue, such issue would be illegitimate. In such circumstances it seems to be agreed that both sisters would be entitled to dower, would both be obliged to perform iddat, and presumably therefore the children of both would be legitimate. Nasab would be established. Yet it is equally clear and certain, that having regard to the prohibition against marrying two sisters at once, if that rests upon a basis of such marriages being incestuous, in the case supposed the children would be the children of incest, or at any rate one of them would though it might be difficult to say which. Again if a man married first

127

A and then while A was still alive, her sister B, and had intercourse with B and begot a child upon her, and the very same night A died, it may be doubted much whether any one would contend that the child so begotten must be illegitimate. Such an example introduces the always illusive and difficult time element. If it really would have the play above attributed to it, then it is clear that the incestuousness of the act which brought the child into being would not be the true determinant. In every case of permanently prohibited women it would. No matter when the act of procreation took place if by reason of consanguinity or affinity the woman was permanently _haram_ to the man, the child born of their union would be illegitimate. An examination of the text-book writers old and relatively modern puts it beyond all doubt that in numerous instances of temporary prohibition, all the legal consequences of marriage may follow, if in fact there has been consummation. In all these cases, there is no incest, and <u>time</u> is always the determinant factor. In dealing critically with a topic which has been subjected to such interminable examination, and fine drawn distinction, the difference between incest and adultery must never be lost sight of. Fornication or adultery was severely punished under the Mahomedan Law, and a great part of the extracts appended to the judgment in <u>Aizunnissa´s case</u> ((1895) 23 Cal. 130) is devoted to this question of punishment. It has little if any relevance to the question we have to answer. It has now been shown, we hope conclusively, that the Quran was incorrectly interpreted by the learned Judges of the Calcutta High Court, and that rightly read, it allows full play to the principles upon which we would decide this case.....

.....A careful analysis of the materials available will show that there is nothing in them prior to the promulgation of the Fatwa-i-Alamgiri, which necessarily impairs the soundness of the doctrine therein enunciated upon this point.....

.....It runs as follows: "If two sisters are married in one and the same marriage, the Kazi will effect separation between them and him (the husband). If the separation takes place before co-habitation nothing will be payable to them (the sisters). But if the separation takes place after co-habitation, each of them will be entitled to the smaller amount of the two, namely, customary and fixed dowers. This is the <u>Muzmirat</u>. But if the two sisters are married by two marriages, the second marriage is <u>fasid</u> (invalid), and it will be obligatory on him to put her away; and if the Kazi comes to know about the existence of such a marriage, he will separate them. If she (the second sister) is separated before consummation nothing will be established amongst the <u>ahkam</u> (legal effects of marriage). But if she is separated after co-habitation she will have the customary dower, and the lower of the two amounts of the customary and fixed dowers will be obligatory, and it will be obligatory on her to observe <u>iddat</u>, and the <u>nasab</u> will be established.....This is in the <u>Muhit of Sarakshi</u>.".....

.....There is no sufficient ground for holding that the clear and explicit doctrine of the Fatwa-i-Alamgiri really conflicts with sound tradition or makes any innovation upon the Mahomedan Law as it had been gradually evolved up to 1660 A.D. Broadly speaking no doubt such a marriage as that of Saidabi in this case is prohibited and would be described as void. <u>Per se</u>, it certainly is void, in the sense that it is expressly forbidden. But since the reason for the prohibition is to be sought in the subsistence of a relation with another, and not in the blood of the woman married, it should not in any classification which aims at logical exactitude, be placed in the same category as those which are founded on incest. By 1660 A.D. the best Mahomedan legal opinion had expressed itself very definitely in favour of regarding such marriages as the one we are dealing with to be <u>fasid</u> only. This opinion seems to us to be founded upon the only intelligible, universal principle, upon which the Courts could deal with marriages some of which must be absolutely void, while others would only be relatively void, or invalid. That principle, as we have stated, is that the test and the only test to be applied is whether the woman in question is permanently or only temporarily <u>haram</u>. In every case of the kind the woman in question must be <u>haram</u>, and the difficulty is to decide when, although <u>haram</u>, she has in fact married a man and the marriage has been consummated, it is to be treated as absolutely void without any legal consequences at all, and when it is to be treated as bad indeed in inception, yet capable of having legal consequences. We see no other ground upon which such a decision can be based with the certainty that it will be uniform and consistent and applicable in every case of doubt than the permanence or otherwise of the prohibition.

It is true that in the case before us, considerations in favour of placing the marriage in one or the other category may so overlap each other as to make it hard to feel that the entire position is logically unassailable. But as contrasted cases diverge further from the point at which, in the present instance, they meet and seem to interpenetrate, the applicability of the test becomes more and more apparent and its use more efficacious.

Taking the whole current of authority and the general trend of informed thought on this subject, it points clearly to some such distinctions having always been recognized by the Mahomedan Law. Where that is so and a particular case on the borderland of such distinctions, to which it may be doubtful whether they can be applied in the ordinary way, arises, surely the Courts would be well advised to accept the authoritative statement of the law as it was then understood by the authors of the Fatwa-i-Alamgiri. It is impossible to say that that statement conflicts with the textual authority of the Quran. Speaking generally, it appears to us to harmonize with the course the law took during the intervening period, and to be in consonance with the soundest practical principles. It has the support of such a great modern text-book writer as Baillie. The eighth chapter of his first book appears to us to reach conclusions by unanswerable reasoning, and while those conclusions may be his own, they are the conclusions of a writer of profound knowledge intimately versed at first hand with all the best writings of Mahomedan lawyers. The modern Mahomedan text-book writers, Ameer Ali, Tyabji, and Abdul Rahim, are in substantial agreement. All authority appears to us to point one way. Against this is nothing but the judgment of the Calcutta High Court in <u>Aizunnissa's case</u> ((1895) 23 Cal. 130), and after having given it and the materials upon which it avowedly rests our most careful and respectful attention, we find ourselves wholly unconvinced by its reasoning and unable to agree with the law it lays down.....

———————

Chapter Three

HUSBAND AND WIFE

The effects of a <u>sahih</u> marriage may be summarised as follows: sexual relations between the spouses are lawful and children born out of such relations are legitimate. Bars of affinity arise between each spouse and certain relatives of the other spouse. The wife acquires a right to dower and maintenance in return for which the husband acquires the right of control over her. Each acquires rights of consortium and inheritance. There is no obligation on the wife to maintain the husband. Unlike other legal systems Muslim law recognises no concept of a merger of the personalities of the spouses nor any doctrine of community of property. They remain quite separate legal persons, the wife retaining her own name and each party retaining his or her own school of law. Each remains sole owner of his or her property and can be convicted of the theft of the other´s. In the Indian subcontinent at least there is a considerable degree of flexibility in the Muslim matrimonial regime for although the rights and obligations of the parties are closely regulated there remains substantial scope for express stipulations in the marriage contract so far as consistent with public policy and the fundamental aims of marriage: this is considered below (1). By custom the husband often takes charge of the management of his wife´s property.

Commenting on this regime, Linant de Bellfonds states: "Apologists of Islam point to this to proclaim the superiority of Islam over those western systems with community of property. But the most critical minds do not fail to remind us that the community of property accompanied, at least at first, the indissoluble form of marriage and that the apparent wisdom of Islam and its liberality on this point is not a recognition of the ability of the woman to run her own affairs but a necessity imposed by the fragility of the conjugal link and to an extent the existence of polygamy." (2) It should also be borne in mind that the spouses´ rights of inheritance are compulsory so long as they remain married: they can neither increase nor decrease each other´s share in their estates, in Sunni law.

Dower

Perhaps the central obligation in marriage is that of payment of the dower (mahr). There has been confusion in the courts as to the nature of dower in Islam (3). The payment of a dower by the husband to the wife is an obligation arising out of their marriage and a result of it: it is not a pre-requisite to the validity of the marriage for the marriage is valid even if the parties agree that no dower shall be paid – such an agreement is ineffective – or if no agreement as to dower is reached (4). In such cases a "proper" dower becomes payable by law, in accordance with a number of clearly defined criteria described below. Mahr is not a consideration for the marriage in the sense of a bride price and it is this characteristic which distinguishes mahr from similar institutions in other systems of law, including the customary law of pre-Islamic Arabia, where the husband paid an agreed sum to the father of the bride. It was this change in the nature of the payment which represented one of the most marked improvements in the status of women brought about by Islam.

A bride will usually be represented by her marriage guardian but a Hanafi bride who is adult and sane may negotiate her own dower just as she may contract her own marriage. A father may contract on behalf of his minor son, but the son will be responsible for the amount agreed, not the father, unless the son dies without property. The dower may be added to by the husband at any time after the first agreement and even after the wife has released the dower debt.

Any property which can be owned lawfully by a Muslim and has a value can be the subject matter of dower. Thus a stipulation to perform services, in Hanafi law at least, is not a valid dower payment and if such a dower were to be agreed the wife would be entitled to a proper dower (5).

In considering the value of the dower two questions must be asked: how much has been agreed upon, and when is that sum payable?

Where there is specified dower, i.e. one has been agreed between the parties, the position is relatively straightforward. The amount payable may be agreed either at the time of the marriage or after it, and there is no upper limit to the amount which can be agreed upon. There is, however, in Hanafi law a minimum figure, that of 10 dirhams, a token sum these days. If the sum is left to be fixed by one of the parties unilaterally it cannot be less than the amount of the ´proper dower´ if fixed by the husband, or more than that amount if fixed by the wife (6). The agreement may be in writing or made orally, but if both parties in a dispute fail to prove that the sum payable is that alleged by them, the court will order payment of the proper dower (7). An

132

agreement that no dower shall be paid is void (8), and in such a case the sum payable is again the proper dower. The dower can also be increased after the date of the marriage, and in certain circumstances released.

The proper dower is payable in the absence of agreement as to a specified dower; or if the whole of the dower agreed upon is unlawful (9), and in the other circumstances mentioned above, as also in the case of a _fasid_ union, where the proper dower is less than the specified dower. In assessing the value of the proper dower, the law lays down a number of criteria (10). These are basically: the status of the bride's family; the bride's personal characteristics, i.e. her age, beauty, wealth, learning and conduct; and the amount agreed in the case of other female members of her family; some attention may also be paid to the position of the husband, but this is very much a subordinate criterion. There may of course be some difficulties in determining exactly what is the proper dower in some cases, where comparisons with equals are hard to draw (11).

Muslim law divides the dower into two types – prompt and deferred. The prompt dower is payable on demand by the wife and failing demand, as a deferred dower; the deferred dower only on the dissolution of the marriage by death or divorce or other agreed event (12). In the absence of agreement as to when the dower is to be paid, though there is some doubt on this point, the position seems to be that in India the court may determine what proportion of the dower shall be prompt and what proportion deferred, by reference to custom, the amount of the dower, and the status of the parties. This seems to be the view of the majority of the authorities (13). It is said by Ameer Ali to be customary in India to divide into half prompt, half deferred (14), but the courts have not, apparently, felt obliged to follow this division (15). In Pakistan, the position has been made quite clear by s10 of the Muslim Family Laws Ordinance 1961 which provides that where no details about the mode of payment of dower are specified in the _nikahnama_, or the marriage contract, the entire amount of the dower shall be presumed to be payable on demand. In practice it will often be agreed, especially in the case of large dower sums, that the greater proportion of it (or even of all of it) shall be payable on death or dissolution of the marriage only.

The dower debt may be satisfied in one of a number of ways: by payment of the debt to the wife herself or if she is a minor to her guardian (16); or by transfer to the wife of some property in lieu of her dower, accepted by her (17). Gifts to the wife by the husband of property during their marriage will not be held to be in satisfaction of the dower debt without proof that the husband intended them as such and that the wife accepted them as such (18), though in some circumstances it may be presumed that a particular payment was made to that end (19). The wife may agree to relinquish the whole or part of her claim, assuming that she does so of her own free will and that there is no stipulation against this in the marriage contract. Such a release may be effected at any time after the marriage ceremony, in whole or in part, conditionally or absolutely, and takes the form of a gift – thus she may effect the release even though not of full age for the purposes of the Indian Majority Act so long as she has attained puberty (20). But such a release would not be valid if made under duress or undue influence (21).

Where the _sahih_ marriage is dissolved by an act of the husband before consummation or because of a _faskh_ on account of the husband's impotence, the wife is entitled to one half of the specified dower (22). If no specified dower had been agreed the wife is entitled to only a small present in such circumstances (23) and this is also the case where a specified dower was only agreed after the marriage which is then terminated in this way before consummation (24). Where the _sahih_ union is dissolved before consummation by an act of the wife, e.g. by exercising her option of puberty, she is entitled to nothing (25). Where the marriage is _fasid_ and dissolved before consummation she is entitled to nothing (26), and this is also the case where the husband was induced to marry her by force or fraud (27), or where he was married as a minor and exercises his option of puberty (28). In the event of the death of one of the parties, however, the full dower (whether it be proper or specified) is payable even without consummation of the _sahih_ marriage (29) – in the case of a _fasid_ marriage the specified or proper dower, whichever is the smaller, is payable once consummation has taken place, but otherwise nothing (30). Once the _sahih_ union has been consummated nothing can operate to the detriment of the wife's right to the dower. For these purposes valid retirement has the same effect as consummation (31).

The most difficult part of the law of dower is that of its enforcement. The position with respect to the prompt dower is however relatively straightforward. If the prompt dower is not paid the wife may sue for it as an unpaid debt. Most often the question of unpaid prompt dower seems to arise in suits brought by a husband for restitution of conjugal rights, to which the wife brings the defence that the dower has not been paid (32). There is no doubt as to the position where there has been no consummation. In such circumstances the courts in both India and Pakistan have held failure to pay the prompt dower to be a complete defence to any such suit, and furthermore this means that the husband remains under an obligation to maintain his wife despite her refusal to consummate the marriage until the dower is paid (33). There is however disagreement as to the position once the marriage has been consummated, both in the classical authorities and in the modern courts. Abu Hanafi held the wife entitled to

refuse intercourse at any time during the marriage until any
dower owed was paid. His two disciples held that the right
was lost on consummation. In Indian courts the view has been
taken that after consummation failure to pay dower is no
defence to a suit for restitution of conjugal rights, but that
the court will grant a decree of restitution (failure to
comply with which renders the wife nashuz and therefore
disentitles her from maintenance) conditional on payment of
the prompt dower, the decree being a discretionary remedy.
The result, then, is a difference of form not substance (34).
In Pakistan the courts have taken the view that the right of
refusal is not lost on consummation and failure to pay the
prompt dower will even then be a defence to a suit for
restitution of conjugal rights (35).

It is quite possible, of course, that the wife will make
no such demand for her prompt dower during the continuance of
the marriage. In this event, on the termination of the
marriage through death or divorce the position with respect to
the prompt dower will be identical to that of the deferred
dower. The position with respect to the deferred dower is
extremely unclear. An unpaid dower is an unsecured debt (36)
and has no priority over other unsecured creditors (37), and
being a simple money claim cannot be attached to any specific
assets of the husband's estate (38). The right to her dower
is however both transferable and heritable, even if not
demanded by the wife during her lifetime. If this were the
only law on the matter the wife's rights in respect of her
deferred dower would be weak indeed. However, the widow whose
dower has remained unpaid at the date of the husband's death
has an additional right in certain circumstances to retain
possession of her husband's estate until such time as the
dower debt is satisfied. This right is not a lien or mortgage
over the property but a mere personal right of retention; and
it is not a right to obtain possession.

To be entitled to retain possession of the property the
widow must have entered into, or been in possession of, the
husband's estate at the time of his death lawfully and without
force or fraud (39). Following some ambiguous dicta in the
decision of the Privy Council in Hamira Bibi v. Zubaida Bibi
(40), the various High Courts of India have given conflicting
decisions on whether the consent, express or implied, of the
husband or his heirs was necessary before her possession could
be deemed lawful. This question is still unresolved but it is
submitted that the better view is that no such consent is
necessary.

Although the widow's right is one of retention not
obtaining possession, if she is unlawfully dispossessed she
may still bring an action to recover the possession she once
had (41).

Even though the right to possession has been held to be
heritable, so that if she dies in possession her heirs may

135

retain that possession until the dower debt is satisfied, they can only do so in cases where their possession is a continuation of hers or they themselves have obtained possession lawfully and without fraud, their right to possession being no better than the widow's (42). And the heirs are not entitled to claim possession where the widow herself never obtained it (43). Again, once having continued or obtained possession lawfully, the heirs can, if subsequently dispossessed, bring an action for recovery of that possession (44).

It is quite clear that the widow's right to possession confers no title in the property: thus she cannot alienate the property itself by sale, gift or mortgage, beyond the share to which she is entitled as heir of the deceased husband (45). There is considerable doubt however as to her rights, if any, to assign the right to retain possession (as opposed to the property itself or the dower debt). One view is that the right to retain possession is so personal that it is wholly untransferable (46). Another, that she is completely free to transfer the right to possess until the dower debt is paid (47). A third view is that she can transfer it provided she also assigns the dower debt itself (48). A fourth view is that she can transfer the right for her lifetime only (49). It does at least seem clear that the assignment of the widow's dower debt does not carry with it the right to possession.

The widow in possession of her deceased husband's property in lieu of her dower debt must account to the heirs for any profits she receives for such possession (50), and will be presumed to have received what rents could with reasonable diligence have been obtained from the property, unless she can prove that the actual amount of profits is smaller (51). However, it seems that it lies in the discretion of the court to award her compensation in the form of interest on the dower debt for forbearing to enforce her right to the dower (52). The fact that the widow is exercising her right of possession does not prevent her from bringing an action against the other heirs of her husband to recover the dower debt, but possibly only on condition that she offers in that suit to give up possession on obtaining a decree (53).

The law of dower must always be judged in the light of the Muslim law's refusal to grant the wife a right of maintenance on the termination of the marriage. There are a number of reasons for the high sums settled for dowers, often much in excess of the means of the husband. The main reason, certainly in modern times, is to provide a disincentive to the husband tempted to exercise his right of _talaq_ in a capricious manner. A high dower sum is also a convenient way of enhancing the wife's entitlement to her husband's estate should he predecease her, over and above her Qur'anic entitlement, which cannot be varied by means of will: though this may equally be a wholly unintended consequence. The announcement of very substantial sums is often motivated by reasons of social prestige both of the husband and the bride's father. This last factor also explains, of course, the practice of sham dowers, publicly announced, behind which exist private agreements for much smaller sums (54).

Whereas the first reason is generally accepted to be both inevitable and desirable so long as the muslim matrimonial regime remains as it is, the second and third reasons have caused much concern. It is widely acknowledged that excessively inflated dower sums can cause severe problems to the issue of the spouses party to such an agreement. However, neither in India nor in Pakistan has there been any attempt on a national level to deal with this particular problem, though there are possibilities, as the Oudh Laws Act 1876 shows, of alleviating it.

Oudh Laws Act 1876: s5

Where the amount of dower stipulated for in any contract of marriage by a Muhammadan is excessive with reference to the means of the husband, the entire sum provided in the contract shall not be awarded in any suit by a decree, in favour of the plaintiff, or by allowing it by way of set off, lieu or otherwise to the defendant; but the amount of the dower to be allowed by the court shall be reasonable with reference to the means of the husband and the status of the wife. This rule shall be applicable whether the suit to enforce the contract be brought in the husband's life or after his death.

What is reasonable is to be determined by reference to the time that the dower is claimed, not the time of the marriage. The Act only applies where the husband resides in Oudh.

The Jammi and Kashmir State Muslim Dower Act 1977F (1920AD) s2 is in identical terms. These provisions do not apply outside Oudh or Jammi and Kashmir. Indeed the institution of dower has been staunchly defended against legislative restrictions by orthodox opinion in both India and Pakistan.

The practice of public dowers announced for reasons of prestige behind which lie private agreements, a practice of some antiquity in the Muslim world, is more easily amenable to reform in the courts. The Fatawa Alamgiri devoted considerable attention to the technicalities of the practice and the practice was much criticised by the Report of the Commission on Marriage and Family laws in 1956 in Pakistan, which advocated its elimination by the simple expedient of always enforcing the terms of the dower publicly announced irrespective of the real agreement between the parties.

137

However, the practice still thrives and the courts show no willingness to find ways of discouraging it (55), no action having been taken by the legislatures of India or Pakistan. The onus of proving the fictitious nature of the amount of dower publicly announced is on the party alleging this but once he has succeeded the court will enforce the private agreement. Nevertheless, it may be very difficult to establish a private agreement if the public announcement takes the form of a deed and it is questionable whether he is entitled to do so in the light of ss91, 92 of the Indian Evidence Act 1872 even where the Muslim doctrine is expressly pleaded (56).

At this point a distinction should be drawn between mehr and the dowry (jihaz), a sum paid by a woman's family to the groom, which is founded in customary practice rather than Muslim law, and which may equally cause problems. This makes an interesting contrast, for in both India and Pakistan steps have been taken against this institution while expressly exempting from any restrictions the Muslim mehr. The only relevance that jihaz may have for the law of Islam is in the law of gifts.

J.L. Esposito. "Women in Muslim Family law" p.87

"Dowry, although not rooted in Islamic law, is a firmly established custom. It consists of property such as clothing, money and jewellery, which the bride's family is obligated to provide. Although the dowry theoretically belongs to the bride, it usually passes to the husband and his family upon marriage and, so, is often an important factor in arranging marriages. In the Indian subcontinent, dowry and lavish weddings have long been recognised as creating serious social problems, since family pride and a desire to provide a suitable marriage often result in the bride's family incurring substantial debts."

West Pakistan Dowry (Prohibition on Display) Act 1967

.....2. Definitions – In this Act, "Dowry" means any property or valuable security as defined in section 3 of the Pakistan Penal Code, given or agreed to be given either directly or indirectly:-

    (i) by one party to a marriage to the other party to the marriage; or

    (ii) by the parents of either party to a marriage or by any other person, to either party to the marriage or to any other person;

at or before or after the marriage, in connection with the marriage of the said parties, but does not include:-

    (a) dower or mahar; or

    (b) any present made at the time of marriage to either

138

party to the marriage in the form of cash, ornaments, clothes or other articles, unless they are made as consideration for the marriage of the said parties.

3. <u>Bar on exhibition of dowry or presents</u> – Whoever intentionally displays or exhibits dowry, or any presents in the form of cash, ornaments, clothes or other articles, made at the time of, or immediately before or after marriage to either party to the marriage, shall be punished with fine which may extend to five thousand rupees.

4. <u>Dowry to be for the benefit of wife or her heirs</u> –
(1)   The dowry given, and all presents made before, at or after the marriage, to the woman in connection with whose marriage they are given or made shall vest in such woman and she shall be deemed to be the absolute owner thereof.
(2)   Where dowry or such presents are received by any person other than the woman in connection with whose marriage they are given or made that person shall transfer the same to such woman –
> (a)   if the dowry or the presents were received before marriage, within one year after the date of marriage; or
> (b)   if the dowry or the presents were received at the time of or after the marriage, within one year of the date of their receipt.

(3)   If any person fails to transfer any property as required by sub-section (2), and within the time provided therefor, he shall be punished with imprisonment which may extend to one year, or with fine which may extend to five thousand rupees, or with both; but such punishment shall not absolve the person from his obligation as required by sub-section (2).
(4)   Where the woman entitled to any property under sub-section (2), dies before receiving it, the heirs of the woman shall be entitled to claim it from the person holding it for the time being.

This legislation proved inadequate, so in 1976 Pakistan enacted legislation more directly aimed at the cause of the problems; and further amended in 1980.

<u>Dowry and Bridal Gifts (Restriction) Act 1976</u>

.....2. <u>Definitions</u> – In this Act, unless there is anything repugnant in the subject or context, –
> (a)   "bridal gift" means any property given as a gift before, at or after the marriage, either directly or indirectly, by the bridegroom or his parents to the bride in connection with the marriage but does not include Mehr;
> (b)   "dowry" means any property given before, at or after the marriage, either directly or indirectly, to

139

the bride by her parents in connection with the marriage but it does not include property which the bride may inherit under the laws of inheritance and succession applicable to her;

(c)   "marriage" includes betrothal, <u>nikah</u> and <u>rukhsati</u>;

(d)   "parents" includes the guardian of a party to a marriage and any person who provides for dowry or bridal gifts and, in the case of a party to a marriage who has no parent, or whose marriage is solemnized in circumstances in which, or at a place at which, no parent is present, such party;

(e)   "present" means a gift of any property, not being a bridal gift or dowry, given before, at or after the marriage, either directly or indirectly, to either party to a marriage in connection with the marriage or to the relatives of the bride or bridegroom but does not include <u>neundra</u> and <u>salami</u>;

(f)   "property" means property, both movable and immovable, and includes any valuable security as defined in the Pakistan Penal Code (Act XLV of 1860); and

(g)   "Registrar" means a <u>Nikah</u> Registrar licensed under the Muslim Family Laws Ordinance, 1961 (VIII of 1961), and such other person as may be designated from time to time to perform the functions of the Registrar.

3. <u>Restriction on dowry, presents and bridal gifts</u> –

(1)   Neither the aggregate value of the dowry and presents given to the bride by her parents nor the aggregate value of the bridal gifts or of the presents given to the bridegroom shall exceed five thousand rupees:

<u>Explanation</u> – The ceiling of five thousand rupees specified in this sub-section does not in any way imply that the dowry, bridal gifts and presents of a lesser amount may not be given.

(2)   No dowry, bridal gifts or presents may be given before or after six months of <u>nikah</u>, and, if <u>rukhsati</u> takes place some time after <u>nikah</u>, after six months of such <u>rukhsati</u>.

4. <u>Restriction on presents</u> – No person shall give to either party to the marriage any present the value of which exceeds one hundred rupees:

Provided that the limit of one hundred shall not apply to the presents given to the bridegroom by the parents of the bride under subsection (1) of section 3:

Provided further that the President, the Prime Minister, Federal Minister, Chief Minister, Minister, Minister of State, Adviser, Governor, Speaker, Deputy Speaker, the Chairman or the Deputy Chairman of the Senate, Parliamentary Secretary, Member of the Senate, National Assembly or Provincial Assembly, Government Servant or an official serving in any corporation, industry or establishment owned, controlled or managed by Government shall not receive any present in connection with his marriage or the marriage of his son or daughter except from his relations (khandan):

> Provided further that this restriction shall not apply to a Government Servant or official serving in the scale below National Pay Scale 17 not exercising in any manner judicial, revenue or executive authority.

5. <u>Vesting of dowry etc., in the bride</u> – All property given as dowry or bridal gifts and all property given to the bride as a present shall vest absolutely in the bride and her interest in property however derived shall hereafter not be restrictive, conditional or limited.

6. <u>Expenditure on marriage</u> – The total expenditure on a marriage, excluding the value of dowry, bridal gifts and presents, but including the expenses on <u>mehndi baarat</u> and <u>valima</u>, incurred by or on behalf of either party to the marriage shall not exceed two thousand and five hundred rupees.

7. <u>Display of dowry, etc</u>. – The parents of each party to a marriage shall, at the time of <u>rukhsati</u>, display all items of dowry, bridal gifts and presents given or received in connection with the marriage so as to be visible to the person attending the <u>rukhsati</u>.

8. <u>List of dowry, etc. to be furnished to Registrar</u> –
(1) The parents of each party to a marriage shall furnish to the Registrar lists of dowry, bridal gifts and presents given or received in connection with the marriage.
(2) The lists referred to in subsection (1) shall be furnished, –
> (a) in the case of property given or accepted before or at the time of the marriage, at the time of the marriage; and
> (b) in the case of property given or accepted after the marriage, within fifteen days of its being given or accepted.

(3) The lists referred to in subsection (1) shall –
> (a) contain details of the property along with the value thereof; and
> (b) be signed or thumb-marked by the persons furnishing to the Registrar and attested by at least two witnesses.

(4) The parents of each party to a marriage shall furnish to the Registrar the details of expenditure incurred on the marriage, duly signed or thumb-marked by them within one week.
(5) The Registrar shall forward the lists furnished under subsection (1) and the details of expenditure submitted under subsection (4) to the Deputy Commissioner within fifteen days of receipt of such list

or details of expenditure.

9. <u>Penalty and procedure</u> –

(1) Whoever contravenes, or fails to comply with, any provision of this Act or the rules made thereunder shall be punishable with imprisonment of either description for a term which may extend to six months, or with fine which may extend to ten thousand rupees, or with both, and the dowry, bridal gifts or presents given or accepted in contravention of the provisions of this Act shall be forfeited to the Federal Government to be utilized for the marriage of poor girls in such a way as may be prescribed by rules made under this Act:

Provided that if both the parents of a party to the marriage contravene, or fail to comply with, any provision of this Act or the rules made thereunder, action under this section shall be taken only against the father:

Provided further that if the parent who contravenes or fails to comply with, any provision of this Act or the rules made thereunder is a female, shall be punishable with fine only.

(2) Any offence punishable under this Act shall be triable only by a Family Court established under the West Pakistan Family Court Act, 1964 (W.P. Act No. XXXV of 1964).

(3) No Family Court shall take cognizance of an offence punishable under this Act except upon a complaint in writing made by, or under the authority of, the Deputy Commissioner within nine months from the date of <u>nikah</u>, and if <u>rukhsati</u> takes place some time after <u>nikah</u>, from the date of such <u>rukhsati</u>.

Dowry and Bridal Gifts (Restriction) Amendment Ordinance 1980

.....1. <u>Short title and commencement</u> –

(1) This Ordinance may be called the Dowry and Bridal Gifts (Restriction) (Amendment) Ordinance, 1980.

(2) It shall come into force at once.

2. <u>Amendment of section 3, Act XLIII of 1976</u> – In the Dowry and Bridal Gifts (Restriction) Act, 1976 (XLIII of 1976), hereinafter referred to as the said Act, in section 3,
–

(a) after subsection (1), the following new subsection shall be inserted, namely:-

"(1-A) No person shall give or accept, or enter into an agreement to give or to accept dowry, bridal gifts or presents of a value exceeding the aggregate value specified in subsection (1)"; and

(b) for subsection (2) the following shall be substituted, namely:-

"(2) No dowry, bridal gifts or presents may be

given before six months or after one month of _nikah_ and, if _rukhsati_ takes place some time after _nikah_ after one month of such _rukhsati_.

3. Omission of section 7, Act XLIII of 1976 - In the said Act, section 7 shall be omitted.

4. Substitution of section 8, Act XLIII of 1976 - In the said Act, for section 8 the following shall be substituted, namely:-

"8. Declaration regarding expenditure to be submitted to Registrar -

(1) The father of the bridegroom or any other person who arranges the marriage shall, within fifteen days of the expiry of the period fixed under subsection (2) of section 3 for giving dowry, bridal gifts and presents, submit a declaration to the Registrar solemnly affirming that the total expenditure on the marriage including dowry, bridal gifts, presents and entertainments did not exceed the limits laid down in this Act.

(2) The Registrar shall forward the declaration submitted under sub-section (1) to the Deputy Commissioner within fifteen days of receipt of such declaration.

8-A. Complaints against violation of the Act - If any person attending a marriage ceremony is satisfied that the provisions of this Act or the rules made thereunder have been contravened in respect of such ceremony, he may submit a complaint, giving full particulars of the contravention, to the Deputy Commissioner."

5. Amendment of section 9, Act XLIII of 1976 - In the said Act, in section 9, -

(a) in subsection (1), for the words "which may extend to ten thousand rupees" the words "which shall not be less than the amount proved to have been spent in excess of the maximum limits laid down in this Act" shall be substituted; and

(b) in subsection (3), for the word "nine" the word "three" shall be substituted.

6. Substitution of section 10, Act XLIII of 1976 - In the said Act, for section 10 the following shall be substituted, namely:-

"10. Power to make rules - The Federal Government, in respect of the Islamabad Capital Territory, and a Provincial Government, in respect of the Province, may, by notification in the official Gazette, make rules for carrying out the purposes of this Act."

This Statute repealed the Act of 1967.

This makes interesting comparison with the Indian legislation:

Dowry Prohibition Act 1961

2. <u>Definition of Dowry</u> - In this Act "dowry" means any property or valuable security given or agreed to be given either directly or indirectly
    (a) by one party to a marriage to the other party to the marriage; or
    (b) by the parents of either party to a marriage or by any other person, to either party to the marriage or to any other person;
at before or after the marriage as consideration for the marriage of the said parties, but does not include dower or mahr in the case of persons to whom the Muslim Personal Law (Shariat) applies.

Explanation I - For the removal of doubts, it is hereby declared that any presents made at the time of a marriage to either party to the marriage in the form of cash, ornaments, clothes or other articles, shall not be deemed to be dowry within the meaning of this section, unless they are made as consideration for the marriage of the said parties.

Explanation II - The expression "valuable security" has the same meaning as in s.30 of the Indian Penal Code.

3. <u>Penalty for giving or taking dowry</u> - If any person, after the commencement of this Act, gives or takes or abets the giving or taking of dowry, he shall be punishable with imprisonment which may extend to six months, or with fine which may extend to five thousand rupees, or with both.

4. <u>Penalty for demanding dowry</u> - If any person, after the commencement of this Act, demands, directly or indirectly, from the parents or guardian of a bride or bridegroom, as the case may be, any dowry, he shall be punishable with imprisonment which may extend to six months, or with fine which may extend to five thousand rupees, or with both:
    Provided that no court shall take cognizance of any offence under this section except with the previous sanction of the State Government or of such officer as the State Government may, by general or special order, specify in this behalf.

5. <u>Agreement for giving or taking dowry to be void</u> - Any agreement for the giving or taking of dowry shall be void.

6. <u>Dowry to be for the benefit of the wife or her heirs</u>
    (1) Where any dowry is received by any person other than the woman in connection with whose marriage it is given, that person shall transfer it to the woman -
        (a) if the dowry was received before marriage, within one year after the date of marriage; or
        (b) if the dowry was received at the time of or after the marriage, within one year after the date

of its receipt; or

> (c) if the dowry was received when the woman was a minor within one year after she has attained the age of eighteen years and pending such transfer, shall hold it in trust for the benefit of the woman.
>
> (2) If any person fails to transfer any property as required by sub-section (1) and within the time limited therefor, he shall be punishable with imprisonment which may extend to six months, or with fine which may extend to five thousand rupees, or with both; but such punishment shall not absolve the person from his obligation to transfer the property as required by sub-section (1).
>
> (3) Where the woman entitled to any property under sub-section (1) dies before receiving it, the heirs of the woman shall be entitled to claim it from the person holding it for the time being.
>
> (4) Nothing contained in this section shall affect the provisions of section 3 or section 4.

T. Mahmood "Muslim Personal Law: Role of the State in the Subcontinent" p.116

"When the Bill leading to the enactment of the Act of 1961 was being debated in parliament, apprehensions regarding its possible effect on the Islamic law of dower (mahr) were expressed by several Muslim members. Accepting their suggestion in the matter, the framers of the Act expressly excluded from the definition of dowry contained in it ´dower or mahr in the case of persons to whom the Muslim Personal Law (Shari´at) applies.´ The penal provisions of the Act of 1961 do not, thus, affect in any way the concept of mahr in Muslim law. While restraining monetary transactions in marriage, the legislature thought it proper to protect the institution of mahr which is regarded in Muslim law as an inseparable part of the contract of marriage and which is, of course, materially different from dowry."

Right to Consortium

The spouses have the right to each other´s consortium. The principal means of enforcing this in India and Pakistan is by suit for restitution of conjugal rights: usually the subject of the suit will be the husband´s demand that his wife cohabit with him. It has been said that the husband must prove strictly all the allegations he makes to justify a decree and that the court will lean in favour of the wife because of the dominant position of husbands (57). Thus the court will not exercise its discretion in his favour in cases

145

where he is guilty of cruelty (58), neglect (59), non-payment of the prompt dower (60), or other improper conduct. The view has been taken in India that the taking of a second wife is in itself cruelty, even if no stipulation against polygamy was made in the marriage contract (61), but the courts of Pakistan have not followed this view (62). Inequality of treatment of one of a number of wives to her prejudice will be a defence to such a suit (63). Unjustified failure to maintain the wife will be a defence to the suit (64): since a denial of conjugal rights which is unjustified is in itself justification of a failure to maintain, the courts often find themselves faced with the ´chicken and egg´ problem of determining whose unjustified conduct came first.

The husband has the right to sexual relations with his wife subject to the restrictions of religion and medical conditions which would endanger her. However the Hanafi school, preferring an objectively easy means of proof, deem only unjustified abandonment of the matrimonial home evidence of her refusal: anything less than this evidence will not permit the husband to suspend his maintenance and ultimately the husband´s only sanction will be _talaq_. The wife would appear to have the right to intercourse only in the consummation of the marriage in the Hanafi school, though failure to maintain sexual relations might well constitute neglect or cruelty. Although in theory the decree for restitution of conjugal rights is equally available to the wife in practice the husband´s power of _talaq_ is such that such a decree may be of no assistance, unless the deferred dower is large enough a disincentive.

The Husband´s Right of Control

This right, though extensive, is not absolute. The husband may select the matrimonial home, though he cannot compel the wife to share her living accommodation with another of his wives, relatives (apart from very young children of another marriage), nor if it is a dangerous place. He may control her movements except to the extent of permitting her reasonable access to her close relatives. He may prevent her from taking up a job of work but may not compel her to work. He may take her on journeys unless such journeys would be unnecessarily dangerous or harmful to her health. If the wife disobeys the husband´s reasonable instructions she becomes _nashuz_ in most schools and therefore disentitled to maintenance, though the Hanafi point of view has already been dealt with. In any event such disobedience entitles the husband first to reprimand her and if this fails to refuse to sleep with her and eventually to beat her, with reasonable force. The wife´s right to maintenance is in one sense consideration for her submission to the husband´s authority.

Maintenance: Content and Quantum of Obligation

Maintenance can be said to comprise food clothing and accommodation but probably extends to other necessaries of life for hygiene (65) and it takes priority over the husband's obligations to maintain his children and other relatives. With respect to accommodation this must be a separate dwelling with its own entrance, exclusive to herself and her husband: she cannot be compelled to share accommodation with another wife or relations etc.

The quantum of maintenance is not an absolute standard: it is determined by reference to the wealth of the spouses. The schools employ different methods of quantifying it but in Hanafi law one must take the median between the wealth of the husband and wealth of the wife as the appropriate measure. Need is not the criterion. This can of course work hardship on an impoverished husband married to a wealthy wife, especially where a substantial portion of what will have been for him a large dower is made prompt. The Shafi'i school takes perhaps the more logical view that the criterion is the husband's wealth alone. Shi'a law adopts the criterion of need. The Hanafi view also has the consequence that a husband will be treating two wives equally only conferring on one a higher level of maintenance than the other if the first is wealthier than the second, even though the first has less need of that maintenance. This does seem rather anomalous.

Although of little significance after the Child Marriage Restraint Acts a husband is not obliged to provide maintenance for a wife who is under the age of puberty and remains with her father: this is the obligation of her father himself. If the woman is capable of consummation however, it is no bar to her right to maintenance that her husband is a minor or cannot cohabit with her. Nor, once consummation has taken place, will the inability of the wife through illness to continue in sexual relations with the husband relieve him of the obligation to maintain her.

There will be no liability to maintain a wife guilty of nashuz (disobedience). A wife is nashiza if without a valid excuse she disobeys his reasonable orders, refuses to cohabit in the house he has chosen, goes on haj without his consent unless it is obligatory for her to go, takes employment outside the house without his consent, or is imprisoned so as to be inaccessible to him (66).

Nevertheless she will not be nashiza if these acts are a response to her husband's failure to pay the prompt dower in its entirety when demanded, when he has failed to house her as the law requires and when he has acted with cruelty in some way or has broken one of the valid stipulations in their marriage contract, e.g. a stipulation that they should not move from a particular locality or that she should have a certain amount of access to her relatives.

147

In both India and Pakistan statute has to some extent
supplemented the Muslim law by providing means of enforcing
the right to maintenance, and in India this right has in one
respect been extended. These are considered below.

Duration of the Right to Maintenance

So long as the wife continues to perform her obligations
under the marriage or has some valid excuse for not doing so,
her right to maintenance endures. On the termination of the
marriage the position varies with the circumstances. Somewhat
unjustly, one might think, the death of the husband at once
brings to an end the right of the wife to maintenance even
though she must observe an ´idda of four months and ten days
during which time she may not remarry. Most of the Hanafi
jurists maintain this position even where, at the time of her
husband's death the wife was pregnant by him (67).

A wife who has been repudiated by her husband remains
entitled to maintenance for the duration of her ´idda, whether
this be revocable or irrevocable repudiation (68). As Linant
de Bellfonds points out, there is a somewhat curious conflict
of principle here. In the revocable repudiation the marriage
continues until the end of ´idda, so one would expect
maintenance to continue as well. But with an irrevocable
repudiation the marriage has ended definitely and there should
logically be no right to it. The other schools follow a more
logical view. A judicial divorce should apply the same rules
as an irrevocable repudiation. Bellfonds ascribes the
illogicality to confusion caused by Qur´an II 241, LXV, 6
(69). If the unilateral conduct of the wife - her apostasy -
causes the termination of the marriage she at once loses her
right to maintenance; though it seems the Caste Disabilities
Removal Act 1850 must reverse the rule that a divorced Muslim
woman who apostasises during her ´idda loses any further
rights to maintenance, and the provisions of s.4 of the
Dissolution of Muslim Marriages Act 1939 render the occasions
on which apostasy of itself can terminate the marriage
extremely rare. Presumably if it were to happen that apostasy
by the wife did cause the irrevocable termination of the
marriage, in one of the rare cases left open by the 1939 Act,
the 1850 Act could not assist her since it would be the
irrevocable termination of the marriage and not her apostasy
which, strictly speaking, had deprived her of any further
right to support from her former husband, unless in this case
too the Hanafi law as applied in the subcontinent takes the
view that both revocable and irrevocable dissolution of the
marriage at the instance of the wife entitle her to a period
of maintenance: given that in Hanafi law no such possibility
of a unilateral divorce by the wife exists, the answer must be
that the Act cannot help.

In the Indian subcontinent it has been held that the

148

wife's right to maintenance extends beyond the period of 'idda consequent upon a talaq, until the time when she receives notice of the talaq if that period is longer (70). It is one possible interpretation of the new Criminal Procedure Code of India that a wife who is divorced acquires the right of maintenance until her remarriage. This is considered below.

In Pakistan, too, some amelioration of the position has been suggested (in Abdul Baqi v. Mst. Nanpera Siddiqi, (1981) P.Cr.L.J. 490) by Zakiuddin Pal J. who held that although after a marriage between the parties had been dissolved by an Order of the Court, the wife was not entitled to further maintenance, where the prompt dower had not been paid she could until such dissolution stay away from her husband and remain entitled to maintenance during that period and the 'idda succeeding the dissolution.

Enforcement of the Right to Maintenance

A wife who has received maintenance in advance is in a strong position in the Hanafi law, where it has been held that once paid to her she acquires it irrevocably, being deemed a gift. The other schools, viewing it as consideration for the wife obeying her husband, require any advance payments to be returned on the termination of the marriage.

A wife seeking to obtain maintenance from an unwilling husband is in a far weaker position. She may sue for maintenance under Muslim law but in practice reliance is placed on statutory means of enforcement both in India and Pakistan.

In Pakistan the wife may choose between the Muslim Family Laws Ordinance 1961, s.9; the Family Courts Act 1964; and the Code of Criminal Procedure 1898, s.488. Under the 1961 Ordinance complete failure on the part of the husband to maintain his wife is not necessary. Even if it is proved that the wife is being maintained by the husband, if the Arbitration Council concludes that he is failing to maintain her adequately or if there is more than one wife, he is not maintaining the complainant equitably, and whether or not the husband and wife are living together, the Council may determine how much should be paid: if that sum is not paid it becomes recoverable as arrears of land revenue (71). Under the Family Courts Act 1964, s.5 "Subject to the provisions of the Muslim Family laws Ordinance 1961 and the Conciliation Courts Ordinance 1961 the Family Courts shall have exclusive jurisdiction to entertain, hear and adjudicate upon matters specified in the schedule" which includes maintenance. Neither of these provisions has any fixed financial limit to the awards it may make. Under s.488 of the Code of Criminal Procedure if any person having sufficient means neglects or refuses to maintain his wife, he may be ordered to make a monthly allowance not exceeding Rs.400, but this is subject to

149

the proviso that if the husband offers to maintain his wife on condition that she lives with him and she refuses the magistrate must consider the grounds and may still order payment if these are justified. No wife living in adultery or refusing to live with her husband without due cause may receive any maintenance under the Code. The fact that the husband has taken a second wife will not be sufficient cause under the Code. A speedy talaq by the husband can effectively frustrate the order for maintenance (72), but failure to comply with an order can lead to one month's imprisonment. In India, s.488 has been amended (by Act IX of 1949) to the extent that if the husband has married another wife the first wife may justifiably refuse to live with the husband and may still claim maintenance. The financial limit is Rs500 per month. The whole Code was repealed and re-enacted with amendments and its replacement, s.125 of the new Criminal Procedure Code 1973, enables the court to award maintenance to a wife, even where that wife is subsequently divorced by the husband, for a period surviving the expiry of ´idda and extending until she either remarries or receives all sums which were payable to her by her personal or customary law on divorce. This surely includes her deferred dower, though the Indian courts and academics have been far from unanimous on this point (73), which revolves around the interpretation of s.127(3) of the Code; we should now look to the decision of the Supreme Court in Baj Tahira v. Ali Hassan (74) in this matter. The relevant provisions of the Code and this decision are reproduced below.

In the absence of a specific agreement the wife is not entitled to claim arrears of maintenance in Hanafi law, though this view is not taken by the other schools and in Pakistan at least there have been some courts willing to abandon this somewhat harsh rule (75), though not in India (76). In the classical Hanafi law, apart from by agreement, the only way in which the wife can claim in respect of past maintenance is where the court has fixed her entitlement, the husband is absent and has left no property or business in consequence of which she has to borrow money on the court's authority. This of course is a serious handicap to the wife.

Contractual Stipulations in Marriage

It is possible to agree a wide variety of stipulations in the marriage contract specifying the obligations of the spouses, both at the time of the marriage and subsequently, so long as the stipulations are not contrary to the fundamental aims of the marriage or to public policy. Where the agreement contains terms, some of which are valid and some of which are not, it will be enforced in respect of the valid stipulations alone if these are severable, but otherwise the whole agreement fails and the marriage continues as if there had been no agreement at all. Examples of stipulations which have succeeded are that the husband shall not during the marriage marry a second wife (77); that he shall pay the wife a certain amount by way of maintenance (78); that he shall maintain her children by a former marriage (79); that they shall not move from a certain town without the wife's consent (80); that the wife be permitted to live away from the husband if he did certain things such as maltreating her or taking to drink (81); that the wife be permitted to visit relations, etc. (82). On the other hand stipulations that the wife might leave the matrimonial home for any reason (83); that she have an unconditional right to maintenance (84), irrespective of her conduct; that she be permitted always to live with her parents (unless perhaps she is one of a number of the husband's wives (85), have been held invalid. The tendency has been to expand the category of valid conditions though as might be expected those relating to polygamy and maintenance have been most common. This device can also be used to enhance the wife's right to terminate the marriage in effect unilaterally within certain limits, since the husband has the right to delegate his power of _talaq_ either to the wife or a third party. An example is the term giving the right to declare _talaq_ for the husband should he marry a second wife (86). Stipulations may also be made governing the payment of dower or provision of servants etc. Again this must not be contrary to public policy. The consequence of a breach of such a condition will depend in large measure on what the marriage contract states to be its consequence. In the absence of any other provision it may lead to the denial to the guilty party of a decree for restitution of conjugal rights. Such stipulations, combined with the provision for dower, may greatly enhance the legal position of the Muslim wife.

Co-Wives in a Polygamous Union

It is an obligation of a husband who is married to more than one wife to show that he is treating them impartially. A wife who is treated worse than other wives of the same husband will have a defence to a suit for restitution of conjugal rights and indeed a cause of action for dissolution of her marriage under the Dissolution of Muslim Marriages Act 1939 (87). Less extreme, she may claim maintenance despite her refusal to cohabit. The question then arises as to the scope of this duty of impartiality. The jurists have uniformly taken an objective view. The principal aspect of the duty concerns maintenance, where the husband must give all his wives food clothing etc. on the same basis of calculation and must give them separate private living accommodation: they cannot be compelled to share such lodgings. Each wife is entitled to an equal amount of the husband's time, not

151

Husband and Wife

necessarily to an equal amount of his sexual favour; but this right is subject to some qualification during the first few days of the husband's marriage to a new wife, and where he must go on a long journey, when he need not take all his wives with him if he chooses to take one for companionship.

<u>NASRA BEGUM (appellant) v. RIJWAN ALI (respondent)</u>
<u>A.I.R. 1980 All. 118 (Seth and Mehrotra JJ.)</u>

SETH, J. - Plaintiff Smt. Nasra Begum has come up in appeal against the order dated 22nd Aug. 1975 passed by the Civil Judge, Bareilly, directing that the plaint filed by her be returned for presentation to proper court.

2. According to the plaintiff, she was married to defendant Rijwan Ali at Bareilly on October 20, 1963, and on that occasion the amount of dower payable to her was fixed at Rs. 50,000. Out of this amount a sum of Rs. 25,000 was to be her prompt dower and the rest her deferred dower. After their marriage the plaintiff and defendant lived at Barabanki and a son was also born to them. Subsequently relations between the plaintiff and her husband got strained and the plaintiff demanded payment of her prompt dower. The defendant instead of paying the money to the plaintiff turned her out of his house. The plaintiff thereupon filed suit No. 6 of 1974 in the court of Civil Judge for recovery of a sum of Rs. 25,000 as her prompt dower and also for possession of certain ornaments.

3. The defendant contested the suit inter alia on the ground that the parties lived at Barabanki, where their marriage was consummated and as the demand for dower is also said to have been made at Barabanki, the court at Bareilly had no territorial jurisdiction to try the suit.

4. The trial court observed that, correctly understood, dower under the Mohammedan Law is something which, notwithstanding any contract to the contrary, the wife, by virtue of entering into marriage contract, is entitled to get from her husband. It is a consideration for conjugal intercourse. Accordingly, the right to dower does not precede the right of cohabitation. It comes into existence at the same time by reason of the same incident of law as the right to cohabitation. The two rights come into existence simultaneously. It, therefore, concluded that the cause of action for a suit for prompt dower arises either at the place where the marriage was consummated or at the place where prompt dower was demanded after such consummation, and not at the place where the marriage was performed (inasmuch as the right to cohabitation and the right to dower come into existence simultaneously only after marriage). As in the instant case, on plaintiff's own showing, the marriage had been consummated at Barabanki and the demand for prompt dower was also made by her at that very place, the courts at
152

Bareilly had no territorial jurisdiction to try the suit. The trial court, therefore, without going into any other controversy raised in the suit, passed the order under appeal directing that the plaint be returned to the plaintiff for presentation before a proper court.

5. Being aggrieved, plaintiff has come up in appeal before this Court and contends that the view of the trial court that in the circumstances, Bareilly court did not have territorial jurisdiction to try the suit, is erroneous, and that the impugned order deserves to be set aside.

6. It is true that under the Mohammedan Law, Mehr or dower means a sum of money or other property which the wife is entitled to receive from the husband in consideration of her marriage. However, the expression ´consideration´ is not to be understood in the sense in which the word is used in the Contract Act. In effect dower is an obligation imposed upon a husband as mark of respect for the wife. Normally the extent of such obligation is determined by the contract entered into between the husband and the wife either before or at the time of marriage. It may be fixed even after the marriage has taken place. If the amount of dower is not fixed or the marriage has been performed on express condition that the wife will not claim any dower, the wife is even then entitled to receive proper dower (mehr-i-misi) from her husband. The wife can refuse to live with her husband and admit him to sexual intercourse so long as the prompt dower is not paid to her (Baillies Digest of Mohammedan Law pages 124-125). We are, therefore unable to agree with the trial court that the right to claim prompt dower does not precede cohabitation and comes into existence along with it.

7. In our opinion in a case where there has been an agreement between the parties at the time of their marriage with regard to the amount of dower payable by the husband, the amount becomes recoverable under the agreement. The agreement between the husband and wife for payment of dower undoubtedly is part of the cause of action for maintaining a suit for its recovery and the place where such agreement was entered into would be a place where a part of cause of action for such suit arises.

8. In the instant case the agreement to pay dower was entered into at the time of marriage at Bareilly. Bareilly courts would therefore, have territorial jurisdiction to try the suit. The order under appeal cannot be sustained and has to be set aside.

ABDUR RASHID (appellant)v. Mst. SHAHEEN BIBI (respondent)
P.L.D. 1980 Pesh. 37. (Karimullah Khan Durrani, J.)

Judgment: - In this writ petition the judgments of the Family Court, Kohat and the District Judge, Kohat on appeal of the former have been assailed. This petition has been moved in the following state of facts.

2. The respondent No. 1 is the legally wedded wife of the petitioner. She had, on 29-3-1978, instituted a suit in the Family Court, Kohat against the petitioner for the recovery of her dower amounting to –

(a) Rs. 5,000 is cash, (b) 8 Tolas of gold valued @ Rs. 6,400, and (c) 1/2 of the house described in the plaint. While a money decree was prayed for the items (a) and (b), decree for possession was sought in respect of item (c) above. This claim was based on an unregistered Kabeen Nama dated 19-5-1977. A counter suit was instituted in the same Court by the petitioner for the restitution of conjugal rights against respondent No. 1.

2. The learned Senior Civil Judge, Kohat as Family Court, on 8-4-1979, decreed both the suits. The petitioner was granted decree for the restitution of conjugal rights against the payment of Rs. 4,600 and the suit of the respondent No. 1 was also granted for the same amount as dower. The rest of the suit of the said respondent was dismissed as the learned trial Court found the Kabeen Nama a forged document and the items (a) and (c) in suit not forming part of the dower.

3. Both the petitioner and the respondent No. 1 took separate appeals to the learned Additional District Judge, Kohat from the judgment and decrees of the Family Court. The learned apellate Court held the Kabeen Nama a genuine document, executed both by the petitioner and his father although not thumb-impressed by the petitioner. On the basis of the same, the learned appellate Court by a common judgment, dated 13-6-1979, dismissed the appeal of the petitioner and accepted that of the respondent No. 1 in that she was awarded an additional decree for the amount of Rs. 5,000 over and above that already granted. In regard to item (c), the 1/2 of the house, it was declared as part of Dower but relief in the form of possession by partition was held to be beyond the competency of the Family Court and that part of the plaint was, therefore, restored to the file of the civil Court. Parties were left to bear their own costs.

4. The petitioner being aggrieved, she now by way of this petition, assailed the decrees of the Courts concerned on two-fold ground:

(1) that the impugned judgments and decrees are without lawful authority and of no legal effect for lack of jurisdiction in the Family Court and the appellate Court in the matter; and

(2) that the Kabeen Nama purported to have been executed both by the petitioner and his father was actually executed by the father alone and, therefore, could not form part of the dower as liability to pay dower is, under the Mohammadan Law, solely on the

husband.

The jurisdiction of the Courts below has been challenged on the ground that it did not extend to passing any order in respect of movable property like a house or the ornaments apart from the agreed amount of dower in cash. It was contended that any matter covering property would be for the civil Courts to decide.

5. To us there does not appear any force in either of the contentions of the learned counsel for the petitioner, firstly because any matter pertaining to the Dower has been brought within the exclusive jurisdiction of the Family Courts by virtue of section 5 of the West Pakistan Family Courts Act, 1964, read with the Schedule appended thereto. Now, it is well-settled law that the Dower of a wife can either be in cash or kind or it may be in the form of the rendition of personal service as was done by Hazrat Moosa, as the dower of his wife, the daughter of Hazrat Shoeb (Peace be upon both of them) - Sura 28 of the Holy Qur´an contains two verses, i.e. Nos. 27 and 28 on the subject. These are rendered into English by the great Muslim Scholar, Mr. Muhammad Marmaduke Pickthal as under:-

> "(27) He said, Lo: I fain would marry thee to one of these two daughters of mine on condition that thou hirest thyself to me for (the term of) eight pilgrimages. Then if thou completest ten it will be of thine own accord, for I would not make it hard for thee. Allah willing, thou wilt find me of the righteous.
>
> (28) He said: That (is settled) between thee and me. Whichever of the two terms I fulfil, there will be no injustice to me, and Allah is Surety over what we say."

Section 285 of the Principles of Muhammadan Law as compiled by Sir D.F. Mulla is as follows:-

> "285. <u>Dower defined - Mahr</u> or dower is a sum of money or other property which the wife is entitled to receive from the husband in consideration of the marriage."

As regards the non-liability of the petitioner for the dower contracted by his father, reliance was placed on section 288 (<u>ibid</u>) which is as under:-

> "A contract of dower made by a father on behalf of his minor son is binding on the son. Such a contract may be made even after marriage provided the son was then a minor. Among Sunnis the father does not, by entering into such a contract, become personally liable for the dower debt, nor is he liable for it merely because he consents to the marriage. But by a recent decision of the Judicial Committee the rule is otherwise among Shias when the minor son has no means of his own."

6. On the authority of the above proposition of law it

was urged that a contract by the father on behalf of a minor
son can only bind that son and as in the instant case, the son
was major, he could not be bound by such a contract as that in
dispute.

7. In the instant case the learned Appellate Court has
come to the conclusion from the evidence on record that
although the petitioner did not thumb-impress the document in
question, it was executed on behalf of both the father and the
petitioner at the time the <u>Nikah</u> was performed and was so
witnessed by the Imam, who performed the <u>Nikah</u>. The
petitioner, it was held, was a party to the same. Moreover,
half of the house belonged to the father and the document in
question having been found executed by him was binding upon
the donor and respondent No. 1, thereby, became lawful owner
of the same.

8. The Family Court or the Court sitting in appeal of
its decrees have exclusive jurisdiction in the matter of dower
and, therefore, these Courts were competent to determine
whether any property movable or immovable in nature, formed
part of the dower or not. No exception can be taken to the
impugned decree on this ground. The delivery of possession by
effecting partition of the suit share has rightly been left to
the civil Court by the learned appellate Court.....

<u>NASIR AHMAD KHAN (appellant) v. ASMAT JEHAN BEGUM (respondent)</u>
<u>P.L.D. 1967 Pesh. 328 (Muhd. Daud Khan, J.)</u>

<u>Judgment</u>:.....Sheikh Bashir Ahmad, Advocate, took great pains
in dilating upon the principle of As-Sum´at, laid down in
Muslim Law. Broadly speaking, this principle recognized that
when a real dower has been fixed between the parties privately
and in some cases publicly the second dower is fixed in
inflated amount just for the enhancement of the prestige of
the family of the bridegroom or for its glorification, but in
such a case the intention was never to enforce the dower
announced in public and the real intention was to enforce the
dower agreed upon privately between the parties. It will be
necessary to quote <u>verbatim</u> the principle of As-Sum´at as laid
down by the learned commentator; at page 426 of the Book
"Mohammedan Law," by Syed Amir Ali:

> "As-Sum´at, according to the Farhang, means literally a
> public announcement of something with the object of
> self-glorification. ´In the language of law´ it means a
> dower announced to the public with the same object. The
> <u>Sharaya-ul-Islam</u> briefly states the Shia doctrine that
> in such cases the private arrangement will constitute
> the lawful dower."

It is further laid down in the Hanafi doctrines at the same
page that:

> The Fatawai Alamgiri gives the Hanafi rules in some

detail:

"If a man were to marry a woman for a certain <u>sadak</u> (dower) settled privately and announce a large amount in public the subject assumes two aspects: first when a dower is settled in private, and the parties then enter into the contract (of marriage) in public for a large amount; if the dower agreed to in public is of the same nature (jins) as that settled privately the difference being only in respect of the one stated in public being more than the one settled in private, and the parties are agreed in its settlement (viz. the private arrangement), or the man has called evidence to prove against her (the woman) or her guardian (if she be a minor) that the dower was that specified privately and the larger amount was Sum´at (for glorification), in that case the dower will be that which was settled in private. If, however, they differ as to the amount settled privately, and the man alleges that it was 1,000 (dirhams) and the women denies that amount, her allegation will be accepted, and the dower will be accepted, and the dower will be that specified in the contract, unless the husband can adduce proof of his allegation."

From the above context it is abundantly clear that the principle of As—Sum´at recognizes the fixation of two agreements with respect to the dower. One agreement is in private for a real amount and the other agreement for inflated amount is in public for the glorification of the bridegroom and his family, and if this is removed, then the real dower, which has been fixed in private would alone be alowed.....

———————

RAHIM JAN (Appellant) v. MUHAMMAD (Respondent)
PLD 1955 Lahore 122. (B.Z.Kaikaus J.)

<u>Judgment</u>:.....The first question that arises for consideration in whether among Hanafis, which the parties are presumed to be, a wife is entitled, even after consummation, to refuse to live with her husband on the ground that her prompt dower has not been paid. On this point there is a difference of opinion between Imam Abu Hanifa and his disciples Imam Muhammad and Imam Abu Yusuf. Imam Abu Hanifa is of the opinion that the consummation of the marriage does not make any difference and that the wife is entitled at any time to refuse to live with her husband until her prompt dower is paid. On the other hand, the two disciples are of opinion that the right of the wife to refuse to live with her husband on account of the non-payment of prompt dower subsists only till the marriage is consummated. The question as to which of these views should be adopted came before a Full Bench of Allahabad High Court in <u>Abdul Kadir v. Salima</u> (I L R 8 All.149). Previously there had

been three cases in the Allahabad High Court, namely, <u>Abdool Shukoar v. Raheemun-nissa</u> (N W P H C Rep., 1874, p.94), <u>Wilayat Husain v. Allah Rakhi</u> (I L R 2 A11.831) and <u>Nazir Khan v. Umrao</u> (Weekly Notes 1882, p.96) in which the view of Imam Abu Hanifa had been followed. In <u>Abdul Kadir v. Salima</u> the facts were that the wife pleaded non-payment of prompt dower in a suit against her for restitution of conjugal rights. At this the plaintiff deposited the amount of the prompt dower in Court. In spite of this the lower appellate Court dismissed the plaintiff´s suit on the ground that on the date when the suit was filed no cause of action for a suit for restitution had arisen. The marriage had been consummated before suit. The question before the Full Bench was whether the suit was maintainable. The Full Bench answered the question in the affirmative but ordered a decree to be passed conditional on payment of the prompt dower. This judgment was followed in Madras, Calcutta and Bombay. A Full Bench of the Punjab Chief Court also followed it in <u>Mst. Salih Bibi v. Rafi-ud-Din</u>(164 P R 1889) and ordered a decree to be passed in favour of the husband on payment of the prompt dower. <u>Abdul Kadir v. Salima</u> has, however, been dissented from in Oudh and Bhopal and has been criticized by Amir Ali in his book on Muhammadan Law.

Although the decree passed in <u>Abdul Kadir v. Salima</u> was conditional on payment of dower observations in the judgment have been quoted as authority for the proposition that after consummation the wife loses the rights to refuse restitution of conjugal rights on the ground of non-payment of dower. In view of the importance of <u>Abdul Kadir v. Salima</u> and also in view of the fact that the Full Bench of the Punjab Chief Court approved of the judgment without itself discussing the point involved it is necessary to determine the extent of the authority of <u>Abdul Kadir v. Salima</u> as a precedent and for this purpose I have to refer to the judgment in some detail. As already stated the question before the Full Bench was whether the suit for restitution of conjugal rights was maintainable although at the time when the suit was filed the dower had not been paid. I give below the various conclusions of Mahmood, J. (whose judgment was adopted by the Full Bench) though I have not stuck to the order in which they are stated by the learned Judge:-

(1) The learned Judge found that there was no proof of any demand for prompt dower having been made by the wife before the suit was filed, and as the right to receive prompt dower did not arise till a demand had been made there could be no objection to the suit.

This would appear from the following passage which appears at page 167 of the report:-

"But the rule enunciated by me need not be applied in its fullest extent to the present case, because here, in the first place, it has not been found that the wife ever demanded her dower before the suit was filed, or

158

that she declined to cohabit with her husband the plaintiff upon the ground that her dower had not been paid. She relied upon allegations of divorce and cruelty, both of which were found by the Court of first instance to be untrue, and upon these findings I hold that she had no defence to the action. The plaintiff, as I have already shown, acquired by the very fact of the marriage the right of cohabitation; he was not bound to pay the dower before it was demanded, and upon the findings of the first Court, the first intimation which he had of such demand was the written defence of his wife (defendant No. 2) in the course of this unfortunate litigation."

(2) On a consideration of the nature of a marriage contract among the Muhammadans and of the rights to which it gives rise the learned Judge came to the conclusion that rights and liabilities of the spouses came into existence simultaneously and one could not be a condition precedent for the other.

He said at page 164 –

"I have already said enough to show that the right of dower does not precede the right of cohabitation which the contract of marriage necessarily involves, but that the two rights come into existence simultaneously and by reason of the same incident of law. The right of the wife to claim maintenance from her husband arises in the same manner as one of the legal effects of marriage, and to say that any of those effects are not simultaneously created by the contract of marriage amounts, in my opinion, to a violation of the fundamental notions of jurisprudence regarding correlative rights and obligations arising from one and the same perfected legal relation. Indeed, so far as the question now under consideration is concerned, the rules of Muhammadan Law leave no doubt when that system of law is consulted as a whole and not upon isolated points. The fact of the marriage gives birth to the right of cohabitation not only in favour of the husband but also in favour of the wife, and to say that the payment of dower is a condition precedent to the vestiture of the right, is to hold that a relationship, of which the rights and obligations are essentially correlative, may come into existence at one time for one party and another time for the other party".

(3) On a consideration of Muslim authorities the learned Judge came to the conclusion that it was the opinion of the two disciples which had been followed in preference to that of Imam Abu Hanifa. The learned Judge found that according to the rule adopted by Muslim jurists the opinion of the disciples when they differed from Imam Abu Hanifa was to prevail against that of Imam

Abu Hanifa.
He said (p. 167):-

> "According to the ordinary rule of interpreting Muhammadan Law, I adopt the opinion of the two disciples as representing the majority of 'the three Masters,' and hold that, after consummation of marriage, non-payment of dower, even though exigible, cannot be pleaded in defence of an action for restitution of conjugal rights; the rule so laid down having, of course, no effect upon the right of the wife to claim her dower in a separate action".

However, it must be stated that this conclusion is not quite consistent with an earlier passage at pages 161-62 where it is regarded as a well-recognized rule of Muhammadan Law that the wife has the right to refuse cohabitation if the husband has not paid the prompt dower. The passage runs (pages 161-62):-

> "The texts cited by the learned pleader for the respondents undoubtedly show, what is a well-recognised rule of the Muhammadan Law of marriage, that the marriage contract having been completed and its legal effects having been established, the right of claiming prompt dower comes into existence in favour of the wife, and that she can use such a claim as a means of obtaining payment of the dower and as a defence for resisting a claim for cohabitation on the part of the husband against her consent. And when I say this, I put the case in favour of the respondents in its strongest possible light, for even upon this question in cases where cohabitation has taken place, the conflict of authority is too great to render it an undoubted proposition of the Muhammadan Law."

The last sentence quite clearly shows that the "well-recognized rule" referred to in the earlier part of the passage includes a case where marriage has been consummated.

It has also to be stated that in spite of his acceptance of the rule that the view of the disciples is to be accepted in preference to the view of Imam Abu Hanifa the learned Judge accepted that so far as going on a journey was concerned, the wife could refuse to do so on the ground that she had not been paid her prompt dower. The learned Judge accepted on this point the opinion of the jurist Abdul Qasim Assaffar, who had followed Imam Abu Hanifa so far as going on a journey is concerned and had followed the two disciples so far as cohabitation is concerned. I might refer in this connection to the following passage in the judgment (p. 162), which is an extract from Fatawa Qazi Khan, and has been quoted with approval:-

> "A wife, having surrendered herself to her husband before the fulfilment (i.e. payment) of dower, subsequently denies herself (to him) for securing

fulfilment of the dower. She has this right in the opinion of Abu Hanifa; but Abu Yusaf and Imam Muhammad maintain that she has not the right of prohibiting him from connubial intercourse, and doubts have arisen in regard to their opinion as to the power of preventing her from journeying. And according to the opinion of Abdul Qasim Assaffar, it is her right that she may prevent him from taking her on a journey."

(4) The learned judge found that in any case it could not be said that there was no cause of action, even if the payment of prompt dower was a condition precedent to the right of restitution.

The question before the Full Bench was whether a cause of action had accrued or not when the suit was filed and this question had to be answered in the affirmative. The learned Judge said at page 170:-

"It is one thing to say that such a defence may be set up under certain conditions: it is a totally different thing to say that ´until the dower was paid no cause of action could accrue to the plaintiff´. The payment of dower not being a condition precedent to the vesting of the right of cohabitation, a suit for restitution of conjugal rights, whether by the husband or by the wife, would be maintainable upon refusal by the other to cohabit with him or her; and in the case of a suit by the husband, the defence of payment of dower could, at its best, operate in modification of the decree for restitution of conjugal rights by rendering the enforcement of it conditional upon payment of so much of the dower as may be regarded to be prompt".

(5) Regarding the marriage contract as a sale and the right of the wife to refuse cohabitation on account of non-payment of prompt dower, a kind of vendor´s lien, the learned Judge held that the right would terminate on consummation as after delivery of goods the lien would cease to exist.

(6) In spite of the fact that the learned Judge had recorded the finding that the wife could not, after consummation, be entitled to plead non-payment of dower as defence to a claim for restitution the learned Judge did not pass an unconditional decree in favour of the plaintiff but passed a decree only conditional on the payment of prompt dower. The reasons for so doing are contained in the passage at page 167, which is the first passage I have quoted from the judgment.

It is clear on a reading of the judgment that all the discussion about the right of the wife to refuse herself on account of non-payment of dower is _obiter_. It is _obiter_ because the learned Judge found that the wife had not demanded prompt dower before suit and as prompt dower becomes payable only on a demand the suit was obviously maintainable. It is an _obiter_ also for the reasons that even if it be accepted

161

that without payment of prompt dower the husband is not entitled to conjugal rights that does not mean that the cause of action had not arisen at all. As the learned Judge put it, it is one thing to say that non-payment of prompt dower is a defence to action for restitution of conjugal rights and another to say that the husband had no cause of action whatsoever. That the husband is entitled to a certain relief only on compliance with a condition precedent does not imply that if before the suit the condition precedent had not been performed there was no cause of action. It should be remembered that the learned Judge was only concerned with the question whether before the suit there was a cause of action and a perusal of the judgment confirms the impression that it is only this question that the learned Judge was trying to determine. That all the remarks about the right of the wife to plead non-payment of the dower as a defence to an action for restitution of conjugal rights, even after consummation, are _obiter_ was recognized by Sulaiman, C.J. in _Anis Begam v. Muhammad Istafa Wali Khan_ (I L R 55 All. 743) to which reference will be made later.

The next important point about the judgment is that the learned Judge though apparently finding in favour of the view of the two disciples did not apply it to the case before him. He directed a decree only on the payment of prompt dower. If really the wife had no right of refusal the husband would be entitled to a decree without the payment of dower. The decree passed really recognizes the right of the wife to dower before restitution of conjugal rights, even after consummation. In spite of the expression of opinion at one place against the view of Imam Abu Hanifa, really the decree is in accordance with the passage where the learned Judge regarded it as a well-recognized rule of Muhammadan Law that the wife was entitled to refuse herself on account of non-payment of dower and the correct basis of the judgment is that the rights arise simultaneously and, therefore, a cause of action for a suit for restitution of conjugal rights exists, even though the wife is entitled to the performance of an obligation in her favour.

Abdul Kadir v. Salima was, as already stated, followed in Bombay, Calcutta, Madras and the Punjab, but it soon became the subject of criticism in other quarters. In Allahabad itself, Maulvi Sami Ullah, who is referred to by Amir Ali in his commentary on Muhammadan Law as "one of the most learned judicial officers in British India", in the case of _Mst. Rasulan and Zahuran v. Mirza Nasimullah Beg_ challenged the view expressed in _Abdul Kadir v. Salima_ with respect to the rule to be followed in case there is a difference of opinion between the disciples and Imam Abu Hanifa as well as with regard to the rights of the wife to refuse herself to the husband after consummation. Amir Ali in his commentary on Muhammadan Law expressed the opinion that _Abdul Kadir v._

<u>Salima</u> proceeded on "wrong analogies" and was "founded on a total misconception of the rules" of Muhammadan Law in case there was a difference of opinion between Imam Abu Hanifa and his disciples. In the Court of the Judicial Commissioner of Oudh in <u>Wajid Ali Khan v. Sakhawat Ali Khan</u> (15 I C 747 = 15 O C 127) Lindsay, J.C. and Rafique A.J.C. dissented from <u>Abdul Kadir v. Salima</u> after an exhaustive discussion of the subject. As regards the rule propounded by Mahmood, J. in case of a difference of opinion between Imam Abu Hanifa and the disciples they came to the conclusion that no such rule had been adopted by Muslim jurists. As regards the rights of the wife after consummation the learned J.C.´s found that the majority of the Muslim jurists had adopted the view of Imam Abu Hanifa. As regards the argument based on the analogy of a sale they held in the first place that the analogy was not applicable and secondly that even if it was applicable the conclusion drawn was unjustified.

In <u>Anis Begam v. Muhammad Istafa Wali Khan</u> a Division Bench of the Allahabad High Court had again to consider the right of a Muhammadan wife to plead non-payment of dower in a suit for restitution of conjugal rights, even after consummation. Sulaiman, C.J. (with whom Thorn, J. concurred) held that there was no rule of interpretation that the view of the disciples was to be preferred to that of Imam Abu Hanifa. Referring to <u>Wajid Ali Khan v. Sakhawat Ali Khan</u> (15 O C 127) the learned Judges said (p. 750):-

> "On pages 144-7 of the report in that case some of the texts have been reproduced to show that, even in the case of a difference the opinion of Imam Abu Hanifa is to be preferred. Of course, there is no such general rule either. As a matter of fact, there does not appear to be any fixed rule: See <u>Irfan Ali v. Bhagwant Kishore</u> (A I R 1929 All. 180 (187)). Different doctors have followed different rules of preference. Those who were more orthodox and, generally speaking, more ancient in many cases preferred the solitary opinion of Abu Hanifa to even the joint opinion of his disciples."

With regard to the argument of Mahmood, J. based on analogy of sale the learned Judge conceded that the inference was unjustified. He said (p. 754):-

> "The line of reasoning based on the analogy of sale has naturally been very severely criticised at pages 148-9 in <u>Wajid Ali Khan´s case</u> ((1912) 15 Oudh Cases 127) by the Oudh Bench, and so also by Mr. Ameer Ali in his Muhammadan Law, Volume II, pages 459-60. No doubt the Muslim commentators have, by way of illustration, applied certain principles governing a contract of sale of goods to the contract or marriage, but that was by way of analogy only. The similarity cannot be pushed too far, nor can the principles governing the sale of goods be applied in all their details. Indeed, if one

163

were to pursue the analogy far enough there would be a reductio ad absurdum."

Having thus agreed that both the bases for the conclusion of Mahmood, J. did not exist the learned Judge proceeded to consider independently of Abdul Kadir v. Salima the question whether the wife was entitled to refuse herself to the husband on account of non-payment of dower even after consummation. He divided Muslim authorities into three groups. In the first group the learned Judge placed the ancient text-books called matan, i.e., Bidaya Tanvir-ul-Absar, Kan-ud-dakaik and Wikayat-ur-rivayah. These he found to be accepting the opinion of Imam Abu Hanifa without even mentioning the difference of opinion. In the second group the learned Judge placed what he called great commentaries. They are Hedaya, Durr-ul-Mukhtar, Bahr-ur-raik, Sharah Vikayah, Fath-ul-Kadir, Tahtawi, Radd-ul-Muhtar and Fatawa-i-Qazi Khan. Of these Durr-ul-Mukhtar adopts what is stated in Tanvir-ul-Absar without mentioning the difference of opinion. The remaining commentaries quote the matan and state the difference of opinion but without expressing any opinion of their own. In the third group the learned Judge placed some later books, i.e., Fatawa Ghiyasia, Jami-ul-Rumuz, Fatawa Himadya and Fatawa Maulvi Abdul Hai. Of these two, i.e., Fatawa Ghiyasia and Fatawa Maulvi Abdul Hai express an opinion in favour of the view of the disciples. After referring to these commentaries the learned Judge reached a conclusion which is thus expressed in the head-note (p. 743):-

"Although the observation of Mahmood, J. in the case of Abdul Kadir v. Salima was an obiter dictum, founded upon a too closely applied analogy of sale of goods and upon a misconceived rule of interpretation of the Muhammadan Law, and although texts and commentaries of ancient jurists of recognized authority could be cited in support of the opposite view, yet it would be dangerous now to go back upon the long course of decisions which throughout India, excluding Oudh, have accepted and followed that dictum, and thereby to unsettle the law by not adhering to the well recognized principle of stare decisis."

Before concluding a review of the case-law I have to refer to Bashiran Bi v. Abdul Wahab Khan, a case of the Bhopal High Court reported in 183 I C 130. The identical question arose in that case. It was first referred to a Mufti under section 111/1 of the Bhopal C.P.C. The question referred to was in the following terms:-

"Was a wife entitled after consummation of marriage to refuse performance of her marital obligations on the ground of her prompt dower having remained unpaid?" The Mufti answered it in the affirmative. A further reference was made to an Assembly of Ulma and they gave the following answer:-

"After consummation of the marriage, and even after birth of children, the right of refusal of person remains with the wife under the circumstances mentioned in the reference. Some of our doctors have held that right of refusal of person is lost after voluntary consummation, but _fatwa_ and practice do not support this view.

In the case under reference it is important to find whether the refusal of person was previous or subsequent to the demand of dower, because a refusal previous to the demand was not lawful. Her right of refusal comes into play only on her making a demand for the exigible dower."

In view of the fact that the answer related only to refusal of person whereas the question involved all marital obligations, M.A. Khan, C.J., who decided the case, went into the question independently and agreed with Imam Abu Hanifa´s view.

As the matter has been exhaustively discussed in Courts that hold opposite views it is not necessary for me to refer in detail to authorities and I will briefly state my conclusions and the reasons therefor.

So far as the rule of interpretation in case of difference of opinion between Imam Abu Hanifa and the disciples is concerned it has been conceded by Sulaiman, C.J. that no such rule exists. As the learned Judge observed (p. 749 of I L R 55 All.) –

"But it would be easy to cite instances in which the opinion of Imam Abu Hanifa alone has prevailed, particularly in matters of prayer and ritual, or of Imam Yusuf in matters of inheritance. There appears to be no such invariable rule which would make the decision depend on the majority of votes only."

In Wajid Ali Khan v. Sakhawat Ali Khan a number of instances have been cited and in fact the old Muslim texts on the very point in dispute would show that the opinion of Imam Abu Hanifa was being preferred to that of disciples. In none of the commentaries referred to by Sulaiman, C.J., is it stated that the opinion of the disciples was to be preferred. On a perusal of the instances given in Wajid Ali Khan v. Sakhawat Ali Khan, as well as the quotations on pages 15 to 17 of Amir Ali´s Muhammadan Law, Volume I, two things become clear. The first is that the weight of the opinion of the master (Imam Abu Hanifa) depends upon what the Court regards his capacity for interpretation and not because of any religious duty to accept that opinion. In some matters, the opinion of the disciples is accepted while in others the opinion of Imam Abu Hanifa is regarded as supreme. The second is that the opinion even of one who is held in great respect can be disregarded when there is a change of circumstances.

As Sulaiman, C.J., and the learned Judges in Wajid Ali

165

<u>Khan v. Sakhawat Ali Khan</u> have pointed out there is no fixed rule adopted by Muslim jurists. Under the circumstances, I would adopt the rule enunciated by Alhawi which is thus referred to at page 188 of Abdur Rahim's Muhammadan Jurisprudence:-

> "Alhawi lays down as the correct rule that in such cases of difference of opinion regard should be had to the authority and reasons in support of each view and the one which has the strongest support should be followed, and this is undoubtedly in strict accord with the principles of Muhammadan jurisprudence apart from the great weight that attaches to that eminent authority."

With respect to the question whether under Muhammadan Law a wife has a right of refusal of person after consummation, it will be observed that the original Muslim authorities which are called <u>matan</u> and are placed by Sulaiman, C.J., in class 1 are all in favour of the right of the wife. Out of the authorities of the second class Durr-ul-Mukhtar is in favour of the wife while the others refer to the conflict without expressing their own views. Out of the authorities of the third class there are only two, Fatawa Ghiyasia and Fatawa Maulvi Abdul Hai, which express an opinion against the wife but neither of these books can be regarded as an authority. They are not mentioned in any treatise on Muhammadan Law. As Abdur Rahim has pointed out at page 189 of Muhammadan Jurisprudence, doubtful authorities should not be followed. This is what the learned commentator says:-

> "In this connection one has to be careful as to the books that he consults. Writings of obscure authors, such as Mula Miskin's commentary on 'Kanz' or Qahastani's commentary on 'Niqaya', and unreliable books, that is, those in which weak versions of the law are reported such as 'Qinyah' by Zahidi should be avoided and the propositions laid down in them can only be accepted if their authority be known."

I cannot accept the statements in the two books mentioned above in preference to what is stated in the <u>matan</u>.

The argument of Mahmood, J. based on the analogy of sale was conceded by Sulaiman, C.J., as leading to an absurd position. I do not feel the need of saying more about it as I am in respectful agreement with the criticism of the argument in <u>Wajid Ali Khan v. Sakhawat Ali Khan</u>.

As regards the basic argument of Mahmood, J. at page 164, which I have already quoted, I have with great respect to record my dissent. The argument put forward is that the rights of the husband and wife arise simultaneously and, therefore, the one cannot be a condition precedent for the other. But it is agreed on all hands that before consummation the payment of dower does constitute a condition precedent. It cannot, therefore, be urged that the performance of an obligation by the husband cannot be a condition precedent for the exercise of a right by him. The real question was not whether the payment of dower constituted a condition precedent at all but whether it ceased to be a condition precedent on account of the wife having once surrendered herself. It was only some kind of estoppel or relinquishment of right by which the right which the wife had might have been terminated. The matter is not discussed in any judgment from this point of view although resort is being had to a priori reasoning. I do not find any principle of justice or reason by which the right of the wife to refuse the performance of marital obligations on account of non-payment of prompt dower may come to an end by her once surrendering herself.

There is also an inconsistency in the Allahabad view. As already stated, Mahmood, J. had accepted the view of Abul Qasam Assattar that after consummation the wife could still refuse to go out on a journey with the husband if her prompt dower was not paid (which otherwise she was not entitled to do) but she could not refuse her body. No effort has been made to explain the principle on which while the wife can use the non-payment of dower as defence against the performance of one marital obligation she cannot do so in respect of another. In this connection I might refer to that verse in Sura Maida which deals with the payment of dower.

It runs:-

> "This day are (all things)
> Good and pure made lawful
> Unto you. The food
> Of the People of the Book
> Is lawful unto you
> And yours is lawful
> Unto them
> (Lawful unto you in marriage)
> Are (not only) chaste women
> Who are believers, but
> Chaste women among
> The People of the Book,
> Revealed before your time, –
> When ye give them
> Their due dowers, and desire
> Chastity, not lewdness,
> Nor secret intrigues,
> If any one rejects faith,
> Fruitless is his work,
> And in the Hereafter
> He will be in the ranks
> Of those who have lost,
> (All spiritual good). – (Holy Quran : V.6)

The least that can be said is that this verse stresses the right of the wife to payment before she can be made the subject of exercise of his rights by the husband.

I may also point out that in Egypt, Turkey and Arabia the

167

right of wife to resist a claim for restitution of conjugal rights exists even after consummation, as will appear from Article 213 of Abdur Rahman's Institutes of Muhammadan Law (which book is based on the Droit Musulman, a Code prepared under a commission from the Egyptian Government by a Council presided over by Kadri Pasha, a Judge of the Mixed Tribunal of Appeals at Alexandria) and an extract from the commentary under that Article which I quote below:-

> 'Article 213 - .....According to Imam Abu Hanifa, the founder of the Hanifa sect of Mussalmans, the wife even after consummation of marriage, can refuse her person to her husband until he has paid in full the prompt portion of the dower. In Egypt, Turkey and Arabia, this rule of law obtains among the Hanifites, and the British Courts in India administered it for nearly a century, as the following notes of their decisions would illustrate.'

There were two grounds for the view of Mahmood, J: preference of the view of the disciples and logical reasoning. Both these grounds were conceded by Sulaiman, C.J., to be non-existent. It is clear from Anis Begam v. Muhammad Istafa Wali Khan that Sulaiman, C.J. stuck to the view of Mahmood, J. only on the basis of stare decisis. The principle of stare decisis may be applied to cases where relying on the existence of a particular state of the law people had entered into transactions so that they would be prejudiced if the law was held to be different, but otherwise it cannot, as pointed out in Ramadayal Munnalal Sonar v. Sheodayal (A I R 1939 Nag. 186 (F B)) and Chandra Binode Kundu v. Sheikh Ala Bux Dewan (58 I C 353) prevent a Court from interpreting the law correctly. It cannot be said that marriage contracts have been entered into on the strength of Abdul Kadir v. Salima and that had the husbands known the law to be different they would either not have entered into marriage contracts at all or would have reduced the amount of dower. Even according to the law, as accepted by the disciples and all Courts, till consummation the wife has always the right to refuse herself if prompt dower is not paid. Also in Abdul Kadir v. Salima the decree had been made conditional on the payment of prompt dower and the law had since then been understood to be that a decree for restitution was to be conditional on the payment of prompt dower. I do not think a recognition of the right of the wife of dower after consummation would, under the circumstances, have the effect of unsettling the law so as to call for the application of stare decisis. The decree in Abdul Kadir v. Salima had in fact recognized the right of the wife though the judgment did contain observations that the right did not exist and the law, as laid down in the commentaries on Muhammadan Law, has been that a decree is to be passed only on payment of dower.

I would explain that I am respectfully in entire agreement with the view of Mahmood, J. that rights arise at the time of marriage. Only, as in cases of specific performance of contracts, the performance of a reciprocal obligation may become a condition precedent. Just as in a suit for specific performance a plaintiff should be "able and willing" to perform his part of the contract so in a case for restitution of conjugal rights the husband has to pay the dower if he wants the restitution of conjugal rights.

I would hold that even after consummation the wife retains the right to refuse the performance of marital obligation till the prompt dower is paid.

Another question that arises is this: Is the wife entitled to this protection only if she expressly refuses the performance of marital obligations on account of non-payment of dower? It is true that unless she makes a demand for her prompt dower the husband is entitled to conjugal rights, but if a demand for prompt dower has been made and the dower is not paid, the refusal of the wife to live with the husband would be justified even though this is not assigned as the reason of her refusal. The husband being in default is not entitled to the exercise of conjugal rights and the failure of the wife to live with the husband cannot be a wrong.

It was urged on behalf of the respondent that even if the husband was not entitled to restitution of conjugal rights on account of non-payment of dower, that would not imply that the husband was bound to maintain the wife. Reliance was placed in this connection on <u>Sadar Din v. Mst. Suban</u> (6 P R 1888 (Cr.)) where an order made under section 488 of the Code of Criminal Procedure was set aside because the wife refused to live with her husband on the ground that her prompt dower had not been paid. The judgment is very short and contains no reference to any work on Muhammadan Law. The whole argument is exhausted in the following two sentences:-

> "The wife may, we suppose, resist her husband on the civil side by a plea of unpaid dower, but if she does, we do not think she can expect her husband to maintain her elsewhere.
>
> We hold, therefore, that she has not shown sufficient cause to justify her refusal to live with her husband, and under the latter part of section 488, Cr.P.C., we set aside the order of maintenance."

The judgment may have been based on the wording of section 488 which requires "a sufficient cause" for the refusal of the wife to live with the husband. While I would not with all respect agree even with this interpretation of "sufficient cause" it is clear that for the decision of the present case the judgment is not of any help. It may be sufficient for repelling the contention put forward to refer to Hamilton's Hedaya, Volume I, page 151, where it is said:-

> "It is proper to observe, that where the woman refuses to admit the husband to a repetition of the carnal act, as above stated, yet she has, nevertheless, (according

169

to Haneefa), a claim to her subsistence as her refusal does not, in this case, proceed from any stubbornness or disobedience, since it is not exerted in resistance to a right, but rather in maintenance of one."

Article 214 of Abdur Rahman's Institutes of Mussalman Law runs:-

"When the wife has not received her prompt dower in full, after having laid claim to it, she is free to leave her husband's house without his permission and without thereby rendering herself rebellious or losing her right to maintenance."

The same is provided in paragraph 53(a) of Wilson's Anglo-Muhammadan Law which I reproduce below:-

"The husband is bound -

(a) To maintain his adult wife in a manner suitable to his wealth, or at least to the mean between his wealth and hers if she is the poorer, quite irrespective of her ability to maintain herself out of her own property, so long as she is undivorced and obedient, and whether obedient or not if she has the right of refusal for non-payment of dower; but he is not bound to maintain a wife who refuses herself to him without reasonable cause or is otherwise disobedient;".

To the same effect is paragraph 277 of Mulla's Muhammadan Law. I may also refer to <u>Najiman Nissa Begum v. Sarajuddin Ahmad Khan</u> (A I R 1946 Pat. 467) where the identical question arose. It was held that the wife was entitled to maintenance and failure by the husband to maintain for two years would entitle the wife to a decree for dissolution of marriage.

I do not, at the same time, find any good reason for refusing maintenance to the wife when the husband does not pay her prompt dower. The husband cannot be allowed to take advantage of his own default and the wife, who is otherwise entitled to maintenance, cannot be deprived of it by the exercise of a right given to her by the law. I find no substance in this contention.

So far the wife is on good ground and had the matters for consideration ended here this appeal would have to be accepted. But there is a matter not argued in the Courts below which I took up <u>suo motu</u> and that is the effect of the decree for restitution of conjugal rights. I had pointed out to the parties at the hearing that the existence of the decree may seriously affect the decision of this case and after giving the matter full consideration I have reached the conclusion that the decree is an insuperable obstacle in the plaintiff's way.

There are two aspects to the effect of this decree. The first is its force as <u>res judicata</u> and the second its effect on account of the right which it establishes. The plea that on account of non-payment of prompt dower the husband was not

170

entitled to an unconditional decree for restitution of conjugal rights was open to the wife in the suit for restitution. True, it need not have been taken at the time when the written statement was filed in that suit for up to that time the wife had not made a demand for prompt dower and her right to refuse performance of marital obligation could only arise when she did make that demand. She was not bound to make the demand when she presented a written statement. However, she did make the demand during the pendency of the suit on the 14th of November, 1949, by filing a suit for dower. Her right to refuse her person did arise then and she ought to have made non-payment of dower a ground of defence in the suit for the decree would establish the right of the husband to restitution of conjugal rights on the date on which the decree was passed. The wife could not in answer to the execution of the decree plead a fact which had happened before the decree. Had no demand for dower been made before the passing of the decree, it would have been open to the wife to make a demand for dower and then to resist execution on the ground that the decree which was valid when passed had been rendered incapable of execution by a subsequent event. She would be unable, however, to take the plea that would make the decree wrong on the date on which it was passed. Such a plea would be barred by the rule of res judicata. I may point out that although res judicata is generally based on a judgment it can be supported even by a decree which embodies the operative part of a judgment. Reference may be made in this connection to Amriteswari Debi v. The Secretary of State for India in Council (I L R 24 Cal. 504 (P C)), Pranal Anni v. Lakshmi Anni and others (I L R 22 Mad. 508 (P C)) and Kaveri Ammall and others v. Sastri Ramier and another (I L R 26 Mad. 104).

A possible argument would be that the right of the wife to refuse the performance of marital obligations would arise only if she made a specific plea of it with her husband, that is, if she said to her husband "I will not live with you till you have paid my prompt dower", and that as she had never taken up this position before the decree was passed against her, it would be open to her to say after the decree that she would henceforth exercise her right and would not go to her husband's house till the dower was paid. The principle of res judicata it may be said would not stand in her way as her fight came into existence after the decree. I have already rejected the basis of this argument when it was urged by the respondent to suit his own purpose. It is sufficient if a demand for prompt dower has been made and it is not necessary that the wife should make the non-payment of dower a ground of her refusal to live with the husband. By the demand the husband becomes a defaulter and loses the right to an unconditional decree. However, I may state that if I were to accept the argument it would not help the wife for admittedly she never told the husband that she refused to live with him

171

because he did not pay the dower. Her position even in the present suit has been that she had been willing to live with her husband who had turned her out of house. I would hold that the plea as to the wife's right to refuse to live with the husband on account of non-payment of prompt dower is barred by <u>res judicata</u>.

The decree also destroys the wife's case in so far as it grants to the husband the right that the wife should go and live with him. The decree directs the wife to perform her marital obligations although in case of disobedience the wife cannot be delivered to her husband and can only be proceeded against under Order 21, rule 32 C. P. C. by attachment of her property. If the husband has the right that the wife should live with him the wife cannot, at least under ordinary circumstances, continue to have a right to be maintained in the place where she chooses to reside.

The result is not at all happy. Here are a husband and wife who have reached a stage where they cannot pull on with one another. There is no charge of any misconduct against the wife, in fact the record is silent as to the reason for the rift between the spouses. It is hard to believe that Muslim Law, so rational and practical, is unable to provide a remedy. But the question as to the rights of the wife in such a situation has not been determined in the present case and I can do no more than record that her right to agitate this matter is not barred, with which observation I dismiss this appeal but leave the parties to bear their own costs throughout.

<u>ITWARI (appellant) v. ASGHARI (respondent)</u>
<u>A.I.R. 1960 All. 684. (Dhavan, J.)</u>

<u>Judgment</u>.....(5) The first question is whether the conduct of the husband in taking a second wife is any ground for the first wife to refuse to live with him or for dismissing his suit for restitution of conjugal rights. Learned counsel for the husband vehemently argued that a Muslim husband has the right under his personal law to take a second wife even while the first marriage subsists. But this right is not in dispute in this case.

The question before the Court is not whether the husband had the right to take a second wife but whether this Court, as a court of equity, should lend its assistance to the husband by compelling the first wife, on pain of severe penalties, to live with him after he has taken a second wife in the circumstances in which he did.

(6) A marriage between Mohammedans is a civil contract and a suit for restitution of conjugal rights is nothing more than an enforcement of the right to consortium under this contract. The Court assists the husband by an order

compelling the wife to return to cohabitation with the husband. "Disobedience to the order of the Court would be enforceable by imprisonment of the wife or attachment of her property, or both". Moonshee Buzloor Ruheem v. Shumsoonissa Begum (11 Moo Ind App 551 (609). Abdul Kadir v. Salima (ILR 8 All 149 (FB)).

But a decree for specific performance of a contract is an equitable relief and it is within the discretion of the Court to grant or refuse it in accordance with equitable principles. In Abdul Kadir's case (ILR 8 All 149 (FB)), it was held that in a suit for conjugal rights, the courts in India shall function of mixed Courts of equity and be guided by principles of equity well-established under English jurisprudence. One of them is that the Court shall take into consideration the conduct of the person who asks for specific performance.

If the Court feels, on the evidence before it, that he has not come to the Court with clean hands or that his own conduct as a party has been unworthy, or his suit has been filed with ulterior motives and not in good faith, or that it would be unjust to compel the wife to live with him, it may refuse him assistance altogether. The Court will also be justified in refusing specific performance where the performance of the contract would involve some hardship on the defendant which he did not foresee, whereas its non-performance would involve no such hardship on the plaintiff.

(7) It follows, therefore, that in a suit for restitution of conjugal rights by a Muslim husband against the first wife after he has taken a second, if the Court after a review of the evidence feels that the circumstances reveal that in taking a second wife the husband has been guilty of such conduct as to make it inequitable for the Court to compel the first wife to live with him, it will refuse relief.

(8) The husband in the present case takes his stand on the right of every Muslim under his personal law to have several wives at a time up to a maximum of four. He contends that if the first wife is permitted to leave the husband merely because he has taken a second, this would be a virtual denial of his right. It is necessary to examine this argument.

(9) Muslim law permits polygamy but has never encouraged it. The sanction for polygamy among Muslims is traced to Koran IV.3:

> "If ye fear that ye cannot do justice between orphans then marry what seems good to you of women, by two's or three's or four's or if ye fear that ye cannot be equitable, then only one, or what your right hand possesses."

This injunction was really a restrictive measure and reduced the number of wives to four at a time; it imposed a ceiling on conjugal greed among males which prevailed among males on an extensive scale. The right to four wives appears to have been qualified by a ´better not´ advice, and husbands were enjoined to restrict themselves to one wife if they could not be impartial between several wives – an impossible condition according to several Muslim jurists, who rely on it for their argument that Muslim law in practice discourages polygamy.

(10) A Muslim has the undisputed legal right to take as many as four wives at a time. But it does not follow that Muslim law in India gives no right to the first wife against a husband who takes a second wife, or that this law renders her helpless when faced with the prospect of sharing her husband´s consortium with another woman. In India, a Muslim wife can divorce her husband, under his delegated power in the event of his taking a second wife. <u>Badu Mia v. Badrannessa</u> (40 ILR 803, AIR 1919 Cal 511 (2)).

Again a Muslim wife can stipulate for power to divorce herself in the case of the husband availing of his legal right to take another wife, <u>Sheikh Moh. v. Badrunnissa Bibee</u> (7 Beng LR App 5 (sic)), <u>Badarannissa Bibi v. Mafiattala</u> (7 Beng LR 442). In <u>Ayatunnessa Beebee v. Karam Ali</u> (ILR 36 Cal 23), it was held that a Muslim wife, who has the power given to her by the marriage contract to divorce herself in the event of the husband taking a second wife does not lose her option by failing to exercise it the very moment she knows that he has done so, for "a second marriage is not a single but a continuing wrong to the first wife."

The court significantly described a second marriage as a "continuing wrong" to the first wife. The implications of these rights of the first wife are unmistakable. To say the least, a law cannot regard the husband´s right to compel all his wives to submit to his consortium as fundamental and inviolate if it permits a wife to make a stipulation that she will break up her marriage on his taking a second wife. Further, the moral foundation of this right is considerably weakened if the law, while tolerating it, calls it "a continuing wrong" to the first wife and permits her to stipulate that she will repudiate her marriage vows on the coming of a second wife.

If Muslim law had regarded a polygamous husband´s right to consortium with the first wife as fundamental and inviolate, it would have banned such stipulations by the wife as against Muslim public policy. But it has done no such thing. On the contrary Muslim law has conferred upon the wife´s stipulated right to dissolve her marriage on her husband taking a second wife a force overriding the sanctity of the first marriage itself.

If Mohammadan Law permits and enforces such agreements it follows that it prefers the breaking up of the first marriage to compelling the first wife to share her husband with the second. The general law, too, recognises the sanctity of such agreements, and it has been held that a contract restraining a

174

Muslim husband from entering into a second marriage during the life time of the first is not void under Sec. 23 of the Contract Act which bans agreements in restraint of marriage.

(11) I am, therefore, of the opinion that Muslim Law as enforced in India has considered polygamy as an institution to be tolerated but not encouraged, and has not conferred upon the husband any fundamental right to compel the first wife to share his consortium with another woman in all circumstances. A Muslim husband has the legal right to take a second wife even while the first marriage subsists, but if he does so, and then seeks the assistance of the Civil Court to compel the first wife to live with him against her wishes on pain of severe penalties including attachment of property, she is entitled to raise the question whether the court, as a court of equity, ought to compel her to submit to co-habitation with such a husband. In that case the circumstances in which his second marriage took place are relevant and material in deciding whether his conduct in taking a second wife was in itself an act of cruelty to the first.

(12) Mr. Kazmi contended that the first wife is in no case entitled to consider the second marriage as an act of cruelty to her. I cannot agree. In Shamsunnissa Begum's case (11 Moo Ind App 551), the Privy Council observed that "the Mohammedan Law, on a question of what is legal cruelty between man and wife, would probably not differ materially from the English Law". It follows that Indian Law does not recognise various types of cruelty such as 'Muslim' cruelty, 'Christian' cruelty, 'Hindu' cruelty, and so on, and that the test of cruelty is based on universal and humanitarian standards that is to say, conduct of the husband which would cause such bodily or mental pain as to endanger the wife's safety or health.

(13) What the Court will regard as cruel conduct depends upon the prevailing social conditions. Not so very long ago in England a husband could inflict corporal chastisement on the wife without causing comment. Principles governing legal cruelty are well established and it includes any conduct of such a character as to have caused danger to life, limb, or health (bodily or mental) or as to give a reasonable apprehension of such a danger. Raydon On Divorce 5th Edition p. 80.

But in determining what constitutes cruelty, regard must be had to the circumstances of each particular case, keeping always in view the physical and mental condition of the parties and their character and social status ibid p. 80. In deciding what constitutes cruelty, the Courts have always taken into consideration the prevailing social conditions, and the same test will apply in a case where the parties are Mohammadans. Muslim society has never remained static and to contend otherwise is to ignore the record of achievements of Muslim civilisation and the rich development of Mohammedan

175

jurisprudence in different countries. Muslim jurisprudence has always taken into account changes in social conditions in administering Mohammedan Law.

"Necessity and the wants of social life are the two all-important guiding principles recognised by Mohammedan Jurisprudence in conformity to which Laws should be applied to actual cases, subject only to this reservation that rules, which are covered by a clear text of the Quran or a precept of indisputable authority, or have been settled by agreement among the learned, must be enforced as we find them. It seems to me beyond question that, so long as this condition is borne in mind, the Court in administering Mohammedan Law is entitled to take into account the circumstances of actual life and the change in the people's habits, and modes of living": Mohammedan Jurisprudence by Sri Abdur Rahim, Tagore Law Lecture - 1908 p. 43.

(14) The most convincing proof of the impact of social changes on Muslim Law is the passing of the Dissolution of Muslim Marriages Act 1939 by which the legislature enabled a Muslim wife to sue for the dissolution of her marriage on a number of grounds which were previously not available. One of them is the failure of the husband who has more wives than one to treat all of them equitably in accordance with the injunctions of the Quran.

It is but a short step from this principle to ask a husband who has taken it into his head to have a second wife during the subsistence of the first marriage to explain the reasons for this conduct and, in the absence of a convincing explanation, to conclude that there is little likelihood of the first wife receiving equitable treatment from him.

"By this Act the legislature has made a distinct endeavour to ameliorate the lot of the wife and we (the Courts) must apply the law in consonance with the spirit of the legislature." - Sinha J., in <u>Mt. Sofia Begum v. Zaheer Hasan</u>, AIR 1947 All 16.

I respectfully agree, and would like to add that in considering the question of cruelty in any particular case, the Court cannot ignore the prevailing social conditions, the circumstances of actual life and the change in the people's habits and modes of living.

(15) Today Muslim women move in society, and it is impossible for any Indian husband with several wives to cart all of them around. He must select one among them to share his social life, thus making impartial treatment in polygamy virtually impossible under modern conditions. Formerly, a Muslim husband could bring a second wife into the household without necessarily meaning any insult or cruelty to the wife. Occasionally, a second marriage took place with the consent or even at the suggestion of the first wife.

But social condition and habits among Indian Mussalmans have changed considerably, and with it the conscience of the
176

Muslim community. Today the importing of a second wife into the household ordinarily means a stinging insult to the first. It leads to the asking of awkward questions the raising of unsympathetic eyebrows and the pointing of derisive fingers at the first wife who is automatically degraded by society. All this is likely to prey upon her mind and health if she is compelled to live with her husband under the altered circumstances.

A husband who takes a second wife in these days will not be permitted to pretend that he did not realise the likely effect of his action on the feelings and health of first wife. Under the law, the husband will be presumed to intend the natural consequences of his own conduct. Simpson v. Simpson, ((1951) I All ER 955). Under the prevailing conditions the very act of taking a second wife, in the absence of a weighty and convincing explanation, raises a presumption of cruelty to the first. (The Calcutta High Court called it a "continuing wrong").

The onus today would be on the husband who takes a second wife to explain his action and prove that his taking a second wife involved no insult or cruelty to the first. For example, he may rebut the presumption of cruelty by proving that his second marriage took place at the suggestion of the first wife or reveal some other relevant circumstances which will disprove cruelty. But in the absence of a cogent explanation the Court will presume, under modern conditions, that the action of the husband in taking a second wife involved cruelty to the first and that it would be inequitable for the Court to compel her against her wishes to live with such a husband.

(16) Mr.Kazmi relied on an observation of the late Sir Din Shah Mulla in his Principles of Mohammedan Law, 14th edition page 246, that:
"cruelty, when it is of such a character as to render it unsafe tor the wife to return to her dominion, is a valid defence"
to a suit for restitution of conjugal rights by the husband. Learned counsel argued that cruelty which would fall short of this standard is no defence. I do not read any such meaning in that eminent author's observation which is really borrowed from the judgment of the Privy Council in Shamsunnissa Begum's case, (11 Moo Ind App 551). But I have indicated that the Privy Council observed in that case that the Mohammedan Law is not very different from the English Law on the question of cruelty.

The Court will grant the equitable relief of restitution in accordance with the social conscience of the Muslim community, though always regarding the fundamental principles of the Mohammedan Law in the matter of marriage and other relations as sacrosanct. That law has always permitted and continues to permit a Mohammedan to marry several wives upto the limit of four. But the exercise of this right has never

177

been encouraged and if the husband, after taking a second wife against the wishes of the first, also wants the assistance of the Civil Court to compel the first to live with him, the Court will respect the sanctity of the second marriage, but it will not compel the first wife, against her wishes, to live with the husband under the altered circumstances and share his consortium with another woman if it concludes, on a review of the evidence, that it will be inequitable to compel her to do so.

(17) Counsel for the appellant argued vehemently that dismissal of the husband's suit against the first wife virtually means a denial of his right to marry a second time while the first marriage subsists. I do not agree. A Muslim husband has always the right to take a second wife. If he does so, he cannot be prosecuted for bigamy, the second marriage is valid, the children of the second wife are legitimate and he is entitled to the enjoyment of his rights (subject to his obligations) under the second marriage.

But it is not at all necessary for the enjoyment and consummation of his rights under the second marriage that he should apportion his consortium between two women. On the contrary, nothing is more likely to mar the conjugal bliss of his second marriage than that his new wife should be asked to share it with the old. The second wife is not likely to view with sympathy her husband's attempt to compel the old wife to return to his consortium and, to put it very mildly, the dismissal of the husband's suit for restitution against the first wife is not likely to break the second wife's heart.

Therefore, if, in his conjugal greed, the husband does not rest content with the enjoyment of his new connubial bliss but, like Oliver, asks for more, and is refused relief by the Court, he cannot complain that his rights under the first marriage have been impaired. The Court will be justified in inquiring whether it will be equitable to compel his first wife to submit to his consortium in the altered circumstances.

(18) Even in the absence of satisfactory proof of the husband's cruelty, the Court will not pass a decree for restitution in favour of the husband if, on the evidence, it feels that the circumstances are such that it will be unjust and inequitable to compel her to live with him. In Hamid Hussain v. Kubra Begum, (ILR 40 All 332): (AIR 1918 All 235), a Division Bench of this Court dismissed a husband's prayer for restitution on the ground that the parties were on the worst of terms, that the real reason for the suit was the husband's desire to obtain possession of the wife's property and the Court was of the opinion that by a return to her husband's custody the wife's health and safety would be endangered though there was no satisfactory evidence of physical cruelty.

In Nawab Bibi v. Allah Ditta, (AIR 1924 Lah 188 (2)), Shadi Lal C.J. and Zafar Ali, J. refused relief to a husband

178

who had been married as an infant to the wife when she was a
minor but had not even cared to bring her to live with him
even after she had attained the age of puberty. In <u>Khurshid
Begum v. Abdul Rashid</u>, (AIR 1926 Nag 234), the Court refused
relief to a husband because it was of the opinion that the
husband and wife had been "on the worst of terms" for years
and the suit had been brought in a struggle for the possession
of property.

(19) These principles apply to the present case. The
lower appellate court has found that the appellant never
really cared for his first wife and filed his suit for
restitution only to defeat her application for maintenance.
In the circumstances, his suit was mala fide and rightly
dismissed.

(20) Lastly, the appellate court, reversing the finding
of the trial court, believed the wife's allegation of specific
acts of cruelty committed by the husband and held that she had
been deserted and neglected by the husband for so many years.
In the circumstances, I concur in the opinion of the District
Judge that it will be inequitable to compel the first wife to
live with such a husband. The appeal is dismissed under O.
41, R. 11, C. P. C.

[Note the disparaging comment on this decision by Derrett
in his book "Religion Law and the State in India": "Itwari v.
Asghari AIR 1960 All. 684 if it is an advance (in the concept
of cruelty in matrimonial causes) is minimal and to hail it as
an advance is to pronounce on the decrepitude of the system"
(at p. 538). An unfairly harsh comment in the light of the
jurisprudential background?]

<u>SYED AHMAD KHAN (appellant) v. IMRAT JAHAN BEGUM (respondent)</u>
<u>A.I.R. 1982 All. 155 (Deoki Nandan, J.)</u>

[The appellant was seeking a decree of restitution of conjugal
rights, which the respondent resisted partly on the ground of
non-payment of dower, and partly on the basis of cruelty in as
much as the husband had, during the suit, married for a third
time]

<u>Judgment</u>.....3. The relevant facts of the case are that the
parties were married in the year 1968. The husband Syed Ahmad
Khan had already a wife living when he married the present
wife Smt. Imrat Begum. The parties are supposed to have lived
and cohabited together only for about a year and it was stated
in the husband's plaint dated the 29th Oct., 1973 for
restitution of conjugal rights (Suit No. 435 of 1973
originally of the court of Munsif, Bisauli) that the wife had
for the last four years neglected and refused to give her
society or to cohabit with the husband without just cause and
had taken to the profession of a teacher at Gunnaur against

179

his wishes, and did not come to live with him in spite of a notice served in July, 1973. It is not necessary to detail the defence set up by the wife.....
.....8. It appears from the reasons given by the trial court for its findings..... .....that the wife was willing to live with the husband even up to the year 1972 and that she could not be said to have been treated cruelly by the husband so as to give her any cause for refusing her society to him. This finding cuts both ways, for it means that while on the one hand the wife could not be said to have withdrawn herself from the society of the husband at least up to the year 1972, on the other hand that there was no good cause for her refusing to join the husband, particularly when the husband served a notice on her as to do so and even followed it up by a suit. The finding that the wife could not complain of any cruelty during the period when she did actually live with her husband cannot be seriously challenged if she was willing to go back to the husband in the year 1972. The fact that she had not lived with the husband at anytime after 1969 shows that she could have had no reasonable ground for believing that it would not be safe for her to live with the husband. Mr. Janardan Sahai pointed out that it was admitted by the husband that he had married a third time during the pendency of this litigation. That may be a good cause for refusing a decree for restitution of conjugal rights, but the learned Judge pointed out that even so a Muslim is entitled to have up to four wives. Since the wife did not live with the husband for a single day after his having married a third time, it cannot be said that the husband does not treat his wife equitably in accordance with the injunction of the Quran. So far as the first wife was concerned the complaint was not that the husband did not treat the wife, who has appealed from the decree of the restitution of conjugal rights, equitably in accordance with the injunctions of the Quran but that the first wife treated her roughly. It therefore appears to me that the wife, who has appealed from the decree of restitution of conjugal rights, cannot be said to have proved that the husband had treated her with cruelty in the sense in which it is explained and defined in the Dissolution of Muslim Marriages Act, 1939. That being so she could not properly resist the husband´s demand for her society which he has followed up with the suit for restitution of conjugal rights.
9. Confronted with this position Mr. Janardan Sahai, learned counsel for the wife, contended that the decree for restitution of conjugal rights, even if it were allowed to stand could not be enforced unless the wife´s demand for payment of her prompt dower was satisfied. On this Mr. Rajeshji Verma objected that after consummation of a marriage non-payment of dower, even though exigible, cannot be pleaded in defence to an action for restitution of conjugal rights, and relied upon for the proposition on a Division Bench

decision of this Court in <u>Rabia Khatoon v. Mohd. Mukhtar Ahmad</u>
(AIR 1966 All 548). Mr. Janardan Sahai countered by saying
that he is not putting forth the demand for dower as a defence
to an action for restitution of conjugal rights. The wife
already has a decree in her favour for recovery of her prompt
dower. The husband was not paying it and in equity the court
ought to have made the satisfaction of the decree for recovery
of dower as a condition for enforcement of the decree for
restitution of conjugal rights. In Smt. Rabia Khatoon's case
(supra) also although non-payment of the dower was not
admitted as a proper defence in the suit for restitution of
conjugal rights which was decreed yet the decree was made
conditional upon payment of the amount of prompt dower by the
husband to the wife.

10. Under the circumstances, it would be equitable, just
and proper to impose a condition that the decree for
restitution of conjugal rights would not be executable unless
the decree for recovery of the prompt dower was satisfied.
This, however, brings me to the question whether the decree
for recovery of dower is sustainable.

11. One of the grounds of objection against the decree
was that the suit was time barred. Apart from the facts found
by the trial court for holding that the claim was not barred
by limitation. I have been referred to the judgment of this
Court in <u>Naeem Begum v. Alam Ali Khan</u> (1979 All LJ 771)
wherein it was held that Section 29 (3) of the Limitation Act,
1963 expressly saves a suit for recovery of dower which is
brought under the Muslim Law of marriage and divorce, from the
law of limitation.

12. On the merits of the claim the husband's defence was
that it had been remitted by the wife. That defence has been
disbelieved by the trial court on an appraisal of evidence, on
the record. The evidence on this point is oral. The trial
court had the opportunity of hearing the witnesses and
watching their demeanour. There is nothing in the facts and
circumstances of the case which may give me reason to think
that the finding is, in anyway, incorrect. Learned counsel
for the appellant has been unable to show that the finding
suffers from any error. The amount of the dower was not
remitted. The correctness of the amount or that the whole of
it was prompt was not challenged by the husband, his whole
defence being that it was remitted.

13. In the result, both these appeals are liable to be
dismissed, subject however, to the modification in the decree
for restitution of conjugal rights that was passed by the
Civil Judge, Budaun, in Suit No. 435 of 1973 originally of the
court of Munsif, Bisauli, to the effect that the decree shall
not be executable and shall not be executed until such time as
the decree for recovery of dower passed in Suit No. 100 of
1975 of the court of the Civil Judge, Budaun, is fully
satisfied. In the circumstances, I would however, direct that

the husband Sayed Ahman Khan shall pay the costs of the wife in both the First Appeal in this Court.

————————

MOHD. ZAMAN (appellant) v. IRSHAD BEGUM (respondent)
P.L.D. 1967 Lah. 1105. (Fazle Ghani, J.)

Judgment.....The brief facts giving rise to the present second appeal are as follows:

Plaintiff Muhammad Zaman was married with Mst. Irshad Begum sometime in the year 1949-50. They lived for sometime together and a daughter was born to them out of this wedlock. In 1951 Muhammad Zaman executed an agreement in favour of his wife Mst. Irshad Begum to the effect that in case he was to take a second wife she will be entitled to receive maintenance in a separate house and even if she wanted to live with her parents he will be liable to pay maintenance to her in her parental home. On the 11th of October 1960 Muhammad Zaman filed a suit for the restitution of conjugal rights against Mst. Irshad Begum and also prayed that a perpetual injunction be issued against Muhammad Bashir, Nawazish Ali and Mst. Aziza Begum so as to restrain them from preventing Mst. Irshad Begum, his wife, from coming to his house. All the defendants resisted the suit and on behalf of Mst. Irshad Begum it was pleaded that the plaintiff Muhammad Zaman had not paid her prompt dower of Rs. 1,000.00 and that he used to ill-treat her and as such her life was in danger and at any rate, the suit for the restitution of conjugal rights was brought by the plaintiff against her as a counter blast to her application which she had moved before the Criminal Court under section 488, Criminal Procedure Code, for the payment of maintenance allowance for herself and for her daughter. Consequent to the above pleadings of the parties the trial Court framed the following issues:-

(1) Whether the plaintiff has not paid dower to the defendant, if so what is its effect?
(2) Whether the suit is _mala fide_ and has been brought to be saved from the maintenance allowance?
(3) Whether the plaintiff has accused the defendant of theft and misappropriation, if so what is its effect?
(4) Whether the plaintiff has any cause of action against defendants Nos. 2 to 4?
(5) Whether the plaintiff executed an agreement in favour of the defendant Irshad Begum that in case the plaintiff marries a second woman, the defendant would be entitled to reside away from him, if so what is its effect?
(6) Relief.

After recording the evidence of the parties the trial Court found that the prompt dower was not paid by the plaintiff to his wife but the decision of the case rested mainly on the

findings on issue No. 5 and it was held that by executing the
agreement (Exh. D.2) the plaintiff unconditionally undertook
"not to take a second wife, and in case he does so, he allows
the defendant to live with her parents". As a result of the
above finding the plaintiff´s suit was dismissed by the trial
Court on the 12th of April 1961. The plaintiff´s appeal
before the learned District Judge was dismissed on the 13th of
July 1961. It was held by the learned lower appellate Court
that the plaintiff had admitted that he had taken a second
wife and as such he was not entitled to the decree for the
restitution of conjugal rights against his wife Mst. Irshad
Begum.

2. In this second appeal, learned counsel for the
appellant mainly relied on one argument. He submitted that
both the Courts below had acted contrary to law inasmuch as
they relied on agreement (Exh. D.2) which is a void agreement
as it contains a stipulation in restraint of marriage and
provides condition for the husband and wife to live separately
from each other. This agreement, according to the learned
counsel, is opposed to public policy, within the meaning of
section 23 of the Contract Act and could not be acted upon.
In support of his contention he relied on Mst. Bai Fatima v.
Ali Muhammad Aiyeb (I L R 37 Bom. 280) and Mst. Bibi Fatima v.
Nur Muhammad ((1921) 60 I C 88). In both these cases it was
held that an iqrarnama which provides and encourages future
separation between husband and wife, must be pronounced as
being against public policy. Since the question decided in
these two cases involves an important question of law, it
needs detailed examination.

3. In the Bombay case Mst. Bai Fatima v. Ali Muhammad
Aiyeb, Batchelor, J., who delivered the judgment of the
Division Bench, relied on his earlier judgment which he had
given when sitting single in Meherally v. Sakerkhanoobai (I L
R 37 Bom. 280) and it was held by him that an agreement made
by a husband with his wife was bad in English Law and as such
was also bad between Muhammadan spouses. The learned Judge
concluded his judgment with the following observations:-

> "It is, as I understand it, as much the policy of the
> Muhammadan Law as of the English law, that people who
> are married should live together and not apart; and if
> that is so, it seems to me that there should be no
> difficulty in applying to Muhammadans the English Rule
> that any agreement such as this, which provides for, and
> therefore encourages, future separation between the
> spouses, must be pronounced void as being against public
> policy."

In the Lahore Case Mst. Bibi Fatima v. Nur Muhammad learned
Judges of the Division Bench relied on the judgment of the
Bombay High Court and it was held that an agreement by a
Muslim husband with his wife that she will live in her
parents´ house was invalid and cannot be utilised by the wife

to defeat the husband's claim for the restitution of conjugal
rights. In this case learned Judges examined the statement of
law as given in Muhammadan Law, Vol. III, 1917 Edition by Sir
Amir Ali and taking into consideration the facts of the case
it was found that the right, if any, in the iqrarnama,
executed by the husband had been waived by the wife because
after the execution of the deed the wife had consented to live
with her husband. However, in this case also it was held that
an agreement between husband and wife to live away from each
other was void as being opposed to public policy.

4. The Bombay case came for examination before the Chief
Court of Oudh in Manzoor v. Azizul (A I R 1928 Oudh 303). In
that case the wife was the first wife of the plaintiff husband
and when both the wives could not pull on well an agreement
was executed by the husband for the payment of maintenance in
a separate house. On a suit by the wife for the maintenance
the husband pleaded that he was not liable to maintain her
under the agreement because she was not living with him as a
wife. The suit of the wife was decreed up to the first
appellate stage and in second appeal before the Chief Court it
was urged that the agreement was without consideration and
against public policy. The learned Judges repelled the
contention and dissenting from the Bombay view observed as
follows:-

> "If a Muhammadan marries a second wife and finds that
> the first wife cannot pull on well with his second wife
> and he does not and cannot provide a separate apartment
> or habitation for her exclusive use, and for the sake of
> preservation of the family peace executes an agreement
> in her favour giving her maintenance, even if she does
> not reside in the same house with him and his second
> wife, that agreement is not in our opinion against
> public policy. This arrangement does not necessarily
> result in separation between husband and wife."

The Lahore High Court in a latter decision Muhammad Ali Akbar
v. Mst. Fatima Begum (A I R 1929 Lah. 660) considered the
judgment of the Bombay High Court in a case where the District
Judge had made an award of Rs. 900 in favour of wife on
account of the arrears of Kharcha-i-Pandan. It seems that
their earlier decision in Mst. Bibi Fatima v. Nur Muhammad was
not cited but the Bombay case was particularly dissented in
the following words:-

> "With all due deference to the learned Judges (of Bombay
> High Court) who decided that case, I do not see why a
> stipulation by the husband to make an allowance to his
> wife in case of separation should be deemed to offend
> against the rule of public policy. Such a stipulation
> encourages their living separate from each other no more
> than their living together by imposing an obligation on
> the husband calculated to prevent him from doing any act
> which would lead to separation."

184

The obligation of the husband which he had undertaken for the payment of <u>Kharcha-i-Pandan</u> at the time of his marriage, was, therefore, enforced.

5. With utmost respect to the learned Judges, who decided the two cases of Bombay and Lahore High Courts, which were cited by the learned counsel for the appellant, I am unable to accept the proposition that an agreement made by the husband with his wife allowing her to live away from him in case of disagreement or when he takes a second wife can in any way be termed as opposed to public policy either under the Muslim Law or within the meaning of section 23 of the Contract Act. A marriage between Muslim male and female is purely of a nature of civil contract and the wife is entitled to protect herself at the hands of her husband in case of their future differences. In the present case the agreement is to the effect that the wife is entitled to receive alimony in the house of her parents or anywhere else where she chooses to reside in case the husband takes a second wife and there is nothing in such an agreement which may be considered to offend against the term "public policy" which is very broad and it is not safe to rely upon it in such cases as a ground for legal decision.

6. Meherally´s case was decided by Batchelor, J. in 1905 but the position of law has undergone a considerable change after the decision of their Lordships of the Privy Council in <u>Nawab Khawaja Muhammad Khan v. Husaini Begum alias Dilbari Begum</u> (7 I C 237) where it was held that:-

> "Where the father of the husband by an agreement executed to the father of the wife bound himself to pay to the wife the fixed allowance and there was no condition that it should be paid only whilst the wife is living in the husband´s home, the wife would be entitled to the allowance even if she refused to live with her husband."

The attention of the learned Judges, who decided the Bombay case in 1912 and the Lahore case in 1925, does not seem to have been drawn to the above-mentioned pronouncement of their Lordships of the Privy Council.

7. The other cases which can be referred in this context are <u>Saeed Khan v. Balatunnisa Bibi</u> (25 C W N 888) where in a suit by the husband for the restitution of the conjugal rights it was held by a Division Bench that a stipulation that a Muhammadan wife may leave her husband´s house on ill-treatment is not opposed to Muhammadan Law. In this case the husband was given a conditional decree to go and perform his marital obligations in the house of his wife´s parents. It was clearly laid down in this case that there is nothing in the Muslim law which can invalidate the agreement of the husband with the wife that wife can live away from the husband in case of disagreement. This case is completely on all fours with the facts of the present case and being directly in point

185

furnishes a complete answer to the argument of the learned counsel for the appellant.

8. In <u>Mst. Sakina Farooq v. Shamshad Khan</u> (A I R 1936 Pesh. 195) in similar circumstances it was held that a Muslim husband could make a stipulation that he will not remove his wife from her parental home and that such an agreement is a valid contract and not opposed to public policy.

9. Taking into consideration the preponderance of judicial dicta on the subject I am of the opinion that if a Muslim marries a second wife and finds that his first wife cannot keep on well with his second wife and he does not or cannot provide a separate and exclusive inhabitation for her for the sake of preservation of family peace and, therefore, executes an agreement giving her a right to maintenance even if she does not live with him and his second wife and lives in the house of her parents the agreement is not in any way opposed to public policy. In the present case the agreement was executed by the appellant to meet such a situation. The appellant has admitted before the trial Court that he has taken a second wife and has also got children from her and he is living with them. In these circumstances it is obvious that this agreement was executed in order to maintain the harmony between his two wives and such an agreement is legally perfect and valid under the law.

10. Learned counsel for the appellant had also raised an alternative contention. He submitted that in case the agreement is held to be valid there is nothing under the law to prevent a husband for getting a decree for restitution of conjugal rights on his suit because at the most the wife can enforce her maintenance in a separate house through a Court of law but the existence of such an agreement or failure of the husband to fulfil the obligations under the agreement is no defence to the plaintiff's suit for the restitution of the conjugal rights against his wife. I regret I am not able to accept this contention of the learned counsel for the appellant. No doubt it is the duty of the wife to follow the husband wherever he desires her to go. But such an obligation of the wife to live with her husband at all times and in all circumstances is not an absolute one. The law recognises circumstances which justify her refusal to live with him. For instance if he has habitually ill-treated her, if he has deserted her for a long time, or he has directed her to leave his house or even connived at her doing so. On all such occasions the husband cannot require his wife to re-enter the conjugal domicile nor the Court of justice can give him assistance to restore him the hand of his wife. The bad conduct or gross neglect of the husband under the Muslim law is good defence to a suit brought by him for restitution of conjugal rights. <u>Buzloor Rahman v. Shumsoonnisa Begum</u> ((1876) 11 Moore's I A 555), Ameer Ali's Muhammadan Law, Vol. II (1929 Edn.) section 11, pp.442-446).

11. No doubt a husband can maintain a suit for the restitution of the conjugal rights in a civil Court against his wife, but the decree of the restitution of the conjugal rights is in the discretion of the Court whose duty it is to find out, if there be a cruelty of a degree rendering it unsafe for her if she is ordered to return to the husband's house. In the present case I find that the appellant has committed breach of the agreement which he has executed in favour of his wife as early as 14th of May 1951. The defendant has asserted in her statement before the trial Court that she was maltreated by the appellant as he used to beat her in the presence of his second wife and has ultimately turned her out of his house. There is no evidence in rebuttal to these allegations and the appellant did not even care to cross-examine her with reference to the allegations which she had levelled against him about the maltreatment, etc. The appellant has failed to provide any maintenance for the defendant wife and her daughter and she was compelled to go to the Criminal Court to enforce the appellant's obligation of maintenance under section 488, Cr. P. C. In these circumstances, I find that the appellant had been guilty of gross failure on his part to perform his obligations imposed on him by the agreement and these circumstances afford a sufficient ground to refuse to the appellant any relief in his suit. I am clear in my mind that the appellant has brought this suit for the restitution of the conjugal rights _mala fide_ and as a counter blast to the application of the respondent for maintenance under section 488, Cr. P. C. I, therefore, do not think that the appellant is entitled to crave for the indulgence of the Court for the grant of the decree for the restitution of the conjugal rights in his favour. Every case, in which the question of conjugal domicile is involved, depends upon its own features and the general principles of the Muslim Law on the subject are that a wife is bound to reside with her husband unless there is a valid reason of her refusal to do so. The sufficiency or validity of the reason in each case is a matter for the consideration of the Court with special reference to the circumstances in which the parties have been residing or they wish to settle in future.

12. In the present case I have no hesitation in saying that the grounds on which Mst. Irshad Begum has separated herself justify her in that step and if a decree for restitution of conjugal rights is granted to the appellant directing the defendant wife to return to the conjugal domicile of her husband I will be perpetrating a grievous injustice by compelling her to live with the appellant in his house with his second wife and her step children.

13. For the aforesaid reasons I do not see any justification to interfere with the judgments and decrees passed by the Courts below. The plaintiff's suit has rightly been dismissed. This appeal has thus no merit and is hereby

dismissed. Since no-one appears for the respondent there will
be no order as to costs.

————————

SARDAR MOHD. (Petitioner) v. NASIMA BIBI (Respondent)
PLD 1966 Lahore 703. (Muhd. Afzal Cheema J.)

Judgement.....2. The facts giving rise to this Writ Petition
may be summarised as follows:
    The petitioner Sh. Sardar Muhammad who is a Head
Constable in the police department was married to respondent
No. 1 on 24th May 1957. The spouses lived happily for about a
year and a quarter and a daughter was born to them. According
to the respondent's allegations, the petitioner brought her to
Gujrat, left her with her parents and never bothered himself
about her again. On 7th February 1962, respondent No. 1
applied to the Chairman Union Committee No. 2, Gujrat under
section 9 of the Family Laws Ordinance, in which she claimed
dower money to the tune of Rs. 4,000, monthly allowance at the
rate of Rs. 80 per mensem in addition to the jewellery,
clothes, furniture, etc., which was given as dowery at the
time of her marriage. It appears that the Chairman issued
three notices to the petitioner under registered cover at his
home address in Union Committee No. 3, in Jalalpur Jattan,
district Gujrat, followed by two notices sent to him through
the Chairman of that Committee. According to the report of
the Chairman, Union Committee, Jalalpur Jattan, one notice was
affixed on the door of the petitioner's residential house.
Finally, a notice was also published in the daily 'Kohistan'
in its issue dated the 30th of March 1962. In spite of all
this, the petitioner failed to respond and as such an
Arbitration Council was constituted without a representative
of the petitioner against whom ex parte proceedings were
taken. As regards the respondent's claim for the dowery and
jewellery she was directed to approach a competent Court, but
her prayer for maintenance was allowed as stated earlier.
This order was unsuccessfully challenged in revision by the
petitioner before the Collector on 2nd October 1963, who
dismissed his petition on 12th November 1963, as time-barred.
    3. The learned counsel for the petitioner has raised the
following contentions before us:
        (1) That the allegations against the petitioner were
        those of total neglect and refusal to maintain and as
        such, section 9 of the Family Laws Ordinance which deal
        with only cases of inadequate maintenance could not be
        invoked.
        (2) That the first impugned order was illegal inasmuch
        as the proceedings were taken against the petitioner ex
        parte by an Arbitration Council which was not properly
        constituted, besides the order appears to have been
        passed by the Chairman in his personal capacity;

(3) That the date of the application before the Chairman was 7th February 1962, whereas the arrears have been granted from 15th July 1961, which was illegal inasmuch as no decree could be passed for past maintenance under Muhammadan Law. Reliance was placed on I L R 6 Cal. 631, Baillie 447 and Hadaya 142. (4) Lastly, that the impugned order clearly stated that the allowance of Rs. 70 per mensem had been granted both for the petitioner´s wife as well as his minor daughter whereas no provision existed in the Family Laws Ordinance for grant of allowance to a child.

4. In order to appreciate the first contention raised by the learned counsel, the two relevant provisions, i.e., the one under section 488 of the Code of Criminal Procedure, and the other in section 9 of the Family Laws Ordinance will have to be considered in juxtaposition, and are reproduced below:

Section 488 of the Criminal Procedure Code:

"488. (1) If any person having sufficient means neglects or refuses to maintain his wife or his legitimate or illegitimate child unable to maintain itself, the District Magistrate, a Sub-Divisional Magistrate or a Magistrate of the first class may, upon proof of such neglect or refusal, order such person to make a monthly allowance for the maintenance of his wife or such child, at such monthly rate, not exceeding four hundred rupees in the whole, as such Magistrate thinks fit, and to pay the same to such person as the Magistrate from time to time directs.

(2) Such allowance shall be payable from the date of the order, or if so ordered from the date of the application for maintenance.

(3) . . . ."

Section 9 of the Muslim Family Laws Ordinance, 1961:

"9. Maintenance – (1) If any husband fails to maintain his wife adequately, or where there are more wives than one, fails to maintain them equitably, the wife, or all or any of the wives, may in addition to seeking any other legal remedy available apply to the Chairman who shall constitute an Arbitration Council to determine the matter, and the Arbitration Council may issue a certificate specifying the amount which shall be paid as maintenance by the husband.

(2) A husband or wife may, in the prescribed manner, within the prescribed period, and on payment of the prescribed fee, prefer an application for revision of the certificate, in the case of West Pakistan, to the Collector, and in the case of East Pakistan to the Sub-Divisional Officer concerned and his decision shall be final and shall not be called in question in any Court.

(3) Any amount payable under subsection (1) or (2), if

189

> not paid in due time, shall be recoverable as arrears of land revenue."

The expression used in section 488, Cr. P. Code is "neglects or refuses to maintain his wife", whereas section 9 of the Ordinance says: "fails to maintain his wife adequately". The two expressions are differently worded and might seemingly have different connotations, but on a close examination the difference between the two is reduced to nothingness. Considering language used in section 488, if a person agrees or offers to give to his wife an inadequate allowance, say Rs. 20, per mensem as against a reasonable amount of Rs. 100 per mensem, his agreement to pay the inadequate sum would certainly amount to a refusal to maintain, as maintenance would mean an adequate, proper and reasonable maintenance, and a person offering an inadequate allowance cannot on that pretext escape or avoid the invocation of section 488, Cr. P. Code. Similarly, although the expression used in section 9 of the Muslim Family Laws Ordinance mentions only the failure on the part of the husband to maintain his wife adequately, a case of total absence of maintenance or refusal to maintain cannot be excluded from the purview of this section as a case of total absence of maintenance does not become identical with one of adequate maintenance. A case of refusal to maintain at all would be a still worse form of inadequate maintenance. In fact, the word ´adequately´ has been employed only to emphasise that the maintenance should be proper and reasonable, and that an inadequate maintenance may be considered no maintenance at all. It is a well settled principle of interpretation of statutes that the interpretation should be beneficial and one which should advance the object of legislation and not the one which should lead to its frustration. Keeping in view the background of the Muslim Family Laws Ordinance which was enacted on the recommendations of the Commission on Marriage and Family Laws, giving rise to country-wide controversy, we are in no manner of doubt that the underlying object in making this provision was to furnish a simpler, cheaper and more expedient remedy to neglected wives than the one which was already available to them under section 488 of the Code of Criminal Procedure. It certainly does not appear to have been the intention of the law-giver to classify cases of maintenance into two different categories, i.e., those of a total absence of maintenance and those of inadequate maintenance. We have thus no hesitation in saying that a case of inadequate maintenance also includes a case of total absence of maintenance and the new remedy now made available to a neglected wife under the Muslim Family Laws Ordinance is not alternative in nature, so as to be invoked by inadequately maintained wives only, but has been made available in addition to a similar remedy already provided in section 488, Cr. P. Code. The two remedies in our view are available to all cases of lack of maintenance whether adequate or inadequate, and we see no reason to hold that both relate to different kinds and categories of such cases.

Coming now to the second contention, regarding the _ex parte_ proceedings and improper constitution of the Arbitration Council, the argument is patently devoid of force as the impugned order clearly shows that every effort was made to serve the petitioner whose substituted service appears to have been properly effected. In his absence there was no question of the nomination of his representatives on the Arbitration Council, and under sub-rule 5(3) of the relevant Rules, proceedings before the Arbitration Council cannot be vitiated on account of the failure of any person to nominate his representative. No doubt, in the impugned order first person has been used by the Chairman giving the impression as if it were an order passed by him in an individual capacity and not by the Arbitration Council as such, but this seems to us to be merely due to inadvertence. The contention has no force.

5. In the next contention, it is argued by the learned counsel that under the Muhammadan Law, a wife is not entitled to a decree for past maintenance, unless the claim is based on a specific agreement, and as such, the Arbitration Council was not competent to grant allowance to respondent No. 1 from 15th July 1961, i.e., the date of the enforcement of the Family Laws Ordinance. The point to be determined by us is whether an Arbitration Council can issue certificate in respect of arrears of maintenance, or to put it more precisely from what date could an allowance be allowed to a neglected wife; from the date when the cause of action arises or the date when she makes the application before the Arbitration Council or the date on which the order is made in her favour. Placing reliance on <u>Abdool Futteh Moulvie v. Zabunnessa Khatun</u> (I L R 6 Cal. 631), it was argued by the learned counsel for the petitioner that maintenance could only be paid to respondent No. 1 from the date of the decree and not even from the date of making application, i.e., 7th February 1962. In this D. B. authority, reliance has been placed on the following observation in Baillie's Digest at page 443:

> "When a woman sues her husband for maintenance for a time antecedent to any order of the Judge or mutual agreement of the parties, the Judge is not to decree maintenance for the past."

Reference has also been made to the Hedaya. We have carefully considered this question and it would be advantageous to reproduce the following passage from Baillie which lends further support to this view:

> "When maintenance has been decreed against a husband at so much the month, or the parties have come to a mutual agreement for so much each month, and several months are allowed to pass without his giving her anything, and she in the meantime raises her maintenance on credit, or disburses it out of her own property, and then either

the husband or the wife happens to die, the whole of what has been so raised or disbursed drops, or can no longer be recovered. And in like manner, if he should repudiate her, any arrears of maintenance that may have accumulated after the decree of the Judge are irrecoverable."

6. A similar view has been expressed at page 142 of Hamilton's Translation of Hedaya:

"Arrears of maintenance not due unless the maintenance have been decreed by the Kazee or the rate of it previously determined on between the parties - If a length of time should elapse during which the wife has not received any maintenance from her husband, she is not entitled to demand any for that time, except when the Kazee had before determined and decreed it to her, or where she had entered into a composition with the husband respecting it, in either of which cases she is to be decreed her maintenance for the time past, because maintenance is an obligation in the manner of a gratuity, as by a gratuity is understood a thing due without a return, and maintenance is of this description, it not being held (according to our doctors) to be as a return for the matrimonial propriety; and the obligation of it is not valid but through a decree of the Kazee, like a gift, which does not convey a right to possession but through seisin, which establishes possession; but a composition is of equal effect with a decree of the Kazee, in the present case, as the husband by such composition, makes himself responsible, and his power over his own person is superior to that of the Magistrate. This reasoning does not apply to the case of dower, as that is considered to be a return for the use of the wife's person.

7. The proposition cannot be questioned that it is incumbent on a Muslim husband to maintain his wife, subject of course to her loyalty and readiness to perform marital obligations. The following passage from Ameer Ali's Muhammadan Law may be reproduced with advantage in which reliance has been placed on Fatawa-i-Alamgiri and Raddul Muhtar:

"If the husband be a minor and the wife an adult, and the incapacity to complete or consummate the contract be solely on his part, she is entitled to maintenance. If the minor has no property, the obligation of maintaining the wife devolves on his father with a right of recovery against him when he is in a position to repay the amount expended on his behalf. When both husband and wife are minors and cohabitation is impossible, there is no liability, for maintenance.

It makes no difference in the husband's liability to maintain the wife, whether he be in health or suffering from illness, whether he be a prisoner of war or undergoing punishment, "justly or unjustly", for some crime, whether he be absent from home on pleasure or business, or gone on a pilgrimage, and whether he be rich or poor. In fact, as long as the status of marriage subsists and the wife is subject to the marital power, she is entitled to maintenance from him. Nor does she lose her right by becoming afflicted with any disease after marriage.

But when she becomes ill before she has taken up her abode in the conjugal domicile there is no obligation on the husband to provide for her maintenance.

8. A woman is also entitled to her maintenance though refusing herself to her husband on the ground that he had not paid her dower, Mulla in his Principles of Muhammadan Law at page 238, 1961 Edn. has observed as follows:-

"Husband's duty to maintain his wife

The husband is bound to maintain his wife (unless she is too young for matrimonial intercourse) so long as she is faithful to him and obeys his reasonable orders. But he is not bound to maintain a wife who refuses herself to him, or is otherwise disobedient, unless the refusal or disobedience is justified by non-payment of proper dower, or she leaves the husband's house on account of his cruelty."

Thus, it is abundantly clear that the husband's obligation to maintain his wife commences with the performance of marriage subject to certain conditions. But the authorities cited earlier and relied upon by the learned counsel for the petitioner seem to lay down in unmistakeable terms that in the absence of an agreement between the spouses or a decree by the Kazee, a wife is not entitled to a decree for past maintenance. The reasoning seems to be that if the wife has somehow managed to get along without maintenance and has not cared to approach the Kazee, a decree for past maintenance may be justifiably refused to her. In other words, the argument is that a person who does not care to promptly seek a legal remedy or has somehow managed to do without it may be afforded a relief only when he seeks it and not for an earlier period of time. This position seems to be rather inconsistent with the view expressed in the above cited authorities that normally obligation to maintain a wife starts from the time of marriage.

9. It appears necessary to appreciate the difference between dower and maintenance. Marriage in Islam being in the nature of a contract, dower is the consideration agreed between the parties which the husband has to pay to the wife either promptly or subsequently in accordance with the terms of the agreement. On the contrary, maintenance is an obligation which is one of the essential incidents of marriage, liable to suspension or forfeiture under certain

circumstances. The two incidents, therefore, proceed on entirely different bases. So far as the payment of dower is concerned, once it is stipulated, its payment becomes obligatory on the husband and even if the wife is divorced by the husband before she is touched, he is bound to pay half of the dower money as would be clear from the following verse No. 236 of Sura Albaqra:

"If you divorce them before consummation but after you have fixed their dower, then there is due half of that fixed"

It could of course, be quite different if the wife voluntarily foregoes the dower.

10. As against this, the obligation of the husband to maintain his wife has been derived from an earlier verse No. 232 of the Sura Albaqra which enjoins upon the father of a suckling child to feed and clothe his wife according to usage:

"But he must pay the women's food and clothing according to what is customary"

This finds further support from the famous tradition of the Holy Prophet (peace be upon Him):

"For those women dependent on you, their food and clothing according to what is customary"

The argument in favour of forfeiture of arrears of maintenance for the past seems to have been based on the assumption that "maintenance is an obligation in the manner of a gratuity" i.e., an _ex gracia_ grant which is paid by way of sympathy and charity which cannot be claimed as of right. This is clearly laid down in Hamilton's Translation of Hedaya of which the relevant portion has been reproduced earlier in this judgment. In all humility and with the utmost respect we find it difficult to endorse this view as the consensus of opinion as shown from the authorities cited earlier seems to be that the maintenance of a wife is the bounden duty of a husband, irrespective of his minority, illness or imprisonment or the richness of the wife, so much so that the obligation devolves on the father of a minor husband with a right of recovery against him when he is in a position to repay the amount as held by Amir Ali on the authority of ´Fatawa-i-Alamgiri´ and Radd-ul-Muhtar, alluded to earlier. It is thus difficult to say that it is in the nature of an _ex gracia_ payment which cannot be claimed for a past period of time.

11. The question of the forfeiture or suspension of maintenance with the passage of time has been discussed by Ibne Qayyum under a separate heading, at pages 149-50 of the Fourth Volume of his famous work _Zaadul Maad_ 2nd Edition, published in Egypt. It is mentioned therein that it was a disputed question. Imam Abu Hanifa the founder of the Hanfi School of thought was definitely in favour of the forfeiture of arrears of maintenance, while on the contrary, the three other Jurists, namely, Imam Shaafi, Imam Ahmad Hanbal and Imam

Malik, unanimously held the view that the arrears of maintenance being a just charge could be realised from the husband.

"People have differed on three versions on the question of forfeiture of maintenance of wives and relatives: whether it stands forfeited or not in both cases or whether maintenance of relations alone forfeits and not that of wives. One view is that it forfeits in both cases with the passage of time and this is the view of Abu Hanifa, and one of the authorities is from Ahmad. The second view is that it does not stand forfeited in either cases, if the relative is a child. This is the Shaafi view. The third view is that it is the maintenance of the relative and not of the wife that forfeits. This is the generally accepted view and was held by Shaafi, Ahmad and Malik."

12. The main argument which formed the basis of the Hanafi view is that Hinda, the wife of Abu Sufian, approached the Holy Prophet complaining about her inadequate maintenance by Abu Sufian, when the Prophet allowed her husband so much as was sufficient to maintain her. From the absence of any reference to past maintenance, it is argued from this that the same stood forfeited. This argument is met by the other school of thought by a counter argument that since Hinda never claimed arrears of maintenance, as such, there was no occasion for the Holy Prophet to allow her a relief which was never prayed for. Another incident on which both sides seem to have relied in support of their respective views is that Caliph Umar wrote to his army officers in distant countries that the Muslim soldiers who were away from their wives should be ordered either to pay maintenance to their wives or divorce them. It was further directed that in the event of divorce they should also remit arrears of past maintenance. It is not disputed that no exception was taken to this directive of Caliph Umar. The argument of the Hanifites is that the payment of arrears was ordered only in case of divorce and not otherwise. On the contrary it is argued by the other schools of thought that this direction of Caliph Umar amounts to a clear dictum in favour of the validity of past maintenance and only in the event of divorce was it insisted that it should be sent along with the divorce, and as such, it does not necessarily mean that it stands forfeited if the wife is not divorced. Further support is lent to the latter view from the fact that the competency of the Kazee to grant maintenance for the past has also been admitted by the Hanafi school of thought as is clear from the following Heading of the excerpt from Hamilton's Hedaya quoted earlier which reads:

"<u>Arrears of maintenance not due unless have been decreed by the Kazee or.....</u>"

Thus the competency of the Courts of today which have stamped into the shoes of the Kazees for the purposes of adjudication

of these matters flows as a necessary corollary therefrom.
The mere fact that a neglected wife has been hesitant in
promptly coming to the Court or has been pursuing alternative
remedies out of Court cannot in all fairness be so construed
as to deprive her of the right of maintenance from the day
when the cause of action accrued to her. The Courts have thus
the jurisdiction to grant such maintenance subject of course
to considerations of limitation and the relevant circumstances
of each case, and we hold accordingly.

13. Even if a different view may be taken from this, and
the period intervening between the time of the accrual of the
cause of action and of filing the suit is excluded there can
be no difference of opinion on the grant of maintenance to a
neglected wife from the date she files an application in
Court. This position is not inconsistent with the one taken
by the Division Bench authority I L R 6 Cal. 631 based on
Baillie's Hedaya, and the apparent inconsistency if any is
capable of being easily reconciled. In the earlier days when
Kazees used to adjudicate upon the rights of the litigants and
performed the same functions which the Courts are now called
upon to perform today, a complainant could get expeditious
relief without loss of time, and it was inconceivable that a
petition could linger on for months and years, as it often
happened in civil litigation of this kind in this country
particularly before the promulgation of the Muslim Family Laws
Ordinance. Thus in those days there was no intervening period
between the date of the filing of the suit and the date of
passing of the decree, and the gap if any would be negligibly
small. That promptitude is certainly very difficult, if not
impossible to achieve in the complicated legal system and
complex social set up of a much more sophisticated society of
today where the Courts have found it difficult to cope with
the ever-increasing volume or mutifarious litigation.

14. In the instant case, maintenance was allowed to
respondent No. 1 from 15th July 1961, i.e., the date of the
promulgation of the Muslim Family Laws Ordinance. It was
argued by the learned counsel for the petitioner that by that
time, even the relevant rules relating to the constitution of
the Arbitration Council and procedure to be followed by it had
not yet been framed, which came into existence only on the
20th of July 1961, and as such, the order could not be
maintained. Having held in favour of the competency of the
Court to grant arrears of maintenance we see no force in this
contention, as once the respondent is found entitled to
maintenance and it is established that the cause of action
accrued to her before the promulgation of the Muslim Family
Laws Ordinance, we see nothing wrong with the impugned order
granting her arrears with effect from the date of the
promulgation irrespective of the fact that the rules were
framed sometime later. In these circumstances, the right
would accrue to the respondent from the 15th of July 1961,

i.e. the date of the promulgation of the Ordinance, as retrospectivity of the rules of procedure could be inferred from that date. The relevant date in fact, is the date of enforcement and not the date on which the Rules were framed, if it had been the intention of the Legislature to make the Ordinance operative with effect from the date of framing of Rules it would have clearly said so. In the absence of such a provision, the retrospectivity of the Rules from the date of enforcement of the Ordinance can be safely presumed.

15. The next point, which is the last contention raised by the learned counsel for the petitioner, has obviously lot of force in it, and we are straightway inclined to concede that position. Muslim Family Laws Ordinance contains no provisions for the maintenance of children unlike the one contained in section 488, Cr. P. C. Section 9 in the relevant section which only deals with the maintenance of neglected wives. This does not appear to us to be an ommission on the part of the law-giver, as the remedy provided in section 9 is made available in addition to the one already in existence under section 488 of the Cr. P. C. Since the respondent invoked section 9 of the Muslim Family Laws Ordinance, she had obviously no right to any maintenance allowance for her minor daughter. As the stipulated allowance at the rate of Rs. 70 per mensem was fixed by the Arbitration Council for both the respondent as well as her daughter, it cannot be sustained under the law, and as such a patent illegality cannot be allowed to be perpetuated merely because the order was challenged in revision beyond limitation.

13. For the foregoing reasons, we accept the petition, quash the impugned orders and remand the case to the Arbitration Council concerned for deciding afresh according to law the allowance which should be paid to the Respondent's wife. The parties are left to bear their own costs.

RASHID AHMAD KHAN (appellant) v. NASIM ARA (respondent)
P.L.D. 1968 Lah. 94. (Sajjad Ahmad, J.)

Judgement.....2. Two points have been urged before us in this petition:
> (1) that the Arbitration Council had no jurisdiction to award arrears of past maintenance; and
> (2) that the representative of the respondent on the Council, namely, her father Ghulam Mustafa Khan had disqualified himself to remain on the council after having become a witness for the respondent and giving evidence in her favour.

3. The first point was considered lately in a Division Bench case of Sardar Muhammad v. Mst. Nasima Bibi (P L D 1966 Lah. 703), decided in writ jurisdiction. One of the questions canvassed in the precedent case was whether the Chairman of

197

the Union Committee had the competency to grant arrears of
past maintenance in proceedings under section 9 of the
Ordinance. The parties in that case were married on the 24th
of May 1957. The respondent-wife was allowed maintenance
allowance at the rate of Rs. 70.00 per mensem for the future
and Rs. 718.00 in lumpsum as arrears in maintenance from 15th
of July 1961, which was the date of the enforcement of the
Ordinance to the 23rd of May 1962, which was the date of the
disposal of the wife's petition. She had filed her
application to the Chairman, Union Committee, on the 7th of
February 1962. It was held in this case that the husband's
obligation to maintain his wife commences simultaneously with
the performance of marriage and being an obligation and not an
ex gratia grant by way of gratuity, it is enforceable even
with respect to the past period of marital life, although it
was not promptly claimed during that period by the wife,
subject to considerations of limitation and the circumstances
of the case itself. We find ourselves in respectful agreement
with the decision cited above, and we see nothing in section 9
of the Ordinance to confine its application only to the grant
of future maintenance not covering the past. Section 9
authorises the issuance of a certificate by the Arbitration
Council, specifying the amount which shall be paid as
maintenance by the husband on his failure to maintain his wife
adequately or equitably with his co-wife, if there is one, or
co-wives, if there are more, on the determination of that
matter when raised before the Council by the neglected wife or
wives. The Ordinance was passed to give effect to certain
recommendations of the Commission that had been set up on
marriage and family laws which provided for some conciliatory
and easy modes for ending unhappy wedlocks and for ensuring
speedy reliefs to the neglected wives against the delinquent
husbands. The action for past maintenance being maintainable
on the part of a wife, subject to limitation and subject to
the claim being otherwise enforceable in a Court of law, and
there being no prohibition for its decision by the Arbitration
Council under the Ordinance as a supplementary agency to the
ordinary forums already existing under the law, it would seem
to be against the intention of the law-giver to hold that the
Arbitration Councils can issue certificates under section 9
only in regard to future maintenance, without having the
powers to do the same in respect of the arrears of past
maintenance. One can imagine a case where a wife may have
hopefully waited for payment to her of her maintenance by the
husband who may have been prevaricating to meet the claim
without expressly denying it and when the wife finally brings
an action under the Ordinance before the Arbitration Council
it would seem unfair to deny to the wife her claim for past
maintenance on the ground that she had not promptly come to
ask for it owing to the false promises held out by the
husband. We are, therefore, unable to find anything in
198

section 9 to draw a line for dividing the jurisdiction of the Arbitration Council for grant of the maintenance between past and future periods.

4. As for the second point, the argument that the father of the respondent was disqualified to remain on the Arbitration Council to deliberate in the final adjudication because of his having made a statement as a witness for the respondent is the tenor and spirit of the Ordinance in regard to the setting up of the Arbitration Councils. "Arbitration Council" is defined in section 2(a) of the Ordinance as a body consisting of the Chairman of the Union Council and a representative of each of the parties to a matter dealt with in the Ordinance. The very constitution of the Arbitration Council under this definition indicates that it is to have one representative or spokesman of either of the parties to a matter before the Arbitration Council and the Chairman has to act as the Umpire. As a representative within the contemplation of the Ordinance he has to be the spokesman of the party represented by him and one can understand that the Ordinance fully recognized that the representative must needs identify himself fully with the cause of the party he represents. The representative walks into the shoes of the party itself and it would be within his normal functions as a representative to make a statement on behalf of his principal. The fact that he makes the statement on oath or otherwise, as a witness or in any other capacity, favouring his party would not, in any manner, effect his capacity to sit on the Arbitration Council and to arbitrate in the matter, his position in the Council being that of a representative of his party throughout although he has to act also as an arbitrator. It is easily understandable that as a representative of one party he cannot be expected to speak for the other party at any stage of the proceedings, and in conceding to him the status of a member of the Arbitration Council, the Ordinance must be deemed to have taken into account his dual capacity as a representative and as a member of the Arbitration Council. We are, therefore, of the opinion that Ghulam Mustafa Khan was not disqualified to remain on the Arbitration Council as its member by the fact that he had made a statement in favour of the respondent which does not, in any way, impair the constitution of the Arbitration Council, nor the decision that has been given by it in favour of the respondent. We dismiss the petition with costs.

BAI TAHIRA (appellant) v. ALI HUSSAIN FISSALLI (respondent)
A.I.R. 1979 S.C. 362. (Supreme Court)

Judgement.....
A Prefatory Statement:
KRISHNA IYER, J.:- In this appeal, by special leave, we

are called upon to interpret a benign provision enacted to ameliorate the economic condition of neglected wives and discarded divorcees, namely S.125, Cr. P. C. Welfare laws must be so read as to be effective delivery systems of the salutary objects sought to be served by the Legislature and when the beneficiaries are the weaker sections, like destitute women, the spirit of Art. 15 (3) of the Constitution must belight the meaning of the Section. The Constitution is a pervasive omnipresence brooding over the meaning and transforming the values of every measure. So S.125 and sister clauses must receive a compassionate expansion of sense that the words used permit.

The Brief Facts:

2. The respondent (husband) married the appellant (wife) as a second wife, way back in 1956, and a few years later had a son by her. The initial warmth vanished and the jealousies of a triangular situation erupted, marring mutual affection. The respondent divorced the appellant around July 1962. A suit relating to a flat in which the husband had housed the wife resulted in a consent decree which also settled the marital disputes. For instance, it recited that the respondent had transferred the suit premises, namely, a flat in Bombay, to the appellant and also the shares of the Co-operative Housing Society which built the flat concerned. There was a reference to mehar money (Rs. 5,000/- and ´iddat´ money, Rs. 180) which was also stated to have been adjusted by the compromise terms. There was a clause in the compromise:

> "The plaintiff declares that she has now no claim or
> right whatsoever against the defendant or against the
> estate and the properties of the defendant."

And another term in the settlement was that the appellant had by virtue of the compromise become the absolute owner of the flat and various deposits in respect of the said flat made with the co-operative housing society.

3. For some time there was flickering improvement in the relations between the quondam husband and the quondam wife and they lived together. Thereafter, again they separated, became estranged. The appellant, finding herself in financial straits and unable to maintain herself, moved the Magistrate under S. 125 of the Criminal Procedure Code, 1973, for a monthly allowance for the maintenance of herself and her child. She proceeded on the footing that she was still a wife while the respondent rejected this status and asserted that she was a divorcee and therefore ineligible for maintenance. The Magistrate, who tried the petition for maintenance, held that the appellant was a subsisting wife and awarded monthly maintenance of Rs. 300/- for the son and Rs. 400/- for the mother for their subsistence, taking due note of the fact that the cost of living in Bombay, where the parties lived, was high, and that the respondent had provided residential

accommodation to the appellant.

4. This order was challenged before the Sessions Judge by the aggrieved husband, who on a strange view of the law that the court, under S. 125, had no jurisdiction to consider whether the applicant was a wife, dismissed the petition in allowance of the appeal. The High Court deigned to bestow little attention on the matter and summarily dismissed a revision petition. This protracted and fluctuating litigation misfortune has led to the appeal, by special leave, before this Court.

The Questions Mooted:

5. Shri Bhandare, appearing for the appellant, contended that the Courts below had surprisingly forgotten the plain provision in the Explanation (b) to Section 125 (1) of the Code which reads:

> "wife" includes a woman who has been divorced by, or has obtained a divorce from, her husband and has not remarried.

On this foundation, he urged that accepting the contention of the respondent that the appellant was a divorcee, his client was still entitled to an allowance. This is obviously beyond dispute on a simple reading of the sub-section and it is curious how this innovative and sensitive provision with a benignant disposition towards destitute divorcees has been overlooked by all the courts below. We hold that every divorcee, otherwise eligible, is entitled to the benefit of maintenance allowance and the dissolution of the marriage makes no difference to this right under the current Code. In the normal course, an order for maintenance must follow, the quantum having been determined by the learned Magistrate at the trial level.

6. However, Shri Sanghi, appearing for the respondent, sought to sustain the order in his favour on three grounds. They are of public importance since the affected party in such a fact-situation is the neglected divorcee. He first argued that S. 125 (4) would apply in the absence of proof that the lady was not living separately by mutual consent. His next plea was that there must be proof of neglect to maintain to attract S. 125 and his third contention was that there was a settlement by consent decree in 1962, whereby the mehar money had been paid and all claims adjusted, and so no claim for maintenance could survive. The third contention is apparently based upon a contractual arrangement in the consent decree read with S. 127 (3) (b) which reads:

> "(b) the woman has been divorced by her husband and that she has received, whether before or after the date of the said order, the whole of the sum which under any customary or personal law applicable to the parties, was payable on such divorce, cancel such order –
>
> (i) in the case where such sum was paid before

such order, from the date on which such order was made,
(ii) in any other case, from the date of expiry of
the period, if any, for which maintenance has been
actually paid by the husband to the woman;"
We must state, however, that there was no specific plea, based
upon the latter provision set up anywhere in the courts below
or urged before us. But if one were to locate a legal ground
to raise the contention that the liability to pay maintenance
had ceased on account of the payment of mehar, it is S. 127
(3) of the Code. So we must deal with the dual sub-heads of
the third ground.

7. The meaning of meanings is derived from values in a
given society and its legal system. Art. 15 (3) has
compelling, compassionate relevance in the context of S. 125
and the benefit of doubt, if any, in statutory interpretation
belongs to the ill-used wife and the derelict divorcee. This
social perspective granted, the resolution of all the disputes
projected is easy. Surely, Parliament, in keeping with Art.
15 (3) and deliberate by design, made a special provision to
help women in distress cast away by divorce. Protection
against moral and material abandonment manifest in Art. 39 is
part of social and economic justice, specificated in Art. 38,
fulfilment of which is fundamental to the governance of the
country (Art. 37). From this coign of vantage we must view
the printed text of the particular Code.

8. Section 125 requires, as a sine qua non for its
application, neglect by husband or father. The Magistrate's
order proceeds on neglect to maintain; the Sessions Judge has
spoken nothing to the contrary; and the High Court has not
spoken at all. Moreover, the husband has not examined himself
to prove that he has been giving allowances to the divorced
wife. His case, on the contrary, is that she has forfeited
her claim because of divorce and the consent decree.
Obviously, he has no case of non-neglect. His plea is his
right to ignore. So the basic condition of neglect to
maintain is satisfied. In this generous jurisdiction, a
broader perception and appreciation of the facts and their
bearing must govern the verdict not chopping little logic or
tinkering with burden of proof.

9. The next submission is that the absence of mutual
consent to live separately must be made out if the hurdle of
S. 125 (4) is to be overcome. We see hardly any force in this
plea. The compulsive conclusion from a divorce by a husband
and his provision of a separate residence as evidenced by the
consent decree fills the bill. Do divorcees have to prove
mutual consent to live apart? Divorce painfully implies that
the husband orders her out of the conjugal home. If law has
nexus with life this argument is still-born.

10. The last defence, based on mehar payment, merits more
serious attention. The contractual limb of the contention
must easily fail. The consent decree of 1962 resolved all

disputes and settled all claims then available. But here is a new statutory right created as a projection of public policy by the Code of 1973, which could not have been in the contemplation of the parties when in 1962 they entered into a contract to adjust their then mutual rights. No settlement of claims which does not have the special statutory right of the divorcee under S. 125 can operate to negate that claim.

11. Nor can S. 127 rescue the respondent from his obligation. Payment of mehar money, as a customary discharge, is within the cognisance of that provision. But what was the amount of mehar? Rs. 5000/-, interest from which could not keep the woman´s body and soul together for a day, even in that city where 40% of the population are reported to live on pavements, unless she was ready to sell her body and give up her soul! The point must be clearly understood that the scheme of the complex of provisions in Chap. IX has a social purpose. Ill-used wives and desparate divorcees shall not be driven to material and moral dereliction to seek sanctuary in the streets. This traumatic horror animates the amplitude of S. 127. Where the husband, by customary payment at the time of divorce, has adequately provided for the divorcee, a subsequent series of recurrent doles is contra-indicated and the husband liberated. This is the teleological interpretation, the sociological decoding of the text of S. 127. The key-note thought is adequacy of payment which will take reasonable care of her maintenance.

12. The payment of illusory amounts by way of customary or personal law requirement will be considered in the reduction of maintenance rate but cannot annihilate that rate unless it is a reasonable substitute. The legal sanctity of the payment is certified by the fulfilment of the social obligation, not by a ritual exercise rooted in custom. No construction which leads to frustration of the statutory project can secure validation if the court is to pay true homage to the Constitution. The only just construction of the section is that Parliament intended divorcees should not derive a double benefit. If the first payment by way of mehar or ordained by custom has a reasonable relation to the object and is a capitalised substitute for the order under S. 125 – not mathematically but fairly – then S. 127 (3) (b) subserves the goal and relieves the obligor, not pro tanto but wholly. The purose of the payment ´under any customary or personal law´ must be to obviate destitution of the divorcee and to provide her with wherewithal to maintain herself. The whole scheme of Section 127 (3) (b) is manifestly to recognise the substitute maintenance arrangement by lump sum payment organised by the custom of the community or the personal law of the parties. There must be a rational relation between the sum so paid and its potential as provision for maintenance: to interpret otherwise is to stultify the project. Law is dynamic and its meaning cannot be pedantic but purposeful.

The proposition, therefore, is that no husband can claim under Section 127 (3) (b) absolution from his obligation under S. 125 towards a divorced wife except on proof of payment of a sum stipulated by customary or personal law whose quantum is more or less sufficient to do duty for maintenance allowance.

13. The conclusion that we therefore reach is that the appeal should be allowed and it is hereby allowed and the order of the trial court restored.

GHULAM RASUL (petitioner) v. COLLECTOR, LAHORE
P.L.D. 1974. Lah 496 (Aftab Hussain, J.)

Judgement.....This petition under Article 201 of the Interim Constitution of the Islamic Republic of Pakistan (now Article 199 of the Constitution of the Islamic Republic of Pakistan, 1973) has been filed to seek a declaration that the order of the Chairman of the Union Committee assessing the arrears of maintenance as payable to respondent No. 2 by the petitioner and the order of the Collector dated 27-3-1973 upholding that order, are without lawful authority and that the order of the Union Committee dated 21-11-65 awarding maintenance to respondent No. 2 stands vacated by cohabitation by the petitioner and the said respondent.

2. The petitioner and respondent No. 2 are husband and wife. On an application made by respondent No. 2 to the Chairman, Union Committee, Sant Nagar Lahore, on 16-10-1965 for grant of maintenance, an order was passed in her favour by the Arbitration Council on 21-11-1965 holding her entitled to receive Rs. 200 p.m. as Maintenance and Rs. 100 p.m. on account of insurance policy. This order was passed on the basis of a compromise between the spouses. On 2-11-68 Mst. Khurshid Begum respondent submitted an application to the Chairman of the Union Committee complaining that only a sum of Rs. 400 was paid to her by the petitioner and requested for recovery of the arrears to be made from him. The Chairman, after calculation of the amount due, issued a recovery certificate for a sum of Rs. 10,100 for the period from 21-11-1965 to 21-10-1968.

3. The petitioner submitted an application to the Collector on 6-1-1969 against this order. The learned Collector provisionally stayed the recovery but subsequently on the application of respondent No. 2 vacated this stay order on the ground that the application was not maintainable under the law. The application was withdrawn by the petitioner on 17-2-1969. Thereafter he filed Writ Petition No. 126 of 1969 which was allowed on 23-11-1972 and the Collector was directed to give a decision after hearing the parties.

4. The case of the petitioner before the Collector was that after the order of the Arbitration Council, the husband and wife had started living together and this rendered the

204

decision of the Arbitration Council a nullity. The learned Collector did not agree with this contention. He held that the petitioner had not been able to give any proof to the effect that he had been maintaining respondent No. 2 adequately during the period in question. Respondent No. 2 had urged before the Collector that the birth of children during the period in dispute was the result of occasional visits of the husband to her house where she was forced to perform matrimonial obligations. The learned Collector appears to have held otherwise as he observed that "the fact that the respondent agreed to stay with the petitioner for years and also performed all matrimonial obligations is a proof to the fact that she was genuinely interested in being maintained by the husband as a wife." He also found that the order of payment of maintenance passed on 21-11-1965 was still operative as it had not been set aside by any competent authority.

The Collector has found it as a fact that there was no evidence before him that during the period in dispute the petitioner had been maintaining the wife adequately. This finding has not been challenged. Under the Order of 1965 the petitioner was liable to pay Rs. 100 towards insurance but there is no averment that this was ever paid by the petitioner to the respondent or the Insurance Company. For this reason the above orders are amply justified.

5. The learned counsel argued on the anology of certain decisions given on the interpretation of section 488 of the Code of Criminal Procedure that the order of the Arbitration Council became a nullity on the date when by compromise the parties started living together. He relied upon <u>Munswami Pillai v. Doraikannu Ammal</u> (A I R 1946 Mad. 222) and <u>Kuppuswami Padayachi v. Jagadambal</u> (A I R 1947 Mad. 423).

Alternatively the learned counsel argued that during the time that the parties had been living together the said order stood suspended.

6. The relevant case-law under section 488, Cr. P. C. has been summed up in a case decided by the West Pakistan High Court in <u>Muhammad Hussain v. Mst. Shakira Begum</u> (P L D 1963 Kar. 122). The Madras view is that where the wife comes and lives with the husband even for a few days, she cannot be allowed to rely on the original order of maintenance passed under section 488, Cr. P. C. or to execute that order against her husband. If she separates again from her husband, she must file another petition on a fresh cause of action. <u>Vankayya v. Raghavamma</u> (A I R 1942 Mad. 1), <u>Munuswami Pillai v. Dorakikannu Ammal</u> (A I R 1947 Mad. 222), <u>Kuppuswami Padayachi v. Jagadambal</u> (A I R 1947 Mad. 423), <u>S. Natesa Pillai v. Jayammal</u> (A I R 1960 Mad. 515). Similar view had been taken by the Rangoon High Court in <u>Ellen Ma Noo v. Villam Po Thit</u> (A I R 1931 Rang. 89). The High Courts of Bombay, Calcutta, Allahabad, Nagpur, Orissa, East Panjab have adopted

a contrary view that re-union and cohabitation between parties does not put an end to an earlier maintenance order. <u>Parul Bala Debi v. Statis Chandra Bhattacharjee</u> (A I R 1923 Cal. 456), <u>Laxman Gajiu v. Sitabai Laxman</u> (A I R 1958 Bom. 14), <u>Pearay Lal v. Mst. Naraini</u> (A I R 1935 All. 977), <u>John P.E. Coelho v. Mrs. Blache Coelho</u> (A I R 1936 Nag. 228), <u>Casinath Panda v. Padambati Debi</u> (A I R 1956 Orissa 199), <u>Mukand Singh v. Mst. Kartar Kaur</u> (A I R 1958 Pb. 422) and <u>Mst. Zauhra Bi v. Muhammad Yusuf</u> (A I R 1930 Lah. 1043). The consistent view of these High Courts, however, is that during the period of re-union the order may remain suspended but otherwise it remains in force till it is cancelled on the ground set out in section 488 (5), Cr. P. C. This was also the earlier Madras view in <u>Kanagammal v. Pandra Nadar</u> (A I R 1927 Mad. 376). In <u>Muhammad Hussain v. Mst. Shakira Begum</u> the West Pakistan High Court adopted the view of the majority of the High Courts in the sub-continent.

7. The view of the Lahore High Court has consistently been that an order under section 488, Cr. P. C. does not come to an end by re-union of the parties or even by a subsequent compromise. In <u>Fazal Din v. Mst. Fatima</u> (A I R 1932 Lah. 115) it was held that a subsequent compromise between the parties could have no effect on the order of payment of maintenance.

If this had been a case under section 488, Cr. P. C. I would have no hesitation in following the view of the majority of the High Courts. In this circumstance I would have found no difficulty in answering the question by holding that during the period of re-union the order of payment of maintenance remains suspended but it is revived after the separation of the parties.

8. All these cases under section 488, Cr. P. C. whether nullifying the order of maintenance or suspending it can somehow be justified on the language of that section. Section 488, Cr. P. C. provides that if any person having sufficient means neglects or refuses to maintain his wife, a Magistrate <u>inter alia</u> may on proof of such neglect or refusal order such person to make a monthly allowance for the maintenance of his wife which shall not exceed a sum of Rs. 400. Subsection (3) of this section provides that if any person so ordered fails without sufficient cause to comply with the order, any such Magistrate may, for every breach of the order issue a warrant for levying the amount due in manner hereinbefore provided for levying fines, and may sentence such person, for the whole or any part on each month's allowance remaining unpaid after the execution of the warrant, to imprisonment for a term which may extend to one month or until payment if sooner made. Proviso (1) to subsection (3) is to the effect that if such person offers to maintain his wife on condition of her living with him, and she refuses to live with him, such Magistrate may consider any grounds of refusal stated by her and may make an order under this section notwithstanding such offer. Proviso

(2) deals with the period of Limitation for application for issuance of a warrant for recovery. Subsection (4) provides that no wife, refusing to live with the husband without any sufficient cause or living in adultery, is entitled to receive any allowance. Under subsection (5) the Magistrate has been empowered to cancel the order if it is proved that the wife had been living in adultery or had refused to live with the husband without sufficient reasons. The wife is, therefore, entitled to maintenance only if she is not living with the husband and refuses to live with him for sufficient reasons. It can, therefore, be urged with force that if she ever starts living with the husband, the order for payment will at least remain in a state of suspension as during that period the wife would not be entitled to any maintenance under section 488, Cr. P. C.

9. The provisions of section 9 of the Muslim Family Laws Ordinance are, however, different. Under this section the wife is entitled to maintenance not only when she is not living with the husband but whenever it is proved that the husband fails to maintain her adequately or where there are more wives than one, fails to maintain the wife seeking maintenance, equitably.

The recovery is also not subject to the condition of failure to comply with the order of payment of maintenance without sufficient cause as has been seen in subsection (3) of section 488, Cr. P.C. Subsection (3) of section 9 of the Family Laws Ordinance provides that any amount payable under subsection (1) of section 2 if not paid in due time, shall be recoverable as arrears of land revenue. The authorities relied upon by the learned counsel for the petitioner or the other authorities about suspension of the order during the period of re-union between the spouses are not, therefore, applicable to a case falling under section 9 of the Family Laws Ordinance. According to this section complete neglect or failure on the part of the husband to maintain the wife is not necessary to be established to attract the provision of this section. Even if it is proved that the wife is being maintained by the husband but the Arbitration Council comes to the conclusion that there is failure to maintain a single wife adequately or in case there is a plurality of wives one of the wives equitably, although the husband and wife are living together, the order of payment of maintenance can be passed. The mere re-union, therefore, does not make any difference. The provision about recovery is couched in mandatory form. If it is once proved that the amount payable has not been paid it shall be recovered as arrears of land revenue. This leaves no doubt that the order of payment of maintenance is neither terminated nor suspended by any act of parties for so long as they remain husband and wife. I am of the view that the order of the Arbitration Council issuing the certificate of recovery and the order of Collector have not been passed without any

207

lawful authority.

10. The learned counsel for the petitioner lastly argued that the Chairman of the Union Committee had not given any show-cause notice before issuing this recovery certificate. This argument is not tenable in view of the decision in the earlier writ petition. This is a matter which could have been urged in that writ petition and it is for this reason that a form was provided to the petitioner to show cause against the order of recovery. I find no merit in this petition which is dismissed with costs.

SIRAJMOHMED KHAN (appellant) v. HAFIZUNNISSA YASINFHAN (respondent)
A I R 1981 S.C. 1972 (Supreme Court)

FAZAL ALI J.....3. So far as the facts found are concerned, there is no dispute and the case will have to be decided on the point of law that arises on the contentions raised by the parties before the courts below as also in this Court. Both the High Court and the Metropolitan Magistrate clearly found that the appellant was physically incapable of having sexual relations with the respondent......

.....5. Mr. Keshwani, learned counsel for the appellant, vehemently contended before us that it is now well settled by a long course of decisions of various High Courts that impotency is no good ground or reason for the wife to refuse to live with her husband and hence the wife is not entitled to maintenance if she refused to live with the husband merely because her husband was impotent. Mr. Keshwani cited a number of decisions in support of his contentions; on the other hand, Mr. Dave, appearing for the respondent, submitted that the various authorities of the High Courts seem to have overlooked the legal effect of the second proviso to sub-section (3) of Section 125 of the Code of 1973 under which a wife could refuse to live with her husband if there was a just ground for doing so. The said proviso may be extracted thus:-

"Provided further that if such person offers to maintain his wife on condition of her living with him, and she refuses to live with him, such Magistrate may consider any grounds of refusal stated by her, and may make an order under this section notwithstanding such offer, if he is satisfied that there is just ground for so doing."

6. We are of the opinion that if the husband was impotent and unable to discharge his marital obligations, how could he fulfil the main object of marriage, more particularly, under the Mahomedan law where marriage is a sacrosanct contract and not a purely religious ceremony as in the case of Hindu Law. This would certainly be a very just and reasonable ground on the part of the wife for refusing to live with her husband, as also in cases under the Hindu Law or

other Laws. In <u>Nanak Chand v. Chandra Kishore Agarwala</u>
((1970) 2 SCR 565) : (AIR 1970 SC 446 at p.448), this Court
held thus:

"Section 488 provides a summary remedy and is applicable
to all persons belonging to all religions and has no
relationship with the personal law of the parties."

7. After having heard counsel for the parties we are
clearly of the opinion that the contention of the counsel for
the respondent is sound and must prevail. It is true that
there are several decisions of the High Courts taking a
contrary view but they seem to have proceeded on a totally
wrong assumption and we are constrained to observe that in
taking such a narrow view they have followed a most outmoded
and antiquated approach. The learned Magistrate mainly relied
on a decision of the Allahabad High Court in <u>Bundoo's case</u>
(1978 Cri LJ 1661) (supra). It is true that Bakshi, J. in
that case seems to have been influenced more by the concept of
neglect rather than by the reasonableness of the ground on
which the refusal of the wife was based. While dwelling on
this aspect of the matter, the learned Judge observed as
follows (at p. 1663):-

"Assuming now for the purpose of argument that Bundoo
was physically incapable of satisfying the sexual desire
of his wife, it cannot be said that this inability
amounted intentionally to disregarding, slighting,
disrespecting or carelessly and heedlessly treating his
wife. In this view of the matter, I am of the opinion
that the element of neglect as envisaged under Section
488 Cr. P. C., old and under Section 125, Cr. P. C. new,
has not been established....."

8. The attention of the learned Judge does not seem to
have been drawn to the provisions of the second proviso nor
has the Judge come to any clear finding that the refusal of
the wife could not fall within the ambit of "just ground" as
contemplated by the aforesaid proviso. Secondly, the learned
Judge mainly relied on an earlier decision of Hidayatullah, J.
(as he then was) in <u>Emperor v. Daulat Raibhan</u> (AIR 1948 Nag
69), in which it was held that a wife was not entitled to live
apart from her husband and claim maintenance on the ground
that her husband was impotent and unable to perform his
marital obligations. In fact, a number of decisions of the
High Courts which were relied upon by the counsel for the
appellant follow the decision of the Nagpur High Court as also
the previous decisions of other High Courts relied upon by
Hidayatullah, J. in the Nagpur case. We shall consider the
legal effect of this decision a little later. So far as the
decision of the Allahabad High Court, on which the Magistrate
had relied, is concerned, the observations of Bakshi J. were
purely obiter. It would appear that there was a clear finding
of fact by the Magistrate, which had been accepted by the High
Court, that the wife failed to prove by convincing evidence

that her husband was impotent. In view of this finding of fact, the question of law posed and decided by Bakshi, J. did not fall for decision at all because if the wife failed to prove that her husband was impotent, the question of her refusal to live with him for a just ground did not arise at all. While adverting to this finding of fact, Bakshi, J. in the aforesaid case (1978 Cri LJ 1661 at p. 1662), observed as follows:-

> "I find from the perusal of judgment of the Magistrate that he has taken into consideration the entire evidence on the record led in connection with this question and he was of the opinion that <u>Smt. Mahrul Nisa failed to prove by convincing evidence that Bundoo was impotent."</u> (Emphasis supplied).

9. In the circumstances, we are not in a position to accept the observations of Bakshi, J. which are in the nature of obiter dictum, in support of the argument of Mr. Keshwani.

10. This brings us now to the consideration of the authorities of other High Courts which seem to have taken the view that impotency is no ground for grant of maintenance to the wife. We would first deal with the decision of Hidayatullah, J. in <u>Daulat Raibhan's case</u> (AIR 1948 Nag 69) (supra). In the first place, the learned Judge thought that the point raised before him was one of first impression and his decision was, therefore, greatly influenced by the fact that there was no direct decision on the point taking a contrary view. In this connection, the learned Judge observed as follows:-

> "No authority has been cited before me in support of the case of the wife that she is entitled to live separate from her husband on account of his impotence."

11. Subsequently, the learned Judge mainly relied on the following observations made in <u>Arunachala v. Anandaymmal</u> (AIR 1933 Nag 688 (1)):

> "I cannot see that Section 488, Criminal P. C. has anything to do with ordinary conjugal rights, it deals with ´maintenance´ only....."

12. The learned Judge seems to have been under the impression that so far as the provisions of Section 488 of the Code of 1898 were concerned they had no bearing on conjugal relations between the husband and the wife. With great respect to the learned Judge we are unable to agree with this process of reasoning. In fact, the fundamental basis of the ground of maintenance under S. 488 is conjugal relationship and once conjugal relationship is divorced from the ambit of this special provision, then the very purpose and setting of the statutory provision vanishes. In the Matter of the Petition of Din Muhammad (1883) ILR 5 All 226, Mahmood, J. very pithily and pointedly observed as follows:-

> "The whole of Chapter XLI, Criminal Procedure Code, so far as it relates to the maintenance of wives,

contemplates the existence of the conjugal relation as a condition precedent to an order of maintenance <u>and, on general principles, it follows that as soon as the conjugal relation ceases, the order of maintenance must also cease to have any enforceable effect</u>." (Emphasis supplied).

13. We find ourselves in complete agreement with the observations made by the eminent Jurist Mahmood, J. which lays down the correct law on the subject. Thus, one of the fundamental premises on which rested the decision of Hidayatullah, J. appears to us to be clearly wrong and directly opposed to the very object of the section (which at the relevant time was Section 488). In <u>Arunachala´s case</u> (AIR 1933 Mad 688 (1)) (supra), which was relied upon by Hidayatullah, J., Burn, J. observed thus:

"I cannot see that Section 488, Criminal P. C. has anything to do with ordinary conjugal rights; it deals with "maintenance" only and I see no reason why maintenance should be supposed to include anything more than appropriate food, clothing and lodging."

14. It would be seen that here also the learned Judge proceeds on a legally wrong premise, viz., that Section 488 had nothing to do with ordinary conjugal rights. Moreover, the Madras decision as also the earlier decision seem to have followed the outmoded and antiquated view that the object of Section 488 was to provide an effective and summary remedy to provide for appropriate food, clothing and lodging for a wife. This concept has now become completely outdated and absolutely archaic. After the International Year of Women when all the important countries of the world are trying to give the fair sex their rightful place in society and are working for the complete emancipation of women by breaking the old shackles and bondage in which they were involved, it is difficult to accept a contention that the salutary provisions of the Code are merely meant to provide a wife merely with food, clothing and lodging as if she is only a chattel and has to depend on the sweet will and mercy of the husband. The same line of reasoning was adopted in an earlier decision of the Madras High Court in <u>Jaggavarapu Basawamma v. Jaggavarapu Seeta Reddi</u> (AIR 1922 Mad 209). Here also, the Judge was of the opinion that food and clothing was sufficient for the maintenance of the wife and even if the husband refused to cohabit that would not provide any cause of action to the wife to claim separate maintenance. In a recent decision in <u>Velayudhan v. Sukmari</u> (1971 Ker LT 443), a single Judge observed as follows:-

"Learned magistrate seems to have concentrated solely on the last-mentioned ground namely, failure of the husband to perform his marital duties, and has held that it is a sufficient ground entitling the wife to live away from the husband, and claim separate maintenance. But I do not think, in the face of authorities cited before me

211

that this is a sufficient ground justifying the award of separate maintenance to the wife. It was observed by Kumaraswami Sastri, J. in <u>Basawamma v. Seetareddi</u> (AIR 1922 Mad 209), that there is nothing in the Code which compels the criminal Court to award separate maintenance to a wife whom the husband agrees to protect and maintain in a manner suitable to her position in life; refusal to cohabit is no ground."

15. Here also, the Judge while noticing that the ground taken by the wife was that the husband has failed to perform his marital duties, found himself bound by the decisions of the Madras High Court in <u>Jaggavarapu Basawamma's case</u> (AIR 1922 Mad 209) (supra). Thus even in this decision though given in 1971 when the entire horizen of the position and status of women had changed, it is rather unfortunate that the Judge chose to stick to the old view.

16. There is however a very formidable circumstance which seems to have been completely overlooked by later decisions while following the previous decisions of the Nagpur or the Madras High Court. Although the second proviso to sub-section (3) of Section 125 of the Code of 1973, which was also a proviso to the old Section 488, clearly provided that it is incumbent on the Magistrate to consider the grounds of refusal and to make an order of maintenance if he was satisfied that there was <u>just ground</u> for refusing to live with the husband, yet this salutary provision which was introduced with the clear object of arming the wife with a cause of action for refusing to live with the husband as the one which we have in the present case, no legal effect to the legislative will and intent appears to have been given by the aforesaid decisions.

17. Another important event which happened in 1949 also seems to have been completely ignored by the recent decisions while following the previous decisions of the High Courts. It would appear that by the Code of Criminal Procedure (Amendment) Act No. 9 of 1949 an additional provision was added after the proviso which may be extracted thus:-

"If a husband has contracted marriage with another wife or keeps a mistress it shall be considered to be just ground for his wife's refusal to live with him."

18. The object of introducing this provision was clearly to widen the scope and ambit of the term 'just ground' mentioned in the proviso. This provision is not exhaustive but purely illustrative and self-explanatory and takes within its fold not only the two instances mentioned therein but other circumstances also of a like or similar nature which may be regarded by the Magistrate as a just ground by the wife for refusing to live with her husband under the Code of 1973. This provision has been incorporated as Explanation to the second proviso to sub-section (3) of Section 125.

19. The decisions of the High Courts given prior to the Amendment of 1949 would no longer be good law after the

introduction of the Amendment which gives, as it were, a completely new complexion to the intendment and colour of the second proviso to Section 488 (now Explanation to the second proviso to sub-section (3) of S. 125) and widens its horizon. It is, therefore, needless to refer to these decisions or to subsequent decisions which have followed the previous cases.

20. A clear perusal of this provision manifestly shows that it was meant to give a clear instance of circumstances which may be treated as a just ground for refusal of the wife to live with her husband. As already indicated by virtue of this provision, the proviso takes within its sweep all other circumstances similar to the contingencies contemplated in the Amending Provision as also other instances of physical, mental or legal cruelty not excluding the impotence of the husband. These circumstances, therefore, clearly show that the grounds on which the wife refuses to live with her husband should be just and reasonable as contemplated by the proviso. Similarly, where the wife has a reasonable apprehension arising from the conduct of the husband that she is likely to be physically harmed due to persistent demands of dowry from her husband's parents or relations, such apprehension also would be manifestly a reasonable justification for the wife's refusal to live with her husband. Instances of this nature may be multiplied but we have mentioned some of the circumstances to show the real scope and ambit of the proviso and the Amending provision which is, as already indicated, by no means exhaustive.

21. In other words, where a husband contracts a marriage with another woman or keeps a mistress this would be deemed to be a just ground within the meaning of the second proviso so as to make the refusal of the wife to live with her husband fully justified and entitled to maintenance. If this is so, can it be said by any stretch of imagination that where a wife refuses to live with her husband if he is impotent and unable to discharge his marital obligation, this would not be a just ground for refusing to live with her husband when it seems to us that the ground of impotence which had been held by a number of authorities under the civil law to be a good ground not only for restitution of conjugal rights but also for divorce? Indeed, if this could be a ground for divorce or for an action for restitution of conjugal rights, could it be said with any show of force that it would not be a just ground for the wife to refuse to live with her husband? The matter deserves serious attention from the point of view of the wife. Here is a wife who is forced or compelled to live a life of celibacy while staying with her husband who is unable to have sexual relationship with her. Such a life is one of perpetual torture which is not only mentally or psychologically injurious but even from the medical point of view is detrimental to the health of the woman. Surely, the concept of mental cruelty cannot be different in a civil case and in a

213

criminal case when the attributes of such a cruelty are the same.

22. In <u>Rita Nijhawan v. Balkishan Nijhawan</u> (AIR 1973 Delhi 200) (Sachar, J.) while dealing with a case of annulment of marriage under the Hindu Marriage Act on the grounds of impotency very poignantly and pithily observed as follows (at p. 209):-

> "Thus the law is well settled that if either of the parties to a marriage being (of) a healthy physical capacity refuses to have sexual intercourse the same would amount to cruelty entitling the other party to a decree. In our opinion it would not make any difference in law whether denial of sexual intercourse is the result of sexual weakness of the respondent disabling him from having a sexual union with the appellant, or it is because of any wilful refusal by the respondent.
>
> ...   .
>
> Marriage without sex is an anathema. Sex is the foundation of marriage and without a vigorous and harmonious sexual activity it would be impossible for any marriage to continue for long. It cannot be denied that the sexual activity in marriage has an extremely favourable influence on a woman´s mind and body. The result being that if she does not get proper sexual satisfaction, it will lead to depression and frustration."

23. We find ourselves in complete agreement with the very practical and pragmatic view that the learned Judge has taken and the principles adumbrated by the Judge apply fully to proceedings for maintenance because as we have said the concept of cruelty is the same whether it is a criminal case or a civil case.

24. As far back as 1906, the Bombay High Court came out with the concept of cruelty which could be considered for exercising jurisdiction under S. 488 of the Code of 1898. In <u>Bhikaji Maneckji v. Maneckji Mancherji</u> ((1907) 5 Cri LJ 334) a Division Bench of the Bombay High Court observed as follows:-

> "Where it is proved that a husband has not <u>refused</u> or neglected to <u>maintain</u> his wife, a criminal Court, acting under the section, has no jurisdiction to make an order upon the husband for her maintenance on the ground that the husband has been guilty of cruelty to her. But that is a very different thing from holding that no evidence of cruelty can be admitted in a proceeding under the section to prove, not indeed cruelty as a ground for separate maintenance, but the conduct and acts of the husband from which the Court may draw the inference of neglect or refusal to maintain the wife. A neglect or refusal by the husband to maintain his wife may be by words or by conduct. It may be express or implied. If there is evidence of cruelty on the part of the husband

214

towards the wife from which, with other evidence as to surrounding circumstances, the Court can presume neglect or refusal, we do not see why it should be excluded. There is nothing in S. 488 to warrant its exclusion, and such has been the practice of this Court..... But the section has been altered and now the Court can pass an order for maintenance where neglect or refusal is proved, even if the husband is willing to maintain the wife, provided the Court finds that there are "just grounds for" passing such an order. The alteration gives a wider discretion to the Court, which means that in passing such an order it is legitimate for it to take into account the relations between the husband and the wife, and the husband´s conduct towards her."

25. This decision, given as far back as 1907, while construing the proviso appears to be both prophetic and pragmatic in its approach and it is rather unfortunate that subsequent decisions have not noticed this important principle of law decided by the Bombay High Court. We fully endorse this decision as laying down the correct law on the subject and as giving the correct interpretation of the proviso to Section 488 particularly the concept of the words ´just ground´.

26. Another decision which had touched the question of ´cruelty´ is the case of <u>Bai Appibai v. Khimji Cooverji</u> (AIR 1936 Bom 138) where the following observations were made:

"If, however, the husband by reason of his misconduct, or cruelty in the sense in which that term is used by the English Matrimonial Courts, or by his refusal to maintain her, or for any other justifying cause, makes it compulsory or necessary for her to live apart from him, he must be deemed to have deserted her, and she will be entitled to separate maintenance and residence."

27. In <u>Gunni v. Babu Lal</u> (AIR 1952 Madh Bha 131), Dixit, J. sounded a very pragmatic note on this aspect of the matter and in this connection pointing out the scope of the Amendment of 1949 observed thus (at pp. 132, 133):

"There is nothing in the Criminal Procedure (Amendment) Act, 1949 to show that it would not be a just ground for the wife´s refusal to live with her husband if the husband has contracted marriage with another wife or taken a mistress before the amendment made in S. 488..... The amendment is clearly intended to put an end to an unsatisfactory state of law, utterly inconsistent with the progressive ideas of the status and emancipation of women, in which women were subjected to a mental cruelty of living with a husband who had taken a second wife or a mistress on the pain of being deprived of any maintenance if they chose to live separately from such a husband. In my view to hold that the amendment is intended to afford a just ground for

215

the wife's refusal to live with her husband only in
those cases where he has after the amendment, taken a
second wife or a mistress is to defeat in a large
measure the very object of the amendment."

28. We find ourselves in complete agreement with the
observations made by the learned Judge. In Mst. Biro v.
Behari Lal (AIR 1958 J & K 47), a decision to which one of us
(Fazal Ali, J. as he then was) was a party, where the
importance of the Amendment of 1949 was also touched, the
following observations were made (at p. 49):-

"Before the amendment, the fact of the husband's
marrying a second wife or keeping a mistress was not by
some High Courts considered a just ground for the first
wife's refusal to live with him, although it was taken
into account in considering whether the husband's offer
to maintain his first wife was really 'bona fide' or
not.

The amendment is clearly intended to put an end to an
unsatisfactory state of law utterly inconsistent with
the progressive ideas of the status and emancipation of
women, in which women were subjected to a mental cruelty
of living with a husband who had taken a second wife or
a mistress on the pain of being deprived of any
maintenance if they chose to live separately from such a
husband."

29. In Sm. Pancho v. Ram Prasad (AIR 1956 All 41), Roy,
J. while dealing with the Hindu Married Women's Right to
Separate Residence and Maintenance Act (19 of 1946) expounded
the concept of 'legal cruelty' and observed thus (at pp. 42,
43):-

"In advancement of a remedial statute, everything is to
be done that can be done consistently with a proper
construction of it, even though it may be necessary to
extend enacting words beyond their natural import and
effect.

...   .

Conception of legal cruelty undergoes changes according
to the changes and advancement of social concept and
standards of living. With the advancement of our social
conceptions, this feature has obtained legislative
recognition that a second marriage is a sufficient
ground for separate residence and separate maintenance.
Moreover, to establish legal cruelty, it is not
necessary that physical violence should be used.
Continuous ill-treatment, cessation of marital
intercourse, studied neglect, indifference on the part
of the husband, and an assertion on the part of the
husband that the wife is unchaste are all factors which
may undermine the health of a wife."

30. The learned Judge has put his finger on the correct
aspect and object of mental cruelty. The fact that this case

did not arise out of the proceedings under S. 125 makes no difference because we have already observed that the concept of cruelty remains the same whether it is a civil case or a criminal case or a case under any other similar Act. The general principles governing acts constituting cruelty - legal or mental - ill-treatment or indifference cannot vary from case to case though the facts may be different.

31. Similarly, while dealing with a case under the Hindu Marriage Act, 1955, a Division Bench of the Karnataka High Court in Dr. Srikant Rangacharya Adya v. Smt. Anuradha (AIR 1980 Kant 8) dwelling on the aspect of impotency and its impact on the wife observed as follows (at p. 13):-

"In these days it would be an unthinkable proposition to suggest that the wife is not an active participant in the sexual life and therefore, the sexual weakness of the husband which denied normal sexual pleasure to the wife is of no consequence and therefore cannot amount to cruelty. Marriage without sex is an anathema. Sex is the foundation of marriage and without a vigorous and harmonious sexual activity it would be impossible for any marriage to continue for long. It cannot be denied that the sexual activity in marriage has an extremely favourable influence on a woman's mind and body. The result being that if she does not get proper sexual satisfaction it will lead to depression and frustration. It has been said that the sexual relations when happy and harmonious vivifies woman's brain, develops her character and trebles her vitality. It must be recognised that nothing is more fatal to marriage than disappointments in sexual intercourse."

32. We find ourselves in entire agreement with the observations made by the learned Judges of the Karnataka High Court which seem to be the correct position in law. Even the learned Judge who had delivered the judgment in the instant case had very rightly pointed out as follows:-

"If the maintenance of a wife is supposed to include only food, shelter and clothing having regard to the conjugal rights and if the just cause on which wife can refuse to stay with the husband and yet claim maintenance, can have reference only to the comfort and safe (safety?) of the wife then it might reduce the wife to the status of a domesticated animal.

In the context of the changing status of women in society such a proposition would seem outdated and obsolete..... In other words, the Court cannot compel the wife to stay with the husband on the ground that the husband though he is forcing her in a situation where her physical and mental well being might be adversely affected, as there is no intention on the part of the husband to inflict that cruelty, she should suffer that predicament without demur and be satisfied with a grab to bite and some rags to clothe her and a roof over her head."

33. We fully endorse the observations made above. Apart from the various decisions referred to above, there is a direct English decision on the point. In <u>Sheldon v. Sheldon</u> ((1966) 2 All ER 257) Lord Denning observed as follows:-

"I rest my judgment on the ground that he has persistently, without the least excuse, refused her sexual intercourse for six years. It has broken down her health. I do not think that she was called on to endure it any longer.

It has been said that, if abstinence from intercourse causing ill-health can be held to be cruelty, so should desertion simpliciter leading to the same result."

34. Thus, from a conspectus of the various authorities discussed above and the setting, object and interpretation of the second proviso to sub-section (3) of S. 125 of the Code of 1973, we find ourselves in complete agreement with the view taken by the learned Judge of the High Court. We hold that where it is proved to the satisfaction of the court that a husband is impotent and is unable to discharge his marital obligations, this would amount to both legal and mental cruelty which would undoubtedly be a just ground as contemplated by the aforesaid proviso for the wife's refusal to live with her husband and the wife would be entitled to maintenance from her husband according to his means. In these circumstances, therefore, it would be pusillanimous to ignore such a valuable safeguard which has been provided by the legislature to a neglected wife.

35. For these reasons, therefore, we find no merit in the appeal which fails and we accordingly dismiss the same without any order as to costs.

36. In view of our decision in this case, it follows that the decisions referred to above in the judgment taking a contrary view must be held to be no longer good law and are hereby overruled.

Chapter Four

DISSOLUTION OF MARRIAGE

<u>Death</u>

The death of either spouse terminates the marriage. A widower may remarry at once but a widow must observe <u>idda</u>, a period of waiting, before remarriage, the principal purpose of this being to assist in the determination of paternity of any children born to her. Any deferred dower becomes payable as has already been considered, but no maintenance is payable to the widow even if she is pregnant at the time of her husband's death: the Qur'anic verse which purported to grant her maintenance for one year was deemed by the jurists to have been superseded by the provision for her of a share in her husband's estate, which might in practical terms be greatly enhanced by her deferred dower. The duration of <u>idda</u> after the husband's death varies with the circumstances but must be observed irrespective of whether consummation took place. Normally it lasts for four months and ten days but if the widow was pregnant at the time of the husband's death it will endure until the birth of the child. After the death of a husband to a <u>fasid</u> marriage the period is just three menstrual cycles.

In the matter of presumed death the classical law and statute diverge. In classical Hanafi law a missing person is deemed to be dead for these purposes only after an extraordinarily long period, when he would have attained 90 years of age, unless he went missing when seriously ill or when in battle or similar dangerous circumstances. Because of the hardship which might be occasioned to a wife by this rule Hanafi doctrine permitted her to have recourse to a Maliki or Hanbali Qadi, who in accordance with the law of those schools may declare someone dead who has been missing for four years after the matter was brought to their attention and a fruitless search made, and, according to the majority view, dissolve the marriage.

In India and Pakistan two statutes are now relevant. Firstly s.108 of the Evidence Act 1872 provides a presumption

219

that a person who has been absent and unheard of for seven years by those who would naturally have heard from him if he had been alive, is dead. The Muslim rule has been held to be one of evidence not substantive law and therefore superseded by the statute (1). Secondly the Dissolution of Muslim Marriages Act 1939 enables a wife to sue for dissolution of her marriage on the ground of her husband´s absence for four years. A dissolution under this Act is not however a declaration of death, so the wife need observe only the idda of divorce.

Talaq

Talaq is the unilateral repudiation of a wife by her husband. No formalities are necessary (2) and there is not even any need of witnesses, though since the burden of proof lies on the person who alleges the talaq they are desirable. The repudiation need not be addressed to the wife who need not even be present (3): in classical law the fact that the talaq is not communicated to her will not invalidate it although until it is so communicated her rights of maintenance will now remain intact (4). Because of their disapproval of divorce the Muslim jurists, especially the Hanafis, took a very strict approach. Only when the husband´s statements are ambiguous is intention relevant (5), for the jurists wished to deter careless and wanton use of talaq. Thus the talaq is effective even when uttered in jest or when intoxicated or when tricked into saying the words or under duress (6). However, to pronounce talaq the husband must have attained puberty and must have the capacity to understand the nature of his acts, though not necessarily their consequences (7). Accordingly a talaq pronounced when insane or asleep, or when intoxicants have been administered without the husband´s consent or knowledge, is ineffective. The husband may if he chooses pronounce talaq using an agent or messenger.

There are a number of forms of talaq. Talaq al-ahsan is the most approved; talaq al-hasan the next approved; and talaq al-bida disapproved. The first two are collectively known as talaq as-sunna.

Talaq al-ahsan is a single pronouncement of divorce during the wife´s period of tuhr (absence of menstrual flow) during which the husband has not had intercourse with her. There then begins an idda period of three menstrual cycles during which time the husband must not have sexual intercourse with his wife. At the end of this time the marriage is dissolved automatically. During the idda period the talaq may be revoked at any time, either expressly or by conduct, e.g. the resumption of sexual relations, unless this is the third occasion on which a talaq has been declared, in which case it dissolves the marriage at once.

Talaq al-hasan is a single repudiation during the wife´s

tuhr during which the husband has not had intercourse with his wife, repeated in the following tuhr and again in the tuhr following that during which time there is no intercourse between them. On the third pronouncement without any intervening revocation, the divorce takes effect immediately.

In either case if the wife does not menstruate time is calculated by the lunar month. Where the marriage has not been consummated the talaq may be declared at any time and is immediately irrevocable. But the ahsan and hasan forms differ in one important respect: whereas because the ahsan form is a single repudiation the couple concerned may if they wish remarry each other at once, unless it is the third such occasion, in the hasan form which involves a three-fold repudiation the parties may not remarry each other until the woman has undergone an intervening and consummated marriage with another man which is subsequently dissolved. The Qur´anic form was designed to place some limit on the husband´s absolute right of divorce so as to improve the condition of wives who might otherwise live constantly under the threat of arbitrary repudiation by tyrranical husbands. However, the strictness of the Hanafi rules combined with this Qur´anic provision can lead to even greater hardship in the context of a repudiation in the disapproved al-bida (innovatory) form of talaq.

The talaq al-bida is effected in one of a number of ways not complying with the requirements of talaq as-sunna, e.g., three pronouncements of talaq in the same sitting or in the same period of tuhr; pronouncement in a period of tuhr in which the husband has had intercourse with his wife; after consummation, during a period of menstruation; or one pronouncement with an added element of finality. It is an unfortunate reflection on Muslim society, or rather the male part of it, that the first of these forms of talaq al-bida, the so called triple talaq, is the only one used in practice and probably the only one known to most Muslim men today. A talaq al-bida is effective and irrevocable immediately.

During the idda period consequent upon a revocable talaq the marriage remains in existence and therefore rights of inheritance survive: intercourse is lawful though it will constitute revocation of the talaq. On the pronouncement of an irrevocable divorce rights of inheritance and intercourse disappear, though the couple may remarry unless it is a third or triple talaq. The deferred dower becomes payable at the time of dissolution and maintenance is payable throughout the idda period whether it be consequent upon a revocable or irrevocable talaq. It is only the third talaq, whether it be al-bida, ahsan or hasan which raises the bar to marriage between the parties.

The classical law remains fully in force in India but in Pakistan there has been considerable statutory intervention aimed at the prevention of hasty dissolutions, through the

221

Muslim Family laws Ordinance 1961. This is considered below.

The husband may delegate his right of talaq to his wife. Such a delegation (tafwid) may be made before, at the time of, or after the marriage takes place. In the absence of any condition to the contrary the Hanafis hold that the wife must exercise the power, if at all, as soon as she learns of it or, where the delegation is made conditional on the occurrence of a particular event, as soon as she learns of that event. Once the husband has delegated that power, although he is still perfectly free to pronounce a talaq himself, he cannot revoke the power he has delegated to his wife. The Hanafis hold that the wife's exercise of the power delegated to her amounts to an irrevocable talaq by the husband - the delegation would after all have little meaning if the husband could revoke the talaq after his wife had pronounced it. It is for the wife to prove both the delegation of the power, the exercise of it and the fulfilment of any conditions to which it was subject, though such conditions will be ignored if they are contrary to public policy. The husband may further delegate his power of talaq to a third person, e.g., the wife's father: but in this case the delegation is revocable.

Alternatively, but less satisfactorily and flexibly for the wife, the husband may pronounce a conditional talaq, i.e., one which without more will take effect on the occurrence of a certain event. If the condition is ambiguous or uncertain or impossible the talaq itself is ineffective. The condition must not be contrary to public policy. The Hanafi jurists state that a talaq pronounced subject to a condition cannot be withdrawn. Common examples of conditions are that the delegation or talaq should be effective, if the husband marries a second wife without the first wife's consent, or fails to pay her maintenance for a set period without good cause.

The advantage for a wife of a conditional or delegated talaq over khul´ or mubara´a (considered below) is the fact that she will not have to return the dower or make a similar payment to the husband for the divorce. It has sometimes been said that in a marriage agreement, unlike a subsequent unilateral delegation by the husband, the delegation to the wife cannot be absolute, but such a clause has been upheld in the courts of Pakistan (8). The objection is presumably that such an unconditional right would be incompatible with the nature of the marriage contract but this is not particularly convincing.

In Pakistan the Muslim Family Laws Ordinance effects a considerable modification of the classical law: nothing comparable exists in India but the scope for judicial reinterpretation and restriction of talaq is revealed by the unreported judgment of Baharul Islam J. in Anwara Begum's case, which is reproduced later in this Chapter.

Muslim Family Laws Ordinance 1961, ss. 7, 8

7. <u>Talaq</u> – (1) Any man who wishes to divorce his wife shall, as soon as may be after the pronouncement of <u>talaq</u> in any form whatsoever, give the Chairman notice in writing of his having done so, and shall supply a copy thereof to the wife.

(2) Whoever contravenes the provisions of sub-section (1) shall be punishable with simple imprisonment for a term which may extend to one year or with fine which may extend to five thousand rupees or with both.

(3) Save as provided in sub-section (5), a <u>talaq</u> unless revoked earlier, expressly or otherwise, shall not be effective until the expiration of ninety days from the day on which notice under sub-section (1) is delivered to the Chairman.

(4) Within thirty days of the receipt of notice under sub-section (1), the Chairman shall constitute an Arbitration Council for the purpose of bringing about a reconciliation between the parties, and the Arbitration Council shall take all steps necessary to bring about such reconciliation.

(5) If the wife be pregnant at the time <u>talaq</u> is pronounced, <u>talaq</u> shall not be effective until the period mentioned in sub-section (3) or the pregnancy, whichever be later, ends.

(6) Nothing shall debar a wife whose marriage has been terminated by <u>talaq</u> effective under this section from re-marrying the same husband, without an intervening marriage with a third person, unless such termination is for the third time so effective.

8. <u>Dissolution of marriage otherwise than by talaq</u> – Where the right to divorce has been duly delegated to the wife and she wishes to exercise that right, or where any of the parties to a marriage wishes to dissolve the marriage otherwise than by <u>talaq</u>, the provisions of section 7 shall <u>mutatis mutandis</u> and so far as applicable, apply.

The effect of the Ordinance is to render every <u>talaq</u> revocable by freezing it for ninety days during which time reconciliation is attempted by the Union Council Chairman – a function now performed by a judge. There has been a substantial amount of case law on its provisions. It has been held that failure to give notice of a <u>talaq</u> in accordance with the Ordinance to the relevant person in authority operates as a revocation by conduct of the <u>talaq</u> (9). The appropriate person is determined by the Rules made under the Ordinance. It is unclear whether failure to serve notice of the <u>talaq</u> on the wife will also have the effect of revocation and whether an indirect communication to her, perhaps through the authorities concerned, will suffice (10). It is clear, however, that a failure to co-operate with the reconciliation

223

re will in no way invalidate the <u>talaq</u> nor will any
by the authorities to form an arbitration council
(11). In the absence of an express or constructive revocation
whether or not arbitration takes place, the <u>talaq</u> will
dissolve the marriage at the end of the ninety day period.
The <u>idda</u> period runs from the end of the ninety days. Where
the wife or a third party has a power of <u>talaq</u> by virtue of
delegation the same procedures must be complied with, notice
being given (presumably) to the husband as well.

Faskh

<u>Faskh</u> is the dissolution of a marriage by judicial decree
and has its basis in the Qur´an Sura IV:35. In the classical
law the schools differed widely as to the permissable scope of
<u>faskh</u>. Hanafi law adopted the extremely restrictive approach
that a woman might obtain a decree from the Qadi ordering her
husband to divorce her only where that husband was incapable
of consummating the marriage. At the other extreme Maliki law
accepted this right in a wide variety of circumstances
including various physical and mental defects, failure to
maintain her, desertion and ill-treatment. The other schools
occupied intermediate positions. It was Maliki law which
inspired the terms of the Dissolution of Muslim Marriages Act
1939 which now governs <u>faskh</u> in India and Pakistan, though the
Act should not be thought of as a codification of the Maliki
law. For the Hanafi wife the Act represents a radical
enhancement of her rights of dissolution and the provisions on
cruelty in particular extend even the classical Maliki law.
It should also be noted that the Act applies to a wife only.
The Hanafi law conceded the right to the wife alone but the
other schools laid it open to both spouses, this difference of
approach being based partly on the idea that in the Hanafi
view only those defects which prevented intercourse altogether
should be allowed to raise a <u>faskh</u> whereas the other schools
regarded the risk of infection of the other spouse with some
serious disorder as good cause for separation. Outside the
Hanafi and Maliki schools (where the separation is in form
effected through <u>talaq</u>) the divorce is effected in form and
substance by the Qadi.

The text of the Dissolution of Muslim Marriages Act 1939,
s.2 followed by a commentary of its individual provisions, is
set out below. Its interpretation raises a number of issues;
with it is a Pakistani amendment in the shape of s.13 of the
Muslim Family Laws Ordinance 1961.

Dissolution of Muslim Marriages Act, 1939

2.   Grounds for decree for dissolution of marriage – A
woman married under Muslim law shall be entitled to obtain a
decree for the dissolution of her marriage on any one or more
224

of the following grounds, namely:

(i)   that the whereabouts of the husband have not been known for a period of four years;

(ii)   that the husband has neglected or has failed to provide for her maintenance for a period of two years;

(iii)   that the husband has been sentenced to imprisonment for a period of seven years or upwards;

(iv)   that the husband has failed to perform, without reasonable cause, his marital obligations for a period of three years;

(v)   that the husband was impotent at the time of the marriage and continues to be so;

(vi)   that the husband has been insane for a period of two years or is suffering from leprosy or a virulent venereal disease;

(vii) that she having been given in marriage by her father or other guardian before she attained the age of fifteen years, repudiated the marriage before attaining the age of eighteen years;

Provided that the marriage has not been consummated;

(viii)that the husband treats her with cruelty, that is to say:

(a)   habitually assaults her or makes her life miserable by cruelty of conduct even if such conduct does not amount to physical ill-treatment, or

(b)   associates with women of evil repute or leads an infamous life, or

(c)   attempts to force her to lead an immoral life, or

(d)   disposes of her property or prevents her exercising her legal rights over it, or

(e)   obstructs her in the observance of her religious profession or practice, or

(f)   if he has more wives than one, does not treat her equitably in accordance with the injunctions of the Quran;

(ix)   on any other ground which is recognised as valid for the dissolution of marriages under Muslim law;

Provided that –

(a)   no decree shall be passed on ground (iii) until the sentence become final;

(b)   a decree passed on ground (i) shall not take effect for a period of six months from the date of such decree, and if the husband appears either in person or through an authorised agent within that period and satisfies the Court that he is prepared to perform his conjugal duties, the Court shall set aside the said decree; and

(c)   before passing a decree on ground (v) the Court shall on application by the husband, make an order requiring the husband to satisfy the Court within a period of one year the date of such order that he has ceased to be impotent, and if the husband so satisfies the Court within such period, no decree shall be passed on the said ground.

3. Notice to be served on heirs of the husband when the husband's whereabouts are not known. - In a suit to which clause (i) of section 2 applies -

(a) the names and addresses of the persons who would have been the heirs of the husband under Muslim law if he had died on the date of the filing of the plaint shall be stated in the plaint.

(b) notice of the suit shall be served on such persons, and

(c) such persons shall have the right to be heard in the suit:

Provided that the paternal uncle and brother of the husband, if any, shall be cited as party even if he or they are not heirs.....

.....5. Rights to dower not to be affected - Nothing contained in this Act shall affect any right which a married woman may have under Muslim law to her dower or any part thereof on the dissolution of her marriage.....

Muslim Family Laws Ordinance 1961

13. Amendment of the Dissolution of Muslim Marriages Act 1939 (VIII of 1939) - In the Dissolution of Muslim Marriages Act, 1939 (VIII of 1939), in section 2:

(a) after clause (ii), the following new clause (iia) shall be inserted, namely:-

"(iia) that the husband has taken an additional wife in contravention of the provisions of the Muslim Family Laws Ordinance, 1961"; and

(b) in clause (vii), for the word "fifteen" the word "sixteen" shall be substituted.

In s.2(i) the provision for suspension of the decree after a finding that the husband had been missing for four years found no place in the Maliki law.

There has been much case law on s.2(ii). A possible reading of this clause is to confer on the wife the unconditional right to maintenance so that in order to succeed in a claim for dissolution of her marriage all a wife need do is to prove that for whatever reason the husband has failed to provide maintenance for a period of two years. In particular this would mean that a failure to provide maintenance which in classical law would be justified on the ground that the wife was nashiza or that the husband had no money with which to provide maintenance would be no defence to a wife's suit for dissolution under the Act. One line of decisions has taken this view (12). On the other hand another line of decisions

226

has maintained that the husband can only be said to neglect or fail to provide maintenance when Muslim law obliges him to provide it and he does not, and thus when Muslim law excuses him he can neither neglect nor fail in this duty (13). It would seem very strange if this provision directed at a remedy for failure to meet a legal duty had by a sidewind altered the nature of that duty itself. The first view of the clause is clearly coloured by a desire to enhance the rights of the wife to a divorce but not only is it inconsistent with the classical law, it is also a remedy in effect obtainable only by the wife with alternative means of supporting herself who is prepared to wait. There is further doubt whether the two year period specified by the Act must immediately precede the suit or not. It does however seem reasonably clear that the term ´neglect´ encompasses not only total but also partial failure to maintain, i.e. a consistent payment of deficient amounts. In this context the Code of Criminal Procedure should be recalled which permits a wife to live away from her husband without losing her right to maintenance where he has taken a second wife (14).

s.2(iii) differs from the classical law of the Maliki school which took a three year period.

s.2(iv) it will be seen has considerable scope for overlap with the other clauses. The principal matrimonial obligations have already been considered.

s.2(v) differs from the classical law in which it was necessary that the wife be ignorant of the impotence of her husband at the time of the marriage. The burden of proof under the Act lies on the husband to show his potency vis-a-vis the wife and the court may only postpone the decree for one year at the application of the husband – he may waive the right, unlike the position in classical law.

s.2(vi) is not as wide in its range of disorders as the classical law of the Maliki school.

s.2(vii) and the option of puberty are considered below.

s.2(viii) is from the point of view of the Hanafi wife the most significant extension of her rights. The classical Hanafi jurists regarded the verses of the Qur´an relied on by the Malikis for their jurisdiction to order dissolution on the basis of cruelty as extending only to the appointment of arbitrators to attempt a reconciliation, not also to effecting a separation if reconciliation was impossible. The statute could be said to have gone to the other extreme by reducing to a minor role the function of arbitration which the Maliki law prescribed before separation though in Pakistan this criticism may be answered to some extent by provisions in the Family Courts Act 1964 for attempts at compromise and conciliation, combined with s.8 of the 1961 Ordinance.

s.2(ix) is directed towards _khul´_, _lian_, _ziar_, etc., considered below.

As for the Pakistan amendment of 1961, there cannot be

227

said to be any basis for this whatsoever in the classical texts.

Khul´ and Mubara´a

Divorce by mutual consent may be effected by khul´ or by mubara´a. These forms of dissolution have their foundation in the Qur´an Sura II:229. The principal distinction is that in khul´ the aversion which causes the desire for dissolution is that of the wife alone whereas in mubara´a the aversion is mutual. In either case the proposal must be made and accepted at the same meeting, but no other formalities need be observed and no witnesses are necessary in Hanafi law. If the proposal is made by the husband he cannot retract it: the wife must be allowed to reply. If the husband purports to suspend the offer it still takes effect at once. The wife may retract any offer before the husband has had a chance to reply, and may suspend it. It is usual but in the classical law not essential for a wife requesting a khul´ to give the husband some compensation - usually her dower; but in mubara´a the husband should not (and it has been said cannot) demand any compensation as the price of his agreement. A khul´, subject to contrary agreement, and a mubara´a, will extinguish all rights accrued between husband and wife as a result of the marriage, e.g. unpaid but due dower but not other debts, e.g. business debts. The purpose of this is to remove what the Muslim jurists assume to have been the most likely cause of the aversion - money problems. The parties must be adult and sane though a marriage guardian may agree on behalf of a minor girl to a khul´ if he takes responsibility for paying compensation out of his own pocket. Nor must the consent of the wife have been obtained by fraud or duress. Failing these two conditions the khul´ will still effect dissolution but the compensation will not be payable. The effect of the khul´ is that of a single and irrevocable talaq. Maintenance remains due, therefore, during idda though as part of the compensation the wife may agree to forgo this, with the exception of her right of residence - this right being expressly conferred by the Qur´an the parties cannot go against it. Unlike talaq, however, khul´ in death sickness is possible - the consent of the parties eliminating any risk of fraudulent disinheritance. The wife cannot forgo custody of the children of the marriage as the price of the khul´. Failure to pay does not invalidate the khul´ but merely entitles the husband to sue for the agreed sum. Because of the very limited circumstances in which a Hanafi wife might in classical law obtain a dissolution of her marriage the husband might in practice be able to extract very considerable compensation for agreeing to the dissolution by khul´. There are conflicting traditions on compensation. In the Qur´an Sura IV:20 it is said that the husband must not accept compensation where it is he who initiates the dissolution by consent. As to accepting compensation greater than the benefits which he has conferred on the wife during the marriage, some jurists regard this as disapproved, some as forbidden, some as permissible. It is said that where there is disagreement as to the amount which should be paid, the Qadi may be asked to fix an appropriate amount. The subject matter of the compensation may be anything which can be the subject matter of dower.

The reason for the different rules relating to offers by the husband and those by the wife is that the Hanafi school look on khul´ and mubara´a as, from the point of view of the husband, a repudiation, but, from the point of view of the wife, a gift of the compensation (the other schools regard it as a bilateral contract).

In Pakistan the law of khul´ was little short of revolutionised by the Supreme Court´s decision in Khurshid Bibi v. Mohammad Amin (15) which established the following propositions: (i) The wife is entitled to a dissolution of her marriage without the consent of her husband if she would otherwise be forced to maintain a hateful union. (ii) If the wife desires this she must repay what she has received from her husband during the marriage, the final decision as to what she must return lying with the court. (iii) The right to dissolution is qualified by the requirement that the court be satisfied that the spouses cannot live together within the "limits of Allah". This is to ensure that, on the one hand, the wife does not exercise her right capriciously and, on the other, that she is not oppressed by her husband in an attempt to recover property he has given her or to avoid the payment of deferred dower necessitated by talaq. (iv) There is no need for the cause of the rift to be investigated, nor the reasonableness of the wife´s request; the court need only concern itself with the question of the seriousness of the breakdown of the marriage and the likelihood of the parties being able to fulfil their marital obligations in the future. (v) The khul´ divorce is a faskh not a talaq: therefore the husband´s consent is irrelevant.

Subsequent cases have endorsed and applied this reasoning and it has been held that the dower and other benefits received by the wife need only be restored when the husband expressly demands their restoration (16): the claim can be waived implicitly by conduct and in any event the value of the property restored must never exceed the amount of the wife´s dower or the property given to her (17). A failure by the wife to pay the compensation decreed does not invalidate the dissolution but merely leaves the husband with an action at law in debt (18). It has been suggested that the khul´ and payment may depend on the fault of the parties, (so that if the breakdown was the fault of the husband he might demand nothing) (19) even though the right to dissolution itself would not: but this seems to have been rejected in subsequent

229

cases (20).

Thus the principal changes brought about by the Supreme Court's decision are the absence of any requirement of consent by the husband and the necessity of paying compensation fixed by the court. The position of this new style khul´ within the Muslim Family laws Ordinance 1961 is unclear. The decree is granted through s.2(ix) of the Dissolution of Muslim Marriages Act 1939. It would appear, on the balance of authority, that the provisions of the Ordinance do apply but that the provisions of s.s. 7 and 8 operate after the decree of khul´ has been granted by the Family Court, not before (21).

None of this has had any effect on the old consensual khul´ and mubara´a, though in Pakistan it seems that whatever the strict terms, the non consensual Khurshid Bibi dissolution is now to be called khul´ and the consensual dissolutions mubara´a. With regard to the consensual dissolution no recourse to s.2(ix) of the 1939 Act is necessary, but again the position with respect to the 1961 Ordinance is unclear. What judicial authority there is suggests that s.8 but not s.7(3) applies, therefore requiring notice to the authorities but not permitting revocation; a curious conclusion.

The Khurshid Bibi decision has been criticised on a number of grounds (22). The court, it is said, misunderstood the classical law according to which both khul´ and mubara´a were consensual; the court wrongly held khul´ to be a faskh when it was in fact a talaq; the court wrongly held idda after khul´ to be different to that after talaq; the court wrongly held that there was no classical authority on whether the husband's consent was necessary for the khul´; the court wrongly sought to apply authorities from the classical law of the other schools to a dispute between Hanafis and moreover achieved a result different from that which would have been achieved had the law of the other schools been applied properly to a dispute between members of those schools. However, whatever may be the juristic validity of the Pakistani courts´ decisions on khul´, the Khurshid Bibi decision is now soundly established and unlikely to be challenged. From the point of view of the wife it is a substantial enhancement of her rights. No such development is apparent in the courts of India, where the classical law applies in full. The problems in developing this new body of law derive from the attempts of the courts to apply classical authorities on cases where the husband consented which do not form a convenient source of principle for cases where he does not consent and where compensation is an essential. The change of approach from talaq to faskh exacerbates this problem.

Khiyar-al-Bulugh

In the classical Hanafi law a minor, male or female, who

230

has been contracted in marriage by his or her marriage guardian who is someone other than the father or grandfather may on attaining puberty repudiate the marriage. This is known as the <u>khiyar-al-bulugh</u> (option of puberty). The reasoning behind excluding this option where the marriage guardian is the father or grandfather is that it is presumed that such persons will not behave carelessly or in bad faith in this respect whereas other more remote guardians might. For this reason perhaps the Hanafi jurists conceded the right even where the marriage guardian was a father or grandfather if it could be shown that he had acted fraudulently or carelessly or in circumstances clearly disadvantageous to the child (23).

The option is lost by a virgin girl on consummation of the marriage with her consent after puberty - nothing done before puberty is relevant - or by a boy or non-virgin girl by express assent (24). In the case of the virgin girl she must exercise her option as soon as she reaches puberty, before two witnesses; this will not be so, however, where she is ignorant of the marriage (as opposed to being ignorant of her right) in which case time begins to run only from her discovery of it. The courts of India have been more generous than the classical jurists in this respect by allowing belated suits on the wife's discovery of her right (25). Neither have the courts looked too hard at the requirement of witnesses (26). Moreover the classical law clearly requires a decree of the Qadi before holding the marriage dissolved but the Indian courts have never consistently applied this rule, perhaps out of a desire to avoid convictions for bigamy (27). The courts have also been generous in their construction of certain acts as repudiation of the marriage by conduct (28).

It is said that a marriage susceptible to the option of puberty is nevertheless valid until that option is exercised.

The option of puberty has in practice been much expanded in India and Pakistan by the terms of s.2(vii) of the Dissolution of Muslim Marriages Act 1939 which provides a statutory alternative to, not a substitute for, the classical regime (29).

"s.2. A woman married under Muslim law shall be entitled to obtain a decree for the dissolution of her marriage on any one or more of the following grounds, namely:-

(vii) that she, having been given in marriage by her father or other guardian before she attained the age of fifteen years [sixteen years in Pakistan], repudiated the marriage before attaining the age of eighteen years."

It will be seen that the principal differences between the classical and statutory regimes are these: the statutory regime is available only to girls, and it makes no distinction between the virgin and non-virgin girl. The option afforded

231

by the statutory regime may be effected irrespective of the identity of the marriage guardian and his conduct. The option arises not on puberty but on the attainment of a specific age. The option must be exercised before the attainment of eighteen years but need not be exercised immediately that it arises. The exercise of the option is deemed to take place before the attainment of the eighteenth birthday by the normal manifestations accepted in the classical law - the fact that the institution of the suit before the court takes place after this is immaterial. A straightforward reading of the Act would indicate the need for a judicial decree: some Pakistani decisions deny this, no doubt out of a desire to avoid convictions for bigamy, but nevertheless wrongly (30). The Act is not clear on the effect of a consummation obtained by duress or obtained by false pretences, but it would surely be no more effective for these purposes than in the classical law (31).

Kafa´a

The equality of the spouses is considered to be desirable but not essential to the Muslim marriage. Lack of equality does however form the basis of a claim for dissolution of the marriage by faskh. For although Hanafi law places no restrictions on the right of an adult woman to contract her own marriage, the interests of her family, which may be damaged by an ill-judged alliance, are recognised in this doctrine, which has no apparent Qur´anic basis. The doctrine provides for the dissolution of the marriage through the Qadi at the instance of e.g. the woman´s marriage guardian in the event of there being some substantial inequality of the spouses prejudicial to the woman´s interests, but also at the instance of the woman herself where the marriage was contracted for her by her guardian, even by the father or grandfather, when she exercises her option of puberty. There is no parallel right in the husband except to the extent that he may invoke the doctrine when seeking to exercise the option of puberty to escape a marriage contracted for him by his father or grandfather, e.g. for an excessive dower. The reason behind this is that the wife is assumed always to take on the social status of her husband, so that he cannot generally be adversely affected by their inequality. The Hanafi school adopts an expansive view as to the scope of the doctrine. The marriage is liable to dissolution on this basis for inequality in any of the following areas; religion, family, profession, freedom, piety, and wealth (no doubt in part, at least, because of the limited capacity of the wife to obtain a dissolution by other means). These matters are to be judged at the time of the marriage taking place; subsequent changes in status are immaterial. The husband´s profession must be compared with that of his wife´s father. Wealth is

232

determined by the husband's capacity to pay the prompt dower and maintain the wife. Some jurists maintain that personal attributes such as beauty and stature are also relevant. The effect of the decree of dissolution is to entitle the wife to her dower only if the marriage has been consummated, consummation also determining whether the idda must be observed. Although there is no time limit on the claim, the pregnancy of the wife appears to bring the right to dissolution on this ground to an end.

Apostasy and Conversion

The question who is a Muslim has already been dealt with in Chapter 1. We are here concerned with the effect of conversion or apostasy from Islam by one of the spouses. Considering first the apostasy of the husband, in the classical law this was regarded as treason and was thereby punishable by death if after three days the husband refused to return to Islam. He must have understood the nature of his act and it should not have taken place under duress. In the case of a wife who apostasises, the penalty is imprisonment. These public sanctions are no longer relevant. The effects of apostasy and conversion in inheritance rights are outside the scope of this book.

Apostasy by either spouse brings the marriage to an end, even if the wife apostasises to a religion which, had she been of that faith at the time of her marriage, would not have prevented her from marrying her husband in the first place (though some Indian commentators deny this). If the marriage comes to an end by reason of apostasy after its consummation the wife is entitled to the whole dower. If it comes to an end before consummation she is entitled to only half of the dower if it was the husband who apostasised, none at all if she is the apostate. Idda is necessary only if the marriage had been consummated. Maintenance is payable during the idda unless the wife is the apostate. Apostasy dissolves the marriage automatically, without any need of intervention by the Qadi. The children of the marriage remain Muslims if in dar al-Islam, but elsewhere they have the choice of which faith to follow. The matter of custody is considered in Chapter 5.

In the Indian subcontinent the position has been modified by s.4 of the Dissolution of Muslim Marriages Act 1939, which provides as follows:

Dissolution of Muslim Marriages Act 1939

s.4 The renunciation of Islam by a married Muslim woman or her conversion to a faith other than Islam shall not of itself operate to dissolve her marriage.

Provided that after such renunciation, or conversion, the

woman shall be entitled to obtain a decree for the dissolution of her marriage on any of the grounds mentioned in s.2.

Provided further that the provisions of this section shall not apply to a woman converted to Islam from some other faith who re-embraces her former faith.

The effect of this provision, then, is that if the wife apostasises the marriage will not of itself be dissolved but that she may (not must) obtain a dissolution on some other ground permitted by the statute (these grounds are considered above). The only exception to this is where she was formerly of another faith and adopted Islam (for instance, on her marriage) but later returns to her former faith (not an entirely new faith) in which case the marriage shall terminate. Her apostasy might however entitle the court, under S.2(ix) of the Act, to grant a decree, since apostasy is within ´any other ground which is recognised as valid for the dissolution of marriages under Muslim law´, and a possible reading of the Act is that its only effect in s.4 is to require a judicial decree rather than permitting an automatic dissolution. The Act clearly has no application to apostasy by the husband.

The traditional position with regard to conversion to Islam in the subcontinent is that where the husband converts to Islam and the wife is of a revealed religion, the marriage remains intact. If she is not of a revealed religion and the conversion of the husband takes place in India (but possibly not now in Pakistan, depending on whether the courts now consider the country to be <u>dar al-Islam</u>) then intercourse at once becomes unlawful and after an <u>idda</u> of three menstrual cycles the union is dissolved. In <u>dar al-Islam</u> a Qadi or his equivalent must offer Islam to the wife (or the husband if he is the non-Muslim spouse) and on that spouse´s third refusal of Islam, the Qadi must separate the spouses. Where a wife converts to Islam the religion of the non-Muslim husband is of course immaterial. The Act of 1939 has no effect on such conversions.

<u>Li´an</u>

The basis of dissolution by <u>li´an</u> is the Qur´an, Sura XXIV: 4, 6-9. The procedure is initiated by the husband´s express or implied accusation of adultery by his wife in a <u>sahih</u> marriage which he cannot substantiate by providing the prescribed number of witnesses (four). The wife responds by denying the accusation and demanding, through the Qadi, that the husband substantiate the accusation by oath taking or admit the falsity of the accusation. If the husband then admits that the accusation is false the marriage remains in existence but in classical law (recently revived in Pakistan, but still obsolete in India) he renders himself liable for

false accusation of unchastity (qazf). The Qadi may keep him
in prison until he makes his choice. If the husband presses
the accusation he must swear the oath four times that the
accusation is true and then a fifth time, cursing himself if
it be false. The wife's response to this is either to admit
the accusation or to deny it by an oath repeated four times,
and a fifth time cursing herself if the denial is false. She
too may be imprisoned if the Qadi wishes, until she chooses.
Admission leaves the marriage intact but liability for zina
will accrue to the wife in the classical law (again revived in
Pakistan, but not in India). However even at this point the
Hanafi law allows the husband to retract though in doing so he
renders himself liable to qazf. If the husband refuses to
retract even at this point the Qadi must separate the parties.
It is accepted by most of the Hanafi jurists that the marriage
does not terminate automatically at this point, the taking of
oaths, but that dissolution is dependent on the decree of the
Qadi, which has the same effect as one irrevocable
repudiation. Even after the dissolution until the oath or
denial is retracted, remarriage between the parties is
prohibited and indeed some Hanafi jurists have maintained that
this raises a perpetual bar between the parties. For the
Li'an procedure to be followed both parties must be adult and
sane. The majority of jurists in the Hanafi school maintain
that there can be no li'an of a non-Muslim woman (34).

The status of li'an in India in modern times is somewhat
unclear (35). The means of procuring a dissolution by li'an
is clearly through s.2(ix) of the 1939 Act. Li'an was
expressly preserved by the Muslim Personal Law (Shariat)
Application Act 1937, but the problem relates, as often, to
the question to what extent procedural and evidential and to
what extent substantive the law of li'an is, in view of the
provisions of the Indian Evidence Act 1872 which purports to
supersede the classical rules of evidence. It must be
conceded that subsequent case law has to some extent distorted
the classical law of li'an. In particular there is a
considerable amount of judicial authority to the effect that
the husband cannot retract his accusation, or that the court
cannot be compelled to permit him to do so, after the evidence
has been presented to the court (36). Secondly, the matter of
oath taking has been held to be superseded by the Indian
Evidence Act 1872 so that the wife now simply has to allege in
her claim for dissolution of the marriage under s.2(ix) of the
1939 Act that her husband has made a false allegation of
unchastity against her (37). Thirdly, the truth or otherwise
of the husband's accusation was not material under the
classical procedure except to the extent that actual proof of
the wife's adultery took the whole matter out of the scope of
li'an, but the modern courts have taken the view that the
dissolution is to be granted at the wife's request only once
it is established that the accusation is false, thereby

235

raising the question of the burden of proof, which has been resolved by making the husband prove the truth of his statements, failing which the court is able to dissolve the marriage (38), (though some of the earlier decisions, quite extraordinarily placed the burden the other way round (39)). Where it is still possible the bona fide retraction of the accusation (i.e. not one simply calculated to defeat the wife's suit) will be accepted (40).

The whole of the li'an procedure might until recently have been dismissed by some as of purely antiquarian interest, but the recent Pakistani legislation may well give it a renewed importance and the whole matter will clearly have to be re-examined by the courts (41). The statutory procedure is reproduced below with the substantive offences which surround li'an, zina, qazf and related matters. Li'an is dealt with expressly in s.14 of the Offence of Qazf (Enforcement of Hadd) Ordinance 1979.

ORDINANCE VII OF 1979
OFFENCE OF ZINA (ENFORCEMENT OF HADOOD)
ORDINANCE, 1979

1. **Short title, extent and commencement** – (1) This Ordinance may be called the Offence of Zina (Enforcement of Hadood) Ordinance, 1979.

(2) It extends to the whole of Pakistan.

(3) It shall come into force on the twelfth day of Rabi-ul-Awwal, 1399 Hijri, that is the tenth day of February, 1979.

2. **Definitions** – In this Ordinance, unless there is anything repugnant in the subject or context –

(a) "adult" means a person who has attained, being a male, the age of eighteen years or, being a female, the age of sixteen years, or has attained puberty;

(b) "hadd" means punishment ordained by the Holy Qur'an or Sunnah;

(c) "marriage" means marriage which is not void according to the personal law of the parties, and "married" shall be construed accordingly;

(d) "Muhsan" means –

(i) a Muslim adult man who is not insane and has had sexual intercourse with a Muslim adult woman who, at the time he had sexual intercourse with her, was married to him and was not insane; or

(ii) a Muslim adult woman who is not insane and has had sexual intercourse with a Muslim adult man who, at the time she had sexual intercourse with him, was married to her and was not insane; and

(e) "tazir" means any punishment other than hadd, and all other terms and expressions not defined in this Ordinance shall have the same meaning as in the Pakistan Penal

236

Code (Act XLV of 1860), or the Code of Criminal Procedure, 1898 (Act V of 1898).

3. <u>Ordinance to override other laws</u> – The provisions of this Ordinance shall have effect notwithstanding anything contained in any other law for the time being in force.

4. <u>Zina</u> – A man and a woman are said to commit ´<u>zina</u>´ if they wilfully have sexual intercourse without being validly married to each other.

<u>Explanation</u> – Penetration is sufficient to constitute the sexual intercourse necessary to the offence of zina.

5. <u>Zina liable to hadd</u> – (1) Zina is zina liable to <u>hadd</u> if –

(a) it is committed by a man who is an adult and is not insane with a woman to whom he is not and does not suspect himself to be married; or

(b) it is committed by a woman who is an adult and is not insane with a man to whom she is not, and does not suspect herself to be married.

(2) Whoever is guilty of zina liable to hadd shall, subject to the provisions of this Ordinance –

(a) if he or she is a muhsan, be stoned to death at a public place; or

(b) if he or she is not a muhsan, be punished, at a public place, with whipping numbering one hundred stripes.

(3) No punishment under subsection (2) shall be executed until it has been confirmed by the Court to which an appeal from the order of conviction lies; and if the punishment be of whipping, until it is confirmed and executed, the convict shall be dealt with in the same manner as if sentenced to simple imprisonment.

6. <u>Zina-bil-jabr</u> – (1) A person is said to commit zina-bil-jabr if he or she has sexual intercourse with a woman or man, as the case may be, to whom he or she is not validly married, in any of the following circumstances, namely:–

(a) against the will of the victim,

(b) without the consent of the victim,

(c) with the consent of the victim when the consent has been obtained by putting the victim in fear of death or of hurt, or

(d) with the consent of the victim, when the offender knows that the offender is not validly married to the victim and that the consent is given because the victim believes that the offender is another person to whom the victim is or believes herself or himself to be validly married.

<u>Explanation</u> – Penetration is sufficient to constitute the sexual intercourse necessary to the offence of zina-bil-jabr.

(2) Zina-bil-jabr is zina-bil-jabr liable to <u>hadd</u> if it is committed in the circumstances specified in subsection (1) of section 5.

(3) Whoever is guilty of zina-bil-jabr liable to hadd shall subject to the provisions of this Ordinance –

(a) if he or she is a muhsan, be stoned to death at a public place; or

(b) if he or she is not muhsan, be punished with whipping numbering one hundred stripes, at a public place, and with such other punishment, including the sentence of death, as the Court may deem fit having regard to the circumstances of the case.

(4) No punishment under subsection (3) shall be executed until it has been confirmed by the Court to which an appeal from the order of conviction lies; and if the punishment be of whipping, until it is confirmed and executed, the convict shall be dealt with in the same manner as if sentenced to simple imprisonment.

7. Punishment for zina or zina-bil-jabr where convict is not an adult – A person guilty of zina or zina-bil-jabr shall, if he is not an adult, be punished with imprisonment of either description for a term which may extend to five years, or with fine, or with both, and may also be awarded the punishment of whipping not exceeding thirty stripes:

Provided that, in the case of zina-bil-jabr, if the offender is not under the age of fifteen years, the punishment of whipping shall be awarded with or without any other punishment.

8. Proof of zina or zina-bil-jabr liable to hadd – Proof of Zina or zina-bil-jabr, liable to hadd shall be in one of the following forms, namely:-

(a) the accused makes before a Court of competent jurisdiction a confession of the commission of the offence; or

(b) at least four Muslim adult male witnesses, about whom the Court is satisfied, having regard to the requirmenets of tazkiyah al-shuhood, that they are truthful persons and abstain from major sins (kabair), give evidence as eye-witnesses of the act of penetration necessary to the offence.

Provided that, if the accused is a non-Muslim, the eye-witnesses may be non-Muslims.

Explanation – In this section "tazkiyah al-shuhood" means the mode of inquiry adopted by a Court to satisfy itself as to the credibility of a witness.

9. Cases in which hadd shall not be enforced – (1) In a case in which the offence of zina or zina-bil-jabr is proved only by the confession of the convict, hadd, or such part of it as is yet to be enforced, shall not be enforced if the convict retracts his confession before the hadd or such part is enforced.

(2) In a case in which the offence of zina or zina-bil-jabr is proved only by testimony, hadd, or such part of it as is yet to be enforced, shall not be enforced if any witness resiles from his testimony before hadd or such part is enforced, so as to reduce the number of eye-witnesses to less than four.

238

(3) In the case mentioned in subsection (1), the Court may order retrial.

(4) In the case mentioned in subsection (2), the Court may award tazir on the basis of the evidence on record.

10. <u>Zina or zina-bil-jabr liable to tazir</u> – (1) Subject to the provisions of section 7, whoever commits zina or zina-bil-jabr which is not liable to hadd, or for which proof in either of the forms mentioned in section 8 is not available and the punishment of qazf liable to hadd has not been awarded to the complainant, or for which hadd may not be enforced under this Ordinance, shall be liable to tazir.

(2) Whoever commits zina liable to tazir shall be punished with rigorous imprisonment for a term which may extend to ten years and with whipping numbering thirty stripes, and shall also be liable to fine.

(3) Whoever commits zina-bil-jabr liable to tazir shall be punished with imprisonment for a term which may extend to twenty-five years and shall also be awarded the punishment of whipping numbering thirty stripes.

11. <u>Kidnapping, abducting or inducing woman to compel for marriage etc.</u> – Whoever kidnaps or abducts any woman with intent that she may be compelled, or knowing it to be likely that she will be compelled, to marry any person against her will, or in order that she may be forced or seduced to illicit intercourse, or knowing it to be likely that she will be forced or seduced to illicit intercourse, shall be punished with imprisonment for life and with whipping not exceeding thirty stripes, and shall also be liable to fine; and whoever by means of criminal intimidation as defined in the Pakistan Penal Code (Act XLV of 1860), or of abuse of authority or any other method of compulsion, induces any woman to go from any place with intent that she may be, or knowing that it is likely that she will be, forced or seduced to illicit intercourse with another person shall also be punishable as aforesaid.....

.....15. <u>Cohabitation caused by a man deceitfully inducing a belief of lawful marriage</u> – Every man who by deceit causes any woman who is not lawfully married to him to believe that she is lawfully married to him and to cohabit with him in that belief, shall be punished with rigorous imprisonment for a term which may extend to twenty-five years and with whipping not exceeding thirty stripes, and shall also be liable to fine.

16. <u>Enticing or taking away or detaining with criminal intent a woman</u> – Whoever takes or entices away any woman with intent that she may have illicit intercourse with any person, or conceals or detains with that intent any woman, shall be punished with imprisonment of either description for a term which may extend to seven years and with whipping not exceeding thirty stripes, and shall also be liable to fine.

17. <u>Mode of execution of punishment of stoning to death</u> –

The punishment of stoning to death awarded under section 5 or section 6 shall be executed in the following manner, namely:-

Such of the witnesses who deposed against the convict as may be available shall start stoning him and, while stoning is being carried on, he may be shot dead, whereupon stoning and shooting shall be stopped.

18. Punishment for attempting to commit an offence – Whoever attempts to commit an offence punishable under this Ordinance with imprisonment or whipping, or to cause such an offence to be committed, and in such attempt does any act towards the commission of the offence, shall be punished with imprisonment for a term which may extend to one-half of the longest term provided for that offence, or with whipping not exceeding thirty stripes, or with such fine as is provided for the offence, or with any two of, or all, the punishments.....

.....21. Presiding Officer of Court to be Muslim – The Presiding Officer of the Court by which a case is tried, or an appeal is heard, under this Ordinance shall be a Muslim:

Provided that, if the accused is a non-Muslim, the Presiding Officer may be a non-Muslim.

22. Saving – Nothing in this Ordinance shall be deemed to apply to the case pending before any Court immediately before the commencement of this Ordinance, or to offences committed before such commencement.

ORDINANCE VIII OF 1979
OFFENCE OF QAZF (ENFORCEMENT OF HADD)
ORDINANCE, 1979

1. Short title, extent and commencement – (1) This Ordinance may be called the Offence of Qazf (Enforcement of Hadd) Ordinance, 1979.

(2) It extends to the whole of Pakistan.

(3) It shall come into force on the twelfth day of Rabi-ul-Awwal, 1399 Hijri, that is, the tenth day of February, 1979.

2. Definitions – In this Ordinance, unless there is anything repugnant in the subject or context, –

(a) "adult", "hadd", "tazir", "zina" and "zina-bil-jabr" have the same meaning as in the Offence of Zina (Enforcement of Hudood) Ordinance, 1979; and

(b) all other terms and expressions not defined in this Ordinance shall have the same meaning as in the Pakistan Penal Code (Act XLV of 1860), or the Code of Criminal Procedure, 1898 (Act V of 1898).

3. Qazf – Whoever by words either spoken or intended to be read, or by signs or by visible representations, makes or publishes an imputation of zina concerning any person intending to harm, or knowing or having reason to believe that such imputation will harm, the reputation, or hurt the

feelings, of such person, is said, except in the cases hereinafter excepted, to commit qazf.

Explanation 1 - It may amount to qazf to impute zina to a deceased person, if the imputation would harm the reputation, or hurt the feelings, of that person if living, and is hurtful to the feelings of his family or other near relatives.

Explanation 2 - An imputation in the form of an alternative or expressed ironically, may amount to qazf.

First Exception (Imputation of truth which public good requires to be made or published) - It is not qazf to impute zina to any person if the imputation be true and made or published for the public good. Whether or not it is for the public good, is a question of fact.

Second Exception (Accusation preferred in good faith to authorised person) - Save in the cases hereinafter mentioned, it is not qazf to prefer in good faith an accusation of zina against any person to any of those who have lawful authority over that person with respect to the subject-matter of accusation -

(a) A complainant makes an accusation of zina against another person in a Court, but fails to produce four witnesses in support thereof before the Court.

(b) According to the finding of the Court, a witness has given false evidence of the commission of zina or zina-bil-jabr.

(c) According to the finding of the Court, complainant has made a false accusation of zina-bil-jabr.

4. Two kinds of qazf - Qazf may be either qazf liable to hadd or qazf liable to tazir.

5. Qazf liable to hadd - Whoever, being an adult, intentionally and without ambiguity commits qazf of zina liable to hadd against a particular person who is a muhsan and capable of performing sexual intercourse is, subject to the provisions of this Ordinance, said to commit qazf liable to hadd.

Explanation 1 - In this section, "muhsan" means a sane and adult Muslim who either has had no sexual intercourse or has had such intercourse only with his or her lawfully wedded spouse.

Explanation 2 - If a person makes in respect of another person the imputation that such other person is an illegitimate child, or refuses to recognise such person to be a legitimate child, he shall be deemed to have committed qazf liable to hadd in respect of the mother of that person.

6. Proof of qazf liable to hadd - Proof of qazf liable to hadd shall be in one of the following forms, namely:-

(a) the accused makes before a Court of competent jurisdiction a confession of the commission of the offence.

(b) the accused commits qazf in the presence of the Court; and

(c) at least two Muslim adult male witnesses, other than

241

the victim of the qazf, about whom the Court is satisfied, having regard to the requirements of tazkiyah al-shuhood, that they are truthful persons and abstain from major sins (kabair), give direct evidence of the commission of qazf;

Provided that, if the accused is a non-Muslim, the witnesses may be non-Muslims:

Provided further that the statement of the complainant or the person authorised by him shall be recorded before the statements of the witnesses are recorded.

7. <u>Punishment of qazf liable to hadd</u> - (1) Whoever commits qazf liable to hadd shall be punished with whipping numbering eighty stripes.

(2) After a person has been convicted for the offence of qazf liable to hadd, his evidence shall not be admissible in any Court of law.

(3) A punishment awarded under subsection (1) shall not be executed until it has been confirmed by the Court to which an appeal from the Court awarding the punishment lies; and, until the punishment is confirmed and executed, the convict shall, subject to the provisions of the Code of Criminal Procedure, 1898 (Act V of 1898) relating to the grant of bail or suspension of sentence, be dealt with in the same manner as if sentenced to simple imprisonment.

8. <u>Who can file a complaint</u> - No proceedings under this Ordinance shall be initiated except on a report made to the police or a complaint lodged in a Court by the following, namely:

(a) if the person in respect of whom the qazf has been committed be alive, that person, or any person authorised by him; or

(b) if the person in respect of whom the qazf has been committed be dead, any of the ascendants or descendants of that person.

9. <u>Cases in which hadd shall not be imposed or enforced</u> - (1) Hadd shall not be imposed for qazf in any of the following cases, namely:-

(a) when a person has committed qazf against any of his descendants;

(b) when the person in respect of whom qazf has been committed and who is a complainant has died during the pendency of the proceedings; and

(c) when the imputation has been proved to be true.

(2) In a case in which, before the execution of hadd, the complainant withdraws his allegation of qazf, or states that the accused had made a false confession or that any of the witnesses had deposed falsely and the number of witnesses is thereby reduced to less than two, hadd shall not be enforced, but the Court may order retrial or award tazir on the basis of the evidence on record.

10. <u>Qazf liable to tazir</u> - Whoever commits <u>qazf</u> which is not liable to <u>hadd</u>, or for which proof in any of the forms

mentioned in section 6 is not available, or for which <u>hadd</u> may not be imposed or enforced under section 9, is said to commit <u>qazf</u> liable to <u>tazir</u>.

11. <u>Punishment for qazf liable to tazir</u> — Whoever commits qazf liable to tazir shall be punished with imprisonment of either description for a term which may extend to two years and with whipping not exceeding forty stripes, and shall also be liable to fine.

12. <u>Printing or engraving matter known to be of the nature referred to in section 3</u> — Whoever prints or engraves any matter, knowing or having good reason to believe that such matter is of the nature referred to in section 3, shall be punished with imprisonment of either description for a term which may extend to two years, or with whipping not exceeding thirty stripes, or with fine, or with any two of, or all, the punishments.

13. <u>Sale of printed or engraved substance containing matter of the nature referred to in section 3</u> — Whoever sells or offers for sale any printed or engraved substance containing matter of the nature referred to in section 3, knowing that it contains such matter, shall be punished with imprisonment of either description for a term which may extend to two years, or with whipping not exceeding thirty stripes, or with fine, or with any two of, or all, the punishments.

14. <u>Lian</u> — (1) When a husband accuses before a Court his wife who is muhsan within the meaning of section 5, of zina and the wife does not accept the accusation as true, the following procedure of lian shall apply, namely:-

(a) the husband shall say upon oath before the Court: "I swear by Allah the Almighty and say I am surely truthful in my accusation of zina against my wife (name of wife)" and, after he has said so four times, he shall say: "Allah's curse be upon me if I am a liar in my accusation of zina against my wife (name of wife)"; and

(b) the wife shall, in reply to the husband's statement made in accordance with clause (a), say upon oath before the Court: "I swear by Allah the Almighty that my husband is surely a liar in his accusation of zina against me"; and, after she has said so four times, she shall say: "Allah's wrath be upon me if he is truthful in his accusation of zina against me."

(2) When the procedure specified in subsection (1) has been completed, the Court shall pass an order dissolving the marriage between the husband and wife, which shall operate as a decree for dissolution of marriage and no appeal shall lie against it.

(3) Where the husband or the wife refuses to go through the procedure specified in subsection (1), he or, as the case may be, she shall be imprisoned until —

(a) in the case of the husband, he has agreed to go through the aforesaid procedure; or

(b) in the case of the wife, she has either agreed to go through the aforesaid procedure or accepted the husband's accusation as true.

(4) A wife who has accepted the husband's accusation as true shall be awarded the punishment for the offence of zina liable to hadd under the Imposition of Hudood for the Offence of Zina Ordinance, 1979.

15. <u>Punishment for attempt to commit offence punishable under this Ordinance</u> – Whoever attempts to commit an offence punishable under this Ordinance or to cause such an attempt to be committed, and in such attempt does any act towards the commission of the offence, shall be punished with imprisonment for a term which may extend to one-half of the longest term provided for the offence, or with such whipping or fine as is provided for the offence, or with any two of, or all, the punishments.

16. <u>Application of certain provisions of Pakistan Penal Code (Act XLV of 1860)</u> – (1) Unless otherwise expressly provided in this Ordinance, the provisions of sections 34 to 38 of Chapter II, sections 63 to 72 of Chapter III and Chapters V and V-A of the Pakistan Penal Code (Act XLV of 1860), shall apply <u>mutatis mutandis</u>, in respect of offences under this Ordinance.

(2) Whoever is guilty of the abetment of an offence liable to hadd under this Ordinance shall be liable to the punishment provided for such offence as tazir.....

.....18. <u>Presiding Officer of Court to be a Muslim</u> – The Presiding Officer, or the Court by which a case is tried, or an appeal is heard, under this Ordinance, shall be a Muslim.

19. <u>Ordinance to override other laws</u> – The Provisions of this Ordinance shall have effect notwithstanding anything contained in any other law for the time being in force.

20. <u>Saving</u> – Nothing in this Ordinance shall be deemed to apply to cases pending before any Court immediately before the commencement of this Ordinance, or to offences committed before such commencement.

<u>Ila</u>

The basis of dissolution by <u>ila</u> is the Qur'an, Sura II : 226,7. If the husband takes an oath that he will not have sexual intercourse with his wife for a period of four months or more and that period expires without his retraction of the oath or any resumption of intercourse there is in Hanafi law an automatic dissolution of the marriage; there is no need of any intervention by the Qadi. The divorce is irrevocable. Although <u>ila</u> must be quite uncommon and largely of antiquarian interest there is no doubt that it is still possible, being expressly preserved by the Muslim Personal Law (Shariat) Application Act 1937.

Zihar

The basis of dissolution by _zihar_ is the Qur´an, Sura LVIII : 2-4. If the husband compares his wife to a woman with whom the husband´s marriage would be _batil_ because she would be permanently forbidden to him, e.g. his mother or sister, then intercourse between the husband and wife is forbidden until the husband performs an act of expiation. If the husband refuses to do such an act of expiation the wife may complain to the Qadi who may imprison the husband until he either does an act of expiation or divorces the wife, though the Qadi may not under Hanafi law decree a dissolution personally. _Zihar_ too must be very uncommon but again it is expressly recognised by the Act of 1937.

Difference of Domicile

Although this ground of dissolution seems obsolete, in the absence of any indication to the contrary it would appear that s.2(ix) of the Dissolution of Muslim Marriages Act 1939 might well be used to obtain such a dissolution. It is necessary for these purposes to distinguish between a factual and a legal domicile. In practice this is a distinction between the cases where a couple are temporarily separated, one in _dar al-Islam_ and the other in _dar al-harb_, which constitutes a legal difference of domicile, and where they are permanently separated, one in _dar al-Islam_, the other in _dar al-harb_, which is a factual separation. The Muslim jurists held that a factual but not a legal separation of this nature was a ground for the dissolution of the marriage.

This is to some extent amended in the modern law. Whereas the classical law held the marriage to be dissolved on the expiry of three menstrual cycles, the provisions of the Dissolution of Muslim Marriages Act 1939 now apply so that a judicial decree is needed and of course the wife alone may seek one under this section.

The definition of _dar al-Islam_ and _dar al-harb_ and the question whether Pakistan is the former is uncertain. _Dar al-Islam_ is that territory in which the law of Islam prevails, the rest of the world being _dar al-harb_.

Conclusions on the Muslim law of Divorce

There is no question that to the western observer the Muslim law of divorce, even allowing for the recent developments in the Indian subcontinent, remains in practice heavily weighted in favour of the husband. It cannot be denied that the classical law of divorce and of _talaq_ in particular is perfectly consistent with the theory of Muslim marriage law and with basic Islamic tenets in general. It is however equally certain that the imbalance was exaggerated by the incorrect and restrictive interpretations of some Qur'anic verses and Hadith, particularly in Hanafi law - a fact perhaps in the minds of those Hanafi jurists who claimed that the law of other schools might be applied where a strict application of Hanafi law could cause hardship to the wife. The distinctive characteristic of Muslim divorce law is the unrestricted right of the husband to repudiate his wife even without cause and by comparison the extremely circumscribed rights of the wife to dissolve her marriage unilaterally. The explanation given by Muslim apologists, that divorce is in the eyes of Allah the most detestable of things and that the responsibility of holding this power and the drastic consequences for the holder of its abuse are so great that it cannot be entrusted to women who are weak in resolve and would use it wantonly and for small cause but must be a burden on men's shoulders alone, reflects the tendency often apparent in Islamic Jurisprudence to extend theological tenets to their logical conclusion without regard for the possible practical hardship and injustice this may cause. Nor has Islamic Jurisprudence successfully explained the continued conferment of the power of _talaq_ on those men who have shown themselves irresponsible in its use, with the limited sanctions of a dower debt payable on divorce in some cases and the denial of remarriage to their divorced wife without her intervening consummated marriage with another man.

It may seem an odd response, when criticising the unrestricted _talaq_, to extend the wife's rights to divorce, thereby further weakening the marriage bond. But this may well be the only way in the short term of relieving the wife of some of the abuse of _talaq_ and consequent ill-treatment to which the Muslim system in practice though quite definitely not in intent lays her open. Even this is deficient in at least one important respect: the lack of alimony and social attitudes to single women in Muslim society mean that many Muslim women prefer the unhappy or polygamous marriage to the status of divorcee. Lest this be thought a hostile or unsympathetic view of the Muslim law which would command no acceptance in the Muslim world it may be pointed out that many Muslim states have taken steps to legislate against the imbalance by restricting the right of _talaq_ or by enhancing the wife's rights to dissolution in court. A number of states in which Maliki law does not prevail have introduced legislation similar to that in the Dissolution of Muslim Marriages Act 1939 concerning physical defects and failure to pay maintenance. Cruelty and polygamy have been made grounds for a judicial decree of divorce and a breakdown of the marriage or even the unilateral wishes of the wife without cause, on payment of some compensation. By contrast India has done nothing to restrict the abuse of _talaq_ and Pakistan has effectively only tinkered with the incidents of _talaq_. The

246

Khurshid Bibi decision while important in its own right
strikes only at a symptom of the real problem. It is still
true to say that the Muslim wife in India and Pakistan lives
under the perpetual threat of divorce and therein lies the
inequality and inevitable instability of Muslim marriage.
Which of these two elements, inequality or instability, is the
greater evil is a matter of opinion and religious conscience
and will determine one's approach to the problem. To those
who believe that an uncontrollable right of talaq to be the
greater evil the position in certain Middle Eastern states
where measures have been taken to require extended periods of
maintenance and judicial decrees compares favourably with the
Muslim Family laws Ordinance 1961. The Muslim law of divorce,
whatever its merits, remains a complicated but fascinating
maze of possibilities.

ALI NAWAZ (Appellant) v. MOHD YUSUF (Respondent)
PLD 1963 S.C. 51. (Supreme Court)

[The question before the Court was whether Christa Renata, a
non-Muslim, non-Pakistani, had been divorced by a Shia Muslim
(the petitioner) and was therefore free to marry the
respondent, and if the requirements of Shia law had been met,
whether those of the Muslim Family Laws Ordinance were also
met.]

S.A. Rahman, J.....32. The alleged talaq could at best be
described as talaq bidat, which is not recognised as valid by
Shia law. (See Baillie's Digest of Muhammadan Law, Part II,
p. 118, Tyabji's Muhammadan Law, Third Edition, Ss. 136-142,
Mulla's Muhammadan Law, p. 662, Fifteen Edition, Amir Ali's
Muhammadan Law, Fourth Edition, Vol. II, p. 533). These
text-book writers, moreover, are unanimous in stating that
according to Shia doctors, the talaq must be orally pronounced
by the husband, in the presence of two witnesses and the wife
in a set form of Arabic words. A written divorce is not
recognized, except in certain circumstances which do not exist
in the present case. The learned trial Judge took the view
that the Document D.1, even if it was executed by the
complainant, was not effective in law to separate the two
spouses because of these provisions of the Shia Fiqh. The
Appellate Bench of the High Court regarded the provisions of
the Shia Fiqh with regard to the presence of witnesses and the
necessity of an oral pronouncement of divorce, as merely rules
of evidence which could be disregarded. The law being,
however, laid down in categorical terms, it is open to
question whether the view taken by the Appellate Bench can be
sustained. The learned Judges do not appear to have adverted
to the point that the alleged talaq was in the heretical form
(Talaqul Bidat) which the Shia dispensation of Islamic Law
does not sanction.

33. Assuming for the sake of argument, that the technicalities of the Shia Fiqh could be ignored in respect of the form of divorce, another obstacle to the document D.1 taking effect from the date of its execution, is raised by the provisions of the Muslim Family Laws Ordinance, 1961. This Ordinance came into force with effect from the 15th July 1961, and by subsection (2) of section 1, declares that it extends to the whole of Pakistan and applies to "all Muslim citizens of Pakistan wherever they may be". Section 3 inter alia declares that the provisions of the Ordinance would have effect, "notwithstanding any law, custom or usage". Section 7 of the Ordinance is pertinent to this case..... .....It is common ground between the parties that the complainant in the case had failed to give notice to the Chairman of the Union Council concerned, in respect of the alleged grant of divorce by him to his wife, as required by this section. The learned trial Judge, therefore, found that, in the face of this section, the talaq failed to operate as such. The learned Judges of the Appellate Bench, however, were of the opinion that the Ordinance itself could not apply to the facts of the case, because Christa Renate was a non-citizen and the Ordinance was meant to apply only to Muslim citizens of Pakistan.

34. A brief examination of the provisions of the Ordinance would seem to be necessary in order to determine its scope. As has been observed above, undoubtedly subsection (2) of section 1 of the Ordinance makes it applicable to all Muslim citizens of Pakistan wherever they may be. The question is whether this means that the provisions of the Ordinance are attracted only if both spouses are Muslim citizens; or even where the husband alone is a Muslim citizen. Mr. Mahmud Ali, on behalf of the respondent, has strenuously argued that the Ordinance would be applicable only where both parties to a marriage are Muslim citizens.

35. Section 5 of the Ordinance provides that every marriage solemnized under Muslim Law, shall be registered, in accordance with the provisions of the Ordinance and for this purpose, the Union Council is authorized to grant licences to one or more persons, to be called Nikah Registrars. Every marriage not solemnized by the Nikah Registrar, is required to be reported to him by the person officiating at the marriage, for the purpose of registration, and contravention of this provision is made punishable with simple imprisonment for a term which may extend to three months, or with fine up to one thousand rupees, or with both. The section appears to be general in character, with the only limitation that the marriage should have been solemnized under Muslim Law. It is impossible to read into it a further limitation that the marriage should necessarily be between two Pakistani Muslims. A marriage entered into by a Pakistani Muslim male with say, an Indian Muslim woman, would seem to fall within the purview

of this section, if it is performed within Pakistan.

36. Section 6 is aimed at restricting polygamy. Subsection (1) thereof reads: "No man, during the subsistence of an existing marriage, shall, except with the previous permission in writing of the Arbitration Council, contract another marriage, nor shall any such marriage contracted without such permission, be registered under this Ordinance." The expression "existing marriage" stands unqualified and would obviously cover the marriage of a Pakistani Muslim male with a Muslim non-citizen or even a non-Muslim lady, if it is recognised as valid by the laws of Pakistan. The expression "another marriage" occurring subsequently in this subsection, should have the same connotation, prima facie. The generality of the words cannot be cut down by importing into this subsection any extraneous considerations. The Ordinance of course only penalises the person in respect of a marriage, celebrated in contravention of the provisions of the Ordinance by making him liable to imprisonment or fine or both but does not invalidate the marriage itself. But that has no bearing on the question we are considering.

37. Coming next to the important section 7 itself, it seems to us that the Legislature had attempted to incorporate the Islamic Law provisions with regard to the two forms of "Talaq-us-Sunnat", viz., "Talaq Ahsan" and "Talaq Hasan", as far as may be, in this section. The first of them is that form in which a single pronouncement of divorce is made during a period of menstrual purity, no intercourse having taken place during that period, and is followed by a period of iddat. The second is one in which the first pronouncement made in similar circumstances is followed by two further pronouncements in succeeding periods, no intercourse taking place at any time during the three periods. Such a divorce becomes irrevocable on the third pronouncement. Whether the result achieved is in strict conformity with Islamic Law is a question which does not fall within the province of this Court to determine by reason of Articles 5 and 6 of the Constitution. The section clearly contemplates a machinery of conciliation whereby a husband wishing to divorce his wife unilaterally, may be enabled to think better of it, if the mediation of others can resolve the differences between the spouses. The talaq pronounced is to be ineffective for a period of 90 days from the date on which notice under subsection (1) of this section is delivered to the Chairman and this period is to be utilized for the attempt at reconciliation. Subsection (6) makes it clear that even if talaq has become effective under the previous subsections, the spouses would not be prevented from re-marrying, without an intervening marriage with a third person, unless such termination is effective for the third time. All that the section requires is that the marriage in question should be dissolvable by means of a talaq and it does not seem necessary

249

to adopt the narrow construction contended for on behalf of the respondent, that the wife mentioned in the section must necessarily be a Pakistani citizen. To suggest, as Mr. Mahmud Ali has done, that unless she is such a citizen she would have no right to appoint an Arbitrator on her behalf, under section 2(a) of the Ordinance, appears to beg the question.

38. Mr. Mahmud Ali also put forward the suggestion that the word "effective", occurring in subsection (3) of this section, means "effective against the husband only", and that if the husband failed to give the required notice to the Chairman, the talaq would be effective at once. This interpretation would make the section itself wholly nugatory. All that the husband has to do then is that he should refrain from giving the requisite notice and the talaq would automatically take effect. This is exactly the mischief which the section seems designed to remedy. The alternative contention raised by the learned counsel that Talaq Bidat is altogether outside the purview of the section is plainly untenable as it takes no account of the words "talaq in any form whatsoever" occurring in subsection (1) of section 7.

39. Mr. Mahmud Ali also tried to maintain that in the present case, to permit the complainant to say that by not giving the notice to the Chairman, the divorce granted by him had been robbed of legal effect, would be tantamount to allowing him to take advantage of his own wrong. Learned counsel referred to pages 200 - 203 of Maxwell´s Interpretation of Statutes, Eleventh Edition, in support of the proposition that on the general principle of avoiding injustice and absurdity, any construction would, if possible, be rejected (unless the policy and object of the Act required it) which enabled a person to defeat or impair the obligation of his contract by his own act or otherwise to profit by his own wrong. But here it is obvious that the object of section 7 is to prevent hasty dissolution of marriages by talaq, pronounced by the husband, unilaterally, without an attempt being made to prevent disruption of the matrimonial status. If the husband himself thinks better of the pronouncement of talaq and abstains from giving a notice to the Chairman, he should perhaps be deemed, in view of section 7, to have revoked the pronouncement and that would be to the advantage of the wife. Subsection (3) of this section precludes the talaq from being effective as such, for a certain period and within that period, consequently, it could not be said that the marital status of the parties had in any way been changed. They would still in law continue to be husband and wife.....

.....40. The sphere of attempted conciliation seems to be further extended by section 8 of the Ordinance to cases of "Talaq Tafviz" and also to other forms of dissolution of marriage at the instance of either party, mutatis mutandis, and this throws further light on the objective aimed at by the Ordinance. It would be idle to speculate what alternative forms of dissolution are contemplated by this section.

41. There is nothing in section 9 of the Ordinance (which relates to maintenance to be provided by the husband for the wife) that could cut down the connotation of the term "wife" to a Muslim citizen of Pakistan alone.

42. To hold that the Ordinance could not be pressed into service except in cases where both spouses were Muslim citizens, would lead to the result that a male Muslim citizen, could with impunity, have more than one wife, without recourse to the provisions of the Ordinance, provided that he confines himself to non-citizen Muslim ladies, for marriage purposes. On this interpretation, if a Muslim male citizen of Pakistan, is already married to a Muslim non-citizen, he could marry another wife, whether a Muslim citizen or not, without incurring any penalty under the Ordinance. Similarly, he could go on divorcing non-citizen Muslim ladies, without limit, if he was so minded. Such absurd results would apparently rob the Ordinance of almost all its utility and the narrow interpretation which leads to such results, would not, in all probability, be in consonance with the intention of the Legislature. The policy of the Ordinance seems to be to provide some curbs on too facile pronouncements of divorce and unnecessary or unjustified plural marriages.....

MUHAMMAD LATIF (Petitioner) v. HANIFAN BIBI (Respondent)
1980 P.Cr.3. 123 (Lahore) (Rustam S. Sidhwa, J.)

Judgement.....2. The brief facts of the case are that Muhammad Latif petitioner married Mst. Hanifan Bibi, respondent No. 1, in 1966. On 13th October 1977, the petitioner divorced the respondent by sending a written talaq to her by registered A. D. post, with notice of the same to the Ilaqa Chairman. Without waiting for the ninety days period to expire as provided under section 7 (3) of the Muslim Family Laws Ordinance, 1961, the petitioner contracted a second marriage on 21st October 1977. On 13th January 1978, the petitioner´s talaq became effective, after the reconciliation proceedings before the Chairman ended in failure. On 13th December 1977, the respondent filed a private complaint against the petitioner under section 6 (5) of the Muslim Family Laws Ordinance, 1961, before the Ilaqa Magistrate, Sadar, Lahore Cantonment, inter alia alleging that her husband had during the subsistence of her marriage contracted a second marriage without securing the previous permission in writing of the Arbitration Council as provided by section 6 (1) of the said Ordinance and was thus liable for prosecution. After recording the necessary preliminary evidence, the petitioner was summoned to stand trial. On 14th February 1978, the Magistrate framed a charge against the petitioner under section 6 (5) of the Muslim Family Laws

Ordinance, 1961. Being aggrieved by the said proceedings, the petitioner filed the present quashment petition, which is now before me for disposal.

3. The learned counsel for the petitioner, in support of his petition, contended that since the private complaint under section 6 (5) of the Muslim Family Laws Ordinance, 1961, had been lodged by the respondent wife and not by the Union Council, as provided in rule 21 of the West Pakistan Rules under the Muslim Family Laws Ordinance, 1961, therefore, the same was incompetent. In this connection, he relied upon Muhammad Islam v. The State (P L D 1967 Pesh. 201), Mst. Maqbool Jan v. Arshad Hassan and another (P L D 1975 Lah. 147) and Fateh Muhammad v. Chairman, Union Committee and others (P L D 1975 Lah. 951). The learned counsel for the petitioner also submitted that notwithstanding the provisions of section 7 (3) of the Muslim Family Laws Ordinance, 1961, the Talaq-i-Badai or Talaq-ul-Bidaat given in writing by the petitioner to his wife became effective on 13th October 1977 under Muslim Personal Law and that the relationship of husband and wife between the parties having ceased on 13th October 1977, the petitioner was competent to contract a marriage a second time on 21st October 1977 without securing the prior permission in writing of the Arbitration Council as required by section 6 (1) of the Muslim Family Laws Ordinance, 1961. It was also contended that though section 7 (3) of the Muslim Family Laws Ordinance had the effect of suspending the effectiveness of the divorce for ninety days for collateral purposes, such as, for the purpose of bringing about a reconciliation between the spouses, it could not destroy the irrevocability of the Talaq-ul-Bida'at or Talaq-i-Badai, which had become effective on 13th October 1977. In this connection Mrs. Parveen Chaudhry v. Senior Civil Judge (P L D 1976 Kar. 416), Abdul Aziz v. Razia Khatoon (1969 D L C 586) and Mst. Fahmida Bibi v. Mukhtar Ahmad (P L D 1972 Lah. 694) were cited. In view of these cumulative facts, it was submitted that no violation of section 6 (1) of the Muslim Family Laws Ordinance was made out and that, therefore, the respondent's private complaint deserved to be quashed.

4. The learned counsel for the respondent wife, who strongly opposed the petition, in dealing with the petitioner's counsel's first objection regarding the competency of the petition, submitted that rule 21 of the West Pakistan Rules under the Muslim Family Laws Ordinance, 1961, was amended on 26th November 1976 by Notification No. SOX-1-15/75-Vol.II, dated 26th November 1976, and that with effect from that date, the Courts were competent to take cognizance of offences under the Ordinance or its Rules on the complaint in writing of any aggrieved party. Since rule 21 was amended on 18th November 1976 and the respondent had filed her private complaint against the petitioner on 13th December 1977, it was submitted that the complaint was competent and

252

that there was no bar to the Ilaqa Magistrate taking
cognizance of the same in law. As regards the remaining legal
submissions made by the learned counsel for the petitioner,
the learned counsel for the respondent submitted that section
7 of the Muslim Family Laws Ordinance, 1961, did not make any
distinction between different forms of pronouncements of _talaq_
and whatever was the form of pronouncement of _talaq_, the said
talaq remained ineffective until after the expiration of
ninety days from the day on which notice was delivered to the
Chairman and that during this period of ninety days, the
marital status of the parties did not, in any way change. In
this connection, learned counsel for the petitioner relied
upon _Ali Nawaz v. Muhammad Yousaf_ (P L D 1963 S C 51), _Mst._
Fahmida Bibi v. Mukhtar Ahmad (P L D 1972 Lah. 694) and _Mst._
Maqbool Jan v. Arshad Hassan (P L D 1975 Lah. 147).

5. The contentions raised by the learned counsel for the
petitioner and the respondent have engaged my serious
attention. As regards the plea of the learned counsel for the
petitioner that the private complaint of the respondent was
incompetent because it was not initiated at the instance of
the Union Council, in view of rule 21 of the West Pakistan
Rules under the Muslim Family Laws Ordinance, 1961, the said
contention has no force as the said rule was amended on 26th
November 1976 by Notification No. SOX-1-15/75-Vol. II of the
same date (see P L D 1977 Punjab Statutes 30) and the words
"Union Council" were replaced by the words "aggrieved party".
In these circumstances, the present petition by the respondent
wife, who is an aggrieved party, is competent in law. As
regards the other legal submissions made by the learned
counsel for the petitioner, the same are all answered in _Ali_
Nawaz Gardezi's case. In this case at page 75, Mr. Justice S.
A. Rehman clearly held that subsection (1) of section 7 of the
Muslim Family Laws Ordinance took into account all forms of
talaq and that no particular form was outside its purview and
that subsection (3) of the same section precluded a _talaq_ from
being effective as such, for a certain period and within that
period "it could not be said that the marital status of the
parties had, in any way, been changed. They would still in
law continue to be husband and wife". In fact, _Mrs. Parveen_
Chaudhry v. Senior Civil Judge (P L D 1976 Kar. 416), _Abdul_
Aziz v. Razia Khatoon (1969 D L C 586) and _Mst. Fahmida Bibi_
v. Mukhtar Ahmad do not support the various propositions
raised by the petitioner. On the contrary they support the
arguments of the learned counsel for the respondent. In the
light of these rulings, I have no hesitation in holding that
though the divorce in the instant case was given on 13th
October 1977 to the respondent wife, yet it remained legally
ineffective for all purposes till 13th January 1978,
notwithstanding the now obsolete principle of Hanfi Muslim
Personal Law, which recognised the heretical Talaq-ul-Bidaat
or Talaq-i-Badai (introduced by the Omeyad Monarchs) as

irrevocable and taking effect immediately on its execution if given in writing. On the principle laid down in <u>Ali Nawaz Gardezi's case</u>, the present <u>talaq</u> remained ineffective upto 13th January 1978 and during this period the marital status of the parties did not undergo any change. In these circumstances, on 21st October 1977, if the petitioner contracted a second marriage during the subsistence of his first existing marriage, he was liable to secure the previous permission in writing of the Arbitration Council.

6. Section 7 (3) of the Muslim Family Laws Ordinance, 1961, by providing a period of ninety days for purposes of bringing about a reconciliation introduces into the Talaq-ul-Bidat or Talaq-i-Badai the provisions of Talaq Ahsan referred to in Sura Al-Talaq of the Holy Qur'an. Section 7 (3) of the 1961 Ordinance is therefore, not repugnant to the injunctions of Islam as laid down in the Holy Qur'an or the Sunnah of the Holy Prophet so as to invite any special examination under Article 203-B of the Constitution of Pakistan. Even otherwise, under the Explanation to Article 203-B of the Constitution, Muslim Personal Law is exempt from any such examination and a provision which makes a material amendment to any particular branch of Muslim Personal Law is as much a part of the personal law itself to earn the exemption as provided by the Explanation. The amendment is a beneficial amendment and brings the provisions of <u>talaq</u> more in conformity with the principle of Talaq Ahsan and therefore, deserves the greatest respect. Being nearest to the Injunction of the Qur'an and the Sunnah of the Holy Prophet, its sanctity is all the more enhanced.

7. From the preliminary evidence recorded, it cannot be said that the present private complaint pending before the Magistrate is one based on no evidence. In these circumstances, no interference is called for.

8. In view of the above, there being no merit in this petition, the same is dismissed.

———————

<u>Mst. FAHMIDA BIBI (Petitioner) v. MUKHTAR AHMAD (Respondent)</u>
<u>PLD 1972 Lahore 694. (Sardar Muhd. Iqbal J.)</u>

<u>Judgement</u>:- The respondent Mukhtar Ahmad instituted a suit for restitution of conjugal rights against the petitioner in the Family Court at Lyallpur. The petitioner pleaded in defence that the Family Court at Lyallpur had no jurisdiction and that she had already been divorced by the respondent and relied on a notice purported to have been given by respondent to the Chairman of Union Committee, Hafizabad and also the certificate of divorce issued by the latter. The respondent denied to have ever given any divorce notice to the Chairman or to have given the divorce to the petitioner. The question of jurisdiction was not made subject-matter of any issue. The

learned Family Judge however, framed the issue: "Whether plaintiff has already been divorced by the defendant.".....

.....2. Learned counsel for the petitioner contends that the certificate issued by the Chairman of the Union Committee that the respondent had divorced the petitioner, his wife, was a conclusive proof of the fact that the petitioner was no more the wife of the respondent, with the result that the suit filed by the respondent for restitution of conjugal rights was not competent and, therefore, the order of the learned Additional District Judge whereby he remanded the case was without any lawful basis.

3. In order to appreciate the contention raised by the learned counsel, it is necessary to examine the relevant provisions of section 7 of the Muslim Family Laws Ordinance.....

.....A divorce thus does not become effective unless the notice is served on the Chairman of the Union Committee or Council and ninety days expire from the date of receipt of the notice by him. The Chairman is required to bring about reconciliation between the parties for which purpose he is to give notice to them to nominate their representatives in order to constitute the Arbitration Council. If any of the parties fails to appear before him, he cannot enforce his attendance nor a default of appearance on the part of any of the parties can be visited with any penal consequence. The divorce, notwithstanding the conduct or attitude of any of the parties, shall become effective after the expiry of ninety days unless the divorce is revoked earlier by the husband. In the event, the parties appear before the Chairman and an Arbitration Council is constituted, but reconciliation does not succeed, the only thing the Council or the Chairman may do, is to record in writing that reconciliation has failed. There is no other function which a Chairman or an Arbitration Council is competent to perform in this behalf. If reconciliation does not succeed or the husband does not revoke _talaq_ before expiry of ninety days, it becomes automatically operative and effective. There is no provision either in the Ordinance or the Rules requiring the Chairman or the Arbitration Council to give a decision or to issue a certificate to make the divorce effective. If the Chairman issued the certificate, it was not under any provision of law and had no legal effect.

4. The case can be examined from another angle as well. If under subsection (3) of section 7 of the Ordinance, the husband revokes the _talaq_ before the expiration of ninety days, the spouses continue in law to be husband and wife. Learned counsel for the petitioner has not pointed out any provision of law, and in fact there is none, under which the husband is to inform the Chairman of his decision that he has revoked the _talaq_. The words "unless revoked earlier, expressly or otherwise" are significant. A husband who pronounces divorce on his wife and has served the Chairman

255

with the notice under section 7 of the Ordinance may simply revoke it and inform his wife of his decision. What will in such a case be the value of a certificate which the Chairman may have issued in his ignorance of the factum of revocation of the divorce? The certificate, therefore, cannot at all be a proof, let alone a conclusive proof, of the divorce, as is alleged in the present case. If the certificate is used as a proof of divorce, it will be inconsistent with the statutory right of the husband to revoke _talaq_ before the expiry of ninety days either "expressly or otherwise". It may be one of the reasons for the Legislature in not providing for the issuance of the certificate of divorce by the Chairman of a Council.....

.....6. The learned counsel contended that if the Chairman or the Arbitration Council does not issue a certificate the entire purpose and object of section 7 of the Ordinance will be frustrated.

We are not called upon to adjudicate on the propriety or expedience of the legislation, our functions being limited only to the interpretation and enforcement of the law. Nonetheless, we have no doubt in our mind that the provisions are in the public interest. They have obviated a lot of complications which had been experienced in the past. The provisions of section 7 are meant to prevent hasty dissolution of marriages by _talaq_ pronounced by the husband unilaterally. Similarly, a recalcitrant husband or wife cannot now successfully raise the plea of divorce in the event a dispute arises between the spouses about their marital rights and obligations, unless it is substantiated by proving that notice as required by section 7 of the Ordinance had been served. There is now no possibility of any dispute about the status of a woman after the death of her husband that she has been divorced during his lifetime. The plea of some of the heirs that certain children of the deceased were born after the divorce and, therefore, were illegitimate also cannot successfully be advanced without proving compliance with section 7 by the husband. The Ordinance has, doubtless, ensured certainty about marital status.

The learned counsel next contended that if the Chairman does not issue the certificate, it may make the position of a wife uncertain and the husband may, notwithstanding the divorce, assert that he had not done so. The apprehension is unfounded, because the notice to the Chairman, if it is proved to have been given by him will furnish a proof of divorce unless the husband can prove that he revoked it before the expiry of ninety days.

Viewed from another angle, it may happen that someone may, in collusion with a wife, forge a notice and send it to the Chairman. He may also not appear before the Chairman to nominate his representative. It may also happen that someone on the basis of a forged notice obtain a certificate from the

Chairman that the marriage has been dissolved. In such cases, to preclude the husband from proving in his case for restitution of conjugal rights that he had not divorced his wife will amount to putting premium on forgery and fraud. There is no bar in law for the husband to contest the genuineness or validity of the notice. If it is proved that the husband did not give the notice, the entire proceedings based on that before the Chairman, under the Ordinance, would be a nullity in the eyes of law. However, in the event the wife successfully proves that the notice was, in fact, sent by him or that when appeared before the Chairman he did not dispute the notice, the divorce will become effective unless he is able to establish that he revoked the divorce before the expiration of ninety days.

8. On the above _vire of_ the matter, I find no force in this petition which is hereby dismissed _in limine_.

MUHD. AZAM KHAN (Appellant) v. AKHTAR UN NISSA BEGUM (Respondent)
P.L.D. 1957 Lah. 195. (Changez J.)

Judgement.....The sole question, therefore, which requires determination is whether in the circumstances of the case the divorce is void being against law and opposed to public policy.

In this connection Mr. Ata Ullah Sajjad, the learned counsel for the respondent, vehemently urged that the parties being Muslims, the rule of decision in matter of divorce shall be the Muslim Personal Law, i.e. Shariat. Section 2 of the West Punjab Muslim Personal Law (Shariat) Application Act (IX of 1948), as amended by section 2 of the Punjab Muslim Personal Law (Shariat) Application (Amendment) Act, 1951, provides:-

"Notwithstanding any rule of custom or usage, in all questions regarding succession (whether testate or intestate) special property of females, betrothal, marriage, divorce, dower, adoption, guardianship, minority, legitimacy or bastardy, family, relations, wills, legacies, gifts, religious usages or institutions including _waqfs_, trusts and trust property, the rule of decision shall be Muslim Personal Law (Shariat) in cases where the parties are Muslims."

It will thus be seen that where the parties are Muslims, the rules of Muhammadan Law in respect of betrothal, marriage, divorce and dower, etc., have been expressly directed to be applied to Muslims. One of these rules is that a divorce pronounced by a husband is valid though pronounced under compulsion. Section 315 of Mulla's Principles of Muhammadan Law (thirteenth edition) lays down:-

"If the words of divorce used by the husband are

257

´express´ the divorce is valid even if it was pronounced under compulsion, or in a state of voluntary intoxication, or to satisfy his father or someone else."

Similarly section 123 of Muhammadan Law by Tyabji (third edition), is as follows:-

"Under Hanafi law a pronouncement of talaq is valid and effects a dissolution of marriage, though made under coercion, or without the intention of dissolving the marriage; provided that under all schools, it has no such effect if pronounced by a person who is involuntarily or for a necessary purpose in a state of intoxication."

This rule of Muhammadan Law is so firmly established that it does not require any further comment on my part. It was recognised and re-affirmed by their Lordships of the Privy Council in Rashid Ahmad and another v. Anisa Khatun and others (59 I A 21), where Lord Thankerton, who delivered the judgment of the Board, observed as follows:-

"Their Lordships are of opinion that the pronouncement of the triple talaq by Ghias-ud-Din constituted an immediately effective divorce, and, while they are satisfied that the High Court were not justified in such a conclusion on the evidence in the present case, they are of opinion that the validity and effectiveness of the divorce would not be affected by Ghias-ud-Din´s mental intention that it should not be a genuine divorce, as such a view is contrary to all authority. A talaq actually pronounced under compulsion or in jest is valid and effective; Baillie´s Digest, 2nd Edition, p. 208; Ameer Ali´s Muhammadan Law, 3rd Edition Vol. II, p. 518; Hamilton´s Hedaya, Vol. I, p. 211."

In that case the Subordinate Judge had held that Ghias-ud-Din had irrevocably divorced Anisa Khatun but the High Court had arrived at the contrary conclusion on the ground that the divorce was fictitious and inoperative because it was a mock ceremony performed by Ghias-ud-Din to satisfy his father, but without any intention on his part that it should be real and effective. Similarly it was held by a Division Bench of the Madras High Court in Vadake Vitil Ismail v. Odakel Bevakutti Umah (I L R 3 Mad. 347), that a khoola divorce is valid though granted under compulsion.

It is, therefore, perfectly clear that talaq, even if it is pronounced under any form of compulsion or by way of jest, becomes effective and irrevocable as soon as it is pronounced.

The underlying reason for this salutary provision of Muhammadan Law is that it emphasises the sanctity of the marriage tie among the Muhammadans. Although it is permissible to the husband to dissolve the marriage by pronouncing talaq without assigning any reason, yet the Holy Prophet said: "Of all things that have been permitted by the law, the worst is divorce". In order to give further

258

opportunity to the husband to ponder over the matter before taking the final step the talaq ahsan and hasan forms are preferred to talaq-ul-bidaat form. And once talaq becomes effective the husband cannot marry again the same woman until she has married another man and the latter has divorced her or died after actual consummation of the marriage.

All these provisions of Muhammadan Law clearly go to indicate that the husband, although free to act, as he likes in the matter, is to take into consideration the grave and serious consequences of his act and is not expected to misuse the power given to him or to trifle with it. He should not pronounce it even under compulsion or coercion, for if he does so, he takes the risk of losing his wife altogether. Such is the sanctity attached to the marriage tie under the Muhammadan Law, although in common parlance it is merely a form of contract with no special spiritual incident attached to it.

It is, therefore, argued by the learned counsel for the respondent that in matter of divorce, in view of the very clear provisions of Muhammadan Law, the provisions of Contract Act do not come into operation. If the provisions of Contract Act were applicable then in view of the provisions relating to free consent, coercion, undue influence, fraud, misrepresentation and public policy, etc., such a divorce would be null and void.

But the consensus of authority seems to favour the view that where the parties are Muslims the rule of decision in matters referred to in section 2 of the West Punjab Muslim Personal Law (Shariat) Application Act will be Muhammadan Law irrespective of any other provisions of any other Act to the contrary.

I am, therefore, clearly of the opinion that whatever the circumstances may be, the talaq which had been given by the plaintiff in writing to the respondent, vide talaqnama Exh. D.1, on the 12th of August 1950, was perfectly valid and legal.

SHRI JIAUDDIN AHMED (Petitioner) v. ANWARA BEGUM
Unreported (1978) (Baharal Islam, J: GAUHATI HIGH CT.)
(Criminal Revision 199 of 1977)

[This potentially revolutionary decision points the way for judges who do wish to exploit more adventurously the possibilities of neo-ijtihad. The dispute revolved around a claim for maintenance by the wife, Anwara Begum. The husband claimed to have divorced his wife by talaq: this was accepted by the examining magistrate who nevertheless granted maintenance on the footing that the definition of wife in Clause (b) of the explanation to s.125 (1) of the Criminal Procedure Code (considered in Chapter 3, above) included a woman divorced by her husband and not yet remarried. The husband petitioned the High Court against this decision.]

Judgement.....6. The first point that falls for consideration is whether there has been a valid talaq of the wife by the petitioner under the Muslim Law. ´Talaq´ is an Arabic word meaning divorce. It carries the literal significance of ´freeing´ or ´the undoing of a knot´. Talaq means divorce of a woman by her husband. Before the advent of Prophet Muhammed the condition of women in the world particularly in Arabia, was very miserable. For all practical purposes women were the properties or chattel, as it were, of men. A man could marry any number of wives and could divorce any of them at any time at his whims or caprice. Islam realised that for peace and happiness of a family and for protection and beneficial upbringing of children, divorce was undesirable. The Holy Quran put strong restrictions on the divorce of women by their husbands.

Though marriage under the Muslim Law is only a Civil contract, yet the rights and responsibilities consequent upon it are of such importance to the welfare of humanity, that a high degree of sanctity is attached to it. But in spite of the sacredness of the character of the marriage-tie, Islam recognises the necessity, in exceptional circumstances, of keeping the way open for its dissolution.

7. There has been a good deal of misconception of the institution of ´talaq´ under the Muslim Law. Both from the Holy Quran and the Hadis it appears that, though divorce were permitted, yet the right could be exercised only under exceptional circumstances. The Holy Prophet is reported to have said: "Never did Allah allow anything more hateful to Him than divorce". According to a report of Ibn ´Umar, he said: "With Allah the most detestable of all things permitted is divorce". (See the Religion of Islam by Maulana Muhammad Ali at Page 671).

In his commentary on the Holy Quran, Maulana Mohammad Ali has said:-

"Divorce is one of the institutions in Islam regarding which much misconception prevails, so much so that even the Islamic Law, as administered in the Courts, is not free from these misconceptions."

Quoted by Prof. M.F. Zafer in his paper Unilateral Divorce in Muslim Personal Laws published in Islamic Law in Modern India, by the Indian Law Institute. The learned author has observed:

"Some Muslim Jurists and scholars point out that from the very beginning of the recognition of the principle of unilateral divorce, forces have been at work which have restricted and limited its free and unnecessary use. As observed by Abdur Rahim:

´If the exercise of a particular right is likely to lead to abuses, the law would guard against

260

such a contingency by imposing conditions and limitations. There are certain limitations imposed by the law upon the right of the husband to dissolve the marriage´.

There is a large and influential body of Muslim jurists who regard <u>talaq</u> emanating from the husband as really prohibited except for necessity and only with the sanction of a Judge administering the Muslim Law.

8. The learned Magistrate relied on the following observation of the Privy Council in the case of <u>Rashid Ahmed v. Mst. Anisa Khatun</u> reported in 36 C.W.N. 305:

"It is not necessary that the wife should be present when the talaq is pronounced".

We are not concerned with this aspect of the matter. What we are concerned with is whether there was otherwise a valid talaq under the Muslim Law.

In the case of <u>Ahmad Kasim Molla v. Khatun Bibi</u> reported in I.L.R. 59 Calcutta 833, Justice Costello held:

"Upon that point, there are a number of authorities and I have carefully considered this point as dealt with in the very early authorities to see whether I am in agreement with the more recent decisions of the courts. I regret that I have to come to the conclusion that as the law stands at present, any <u>Mahomedan may divorce his wife at his mere whim and caprice</u>". (Emphasis added).

Following Macnaghten who held that "there is no occasion for any particular cause for divorce, and mere whim is sufficient"; and Justice Batchelor in the case of <u>Sarabai v. Rabiabai</u> (I.L.R. 30 Bombay 537) he held:

"It is good in law, though bad in theology".

The learned Judge quoted the following from Ameer Ali´s Treatise on Mahomedan Law:

"The Prophet pronounced talak to be a most detestable thing before the Almighty God of all permitted things. If talak is given without any reason it is stupidity and ingratitude to God".

He has also quoted from Ameer Ali´s Treatise on Mahomedan Law the following passage:

"The author of the Multeka (Ibrahim Halebi) is more concise. He says: "The law gives to the man primarily the power of dissolving the marriage, if the wife, by her indocility or her bad character, renders the married life unhappy; but in the absence of serious reasons, <u>no Musalman can justify a divorce</u> either in the eyes of the religion or the law. If he abandon his wife or put her away from simple caprice, he draws upon himself the divine anger, for ´the curse of God´, said the Prophet, ´rests on him who repudiates his wife capriciously´." (Emphasis added).

Costello, J. in his learned Judgment has also referred to the case of <u>Asha Bibi v. Kadir Ibrahim Powther</u> (I.L.R. 33 Mad.

261

22) where Munro and Abdur Rahim JJ. held:

> "No doubt an arbitrary or unreasonable exercise of the right to dissolve the marriage is strongly condemned in the Koran and in the reported sayings of the Prophet (Hadith) and is treated as a spiritual offence. But the impropriety of the husband's conduct would in no way affect the legal validity of a <u>divorce duly effected by the husband</u>." (Emphasis added).

It may be noticed that the learned Judges, Munro and Amir Ali, in my respectful opinion, advisedly used the expression ´Divorce duly effected´ in the Judgment. No divorce is duly effected if it is in violation of the injunction of the Quran. Costello, J. has also referred to a decision of the Privy Council reported in I.L.R. 5, Rangoon, 18, in which it has been held:-

> "According to that law (that is, the Muslim law), a husband can effect a divorce whenever he desires".

But the Privy Council has not said that the divorce need not be duly effected, or no procedure enjoined by the Quran need be followed.

The learned Judge, however, preferred Macnaghten and Batchelor J. (in I.L.R. 30 Bom. 537) to Amir Ali and Munro and Abdur Rahim J.J.

9. It is therefore necessary to refer to the relevant verses of the Holy Quran which is the primary source of the Muslim Law, on the relationship between the husband and the wife and divorce of the wife by the husband.

The Holy Quran ordains: (English translation from A. Yusuf Ali's The Holy Quran):

"128. If a wife fears
       Cruelty or desertion
       On her husband's part,
       There is no blame on them
       If they arrange
       An amicable settlement
       Between themselves;
       And such settlement is best;
       Even though men's souls
       Are swayed by greed.
       But if ye do good
       And practise self-restraint.
       God is well-acquainted
       with all that ye do.
129.   Ye are never able
       To be fair and just
       As between women,
       Even if it is
       your ardent desire:
       But turn not away
       (From a woman) altogether,
       So as to leave her (as it were)

Hanging (in the air).
If we come to a friendly
Understanding, and practise
Self-restraint, God is
Oft-forgiving, Most Merciful.
130.   But if they disagree
(And must part), God
Will Provide abundance
For all from His
All reaching bounty:
For God is He
That careth for all
And is wise."
(Sura IV, Verses 128 to 130)
The Holy Quran has further ordained:
"229. A divorce is only Permissible twice: after
that, the Parties should either hold
Together on equitable terms,
Or separate with Kindness,
It is not lawful for you
(Men), to take back
Any of your gifts (from your wives),
Except when both parties
Fear that they would be
Unable to keep the limits
Ordained by God.
If ye (Judges) do indeed
Fear, that they would be
unable to keep the limits
Ordained by God,
There is no blame on either
Of them if she give
Something for her freedom.
These are the limits
Ordained by God;
So do not transgress them.
If any do transgress
The limits ordained by God,
Such persons wrong
(Themselves as well as others).
230.   So if a husband
Divorces his wife (irrevocably),
He cannot, after that,
Re-marry her until
After she has married
Another husband and
He has divorced her.
In that Case there is
No blame on either of them
If they re-unite, provided
They feel that they

can keep the limits
Ordained by God.
Such are the limits
Ordained by God,
Which He makes plain
To those who understand.

231. When ye divorce
Women, and they fulfil
The term of their ('Iddat),
Either take them back
On equitable terms
Or set them free
With kindness;
But do not take them back
To injure them, (or) to take
undue advantage;
If any one does that,
  - He wrongs his own soul.
Do not treat God's signs
As a jest,
But solemnly rehearse
God's favours on you,
And the fact that He
Sent down to you
The Book
And Wisdom,
For your instruction.
And fear God,
And know that God
Is well acquainted
With all things.

232. When ye divorce
Women, and they fulfil
The term of their ('Iddat),
Do not prevent them
From marrying
Their (former) husbands,
If they mutually agree
On equitable terms.
This instruction
Is for all amongst you,
Who believe in God
And the Last Day
That is (the course
making for) most virtue
and purity amongst you.
And God knows,
And yet know not."
(Sura-II, Verses 229-232).

10. The learned Commentator, Abdullah Yusuf Ali
commenting on the subject of 'Talaq' has observed:

264

"Islam tried to maintain the married state as far as
possible, especially where children are concerned, but
it is against the restriction of the liberty of men and
women in such vitally important matters as love and
family life. It will check hasty action as far as
possible, and leave the door to reconciliation open at
many stages. Even after divorce a suggestion of
reconciliation is made, subject to certain
precautions..... against thoughtless action. A period
of waiting (iddat) for three monthly courses is
prescribed, in order to see if the marriage
conditionally dissolved is likely to result in issue.
But this is not necessary where the divorced woman is a
virgin..... It is definitely declared that women and men
shall have similar rights against each other".
(Emphasis added).
Yusuf Ali has further observed:
"Where divorce for mutual incompatibility is allowed,
there is danger that the parties might act hastily, then
repent, and again wish to separate. To prevent such
capricious action repeatedly, a limit is prescribed.
Two divorces (with a reconciliation between) are
allowed. After that the parties must unitedly make up
their minds, either to dissolve their union permanently,
or to live honourable lives together in mutual love and
forbearance - to ´hold together on equitable terms´
neither party worrying the other nor grumbling nor
evading the duties and responsibilities of marriage."
Yusuf Ali proceeds:
"All the prohibitions and limits prescribed here are in
the interests of good and honourable lives for both
sides, and in the interests of a clean and honourable
social life, without public or private scandals....."
...   .
"Two divorces followed by re-union are permissible; the
third time the divorce becomes irrevocable, until the
woman marries some other man and he divorces her. This
is to set an almost impossible condition. The lesson
is: if a man loves a woman he should not allow a sudden
gust of temper or anger to induce him to take hasty
action.....
If the man takes back his wife after two divorces, he
must do so only on equitable terms, i.e. he must not put
pressure on the woman to prejudice her rights in any
way, and they must live clean and honourable lives,
respecting each other´s personalities....."
The learned Commentator further observes:
"The termination of a marriage bond is a most serious
matter for family and social life. And every lawful
device is approved which can equitably bring back those
who have lived together, provided only there is mutual

265

love and they can live on honourable terms with each other. If these conditions are fulfilled, it is not right for outsiders to prevent or hinder re-union. They may be swayed by property or other considerations."

11. The Holy Quran has ordained a condition precedent to divorce in Sura IV Verse 35:

<u>"If ye fear a breach</u>
<u>Between them twain.</u>
<u>Appoint two arbiters.</u>
<u>One from his family.</u>
<u>And the other from hers;</u>
If they wish for Peace,
God will cause
Their reconciliation:
For God hath full knowledge,
And is acquainted
With all things."

Thus runs the commentary of Yusuf Ali on the above verse:- This is

"An Excellent plan for settling family disputes, without too much publicity or mud-throwing, or resort to the chicaneries of the law. The Latin countries recognise this plan in their legal system. It is a pity that Muslims do not resort to it universally, as they should. The arbiters from each family would know the idiosyncracies of both parties, and would be able, with God´s help, to effect a real reconciliation."

Maulana Mohammad Ali has commented on the above verse thus:-

"This Verse lays down the procedure to be adopted when a case for divorce arises. It is not for the husband to put away his wife; it is the business of the Judge to decide the case. Nor should the divorce case be made too public. The judge is required to appoint two arbitrators, one belonging to the wife´s family and the other to the husband´s. These two arbitrators will find out the facts but their objective must be to effect a reconciliation between the parties. If all hopes of reconciliation fail, a divorce is allowed. But the final decision rests with the judge who is legally entitled to pronounce a divorce. Cases were decided in accordance with the directions contained in this verse in the early days of Islam."

The same learned author commenting on the above verse (IV:35) in his the Religion of Islam has observed:-

"From what has been said above, it is clear that <u>not</u> <u>only must there be a good cause for divorce, but that</u> <u>all means to effect reconciliation must have been</u> <u>exhausted before resort is had to this extreme measure.</u> <u>The impression that a Muslim husband may put away his</u> <u>wife at his mere caprice, is a grave distortion of the</u>

Islamic institution of divorce." (Emphasis added).
Fyzee denounces talaq as "absurd and unjust". Abdur
Rahim says:-

"I may remark that the interpretation of the law of
divorce by the jurists, specially of the Hanafi School,
is one flagrant instance where because of literal
adherance to mere words and a certain tendency towards
subtleties they have reached a result in direct
antagonism to the admitted policy of the law on the
subject."

12. Mohammad Ali has observed:-

"Divorce is thus discouraged:-
'If you hate them (i.e. your wives), it may be
that you dislike a thing while Allah has placed
abundant good in it.' Remedies are also suggested
to avoid divorce so long as possible.
'And if you fear a breach between the two (i.e.
the husband and the wife), then appoint a judge
from his people and judge from her people; if they
both desire agreement, Allah will effect harmony
between them.'

It was due to such teachings of the Holy Quran that the
Holy Prophet declared divorce to be the most hateful of
all things permitted..... The mentality of the Muslim is
to face the difficulties of the married life along with
its comforts, and to avoid the disturbing disruption of
the family relations as long as possible, turning to
divorce only as a last resort."

The learned author has further observed:-

"The Principles of divorce spoken of in the Holy Quran
and which in fact includes to a greater or less extent
all causes, is the decision no longer to live together
as husband and wife. In fact, marriage itself is
nothing but an agreement to live together as husband and
wife, and when either of the parties finds him or
herself unable to agree to such a life, divorce must
follow. It is not, of course, meant that every
disagreement between them would lead to divorce; it is
only the disagreement to live any more as husband and
wife....."

He then refers to the condition laid down in Sura IV
Verse 35.

The learned author proceeds:-

"The 'Shiqaq' or breach of the marriage agreement may
also arise from the conduct of either party; for
instance, if either of them misconducts himself or
herself, or either of them is consistently cruel to the
other, or, as may sometimes happen there is
incompatibility of temperament to such an extent that
they cannot live together in marital agreement. The
'Shiqaq' in these cases is more express, but still it

will depend upon the parties whether they can pull on or not. <u>Divorce must always follow when one of the parties finds it impossible to continue the marriage agreement and is compelled to break it off</u>. At first sight it may look like giving too much latitude to the parties to allow them to end the marriage contract thus, even if there is no reason except incompatibiity of temperament, but this much is certain that if there is such disagreement that the husband and the wife cannot pull together, it is better for themselves, for their offspring and for society in general that they should be separated than that they should be compelled to live together. No home is worth the name wherein instead of peace there is wrangling; and marriage is meaningless if there is no spark of love left between the husband and the wife. It is an error to suppose that such latitude tends to destroy the stability of marriage, because marriage is entered into as a permanent and sacred relation based on love between a man and a woman, and divorce is only a remedy when marriage fails to fulfil its object."

With regard to the husband's right of pronouncing divorce the learned author has found:-

"Though the Holy Quran speaks of the divorce being pronounced by the husband, <u>yet a limitation is placed upon the exercise of this right.</u>"

He then refers to the Procedure laid down in Sura IV Verse 35 quoted above, and says:-

"It will be seen that in all disputes between the husband and the wife, which it is feared will lead to a breach, two judges are to be appointed from the respective people of the two parties. These judges are required first to try to reconcile the parties to each other, failing which divorce is to be effected. Therefore, though it is the husband who pronounces the divorce, he is as much bound by the decision of the Judges, as is the wife. This shows that the husband cannot <u>repudiate the marriage at will</u>. The Case must first be referred to two Judges and their decision is binding..... The Holy Prophet is reported to have interfered and disallowed a divorce pronounced by a husband, restoring the marital relations (Bu.68 : 2). It was no doubt a matter of Procedure, but it shows that the authority constituted by law has the right to interfere in matters of divorce."

The learned author has further observed:-

"Divorce may be given orally, or in writing, but it must take place <u>in the presence of witnesses</u>."

13. A perusal of the Quranic verses quoted above and the commentaries thereon by well-recognized Scholars of great eminence like Mahammad Ali and Yusuf Ali and

the pronouncements of great jurists like Ameer Ali and
Fyzee completely rule out the observation of Macnaghten
that "there is no occasion for any particular cause for
divorce, and mere whim is sufficient", and the
observation of Batchelor, J. (I.L.R. 30 Bom. 537) that
"the whimsical and capricious divorce by the husband is
good in law, though bad in theology". These
observations have been based on the concept that women
were chattels belonging to men, which the Holy Quran
does not brook. Costello, J. in 59 Calcutta 833 has
not, with respect, laid down the correct law of talaq.
In my view the correct law of talaq as ordained by the
Holy Quran is that talaq must be for a reasonable cause
and be preceded by attempts at reconciliation between
the husband and the wife by two arbiters – one from the
wife's family the other from the husband's. If the
attempts fail, talaq may be effected.

14. The modern trend of thinking is to put
restrictions on the caprice and whim of the husband to
give talaq to his wife at any time without giving any
reason whatsoever. This trend is in accordance with the
Quranic injunction noticed above, namely, that normally
there should be avoidance divorce, and if the
relationship between the husband and the wife becomes
strained, two persons – one from each of the parties
should be chosen as arbiters who will attempt to effect
reconciliation between the husband and the wife; and if
that is not possible the talaq may be effected. In
other words, an attempt at reconciliation by two
relations – one each of the parties, is an essential
condition precedent to 'talaq'.

15. The view I have taken gets strong support from
a Judgment of Krishna Ayer, J. (now of the Supreme
Court) in the Case of A. Yusuf Rawther v. Sowramma,
reported in AIR 1971 Kerala 261. The learned Judge has
observed:-
"The interpretation of a legislation, obviously intended
to protect a weaker section of the community, like
women, must be informed by the social perspective and
purpose and, within its grammatical flexibility, must
further the beneficient object. And so we must
appreciate the Islamic ethos and the general
sociological background which inspired the enactment of
the law before locating the precise connotation of the
words used in the statute.....
Since infallibility is not an attribute of the
judiciary, the view has been ventured by Muslim jurists
that the Indo-Anglian judicial exposition of the Islamic
law of divorce has not exactly been just to the Holy
Prophet or the Holy Book. Marginal distortions are
inevitable when the Judicial Committee in Downing Street

has to interpret Manu and Mahammad of India and Arabia. The soul of a culture - law is largely the formalised and enforceable expression of a communiy's culture norms - cannot be fully understood by alien minds. <u>The view that the Muslim husband enjoys an arbitrary, unilateral power to inflict instant divorce does not accord with Islamic injunctions..... Indeed a deeper study of the subject discloses a surprisingly rational, realistic and modern law of divorce</u>."

The learned Judge proceeds:-

"It is a popular fallacy that a Muslim male enjoys, under the Quranic law, unbridled authority to liquidate the marriage. The whole Quran expressly forbids a man to seek pretexts for divorcing his wife, so long as she remains faithful and obedient to him, "If they (namely, women) obey you, then do not seek a way against them" (Quran IV 34)..... Commentators on the Quran have rightly observed - and this tallies with the law now administered in some Muslim countries like Iraq - that <u>the husband must satisfy the court about the reasons for divorce</u>. However, Muslim Law, as applied in India, has taken a course contrary to the spirit of what the Prophet or the Holy Quoran laid down and the same misconception vitiates the law dealing with the wife's right to divorce."

Quoting Dr. Galwash the learned Judge has observed:-

"Marriage being regarded as a Civil Contract and as such not indissoluble, the Islamic law naturally recognises the right in both the parties, to dissolve the contract under certain given circumstances. Divorce, then, is a natural corollary to the conception of marriage as a contract....."

"It is clear, then, that Islam discourages divorce in principle, and permits it only when it has become altogether impossible for the parties, to live together in peace and harmony. It avoids, therefore, greater evil by choosing the lesser one, and opens a way for the parties to seek agreeable companions and, thus, to accommodate themselves more comfortably in their new homes."

Further quoting Dr. Galwash the learned Judge says:-

".....divorce is permissible in Islam only in cases of extreme emergency."

16. In the instant Case the Petitioner merely alleged in his written statement before the Magistrate that he had pronounced talaq to the Opposite Party; but he did not examine himself, nor has he adduced any evidence worth the name to prove 'talaq'. There is no proof of Talaq, or its registration. Registration of marriage and divorce under the <u>Assam Moslem Marriages and Divorces Registration Act, 1935</u> is <u>voluntary, and unilateral</u>. Mere registration of divorce (or

270

marriage) even if proved, will not render valid divorce which is otherwise invalid under Muslim Law.

17. Relying on some decisions (AIR 1939 All 592, 1975 Crl. L.J. 1884 and 1977 Crl. L.J. 43) Mr. Saikia appearing for the Petitioner submits that if the husband fails to prove ´talaq´ before the wife´s petition under Section 125 of the Code, ´talaq´ will be valid and take effect from the date of his mention of talaq made in his written statement, saying that he has divorced her. With respect I am unable to subscribe to the above view, as this view appears to be contrary to the Quranic injunction on the subject referred to above.

18. The last submission of Mr. Saikia that as the petitioner has paid all dues at the time of the talaq, the wife is not entitled to maintenance under Section 125 read with Sub-Section (3) of Section 127 of the Code, has no basis, firstly because except the mere allegation, there is no proof of such payment; secondly because, as the petitioner has failed to prove ´talaq´, the question of his payment of all dues ´at the time of talaq´ does not arise.

19. In the result this application fails and is rejected. The Rule is discharged.

Mst. KHURSHID BIBI (Appellant) v. BABOO MUHD. AMIN (Respondent)
PLD 1967 S.C. 97. (Supreme Court)

S.A. Rahman, J.....The question arises whether the wife is entitled, as of right, to claim khula despite the unwillingness of the husband to release her from the matrimonial tie, if she satisfies the Court that there is no possibility of their living together, consistently with their conjugal duties and obligations.

Learned counsel for the appellant, Mr. Ghazanfar Ali Gondal, strongly relied on Mst. Balqis Fatima v. Najmul Ikram Qureshi as authority for the view that, under Muslim Law, the wife is entitled to khula, as of right, if she satisfies the conscience of the Court that it will otherwise mean forcing her into a hateful union. A Full Bench of the West Pakistan High Court held, in that case, that the wife is entitled to dissolution of her marriage, on restoration of what she received in consideration of marriage, if the Judge apprehends that the parties will not observe the "limits of God". This latter limitation is an important one and it is only in cases where a harmonious married state, as envisaged by Islam, will not be possible, that such a decree for khula will be granted. If the rift between the parties is a serious one and there is danger of the wife transgressing the Islamic injunctions, in case the dissolution is not ordered, then there would be plain necessity for the grant of khula. This conclusion was arrived

271

at, after a review of the Qur´anic injunctions on the subject, the relevant Ahadith, previous case-law, and the opinions of legists and commentators of the Qur´an. The view expressed in Mst. Umar Bibi v. Muhammad Din (I L R (1944) 25 Lah. 542) by a Division Bench of the Lahore High Court and endorsed in the Full bench case of Mst. Sayeeda Khanam v. Muhammad Sami (P L D 1952 Lah. 113), to the effect, that incompatibility of temperament, is not a ground for dissolution of marriage and that it is not possible for a Court to grant a khula decree, unless the husband consents thereto, was dissented from.....
.....The fundamental laws of Islam are contained in the Qur´an and this is, by common consent, the primary source of law for Muslims. Hanafi Muslim jurisprudence also recognises hadith, ijtehad and ijma as the three other secondary sources of law. The last two really fall under a single category of subsidiary reasoning, ijtehad being by individual scholars and ijma being the consensus of scholars who have resorted to ijtehad in any one age. That this is the order of priority, in their importance, is clear from the well-known hadith, relating to Muadh-ibn-e-Jabal who was sent by the Prophet as Governor and Qazi of Yemen. The Prophet asked him, how he would adjudicate cases. "By the Book of God", he replied. "But if you find nothing in the Book of God, how?" "Then by the precedent of the Prophet". "But if there be no precedent?" "Then I will diligently try to form my own judgment." On this, the Prophet is reported to have said "Praise be to God who hath fulfilled in the messenger sent forth by his apostle that which is well-pleasing to the apostle of Allah."

The four orthodox schools of Sunni fiqh were headed by Imam Abu Hanifa, Imam Malik, Imam Shafei and Imam Ahmad-bin-Hanbal. The learned Imams never claimed finality for their opinions, but due to various historical causes, their followers in subsequent ages, invented the doctrine of taqlid, under which a Sunni Muslim must follow the opinions of only one of their Imams, exclusively, irrespective of whether reason be in favour of another opinion. There is no warrant for this doctrinaire fossilization, in the Qur´an or authentic Ahadith. In the Almital-wan-Nihal (page 39) it is stated that the great Abu Hanifa used to say "This is my opinion and I consider it to be the best. If someone regards another person´s opinion to be better, he is welcome to it ("for him is his opinion and for us ours").

A few words may now be said about the concept of marriage in Islam. As is well-settled, marriage among Muslims is not a sacrament, but in the nature of a civil contract. Such a contract undoubtedly has spiritual and moral overtones and undertones, but legally, in essence, it remains a contract between the parties which can be the subject of dissolution for good cause. In this respect, Islam, the Din-al-Fitrat, conforms to the dictates of human nature and does not prescribe the binding together of a man and woman to what has been described as "holy dead-lock".

The husband is given the right to divorce his wife, though, of course, arbitrary divorces are discountenanced. There is a saying of the Prophet to the effect that "the most detestable of lawful things in Allah's view is divorce" (Abou Daood). Similarly, the wife is given the right to ask for khulain cases of extreme incompatibility though the warning is conveyed by ahadith against too free exercise of this privilege, one of which says that women asking for khula will be deprived of the fragrance of paradise (Trimizi). The warning both to man and woman in this regard, is obviously placed on the moral rather than the legal plane and is not destructive of their legal rights.

The Qur'an also declares: "Women have rights against men, similar to those that the men have against them, according to the well-known rules of equity". It would, therefore, be surprising if the Qur'an did not provide for the separation of the spouses, at the instance of the wife, in any circumstances. The Qur'an expressly says that the husband should either retain the wife, according to well-recognised custom - (Imsak-un-bil-ma'roof) or release her with grace - (Tasree-hun-bi-ihsan). The word of God enjoined the husband not to cling to the woman, in order to cause her injury. Another hadith declares - Lazarar-un-wa-la-zarar-fil-Islam ("Let no harm be done, nor harm be suffered in Islam"). In certain circumstances, therefore, if the husband proves recalcitrant and does not agree to release the woman from the marital bond, the Qazi may well intervene to give redress and enforce the Qur'anic injunctions.

As was pointed out by Kaikaus, J. in Mst. Balqis Fatima's case the foundation of the law relevent to khula is contained in the Qur'anic verses, which may be translated as follows:

"Such divorce may be pronounced twice; then, either retain them in a becoming manner or send them away with kindness. And it is not lawful for you that you take anything of what you have given them, unless both fear that they cannot observe the limits prescribed by Allah. But, if you fear that they cannot observe the limits prescribed by Allah, then it shall be no sin for either of them in what she gives to get her freedom. These are the limits presribed by Allah, so transgress them not; and who so transgresses the limits prescribed by Allah, it is they that are the wrong-doers."

We may first consider the opinions of the commentators of the Qur'an as to the meaning of these verses, bearing on khula. The words "if you fear" are addressed to the community or "those in authority from among you", and include the Qazi, who represents the community, for adjudication of disputes.....
.....By the phrase "Limits of Allah",..... .....reference is intended to the injunctions regarding the performance of

conjugal obligations while living together.....
.....The question whether _khula_ is to be equated with _talaq_,
or it is a form of dissolution of marriage in a category of
its own, has been the subject of controversy amongst the
jurists. Ibn-i-Rushud, in his Badaya-tul-Mujtahid, says that
most of the _ulema_ and Imam Malik and Imam Abu Hanifa are of
the opinion that _khula_ is equivalent to _talaq_. On the other
hand, Imam Shafe´i, Imam Ahmad, Imam Daood and out of the
Companions, Ibn-e-Abbas were of the view that _khula_ amounts to
fiskh-1-nikah (cancellatin or dissolution of marriage) and not
talaq. Imam Shafe´i had also stated on another occasion that
if the husband intended _talaq_, even in a contract of _khula_, it
would operate as _talaq_ and if he had the intention of
fiskh-i-nikah, it will have effect as such. Ibn-e-Hajar
Asqlani in his books (Alderaya-fi-Takhrija-Ahadith-ul-Hidaya
and Fat-hul-Bari) prefers the opinion of Ibn-e-Abbas on this
point and casts doubt on the authenticity of the _hadith_ which
equates it with irreversible divorce. He relies in this
connection on a Tradition of the Prophet, which specified that
Sabet-bin-Qais´s wife, after the grant of _khula_, was ordered
to pass one period of menstruation as her _iddat_ and this would
not be so if _khula_ were _talaq_. He reiterates this position in
Talkhisul Habir Vol. III, p. 205. On the other hand, the
authorities quoted, on behalf of the respondent, including the
Hedaya, take the view that there is no difference between
khula and _talaq_. This question need not detain us further.
There are good reasons for the view that _khula_ is separation
and not _talaq_, as the right of the husband to take back the
wife after _khula_, does not exist, as it does in the case of
talaq-i-raja´i and the period of Iddat is different in the two
cases. The relevant _Ahadith_ are discussed by Shaukani in
Kitab-ul-Khul Vol. III, p. 260 of his celebrated work
Nail-al-Autar and he reaches the conclusion that _khula_ is not
a type of _talaq_, but is a category apart from it. If this
opinion is accepted, then it is clear that _khula_ is not
dependent on the will of the husband alone. But even if _khula_
be regarded as _talaq_ as seems to be the view of some of the
orthodox Hanafi Jurists, the question arises whether the wife
is not entitled, in appropriate cases, to demand a _khula_
divorce from the husband, in the fact of the latter´s
opposition. This problem finds no express treatment in the
treatises of these Hanafi Jurists who content themselves by
saying that divorce is the right of the husband.
It must be admitted that this is also a controversial
question.....
.....This difference arises owing to the fact that two
situations are contemplated by the writers. One is where
khula takes place as a result of the mutual consent of the
spouses, which is technically called _mubara´t_. In such a case
it appears that no reference to the Qazi is necessary but
where the husband disputes the right of the wife to obtain
274

separation by <u>khula</u>, it is obvious that some third party has
to decide the matter and, subsequently, the dispute will have
to be adjudicated upon by the Qazi, with or without assistance
of the <u>Hakams</u>. Any other interpretation of the Qur´anic verse
regarding <u>khula</u> would deprive it of all efficacy as a charter
granted to the wife. It is significant that according to the
Qur´an, she can "ransom herself" or "get her release" and it
is plain that these words connote an independent right in her.

The Qur´anic injunctions must be interpreted in the light
of well-known <u>ahadith</u>. The classical instance of <u>khula</u> is
that of the wife of Sabet-bin-Qais-bin-Shamas. That tradition
is to be found in various collections of <u>ahadith</u>, including
Bokhari, Abu Daood, Nasai, Ibn-e-Maja and Tirmizi. But there
are two versions, one referring to Jamila, daughter of a
sister of Abdullah bin Abi Salool (in some versions, daughter
of Abdullah) and the other to Habiba, daughter of Sahl. It is
said by some commentators that the two cases relate to two
different wives of the same person. Jamila came to the
Prophet, according to this tradition, and said that she had no
reason to reproach Sabet-bin-Qais, in respect of his morals or
his faith, but she disliked him and after going into the fold
of Islam, she did not want to commit infidelity. The Prophet
asked her whether she was prepared to return the garden given
by her husband to her, in dower. She answered in the
affirmative. The Prophet then directed the husband to accept
the garden and to give her a divorce according to one version.
Another version given by Bokhari, has it that when she agreed
to return the garden to her husband, the Prophet ordered "Qais
and he" separated her. From still another version given by
Hazrat Aisha Siddiqa, (related by Abu Daud) it seems that
Habiba was also subjected by her husband to physical violence
during the previous night but this fact was not put forward by
the woman, apparently, as ground for her release. Abu Daood
also talks of two gardens being returned, which had been
originally gifted by the husband. The two different versions
may be reconciled by the suggestion that, due to her aversion,
Habiba was not willing to perform her marital obligations and
was beaten by her husband in consequence. The generally
accepted account of <u>Jamila´s case</u> as well as that of Habiba
makes it clear that the only ground on which the Prophet
ordered the woman to be released from the marriage bond, was
her intense dislike of her husband. According to one text,
she clarified that she found him to be ugly and repulsive, and
in another that she felt like spitting at him. The Prophet
being convinced that the spouses could not live together in
conformity with their conjugal obligations, ordered the
husband to separate her. Hakim in Almustadrak, Ibne-Abdul
Barr in <u>Al-Istiab</u>, Shaukani in Nail-ul-Autar the last-named
(relying on Dar Qatani´s version), are categorical in saying
that it was the Prophet who ordered the separation. As has
been observed above, Ibne Hajr Asqalani shares this opinion

and doubts the authenticity of the <u>hadith</u> which specifies that this was a case of <u>talaq</u>. Ibne Hazm in Al Mohalla upholds the Qazi's right to effect separation by <u>khula</u> after efforts at conciliation through <u>Hakams</u> have failed. It is not possible to consider this act of the Prophet, except as one conceding the right of the wife, in circumstances of extreme discard.

The opinion of Allama Ibne Rushud on this point has already been quoted in support of the thesis that <u>khula</u> is a right of the wife. Amir Ali in his Muhammadan Law, Vol. II, p. 466, and M. Muhammad Ali in his Religion of Islam, p. 676, express themselves in similar terms. Some other modern opinions will be found collected in Kaikaus, J.'s judgment in <u>Balqis Fatima's case</u> including one by Wilson in his Anglo-Muhammadan Law. Kaikaus, J. has also cited the case of a woman who sought divorce from her husband in Hazrat Umar's time and after testing the seriousness of her demand by confining her in a dirty prison, he ordered her to be separated from her spouse. A modern priest of Egypt, Ali Khafif in his book Furaq-al-Zauj-fi-al Mazahib al Islamia strongly supports the wife's right to <u>khul'</u> when discord is established. I may add, however, that opinions of living authors are not entitled to as much weight as those who have joined the majority, since the possibility of their changing their views before death cannot be excluded.

The present trend of legislation in Muslim countries which may provide indication of Ijma's in modern times, may also be examined. The right of the wife to obtain separation from her husband on any ground of injury, is recognised in Iraq by section 40 of Qanun-ul-Ahwal-al-Shakhsiya of 1959, in Egypt by section 6 of Law No. 25 of 1929, in Tunis by section 25 of Mujalla-tul-Ahwal-ul-Shakhsiya, in Morroco by section 56 of Mudawwana-tul-Ahwal-ul-Shakhsiya-al-Maghrib, in Jordan by section 96 of Qanun-o-Huquq-al-Alla-tul-Urdani and in Syria by section 112 of Qanun-ul-Ahwal-ul-Shakhsiya-Assuri. In some of these Codes it is provided that the matter will first be referred to <u>Hakams</u> and the final decision will rest with the Court.

The argument was raised on behalf of the respondent, that the case should be decided only in accordance with the opinions of Hanafi doctors, who contemplate the grant of a divorce on the part of the husband even in the case of <u>khula</u> and not separation such as could be ordered by a Qazi. The authorities referred to, however, do not discuss what would happen in case the husband is reluctant to divorce the wife but the relations between the spouses have deteriorated so considerably that they could not be expected to live together within the limits of Allah. Such a position is expressly dealt with in books of other Sunni sects – the Malikis, the Shafe'is and the Hambalis. It is permissible to refer to those opinions which are consistent with the Qur'anic injunctions. A certain amount of fluidity exists, even among

276

orthodox Hanafis in certain matters. In the case of a husband who has become _mofqudulkhabar_ (absent without news) for instance, Malikis opinion can be resorted to by a Hanafi Qazi, as is mentioned in Radd-ul-Muhtar.

There is a _hadith_ of the Prophet, concerning Barairah who was married to a slave, named Mughis. She did not live with her husband who followed her disconsolate and weeping, in public. The Prophet advised her to go back to her husband. She asked "Is this an Order?" The Prophet said that it was merely a recommendation. She then declined to go back to her husband, saying: "I have no need of him." This shows that a woman cannot be compelled, if she has a fixed aversion to her husband, to live with him.....

After a discussion of the original sources, I have, therefore, reached the conclusion that the view, taken by Kaikaus, J. in _Balqis Fatima´s case_, that the relevant verse of the Qur´an gives the right of _khula_ to the wife subject to the limitation mentioned therein is correct.

In the present case, on the facts, it has been found that there is no possibility left, of the parties residing together in amity and goodwill. There has been litigation between them. The wife had to be brought away from the husband´s house, on a warrant, issued under section 100, Criminal Procedure Code. She may have taken an intense dislike to her husband, after he contracted his second marriage, but ever since that time, she has consistently declined to share the connubial bed with him. In the circumstances, it would be idle to have recourse to the formality of appointing _Hakams_ to attempt a reconciliation between them, considering that a Panchayat, convened by the defendant´s father, also failed, in this respect. I would, therefore, hold that the plaintiff is entitled to separation from her husband, by _khula_, in the circumstances of the instant case.

The next question is on what terms, such a decree should be granted to her. Unfortunately, in the trial Court, the question of terms was not gone into, on either side, and the trial Judge also failed to advert to this aspect of the matter. There is no material on the file, from which it can be ascertained how much money, if at all, the husband had given to the wife, on the occasion of the marriage, and on receipt of what compensation he would be willing to grant her _khula_. The pleadings of the parties show that the dower, whatever its amount was, had not yet been paid to the wife. She merely express her willingness to relinquish her dower, but the husband said, he was not agreeable even, on this condition, to grant her _khula_. He did not plead that he had actually paid her the dower. Though, according to the _Hedaya_, it is abominable on the part of the husband to have more than the dower itself, in a case of separation by _khula_, yet if he insists, it is legally permissible for him to demand something more than the dower, and to the extent that he might have been out of pocket, in respect of gifts, given to the wife on marriage, he may, in law, demand restitution. This would necessitate an enquiry into the facts and the final decision as to what compensation must be paid by the wife for her relief, must rest with the Court. I would, therefore, allow the appeal and send back the case to the trial Judge, with the direction the parties may be permitted to lead evidence to what gifts, if any, and of what value, were given by the husband to the wife, on the occasion of the marriage, so that if the husband wants to take more than the dower, the condition may be imposed on the wife, to pay the additional sum, expended by the husband to her, to the grant of khula. The parties may be left to bear their own costs throughout in the circumstances of the case.....

HAMOODUR RAHMAN, J. - I agree.

MUHAMMAD YAQUB ALI, J. - I agree.

.....FAZLE-AKBAR, J. - I have had the advantage of reading the judgment prepared by my learned brother S.A. Rahman, J. As I entirely agree with the line of reasonings in his judgment, I concur in the order proposed by my learned brother.

S.A. MAHMOOD, J. - This appeal by Special Leave is by Mst. Khurshid Bibi against the dismissal of her second appeal by the High Court, which raises for decision an important question of law, namely, whether a Muslim wife, whose husband refuses to divorce her, can be granted a decree for dissolution of marriage by a Court by khula, if she satisfies the Court that it is impossible for the spouses to live together in amity, and to perform their marital duties and obligations, enjoined on them by Islam.

2. I have had the advantage of perusing the elaborate and exhaustive judgment, recorded by my learned brother S.A. Rahman, J. after extensive research into the sources of Islamic Law, the original texts, Ahadith and opinions of eminent Jurists, Legists and Juris-consults, and though I concur with his conclusions and have little to add to the wealth and weight of authority quoted by him, I would, in view of the importance of the question involved, like to state some reasons of my own.....

.....9. The learned counsel for the appellant has contended that the Holy Qur'an having by Verse 2:229 (Sura Baqr) conferred on women the right to obtain dissolution of marriage by khula and the right being equally established by Shariat, Mst. Khurshid Bibi is, in the circumstances established, entitled to a decree for dissolution of marriage from the Courts, which have replaced the Qazi, as interpreted by the Full Bench in Mst. Bilqis Fatima v. Najam-ul-Ikram Qureshi. It is emphasised that the Courts in Pakistan are bound to give effect to the correct interpretation of this verse, regardless of the opinions, which may have been expressed by some of the Jurists, for the Qur'an enjoins obedience to God, as the duty of all Muslims (ati-ullah-wa-ati-ur-rasool). It was argued

278

that as Verse 2:229 was not placed before nor was considered by the Full Bench, in deciding Mst. Saeeda Khanum v. Muhammad Sami, which holds that incompatibility of temperaments, aversion, or dislike cannot form a ground for a wife to seek dissolution of her marriage at the hands of a Qazi or a Court, but is to be dealt with under the powers possessed by the husband as well as the wife under Muslim Law, as parties to the marriage contract, and it was also not placed before the Division Bench in Mst. Umar Bibi v. Muhammad Din (I L R 1944 Lah. 542) these cases are easily distinguishable, and are not correctly decided. He also stressed that the conclusion in the two cases that it was not possible for a Court to grant a khula divorce unless the husband consents to it, was expressly dissented from in the later Full Bench case of Mst. Umar Bibi v. Muhammad Din. The learned counsel also referred us to page 158 of Urdu translation of Bedayat-ul-Mujtahid by Allama Ibne Rushud (an independent thinker and philosopher) published by Idarat-ul-Muslemin, Rabwah, in which having stated the meanings of khula, and the conditions in which it was permissible, the learned Author expressed the view that –

> "And the philosophy of khula is this, that khula is provided for the woman, in opposition to the right of divorce vested in the man. Thus, if trouble arises from the side of the woman, the man is given the power to divorce her, and when injury is received from the man's side, the woman is given the right to obtain khula".

10. The learned counsel for the respondent herein conceded that dissolution of marriage by khula is permitted in Islam, but emphasised that it was essential for the husband to pronounce a talaq for khula to take place, because firstly khula signifies an agreement between the spouses for dissolving a connubial connection in lieu of a compensation paid by the wife to the husband out of her property, by which he is induced to liberate her as stated at page 112 of Hamilton's translation of Hedaya, 2nd Edition by Grady; secondly, because it is a talaq irreversible, which is pronounced by the husband; and, thirdly, because in the Qur'anic Verse 238 in Part XX of the Holy Qur'an reproduced below is stated that the tie of marriage is in "his" meaning "husband's" hands:–

> "And if you divorce them before you have touched them, but have settled for a dowery, then half of what you have settled shall be due from you, unless they remit, or her, in whose hand is the tie of marriage, should remit. And that you should remit is nearer to righteousness. And do not forget to do good to one another. Surely, Allah sees what you do."

The learned counsel also drew our attention to some commentaries of the Holy Qur'an taking the view that the person in the expression "person in whose hand is the tie of marriage" means the husband, but this view is not universally

279

accepted. Some Commentators express the view that they refer
to the guardian of the woman, which is more consistent with
the context. He not only sought support from
Tafseer-i-Mazhari, Inaya, which is a commentary of Hedaya,
Raddul Muhtar, Tafseer-ul-Medarik, Tafseer-ul-Ahmadiya and
Tafseer-i-Kabir for the contention that khula means
talaq-i-bain, i.e., an irreversible divorce, but also referred
to certain Ahadith view a view to prove that if the Holy
Prophet in ordering the release of the wife by khula directed
the husband to give her talaq, the pronouncement of talaq by
the husband is a necessary condition of khula.

11. This suit was instituted on the 22nd of February 1960
when section 2 (ix) of the Dissolution of Muslim Marriages Act
VIII of 1939 (repealed by the West Pakistan Muslim Personal
Law (Shariat) Application Act V of 1962, on the 31st December
1962) provided that divorce may be claimed on any ground
recognised as valid for the dissolution of marriage under the
Muslim Law. The Subordinate Courts, the District Judges and
the Judges of the High Courts, in Pakistan, occupy a position
akin to that of a Qazi, since they could effect a divorce on
any ground on which it could be granted under the Muslim Law,
Mst. Umar Bibi v. Muhammad Din (I L R 1944 Lah. 542).

12. The basis and foundation of khula is Verse 2:229 of
the Holy Qur'an, though the word khula finds no mention
therein or in the Holy Qur'an. It has been translated as:

"Divorce must be pronounced twice; then either retain
them in honour or release them with kindness. And it is
not lawful for you that you take back from women
anything out of what you have given them unless they
both fear that they cannot observe the limits imposed by
Allah. But if you fear that they cannot keep within the
limits prescribed by Allah, then it is no sin for either
of them in what she gives up to be free, (i.e., ransomes
herself). These are the limits imposed by Allah.
Transgress them not. For who so transgresses Allah's
limits, it is they who are the wrong-doers."

13. It is accepted by the Jurists and Commentators that
"you" in the words "if you fear" in the relevant verse refers
to ulil-amr, and includes the Qazi, who represents the
community for adjudication of disputes between the parties.
Ample authority in support of this view having been quoted by
S.A. Rahman, J. in his judgment, it is unnecessary for me to
repeat it here. I may, however, add that the words "if you
fear" by which the relevant part of the verse commences, also
appear in the well-known verse 35, section 6, Chapter IV of
the Holy Qur'an in the context of shiqaq (schism or breach)
between the spouses:-

"And if you fear a breach between the two, then appoint
an arbiter from his people and an arbiter from her
people; if they both desire agreement, Allah will effect
harmony between them; surely Allah is knowing Aware."

Here also it is generally accepted that the word "you" refers to ulil-amr. The word "you" can have no reference to the spouses, who are referred to in the relevant verse as "they two" and "them two". Therefore, the verse, in the relevant part, reads:-

"But if the Qazi fears that they will not be able to keep within the limits prescribed by Allah, then it is no sin for either of them in what she gives up to be free."

14. The following conclusions follow from a careful analysis of the verse:-

15. Firstly, the words "if you fear" involve by necessary implication a reference to the Qazi and adjudication by him. The occasion for a reference to him arises only where the husband refuses to release his wife, when she demands a divorce, for if the matter is mutually agreed upon between the parties, the husband will divorce her, and there will be no reference to the Qazi, and no occasion for him to arrive at the conclusion that the parties will not keep within the limits of Allah. In consequence, the verse is a rule of decision in cases where the husband refuses to release his wife, and is not in express terms applicable to cases of khula by mutual agreement where there is no reference to the Qazi. In khula, under the verse, the husband is permitted to accept what the wife may give him to be free and this is an exception to the general rule stated in cases of divorce by the husband in verse 2:229 and verses 19 and 20 of Sura Al-Nisa that it is not lawful for him to take back any part of what he has given to the wife, but it is lawful "if the Qazi entertains the fear". Therefore, the verse contemplates an adjudication by the Qazi as justification for the husband's accepting what his wife gives him for being free. The provision of adjudication in the verse is evidence of Divine wisdom, for it ensures on the one hand that there are not too many, too frequent and unrestricted dissolution of marriages (and thus there need be no fear of frequent breaking of family ties, as was expressed by M. Jan, J. in Mst. Saeeda Khanum v. Muhammad Sami), and on the other that the wife is not oppressed in order to deprive her of her property. Dr. Sabuni in his book "Madi Hurriat-uz Zaujain Fittalaq" at page 572 states:-

"A large section of Muslim Jurists believe that khula is lawful only if there is dislike on the part of the wife so that the husbands do not start oppressing their wives to make them seek khul, so as to get back the property they gave them."

All this does not mean that khula by mutual arrangement is not lawful, for as stated in Hedaya, the justification for such khula is in the words of the verse "there is no blame on them two in what she gives up to be free."

16. Secondly, it confers a right and a privilege on the wife to seek dissolution of marriage. Khula is thus a right

conferred on the wife. In the prior verse 2:228 the Holy
Qur´an itself mentions "women have rights against men similar
to those that men have against them, according to the
well-known rules of equity". The opinion of Allama Ibne
Rushud that khula is a right of the wife has already been
cited. Ameer Ali in his book "Muhammadan Law, Chapter 6,
Volume II, at page 466, of 1965 Edition has emphasised that
previous to Islamic Legislation the wives had no right to
claim dissolution of marriage on any ground whatsoever, and as
a rule neither the Hebrews nor the pre-Islamic Arabs
recognised the right of divorce for women, but the Qur´an
(meaning verse 2:229) allowed them this privilege. Mian Sir
Abdur Rashid, Retired Chief Justice of Pakistan, as Chairman
of the Commission on Marriage Laws, has, in his report,
reached the conclusion that the consensus of opinion is that
Islam has granted a right of khula to the woman, if she
forgoes the mehar or a part of it, if it is demanded by the
husband. Maulana Muhammad Ali in his book "Religion of Islam"
states that the right of the wife to claim divorce is not only
recognised by the Holy Qur´an and Hadith, but also in fiqh.
The view stated in Aziz Ahmad´s Muslim Law at page 235 also is
that the Court has the power to grant khula, if it is so moved
by the wife. Kaikaus, J. also relied on a similar opinion of
a living Author, Maulana Abul A´la Maudoodi in his book
"Haquq-uz Zaujain", and though the latter´s views on questions
of Muslim Law, are entitled to respect, his opinion is not so
weighty as of those, who· are no more amongst us, as the
possibility of a change in his opinion cannot be ruled out.
Al Khafif strongly supports the right of the wife to khula
when discord between the spouses is established. The right is
not, however, an absolute right by which the wife can herself
dissolve the marriage, but is a controlled right. The success
of her right depends upon the Qazi´s reaching the conclusion
that the spouses cannot live within the limits of God, this
being the rule of decision provided for his guidance.

17. Thirdly, the verse, by making it not lawful for the
husband, where he pronounces a talaq to take back anything
from the wife and permitting it where she seeks khul,
indicates that talaq is in a category different from khula.
There is a clear distinction between the two, for khula is the
right of the wife, and talaq is the right of the husband. A
talaq is pronounced by the husband on his own, but khula under
the verse is sought by the wife and is effected by the order
of the Qazi for a consideration to be paid by her. The nature
and character of talaq and khula are different, though their
effect may be the same, namely, dissolution of the marriage
tie, but it will be shown later that their respective effects
are even different, and khula effects a dissolution of
marriage and not a talaq. In cases of khula by mutual
agreement, a talaq is usually pronounced by the husband, but
this is pronounced to effect a dissolution of the marriage
282

tie, and though it is in the form of a _talaq_, what is brought about is in effect a _khula_. _Khula_ is not the same thing as _talaq_ and the two cannot be equated.

18. Fourthly, as the verse confers a right on women to seek dissolution of marriage, names the Qazi as a Judge of the cause and provides the rule of decision, it virtually adds a ground for dissolution of marriage, and thus authorises the Qazi to dissolve the marriage in appropriate cases, even without or against the will of the husband. When it confers a right to sue on women, and provides a forum and a rule for dissolution of marriage, it is the Qazi and not one of the parties to the cause, who can have the authority to decide the cause, for otherwise, the reference of the cause to him, serves no purpose and the verse has no objective. If the husband's consent is necessary, the verse has no efficacy or usefulness as a right conferred on women.

19. Obviously, therefore, the dissolution cannot rest on the consent of the husband, but must depend on the order of the Qazi. When he has the power to order dissolution of marriage and to enforce his decision in cases of li'an, ila and inin and where the husband becomes Mafqood-ul-Khabar (absent without news) even without and against the consent of the husband, as is supported by Hedaya, Raddul Muhtar, Ahkam-ul-Qur'an and Jasas, and when dissolution can take effect without his pronouncing a _talaq_, the Qazi must have the power to dissolve the marriage by _khula_ also, independent of the husband's consent and his pronouncing a _talaq_. Ibne Hazan in "Al-Mohalla" supports the Qazi's right to effect separation by _khula_ after efforts at reconciliation have failed.

20. The verse is thus, in particular, a rule of decision in cases where reference to the Qazi is necessitated by the refusal of the husband to divorce his wife and in such cases dissolution is by the order of the Qazi and is not dependent on the consent of the husband or on his pronouncing a _talaq_. There are no words in the verse indicating that the consent of or _talaq_ by the husband is necessary for _khula_.

21. The recorded traditions of _khula_ by the Holy Prophet and the Caliphs lend strong support to the above conclusions. The classical instance of _khula_ is that of the wife of Sabit bin Qais to be found in various collections of Ahadith including Bukhari, Tirmizi, Abu Daud, Nisai and Ibne Maja, but there are two versions, one referring to Jamila and the other to Habiba. Some Commentators say that they relate to two different wives of the same Sabit. The instance of Jamila, as stated in Mishkat-ul-Mussabib, (Volume II, page 703) is that Jamila went to the Holy Prophet and said that she did not blame her husband Sabit bin Qais about his character or piety, but she feared "heresy in Islam". The Holy Prophet asked her if she was prepared to return the garden given to her as dower, and on her replying "yes, Oh Prophet of God, and even more", the Prophet said: "No more, but you return the garden

283

that he gave you". She agreed and the Prophet said to Sabit: "Take the garden and divorce her". According to another version in Bukhari, when she agreed to return the garden, the Prophet ordered Sabit and he separated her. The other tradition of Habiba, as stated by Imam Malik and Abu Daud, is that one day early in the morning, when the Holy Prophet came out of his house, he found Habiba standing there. He enquired from her what the matter was. She said: "I and Sabit can never pull on together." When Sabit appeared, the Holy Prophet said: "This is Habiba daughter of Sahal. She has stated what God wished she should state." Habiba said: "Oh Prophet of God, let Sabit take from me whatever he has given me, for that is all with me." The Holy Prophet ordered Sabit to take back what he had given her, and to release her. In some versions the words used by him are mentioned as "<u>khale sabilaha</u>" and in others "<u>fariqha</u>", which both mean "divorce her". About this very instance, there is another version reported by Abu Daud and Ibne Gharir as coming from Hazrat Aisha, stating that Sabit had beaten Habiba and broken her bone, but it is clear enough that she made no complaint on this score, and demanded dissolution of her marriage on account of her aversion for his ugliness. The case is one, therefore, of <u>khula</u> in which there was an order of separation by the Holy Prophet.

22. In the days of the Holy Prophet, as reported by Ibne Abbas in Mishkat, Volume II, page 702, Barirah was married to Mughis, who was intensely in love with her, and used to roam about the lanes of Madina, weeping and crying in quest of her. One day the Holy Prophet expressed a wish to her that she should go back to her husband. "Is this an order" asked Barirah, and as the Holy Prophet said: "No, I am only trying to intercede", Barirah did not go back to her husband. This instance has been used in <u>Mst. Saeeda Khanum v. Muhammad Sami</u> as implying that as the Holy Prophet did not force Barirah to go back to her husband, he was not likely to force Sabit bin Qais to divorce his wife. With the greatest respect, it appears to me that this instance instead of reflecting adversely on the efficacy of the cases of Jamila and Habiba, as instances of <u>khula</u> under the orders of the Holy Prophet, enhances their value. The difference between those cases and the case of Barirah is that in those cases the wives approached the Holy Prophet, demanding a dissolution of their marriage, while there was no such demand by Barirah, and the Holy Prophet decided the cases referred to him as head of the State of Islam, and ordered the husband to release them on restoration of benefits conferred. Thus, <u>khula</u> was decreed by the Holy Prophet on the ground that the wives having developed intense hatred for their husband, it had become impossible for them to live with him and to perform their marital obligations. No clearer proof can be had of Qazi´s power and authority to dissolve a marriage in appropriate case by <u>khula</u>.

In the case of Barirah, there being no cause before him as a Qazi or a Judge, he gave no order and merely tendered an advice. Her instance also proves that the Holy Prophet was not in favour of forcing an unwilling wife to live with her husband, where there is hard aversion.

23. The two instances of khula of the days of Khulafa-i-Rashidin cited by Kaikaus, J., in Mst. Bilqis Fatima v. Najam-ul-Ikram Qureshi, are these:-

(1) A woman along with her husband appeared before Hazrat Umar, a companion of the Holy Prophet, wanting a divorce, and though he advised her to live with her husband, she refused. The Caliph shut her up in a dungeon, full of refuse, and when, after being kept there for three days, she was brought before him, asked her how she had fared. She replied: "I swear by God, I have never passed more peaceful nights." This answer is clearly indicative of what misery and torture her life had become with her husband. At this, Hazrat Umar said to the husband: "Give her khula even if it be in lieu of her earrings" (Kushf-ul-ghuma).

(2) Another instance is of the days of Hazrat Usman, a companion of the Holy Prophet. This is the case of Rabi, daughter of Maooz. When she approached him for separation from her husband, Hazrat Usman ordered her husband to take all that she had and to grant her a divorce.

24. If in each of these cases, the Holy Prophet and the Caliphs, in ordering dissolution, directed the husband to pronounce a talaq, this was the form in which it was decreed, but from the form of the order it cannot reasonably be argued that pronouncement of a talaq by the husband is a necessary condition of khula, though it could have been urged that the Courts should follow the same form in making the order. So long as the order was made by the Holy Prophet and the Caliphs in exercise of the authority of the State or Judge, the form of the order is not destructive of the source or substance of the authority of the Qazi, nor makes the pronouncement of talaq a necessary condition of khula. The question of the form in which the order should be made by the Courts is not one of substance and is not, in any case, of any particular importance, in the instant case, as the Courts have power, by their own authority, to dissolve a marriage on the grounds stated in section 2 of the Dissolution of Muslim Marriages Act, VIII of 1939, and if they were to order khula under subsection (IX), a talaq by the husband is not necessary.

25. The word "khula" literally means to put off, as a man is said to khula his garment, when he puts it off. Verse 187, Chapter II of the Holy Qur´an recites "you are garment or apparel for them and they are garment for you", meaning that the husband is a garment for the wife and vice versa. "Khula", therefore, should mean the putting off or doffing of

285

the cloak of marriage. According to the Kilaya, Volume II, page 278, "khula" means to put off, as a man is said to khula his garment when he puts it off. According to Durrul Mukhtar (at page 256), it means in law "demission or laying down by a husband of his right and authority over his wife for an exchange to take effect on her acceptance by means of the words khula, and it is sometime validly effected by the words of sale and purchase. Its condition is that of talaq or repudiation, and its effect one irrevocable repudiation". According to Hedaya (page 112) of Hamilton's Translation by Grady), relied upon by the learned counsel for the respondent, "khula" signifies an agreement between the spouses for dissolving a connubial connection in view of a compensation paid by the wife to the husband out of her property. The reason stated in it in justification of such khula is that whenever enmity takes place between husband and wife and they both see season to apprehend that the ends of marriage are not likely to be answered by a continuance of their union, the woman need not scruple to release herself from the power of her husband, by offering such a compensation, as may induce him to liberate her, because the word of God says: "No crime is imputed to the wife or her husband, respecting the matter in lieu of which she hath released herself" (these words are from verse 2:229), that is to say, there is no crime in the husband's accepting such compensation, nor in the wife's giving it". The discussion in Durrul Mukhtar, Hedaya, the relevant Chapter in Fatawa-i-Alamgiri, Volume II, in which a large number of authorities, a'ima and their disciples are quoted as to the manner in which dissolution of marriage by khula takes place, the consideration for khula, its quantum, the validity of consideration, and rights which flow from such a divorce impart the impression that divorce by khula is an act of the husband, and not a unilateral exercise of a right by the wife. It is also a necessary condition of khula that a desire for separation should emanate from the wife. In Mst. Saeeda Khanum v. Muhammad Sami the Full Bench of the Lahore High Court, following the above, defined khula as dissolution of a marriage by agreement between the parties for a consideration paid or to be paid by the wife to the husband. The emphasis in the above opinions of the Jurists and Commentators on mutual agreement between the spouses, indicates the category of cases to which they relate. These are cases of khula without reference to a Qazi or Court, where without the consent of the husband and his pronouncing a talaq, dissolution of the marriage tie is not possible. It is these considerations which provide the reasons for their opinions that khula is the act of the husband, and it cannot be effected without his pronouncing talaq.

26. There are thus two classes of cases of khula: (1) by mutual agreement, and (2) by order of the Qazi or Court, where dissolution of marriage takes place on the husband's

pronouncing a <u>talaq</u> in the first class of cases, and by the order of the Qazi or the Court in the second. Sanction for <u>khula</u> under the orders of the Qazi is to be found in the express words of verse 2:229 of the Holy Qur´an, which is the word of God. Cases of <u>khula</u> by mutual agreement do not strictly fall under the terms of the verse itself, but what is so effected is also <u>khula</u> and justification for such cases has been found by the Jurists by a process of reasoning and deduction from the words of the verse, referred to in Hedaya and mentioned above, or from the contract between the parties. The principle so deduced amply justifies the conclusion drawn by the Jurists that <u>khula</u> by mutual agreement is permitted in Islam, but the concept of <u>khula</u> derived from instances of mutual agreement should not, in any event, be used to confuse the issue, and made to bear on cases of <u>khula</u> under the orders of the Qazi, which are expressly covered by the verse of the Holy Qur´an.

27. S.A. Rahman, J. in his judgment has admirably brought out the difference in the views of the Jurists and pointed out that these differences arise owing to the fact that two situations come into existence: (1) where <u>khula</u> takes place as a result of the mutual consent of the spouses, which is technically called <u>mubarat</u>. In such cases no reference to the Qazi is necessary, and (2) where the husband disputes the right of the wife to obtain separation by <u>khula</u>, a third party must decide the matter, and it will have to be adjudicated upon by the Qazi, and any other interpretation of the Qur´anic verse would deprive it of all efficacy as a charter granted to the wife. He has also detailed the trend of present legislation in Muslim countries, of the world indicating <u>ijma</u>, in modern times tending to recognise the right of the wife to obtain dissolution of her marriage.

28. The Holy Qur´an, which is the embodiment of Divine will, is the fundamental source of Islamic Laws. The laws in it are decrees and commandments of Divine Origin and not only have super-eminence over other sources of Muslim Law, but cannot be changed or altered by human agency. Verse 2:229 falls in the category of Qur´anic Law. Ahadith come next in importance. The Hanafi Muslim Jurisprudence recognises <u>ijtehad</u> and <u>ijma´</u> as the remaining two sources of Islamic Laws but they are subsidiary reasoning really falling under a single category, <u>ijtehad</u> being by individual scholars and <u>ijma´</u> by consensus of scholars indulging in <u>ijtehad</u> in any one period. The opinions of Jurists and Commentators stand on no higher footing than that of reasoning of men falling in the category of secondary sources of Muslim Law, and cannot, therefore, compare in weight or authority with, nor alter the Qur´anic law or the Ahadith. If the opinions of the Jurists conflict with the Qur´an and the Sunnah, they are not binding on Courts, and it is our duty, as true Muslims, to obey the word of God and the Holy Prophet (<u>ati-ullah-wa ati-ur-Rasool</u>).

Verse 2:229, which expressly covers cases where the husband refuses to divorce his wife, has been interpreted above, and the opinion of Jurists expressed in case of khula, whether by mutual agreement or otherwise which are to the contrary, are not binding on us, particularly if they are expressed in cases of khula by mutual agreement, which are somewhat different from those by judicial decree, where talaq is not pronounced.

29. Even on the question whether khula is to be equated with talaq or whether it is a form of dissolution of marriage, there is difference of opinion among the a'ima and Jurists. Ibne Rushud states in Badaya-tul-Mujtahid that most of the Ulema, Imam Malik and Imam Abu Hanifa are of the opinion that khula is equivalent to talaq, but Imam Shafi'e, Imam Ahmad, Imam Daud, and out of the companions, Ibne Abbas, express the view that khula amounts to fiskh-i-nikah, i.e. cancellation or dissolution of marriage and not talaq. Imam Shafi'e also states on a different occasion that if the husband intended a talaq, even in a mutual agreement of khula, it would operate as a talaq, and if he had intended it to be a fiskh-i-nikah, it would operate as such. Ibne Hajar Asqlani in his book "Alderaya-fi-Takhrija-Ahadith-ul-Hidaya wa Fathul-Bari" favours the opinion expressed by Ibne Abbas and doubts the authenticity of the hadith, which equates it with irreversible divorce, relying on a tradition of the Holy Prophet that the wife of Sabit bin Qais on the ground of khula was ordered by the Holy Prophet to pass one period of menstruation as her 'iddat, which was different from that in talaq. He reiterates it in Talkhisul Habir, Volume III, page 205. The Hedaya and other authorities make no difference between khula and talaq.

30. Thus, the Ulema and Jurists are not all agreed that khula is equivalent to a talaq, but those who have so stated (Imam Malik and Imam Abu Hanifa) and others have ignored the injunctions and prohibition in verse 2:229 and Verses 19 and 20 of Sura Al-Nisa of the Holy Qur'an, for if it is a talaq, it is not lawful for the husband to accept what the wife gives him to be free, as a consideration for khula but if it is khula it is lawful. It is lawful, because it is the wife who exercises her right of khula. Therefore even if a talaq is pronounced to effect khula, what is effected all the same is khula. This view is not only consistent with the Qur'anic injunctions, but has the advantage of saving cases of khula from the prohibition in the Holy Qur'an and this conclusion must be preferred. But even if it be conceded for the sake of argument that where a husband pronounces a talaq, it is equal to irreversible divorce, khula by judicial decree is still not equivalent to a talaq, because a talaq is not pronounced by the husband therein, nor is it a pre-requisite of khula in such cases.

31. In interpreting verse 2:229, it has been shown that khula is so characteristically different from talaq that the two cannot be equated. Talaq is the right of the husband and
288

khula is the right of the wife. Khula is sought and procured by the wife either from the husband or from the Qazi by payment of consideration. She either buys her freedom by inducing her husband to release her or persists in her demand before the Qazi, which results in the dissolution by the Qazi. Therefore, khula is an act of the wife in exercise of her right and cannot legitimately be said to be an act of the husband. The opinions and definitions of khula, adopted by Jurists are misleading when they convey the impression that khula is the act of the husband, and they do not also include cases of khula by the Qazi or the Courts, but if it is defined as putting off or doffing of the cloak of marriage by the wife, this definition will cover not only cases of khula by mutual arrangement, but also those which are enforced by the Qazi and the Courts, and will also not violate the prohibition in the Holy Qur´an. There is, therefore, no justification for the Jurists equating khula with talaq, or treating khula as an irreversible divorce, instead of a separation of the spouses.

32. Khula by a judicial decree, is thus a dissolution of marriage by the Qazi at the demand of the wife and for this conclusion, support is available in the opinions of Imam Shafi´e, Imam Ahmad, Imam Daud, and out of the companions of Ibne Abbas, who call it fiskh-i-nikah, i.e. dissolution of marriage and not a talaq. Ibne Hajar Asqlani supports their view. That khula is in fact a dissolution, and not talaq, is shown also by the that after khula the right of the husband to take back the wife does not remain, as it does in the case of a talaq-i-raja´, and the period of iddat is also different in either case. In the case of Jamila, the Holy Prophet ordered her to observe one period of menstruation as her iddat, which is different from talaq. On a discussion of the relevant Ahadith, Shankani in "Kitab-ul-Khula", Volume III, page 260 of his celebrated work "Nail-ul-Autar", has reached the conclusion that khula is not exactly a talaq, but is in a different category.

33. The pronouncement of a talaq by the husband even in cases of khula by mutual agreement is not essential in every case, because it has been held by the Courts that for the purpose of dissolving a marriage under khula or mubarat, which is dissolution of marriage by mutual agreement for a consideration to be paid by the wife, when there is mutual aversion, it is sufficient that the husband should propose to pronounce a talaq or otherwise to dissolve the marriage for a consideration, and that the wife should accept the proosal, in which case it is not necessary that talaq should be pronounced by him, because the contract itself dissolves the marriage (Muhammadan Law by Tayabji, Third Edition, sections 162 and 163).

34. The question whether the wife is not entitled in appropriate cases to demand a khula divorce from the husband in face of his refusal finds no express treatment in the

289

treatises of Hanafi Jurists, who merely content themselves by
saying that divorce is the right of the husband. As is stated
by S.A. Rahman, J. in his judgment, Dr. Sabuni has summarised
the various opinions on this question at page 621 of his book
"Madi Hurriat-uz-Zaujain Fittalaq" and in particular, to what
is related from Umar-ibn-Al-Khatab through the authority of
Behaqi, that "when women desire <u>khul</u> do not deny it", Sha´rani
in his book "Almizan-ul-Kubra", Volume II, page 117, also
states:

> "Imams agree in that the woman, if she dislikes her
> husband because of his ugliness or misconduct, she has a
> right to seek <u>Khul´</u> by payment of compensation."

Malik, Auzai and Ishaq are of the opinion that no Hakams are
required, nor permission of the spouses. Kufies, Sha´fi and
Ahmad have said that their permission is necessary as the
right to divorce is in the hands of the husband. If he
permits, well and good, otherwise the <u>Court will divorce on
his behalf</u>.

35. It was argued before us that as the parties must be
presumed to belong to the Hanafi Sect, the case must be
decided according to the doctrine of <u>khula</u>, as interpreted by
the Hanafi Jurists. It has already been pointed out that the
problem, where the husband refuses to divorce his wife on her
demand, finds no express treatment in the treatises of Hanafi
Jurists, who content themselves by saying that <u>talaq</u> is the
right of the husband, which is undeniable, but their
observation has no material bearing on cases of <u>khula</u> by
judicial decree. There is also no justification for a strict
doctrination, ruling out the opinions of Imam Malik, Imam
Shafe´i and Imam Ahmad bin Hanbal, who head the School of
Sunni Fiqh, along with Imam Abu Hanifa, for the Imams never
claimed finality for their opinions. When there exist
opinions of Shafie´s, Malikies and Hanbalies in cases, where
it is impossible for the spouses to live together and the
husband is reluctant to release his wife, and when these
opinions are consistent with the Qur´anic injunctions, there
can be no valid objection to relying on them.

36. There are no basic ideological reasons militating
against the view that the Holy Qur´an in conferring a right on
woman to seek dissolution of marriage and providing the forum
and rule of decision authorised the Qazi to dissolve a
marriage by <u>khula</u>. In Islam, marriage is a contract and not a
sacrament, and whatever sanctity attaches to it, it remains
basically a contractual relationship between the parties.
Islam, recognising the weaknesses of human nature, has
permitted the dissolution of marriage, and does not make it an
unseverable tie, condemning the spouses to a life of helpless
despair. The Qur´anic legislation makes it clear that it has
raised the status of women. The Holy Qur´an declares in Verse
2:228 that women have rights against men similar to those that
men have against them. It conferred the right of <u>khula</u> on

women as against the right of <u>talaq</u> in men. On the one hand, it put fetters on the unbridled exercise of power of divorce by the husband by providing for appointment of arbiters in verse 35, section 6, Chapter IV, in case of breach between the spouses, and on the other, conferred a right on women to seek dissolution of their marriage before the Qazi, the success of the right depending upon his order. The trend of Qur'anic legislation is clearly in favour of the freeing of the wife, where the marriage tie cannot serve the objects of marriage, namely, <u>sukun, moaddat</u> and <u>rehmat</u>(peace of mind, love, kindness, sympathy and compassion) specified in verse 21, Chapter XXX, Part 21 of the Holy Qur'an. If its objects cannot be served by a marriage, should it continue, though it be purposeless and even harmful, or is it not better that it be dissolved, so that the evil consequence of an impossible marriage relationship are avoided.

37. When the Holy Qur'an conferred on women a status of equality with men in their rights by stating women have rights against men similar to those that they have against them according to the well-known rules of equity it was natural and logical that she should have been conferred the right of <u>khula</u>, as compared to the right of <u>talaq</u> existing in men. Verse 2:229 of the Holy Qur'an requires that the husband should either retain the wife in honour according to the well-recognised custom or release her with grace, so that detaining them wrongfully is sinful. It further enjoins on the husband not to cling to the woman in order to cause her injury. Allah further commands in verse 19, Sura Al-Nisa (iv):-

"Nor should ye detain them that ye may take away a part of what ye have given them."

Thus the Holy Qur'an prohibits the wrongful or unwilling retaining of women, and favours their release. According to a <u>hadith</u> "let no harm be done, nor harm be suffered in Islam". If the Qazi is satisfied that relations between the spouses are so embittered that a marriage relationship between the spouses consistent with the tenets of Islam is not possible, and a reconciliation is out of question, the husband's clinging to her would be injurious to her, and since she would be prejudiced by the continuance of the marriage, the express words of the Holy Prophet clothe the Qazi with ample authority to dissolve the marriage "If a woman be prejudiced by marriage, let it be broken off" (Sahi-ul-Bukhari), as quoted by Ameer Ali in Muhammadan Law, Volume II (1965 Edition) at page 478.

38. The nature and extent of the power and authority of the Qazi to order dissolution of marriage is to be found in the following words of Mujalla-tul-Ahkam:-

"Hakim (Judge) is that person who is appointed by the Sultan to finally adjudicate upon and determine disputes and claims between the contestants according to

291

Shariat".

Mabsoot, Volume V, at page 97 states:-

"The Qazi has the power to prevent <u>zulm</u> by effecting separation".

Hedaya makes this further clear by stating in Volume II at page 323 as follows:-

"As Allah has enjoined that the husband should either retain the wife according to the well-recognised custom or release her with grace if she is not kept accordingly, it is necessary for him to release her with grace, or the Qazi will release her on his behalf."

Raddul Muhtar, which is a commentary of Hedaya, states that if the husband refuses to divorce his wife, she will make an application to the Qazi, and if her husband's refusal to divorce her is <u>zulm</u>, the Qazi will act on his behalf for relieving her of <u>zulm</u> and it is permissible for the Qazi to dissolve the marriage.

39. The views, which I have quoted above, give the power of dissolution to the Qazi, as agent of or acting for the husband, in the belief that the words "in whose hands is the marriage tie" in verse 238 of Sura Baqr, Part II of the Holy Qur'an, refer to the husband, and it was the husband alone, who had the power of divorce, and this power could only be exercised by him or his agent. The Commentators are not all agreed that these words necessarily refer to the husband, for they refer to the guardian of the woman, but even if they do, they only mean that he has the power to dissolve a marriage which is a truism, for it is he who can pronounce a <u>talaq</u>, but these words do not imply that the Qazi does not have the power to dissolve a marriage in appropriate case, or that the power in the Qazi, where it exists, can be rendered nugatory by the husband's refusal to divorce his wife. The Qazi ordinarily derives his authority from the State and not from the husband (though some Jurists by reason of confusion of thought hold to the contrary) when he orders dissolution as, e.g., in <u>ila, lian, inin</u>, etc. That <u>talaq</u> by the husband is not necessary for dissolution of marriage by <u>him</u> is illustrated by the cases where the husband disappears and becomes Mafqudul Khabar. There, as in other cases, the Qazi can dissolve the marriage tie at the instance of the wife without the husband pronouncing a <u>talaq</u>. Therefore, authority vests in the Qazi to dissolve a marriage independent of the consent of the husband, whose refusal to pronounce a <u>talaq</u> makes no difference to his powers and authority. When a wife seeks <u>khula</u> from the Qazi, he is named as a Judge by the Qur'anic verse 2:229 and he is thus empowered to decide the cause, independent of and even without the consent of the husband. His authority to dissolve a marriage by <u>khula</u>, where the wife seeks <u>khula</u>, and where he is satisfied that continuance of marriage tie is improper, harmful or likely to condemn the Spouses to a life of adultery, Sin and misery, and that the

parties cannot keep within the limits of Allah, has no limitations of consent of the husband, or his pronouncing a talaq.

40. In Mst. Saeeda Khanum v. Muhammad Sami, the learned A.C.J. (as he then was) relied on two traditions as showing that they were inconsistent with the Holy Prophet's decreeing a divorce in the case of Jamila. These traditions are:-

(1) "Soaban reported that the Messenger of Allah said: 'Whichever woman asks for divorce from her husband without fault, the fragrance of paradise is unlawful for her.'"

(2) "Ibne Omar reported that the Apostle of Allah said: 'The most detestable of lawful things near Allah is divorce.'"

These traditions are obviously intended to serve as a check on a moral plane against the free and wanton exercise of either the right of divorce by the husband or the right of khula by the wife, but do not forbid or make sinful either the pronouncing of talaq or the seeking of divorce by the wife from a Qazi. Sir Rowland Wilson in his book "Anglo-Muhammadan Law" has this to say about the first tradition:-

"The hadith in Tirmizi (1,368) that a woman who demands khula without necessity, will lose heaven, implies that legally she can make good her demand, possibly without other reason than alleged aversion or in modern equivalent incompatibility, but at least when she satisfactorily shows to impartial parties the impossibility of a happy married state."

41. The learned A.C.J. by referring to the traditions of Jamila, as narrated by Imam Razi in his commentary on the Holy Quran entitled "Tafseer-ul-Kabir", Volume II, under Verse 35, Chapter IV of the Holy Qur'an, also held that it was a case of khula by mutual agreement and not by judicial decree, for it was evident that as the case came before the Holy Prophet, the wife on the one side expressed a desire for separation from her husband, and the husband on the other, put forward a claim for return of the garden he had given to her, without protesting against his wife's behaviour, and indeed by asking for a consideration, he expressed his willingness that the marriage bond should be broken in return for an advantage to be received by him. Since the Holy Prophet discovered that there was agreement between the parties, he gave a direction, which stands as a guidance for all other Muslim married couples for all times. It should be noted that the learned A.C.J., though holding that it was not an order, has himself characterised it as a "direction" by the Holy Prophet. The learned Judges in Mst. Umar Bibi v. Muhammad Din accepted without question that it was the Holy Prophet who ordered Sabit to divorce his wife in words "talaqaha tatliqa", which mean "give her an irrevocable divorce". With the utmost respect to the learned A.C.J. it may be pointed out that

293

though his conclusion is feasible, it is more reasonable to infer judging by human nature conduct, that Sabit was forced by circumstances to ask for the return of the garden. He must have asked for the garden not because he wanted to divorce her, and preferred the advantage of return of the garden to retaining her, for it is clear beyond doubt that he was intensely in love with her, but because it must have become clear to him that there was no way out of the situation, as the Holy Prophet was bound to separate Jamila from him. Hakim in "Al-Mustadrak", Shaukani in "Nail-ul-Autar", relying on Darkatani´s version, and Ibne Abdul Bar in "Al-Istiab" categorically state that it was the Holy Prophet who ordered the separation. Ibne Hajar Askalani shares this opinion, and doubts the authenticity of the <u>hadith</u> specifying this case as one of <u>talaq</u>.

42. In verse 35, section 6, Chapter IV, the Holy Qur´an provides that if there be <u>shiqaq</u> between the spouses, <u>Hakama</u> or arbiters be appointed, one from each side. This was intended to be a restriction on the free exercise of the right of divorce by the husband, and was in the nature of a protection afforded to the wife. The Jurists disagree on the question whether the <u>Hakama</u> have authority to effect separation of the spouses as would appear from page 265, Volume 19 of Umdatul Qari, printed by Municipal Press in Egypt and this power was held to be lacking in <u>Mst. Umar Bibi v. Muhammad Din</u> and in <u>Mst. Saeeda Khanum v. Muhammad Sami</u>, and this was one of the reasons for taking the contrary view, but the question is hardly of any importance for the interpretation of Verse 2:229, because even if the opinion be formed that if Hakama are not satisfied about <u>shiqaq</u> and they do not agree as to separation, a divorce cannot be effected by them unless authorised by the husband the conclusion cannot affect the power in the Qazi to dissolve a marriage, where he has the necessary apprehension. The lack of authority in the <u>Hakama</u> cannot affect the authority in the Qazi (and the Court,) to dissolve marriage by a <u>khula</u> which is conferred by a Qur´anic verse.

43. The reasons stated by the learned A.C.J. in <u>Mst. Saeeda Khanum v. Muhammad Sami</u> have been examined with care by Kaikaus, J. in <u>Mst. Bilqis Fatima v. Najam-ul-Ikram Qureshi</u>. With his conclusions, I agree with respect. The fact that neither verse 2:229, nor instances of <u>khula</u>, except that of Jamila, were placed before the Full Bench which decided <u>Mst. Saeeda Khanum v. Muhammad Sami</u> or before the Division Bench, which decided <u>Mst. Umar Bibi v. Muhammad Din</u>, and the reasons recorded by Kaikaus, J. afford sufficient justification for departing, I say so with great respect, from the contrary view taken in the two cases.

44. The instant case is one in which Mst. Khurshid Bibi has sought dissolution of marriage under subsection (ix) of section 2 of the Dissolution of Muslim Marriages Act on the

ground of khula, which is recognised as valid for the dissolution of marriage under Muslim Law, and it has been shown that khula can be ordered by the Qazi even against the will and consent of the husband and without his pronouncing a talaq. It has been established that it is impossible for the spouses to live "within the limits of God", which phrase means the performance of marital obligations while living together. The purpose of the appointment of Hakama has been served by the Panchayats which were arranged by the respondent's father, and as all efforts at reconciliation have failed, the appointment of Hakama for the same purpose will be futile. Mst. Khurshid Bibi appellant is, therefore, entitled to a decree for dissolution of marriage under the terms of verse 2:229.

45. Verse 2:229 of the Holy Qur'an implies that the wife has to pay compensation to the husband in order to obtain dissolution of marriage by khula. This conclusion clearly emerges from its words "what she gives up to be free" or "by what she ransomes herself". According to Hedaya, it is abominable on the part of the husband to take from his wife more than what he had given or settled upon her, namely, her dower. Jamia Saghir states that if the husband takes more than the dower it is strictly legal, as the text of the Holy Qur'an is expressed generally, but the reason for its Justification is that being based on contract, it is not illegal. This is legal, because the wife agrees to give more than what she received in lieu of the marriage.

46. The instances of khula, which have been cited above, show that the wife has to return the benefits of the marriage and illustrates that the wife has to refund no more than what she has received, for though Jamila was willing to give more than the garden given to her by her husband, the Holy Prophet said: "No, only the garden." It is a further check on the wife's exercise of the right of khula that, as a general rule, she cannot retain the benefits, i.e., the consideration of the marriage, the same as the husband cannot take back whatever he has given to the wife in consideration of the marriage, if he divorces her, which is a corresponding restraint on his right. Therefore, it is necessary for the Court to ascertain in a case of khula what benefits have been conferred on the wife by the husband as a consideration of the marriage, and it is in the discretion of the Court to fix the amount of compensation, as is indicated by the instances of khula cited above.

47. In the instant case, the wife has offered to give up the dower and the evidence and the pleadings of the parties indicate that it has not been paid to her. Therefore, the question remains whether she has received any other benefit of the marriage, which she has to restore. In other words, what are the terms on which a decree for dissolution of her marriage should be granted to her? Though the first Court granted her a decree for dissolution of her marriage, it did

not consider or indicate the terms and conditions on which it was to operate. Even though the question was specifically included in the fourth issue, the parties have not led any evidence as to the benefits conferred by the respondent herein on the appellant as a consideration of the marriage, or as to the amount of consideration, which the respondent is entitled to be restored as a condition of the grant of khula. On this question, all that we have on the record is the assertion of the appellant in the plaint that the respondent herein incurred no expense on the marriage and of the respondent herein in his written statement that he incurred an expense of Rs. 2,000 on the marriage, but this was not stated in evidence, which is silent on the question of what were the benefits conferred by the respondent on the appellant in consideration of the marriage. Since the possibility cannot be ruled out that if Rs. 2,000 were spent on the marriage, the expense may include the cost of benefits conferred on the wife, I agree that this case be remanded to the trial Court with a direction to allow the parties to lead evidence as to the benefits, if any, conferred by the respondent herein on the appellant as a consideration of the marriage, and that the parties bear their own costs throughout..

Mst. DAULAN (Appellant) v. DOSA (Respondent)
PLD 1956 (W.P.) Lahore 712. (Kaikaus J.)

Judgement.....Mst. Daulan appellant filed a suit against Dosa respondent for cancellation of her marriage on the ground that the marriage had been performed under coercion and undue influence and that in any case her marriage having been performed by a guardian, she, having attained puberty about twenty days before the suit, was entitled to a dissolution.

The defendant-respondent denied the allegations of coercion and undue influence and objected that the plaintiff not having attained the age of fifteen years the suit was premature. He pleaded too that the plaintiff had not attained puberty. Various other issues were raised with which we are not now concerned. The learned Subordinate Judge did not find any evidence on the issue of coercion and undue influence and decided the issue against the plaintiff. On the question, however, of the exercise of the option of puberty the learned Judge came to the conclusion that the plaintiff, though only twelve or thirteen years of age, had attained puberty and that the suit was not premature. In view of these findings he decreed the suit. On appeal the learned District Judge came to the conclusion that on a proper interpretation of section (2) (vii) of the Dissolution of Muslim Marriages Act, 1939, the option granted by that subsection could only be exercised after the completion of fifteen years. Without going into the question as to whether the plaintiff had in fact attained puberty or not he accepted the appeal and dismissed the suit. The plaintiff has appealed.....

.....On the merits the decision of the question whether option to repudiate the marriage can be exercised before completion of fifteen years depends upon the interpretation of section 2 (vii) of the Dissolution of Muslim Marriages Act, 1939.....

.....Learned counsel for the appellant argues that the section nowhere lays down that in order that a woman may be entitled to repudiate the marriage performed by her guardian she must have attained the age of fifteen years. According to him all that is required is that she should have repudiated the marriage before she attains the age of eighteen years. There is no doubt that the section nowhere lays down in so many words that this repudiation cannot come before the attainment of the age of fifteen years. The result of this interpretation, however, would be that if the marriage of a girl of six was performed by her guardian, the very next day she could by her repudiation dissolve it. The Muslim Law on the subject before the enactment of the Dissolution of Muslim Marriages Act, 1939 (shorn of some details not at present relevant) was that a woman whose marriage had been performed by her guardian could on the attainment of puberty repudiate the marriage provided she had not, after the attainment of puberty, consented to or acquiesced in it. To accept the interpretation of the learned counsel for the appellant would be to give to every girl who has not yet attained puberty an option of repudiating her marriage which is neither in consonance with Muslim Law nor would be justified on any principle. The option of puberty of Muhammadan Law is only a right given to a minor party to a contract to avoid the contract entered into by her guardian on becoming <u>sui juris</u>. As the preamble shows, the Dissolution of Muslim Marriages Act, 1939, does not purport to effect any change in Muhammadan Law but to clarify and consolidate it. We will not, therefore, adopt any interpretation which effects a fundamental change unless we are forced to do so. Clause (vii) is capable of an interpretation that repudiation takes place when the age of fifteen has already been reached. The words 'before she attained the age of fifteen years' can quite properly be interpreted as implying that she has already attained the age of fifteen when she repudiates the marriage.

Under Muslim Law there is a presumption of attainment of puberty at the age of fifteen, but this presumption is rebuttable. Clause (vii) of section 2 adopts fifteen as the fixed age of puberty without an opportunity of rebuttal. This clause does not speak of puberty at all, but only of an age though in fact it deals with the option arising at puberty, and the only way in which it can be reasonably interpreted is that a woman who has before the age of fifteen years been given away in marriage by her guardian is allowed to repudiate her marriage for a period of three years after she attains the

297

age of fifteen and before she attains the age of eighteen. The clause eliminates the fight over proof of puberty.

I may mention a possible argument. The word ´repudiation´ it may be argued would imply puberty on the part of the person repudiating. The result of this interpretation would, however, be that although the repudiation comes after fifteen it will be open to the husband to prove that puberty had not been yet attained and to defeat the suit on that ground. The clause does not contemplate such a defence and gives a right after fifteen which is not subject to disproof of puberty. I would, therefore, agree with the learned District Judge with respect to the interpretation he has placed on the clause.

That, however, does not conclude the matter. Next question to be determined is: Does this clause contain the whole of the Muslim Law regarding option of puberty? Is this clause exhaustive and has a woman no right beyond the limits of this clause of repudiation of her marriage performed by her guardian before she attained puberty? As already stated, the Dissolution of Muslim Marriages Act, 1939, is designed to clarify and consolidate the provisions of the Muslim Law. As it is a consolidating Act it may be argued that there should be no relief beyond its provisions. However, the Act is careful and after enacting in section 2, eight clauses, which contain grounds for dissolution of marriages, provides a ninth clause which runs:-

"(ix) on any other ground which is recognised as valid for the dissolution of marriages under Muslim Law:"
It is obvious that the intention was to preserve every ground of dissolution available in Muhammadan Law.

The consequences of regarding this clause as exhaustive would be the following:-

(1) A woman, who is married before she has attained puberty, but on the completion of fifteen years, would be left entirely without a remedy. If a girl attained puberty when she was fifteen years and two days of age, and on the day when she attained the age of fifteen years or the next day she was given in marriage by her guardian, this clause would afford her no relief.
(2) A girl, who attains puberty at the age of eleven or less but has already been given in marriage by her guardian, will be forced either to accept her husband or to wait for four years or more. If she repudiates her marriage before fifteen, according to this clause, marriage will still be valid, though according to Muhammadan Law it stood dissolved by her repudiation.
(3) A woman who is not aware of the marriage till the age of eighteen, would be entirely without a remedy, though the marriage may never have been consummated.
I do not think these are results which were at all contemplated by the legislature. The legislature is presumed

298

not to make any far-reaching changes in the existing law without making itself amply clear and in the present case the Act only purports to clarify the law and has provided a saving clause in section 2, keeping all existing grounds of dissolution intact. It may also be pointed out that clause (vii) deals only with respect to the option of puberty of a woman while the Muslim Law grants option of puberty not only to a girl but also to a boy whose marriage had been performed during his minority by his guardian.

While, therefore, I agree with the learned District Judge that clause (vii) by itself does contemplate only repudiation after fifteen, I am satisfied that this clause does not exhaust the whole of the right which a Muslim woman has with respect to a marriage performed by a guardian before the attainment of puberty, and that all rights of dissolution by exercise of the option of puberty available under Muhammadan Law are intact. The learned District Judge having decided on a preliminary ground the case will have to go back to him for a decision on merits.

I may point out that now that the plaintiff can claim only under the general Muhammadan Law her right will be subject to all the limitations and conditions of Muhammadan Law except to the extent to which they may be held to have been removed by ´clarification´ in the Dissolution of Muslim Marriages Act, 1939. This marriage was performed by the father. Under Sunni Law the marriage performed by a father or grandfather was not subject to the option of puberty unless it was shown to be performed negligently or fraudulently. The reason for this distinction is stated in the <u>Hedaya</u> to be that the father and grandfather are presumed not to act from sinister motives. Really it is a presumption of fact rebutted by proof that the benefit of minor had not been safeguarded. There are allegations in the plaint as to the circumstances under which the marriage was performed though they were not made with the object of showing that the marriage, though performed by the father, was subject to the option of puberty. It can be urged that by clause (vii) the legislature has clarified that a father is in this respect on the same footing as the guardian. The point not having been argued before me I express no opinion. All these are matters for the learned District Judge to decide. There is one thing, however, which I want to make clear. Should the plaintiff´s right to get this marriage dissolved be subject to proof that the marriage was negligently or fraudulently performed and these facts be not proved, she will not lose her remedy altogether but will only have to wait till she attains the age of fifteen years when she could file a suit on the ground that she has repudiated the marriage after she attained the age of fifteen years.

This appeal is accepted and the case remanded to the learned District Judge, Sargodha, for a redecision. Parties shall bear their own costs of this appeal.

MOHD. AMIN (Appellant) v. SURRAYA BEGUM (Respondent)
P.L.D. 1970 Lah. 475. (M.A. Cheema, J.)

Judgement.....2. The brief facts of the case are that the
parties were admittedly married on 18-4-1958 in Lahore when
Rukhsati did not take place. It appears that after having in
vain tried to prevail upon the parents of the respondent to
send her with him the appellant at long last filed a suit for
the restitution of conjugal rights on 24-4-1962. On receipt
of notice, the respondent also brought a suit for dissolution
of marriage on grounds of exercise of option of puberty, the
appellant's association with woman of ill-repute and on the
basis of Khula´.....

.....4. The learned counsel for the appellant raised the
following contentions before me:-
> (1) That the learned Courts below had erred in deciding
> issue No. 1, relating to the competency and
> maintainability of the suit for dissolution of marriage
> filed by the respondent in her favour, inasmuch as the
> mandatory provision contained in section 8 of the Family
> Laws Ordinance had made it obligatory on the respondent
> to have recourse to the procedure laid down in section 7
> ibid.....

.....5. On the contrary, it was contended on behalf of the
respondent that the Muslim Family Laws Ordinance hereinafter
called the Ordinance, did not oust the jurisdiction of the
civil Courts and the existence of such an ouster by
implication was not warranted by any known and established
principles of interpretation; that even otherwise section 8 of
the Ordinance referred to "dissolution of marriages otherwise
than by talaq" and, as such, this provision could not be
attracted to the facts of the instant case in which the suit
of the respondent was decreed on ground of repudiation of
marriage by exercise of option of puberty; and that it was the
appellant himself who dragged the respondent to the civil
Court, who was thus constrained to invoke that jurisdiction
and for that reason as well the bar created by section 8 would
not be attracted.

6. In order to appreciate the merit of the first legal
contention raised by the learned counsel for the appellant, it
would be necessary to reproduce section 8 of the Ordinance.
It reads thus:
> "8. Where the right to divorce has been duly delegated
> to the wife and she wishes to exercise that right, or
> where any of the parties to a marriage wishes to
> dissolve the marriage otherwise than by talaq, the
> provisions of section 7 shall, mutatis mutandis and so
> far as applicable, apply."

300

It may be observed that the procedure laid down in section 7 referred to in the above provision briefly is that the husband wishing to divorce his wife shall after the pronouncement of talaq give a notice to the Chairman of his having done so and shall also send a copy thereof to his wife. A contravention of this provision is made punishable with simple imprisonment which may extend to one year or with fine which may extend to five thousand rupees or with both. The talaq so pronounced by him shall take effect on the expiration of ninety days from the date of delivery of notice to the Chairman who, within thirty days of the receipt of notice, shall constitute an arbitration council for the purpose of bringing about a reconciliation between the parties. If the wife is pregnant at the time of the pronouncement of talaq it does not become effective until the expiration of ninety days or delivery whatever be later.

7. It was contended by the learned counsel that in the instant case the respondent having sought dissolution of her marriage on grounds of option of puberty and Khula´, the expression "wishes to dissolve the marriage otherwise than by talaq" as occurring in section 8 would be attracted with full force to her case, leaving her with no option but to adopt the procedure laid down in section 7 mutatis mutandis. It was next argued that notwithstanding the fact that the ground of Khula´ was patently hit by section 8 of the Ordinance as found by the trial Court had nonetheless deemed it proper to give a finding on this issue without insisting on the amendment of the plaint. It was asserted that while determining the question of the competency of a suit the plaint as a whole had to be taken into consideration and a suit might well be rendered incompetent simply on account of the inclusion of a single objectionable ground in the plaint, the other grounds being wholly unexceptionable. Reliance was placed in this regard on the provisions contained in Order VI, rules 1, 2, 6 and 17 and Order VII, rule 1, clauses (e) and (g). Rahmat Bibi v. Ramzani (P L D 1967 Lah. 1074) was also cited as an authority in point.

8. Having carefully considered the contention, I am clearly of the view that it has no force and has got to be overruled for more than one reason. In the first instance, there is nothing to indicate in the Muslim Family Laws Ordinance which could be construed as amounting to an ouster of the jurisdiction of civil Courts. It was not till the 18th of July 1964, when the West Pakistan Family Courts Act hereinafter called the Act, came into force that under section 5 ibid jurisdiction of ordinary civil Courts in matters relating, inter alia, to dissolution of marriage and restitution of conjugal rights was taken away and vested exclusively in the Family Courts, established under section 3 ibid. [See Appendix I for the text of this Act]. This conferment of exclusive jurisdiction was of course subject to

301

the provisions of the Muslim Family Laws Ordinance, 1961, as clearly provided in the opening clause of section 5 of the West Pakistan Family Courts Act. If, however, section 8 of the Ordinance were so construed as leading inferentially to the ouster of jurisdiction of civil Courts the subsequent vesting of exclusive jurisdiction in the Family Courts would be obviously repugnant to such a construction of the provision contained in section 8 of the Ordinance in which case the latter would prevail. The mere fact, therefore, that the Family Courts as constituted under the Act were given the exclusive jurisdiction to try _inter alia_ suits for dissolution of marriage would clearly indicate that the law-maker had not in view either by express provision or by necessary intendment the ouster of the civil Court's jurisdiction and as such the provision shall have to be given a restricted meaning with its application being confined only to the adoption of the procedure laid down in section 7 of the Ordinance to prevent hasty dissolution of marriages by affording opportunities to the parties to bring about reconciliation through the good offices of the Arbitration Council. Section 21 of the Family Courts Act offers further guidance in this regard by which the apparent conflict between section 8 of the Family Laws Ordinance and section 5 of the Family Courts Act is resolved and the two provisions are so harmonized as to be able to stand together. It reads as follows:-

"21. - (1) Nothing in this Act shall be deemed to affect any of the provisions of the Muslim Family Laws Ordinance, 1961, or the rules framed thereunder; and the provisions of sections 7, 8, 9 and 10 of the said Ordinance shall be applicable to any decree for the dissolution of marriage solemnized under the Muslim Law, maintenance or dower, by a Family Court.

(2) Where a Family Court passes a decree for the dissolution of a marriage solemnized under the Muslim Law, the Court shall send by registered post, within seven days of passing such decree, a certified copy of the same to the appropriate Chairman referred to in section 7 of the Muslim Family Laws Ordinance, 1961 and upon receipt of such copy, the Chairman shall proceed as if he had received an intimation of _talaq_ required to be (given) under the said Ordinance.

From the above it would be seen that when a Family Court passes a decree for dissolution of marriage solemnized under the Muslim Law it is placed under a legal obligation to send a copy of the same to the Chairman concerned, who shall then have recourse to the procedure laid down in section 7 of the Muslim Family Laws Ordinance treating the decree as an intimation of _talaq_. As a necessary corollary from this it would follow that prior to the coming into force of the Family Courts Act, the ordinary civil Courts had the jurisdiction to try the suit for dissolution of marriage as there can be no ouster of jurisdiction by implication unless there is an express provision to this effect or one leading to an inference of necessary intendment. I am, therefore, clearly of the view that the Court had the jurisdiction to entertain the respondent's suit for dissolution of marriage which was instituted on the 24th of April 1962, before the constitution of the Family Courts. A question might well arise as to how could the provisions of section 8 of the Ordinance be invoked in such a case. This obviously presents some difficulty and is not easy to answer. With the utmost respect it may be observed that perhaps being conscious of this lacuna, the Legislature in its wisdom enacted section 21 of the Family Courts Act in order to harmonize the two provisions.

8. It was argued on behalf of the respondent that the expression "wishes to dissolve the marriage otherwise than by talaq" clearly envisaged a case where a marriage was sought to be dissolved by a decree of the Court and did not comprehend within its compass declaratory suit based on repudiation of marriage in exercise of the option of puberty. It was submitted that the distinction between a suit for a declaration and one for dissolution of marriage was patently clear having different implication. In a case where a declaration of dissolution of marriage was sought on ground of Khiarul Balugh, the Court had only to recognize the dissolution of marriage which came into force with effect from the date of the decree, and if in the meantime, the repudiator had contracted a second marriage it would be perfectly valid. On the contrary, in a case for dissolution of marriage, the marriage stood dissolved on the date when the decree was passed. Reliance was placed in this regard on Muni v. Habib Khan (P L D 1956 Lah. 403). In this authority, B.Z. Kaikaus, J. observed as follows:-

"Repudiation of marriage by the exercise of option of puberty puts an end to the marriage without the aid of any Court and when the matter comes to Court, the Court does not dissolve the marriage by its own act but recognizes the termination of marriage."

It was emphasised that since section 8 refers to dissolution of marriage and not to repudiation, the provision was not applicable to a case of repudiation by Khiarul Balugh. The argument on the face of it appears to be quite attractive, but on a closer examination loses much of its charm. In answer to this, it can be argued that the expression "wishes to dissolve the marriage otherwise than by talaq" as occurring in section 8 of the Ordinance is in full accord with the phraseology employed in section 2 of the Dissolution of Muslim Marriages Act of 1939..... .....Ground (vii) of the above grounds relates to repudiation of marriage in exercise of the option of puberty. From this it could be reasonably inferred that notwithstanding the declaratory form of the suit, filed on the basis of Khiarul Balugh, it amounts in effect to seeking a

303

decree for dissolution of marriage and the date of its being operative or effectual would be immaterial. Further support would be lent to this view by the conferment of exclusive jurisdiction on Family Courts constituted under Act XXXV of 1964 to try _inter alia_ suits for dissolution of marriage. A suit based on the ground of _Khiarul Balugh_ is essentially one for dissolution of marriage and it cannot be argued with any modicum of reasonableness that the heading "dissolution of marriage" excludes a declaratory suit for dissolution of marriage based on exercise of option of puberty. I am, therefore, inclined to think that the expression used in section 8 also envisages a suit of the latter category. As stated earlier section 21 of the Family Courts Act resolves the conflict between section 8 of the Muslim Family Laws Ordinance and section 5 of the Family Courts Act on points of jurisdiction and procedure.

9. The next argument that the ground of _khula´_ having been concurrently found by the Courts below to be hit by section 8 of the Ordinance, would have inevitably resulted in the respondent being non-suited, has no force either. No doubt the Courts below had found issue No. 6 relating to _Khula´_ against the respondent on the ground that in order to press into service she should have had recourse to the procedure laid down in section 7 and made an application to the Chairman of the Union Committee concerned. Irrespective of the correctness or otherwise of this finding, I cannot persuade myself to agree with the learned counsel that if one of the several grounds taken for dissolution of marriage in a suit is not competent which again is a question to be determined at the trial, a plaintiff would be non-suited unless he amends the plaint. If the suit for the dissolution of marriage had been filed by the respondent on the sole ground of _Khula´_ which was deemed to have been hit by section 8 of the Muslim Family Laws Ordinance, a preliminary objection to the competency of the suit in that form could have been legitimately taken. But in a case where several grounds are pressed into service including that of _Khiarul Balugh_ which as found earlier is not hit by the provisions contained in section 8 _ibid_ the respondent could not be non-suited. The authority _Rehmat Bibi v. Ramzani_ relied upon by the learned counsel proceeds on entirely distinguishable facts and does not advance the case of the appellant. The facts of that case were that the parties were married at Multan but subsequently lived at Bahawalpur which was the ordinary place of residence of the husband. The wife brought a suit for dissolution of marriage on ground of cruelty and on the basis of _Khula´_ at Multan where the marriage was admittedly contracted. The Civil Judge, Multan, overruled the objection on the question of jurisdiction and dissolved the marriage of the parties. The learned Additional District Judge, Multan, however, took the view that the Civil Courts at Multan had no jurisdiction

304

to try the suit. This judgment was set aside by my learned
brother Sardar Muhammad Iqbal, J. in revision. The learned
counsel for the appellant relied on the following observation
made therein:-

"A cause of action is the sum total of all those
allegations upon which the right to the relief claimed
is founded. It includes every fact which it would be
necessary to prove, if traversed, in order to enable a
plaintiff to sustain his action."

But his Lordship went on to observe that:-

"It is, therefore, to be ascertained from the
allegations in the plaint as to what is the cause of
action in each case. In a suit for dissolution of
marriage, it has always to be alleged that the plaintiff
was the wife of the defendant because unless there is a
marriage, there cannot be any dissolution. The factum
of marriage, therefore, furnishes a part of the cause of
action in such a case and a suit for dissolution is
competent at a place where the marriage takes place."

Thus the subsequent observation reproduced above clearly
militates against the divisibility of cause of action. Again
if several grounds are available to a plaintiff at the time of
the institution of the suit he cannot, under Order II, rule 2,
C.P.C., withhold some of them to be pressed in a subsequent
suit. The contention is, therefore, devoid of force and is
overruled.

9. The finding that a suit for dissolution of marriage
brought on grounds of <u>Khiar-ul-Balugh</u> is not hit by the
provision contained in section 8 of the Ordinance making it
incumbent on the party seeking dissolution to have recourse to
procedure contained in section 7 <u>ibid</u> can be upheld on yet
another ground. Having once repudiated the marriage by a
proper exercise of her option of puberty a Muslim woman is
under no obligation to wait for the decree of the Court for
contracting a second marriage and instances are not wanting
where before the matter has come up before the Court the woman
has already gone in for a second marriage and has even born
children in the subsequent wedlock as is stated to have
happened in the instant case. Obviously the object of having
recourse to the procedure laid down in section 8 of the
Ordinance, namely, to bring about reconciliation having
already been irretrievably defeated there would be no question
of invoking that procedure. Again this view is also in accord
with the established principles of interpretation. Obviously,
the object of the Muslim Family Laws Ordinance was to
discourage avoidable plurality of wives, hasty and impulsive
pronouncement of <u>talaq</u> by "impetuous and capricious husbands"
and to liberalise the law in this regard for the estranged
spouses, particularly, for the benefit of the weaker sex. If,
however, in a case like this where an estranged wife is
dragged to the Civil Court by a husband seeking restitution of

conjugal rights, the construction placed by the learned counsel on section 8 which even otherwise is questionable as discussed earlier, would force the wife to fight on two fronts instead of seeking a declaration in the same Court to which she has been summoned per force. I am, therefore, clearly of the view that the respondent's suit was not hit by section 8 of the Ordinance. The contention is, therefore overruled.

Chapter Five

PARENT AND CHILD

The legal relationship of parent and child depends on
that child's legitimacy, so far as the father is concerned: a
child is in law always related to its mother even if
illegitimate. Legitimacy is important: the entitlement of a
child to maintenance and inheritance from its father, the
right of the father to custody, guardianship, inheritance and
perhaps maintenance in cases of extreme hardship, will depend
on the legitimacy of the child. Determining the legitimacy of
a child takes on added significance when it is remembered that
adoption and legitimation are unknown in Muslim law(1).
Legitimacy may be established in a number of ways. Firstly,
by birth out of the sahih marriage. What constitutes a sahih
marriage has already been considered(2). But a fasid marriage
too will give rise to legitimacy and according to some jurists
even a batil marriage where shubha may be pleaded(3). The
relevant time for determining legitimacy is that of
conception, not birth. But the Muslim law has been extremely
generous in its presumptions as to the duration of gestation.
In Hanafi law a child born within six months of the
commencement of the marriage is presumed not to be born of
that marriage in the absence of acknowledgement by the
husband: thereafter it is presumed to be of that marriage
unless disclaimed by the husband. A child born after the
termination of the marriage will be presumed to be born of the
marriage if born within two years. However, some doubts have
been raised in the Indian subcontinent as to the status of
these presumptions in the light of the Indian Evidence Act
1872, s.112, which must be considered.

The 1872 Act provided by s.112 that "the fact that any
person born during the continuance of a valid marriage between
his mother and any man, or within two hundred and eighty days
after its dissolution, the mother remaining unmarried, shall
be conclusive proof that he is the legitimate son of that man
unless it can be shown that the parties to the marriage had no
access to each other at any time when he would have been
begotten." By s.2 the Act purported to repeal "all rules of

307

evidence not contained in any Statute, Act or Regulation in force in any part of British India." In 1938 s.2 was repealed. To further complicate matters the General Clauses Act 1936 provides: "Where any Central Act or Regulation made after the commencement of this Act repeals any enactment by which the text of any Central Act or Regulation was amended by the express omission insertion or substitution of any matter, then, unless a different intention appears, the repeal shall not affect the continuance of any such amendment made by the enactment so repealed and in operation at the time of such repeal." Finally, the position of Pakistan and India may be distinguished in that the Pakistan Muslim Personal law (Shariat) Application Act of 1962, unlike the Indian Act, includes in its enumeration of matters to be governed by Muslim law both legitimacy and bastardy(4).

The choice between the statutory and Muslim law regimes has considerable practical significance. S.112 might be said to treat fornication more generously than adultery, the Muslim rules the converse. A child born one month after the marriage of a couple is under the Act legitimate, in the absence of proof of non access, but under Muslim law presumed not to be of that marriage unless acknowledged. A child born one year after the termination of the marriage is under the Act presumed neither legitimate nor illegitimate, but the burden of proof lies on the person alleging legitimacy: under Muslim law it is presumed unless disclaimed. Although the point may be considered open it is arguable that the Act applies in India(5), the Muslim law in Pakistan(6), but a further complication may be that a child who is born during the continuance of or after a _fasid_ marriage must in any case be dealt with under Muslim law since the Act expressly applies only to valid marriages.

A second means of establishing legitimacy is acknowledgement of the child by the husband under certain conditions. The relationship of father and legitimate child must have been legally and physically possible, so there must be an age difference of twelve and a half years and a marriage with the child's mother. The paternity of the child must be unknown or at the very least doubtful so that there is no proof that the child is the offspring of unlawful sexual relations. There must be no rebuttal of the acknowledgement. The acknowledgement may however be express or implied, though the statement or conduct relied on must have been intended to have some legal effect. These are rules of substantive law, not evidence. Once made, the acknowledgement is irrevocable. The effect of a valid acknowledgement is to confer all the benefits and the obligations of legitimacy(7).

The consequences of a finding of illegitimacy are severe. The child will lack any right of inheritance or maintenance from its father in Muslim law, lacking any legal relationship with him. His only connection recognised in law is with his mother. Muslim penal law prescribes severe punishments for the parents, zina, on meeting high standards of proof, though today these are only applicable in Pakistan(8). However, the Criminal Procedure Code s.488 (s.125 in the Indian Code of 1973) provides that a father may be compelled to provide maintenance for his illegitimate child while it is a minor and even on attaining majority if (not being a married daughter) that child is through some physical or mental abnormality unable to maintain itself. An agreement to maintain an illegitimate child will not be void(9). The Muslim law obliges the mother to maintain her child and she has custody of it.

Islam does not recognise the institution of adoption, though it was practised in pre-Islamic Arabia and certain customary practices exist in India (10). For the Muslim law any purported adoption is wholly ineffective. Attempts in India to introduce a statutory regime of adoption have failed(11).

<u>Tanzil-ur-Rahman, "A Code of Muslim Personal Law", Vol. I, p.716</u>

It is a well known fact that the Prophet, (peace be on him) had adopted Zaid Bin Haritha as his son. When Zaid divorced his wife, Zainab, the Prophet, after the completion of her term of probation, married her under God´s command. The Jews began to taunt him that he had contracted marriage with the divorced wife of his "son." The Qur´anic verse was then revealed, "Muhammad is not the father of any one of your men." Zaid Bin Haritha whom the Prophet had adopted had not become his son in fact so as to prohibit the Prophet from marrying his divorced wife. The rule that emanates from this verse is that the adoption of some one as son does not legally give him the status and rights of a son. If a person, therefore, is an adopted son he shall not have the same rights as the real son has against his parents ; for instance, the right of maintenance and Inheritance. Likewise, one who adopts cannot as well inherit from the property of his adopted son. Indeed a will to the extent of one-third of his estate may, however, be made in the adopted son´s favour as in case of any stranger.

Some people, in modern times, are trying to legalise adoption in Islam in such manner that the rights of a real child be conferred on the adopted one as well, and in support of their view cite "<u>Aqd Muwakhat</u>" of Prophet´s time. When he migrated from Mecca to Madina the Prophet had ordered that the <u>Muhajirin</u> and <u>Ansar</u> enter into a contract of brotherhood (´<u>Aqd Muwakhat</u>) with each other. In consequence thereof, the contracting persons used to become as brothers and inherited from each other. But basing the argument on this event is invalid now inasmuch as the Qur´anic verse later revealed explained: "And those who accept faith subsequently, and adopt exile, and fight for the faith in your company, they are of you. But kindred by blood have prior rights against each other in the book of Allah." Thus the real kindred shall be the heirs of each other and the rule of inheritance through ´Aqd Muwakhat stood repealed. Some people appear to be in favour of introducing inheritance between the adopter and the adopted on the basis of a contractual relationship but a system of inheritance in Islam cannot be introduced on the basis of a contract except in case of ´Aqd Muwakhat which situation under the present conditions does not exist. Indeed the one who adopts a son or daughter may make a will to the extent of one-third of his property in favour of the adopted one as he is legally entitled to do so in favour of a stranger, or to the extent of entire property if there is no heir at all.

The Obligation of Maintenance

The obligation to maintain one´s child extends beyond food, clothing and lodging to education and preparation for adulthood. The father alone is liable to maintain his legitimate children, but the nature of this liability differs somewhat from that to maintain his wife. The child´s disobedience or the fact that it is in the custody of its mother does not release the father from his obligation to maintain. However, if the child has property of its own from which it may be maintained the father is not obliged to maintain the child from his own funds. Further, if the father is too poor to maintain his child and he cannot earn enough to do so the liability to maintain the child then falls on the mother if she has sufficient property although if she does expend money to this end the father comes under an obligation to reimburse her when he is able to do so. Failing the mother, the child´s grandparents and thereafter others entitled to inherit from the child become liable(12).

With regard to a daughter this right endures until she marries. Although there is some doubt in this matter it appears that on her divorce or on the death of her husband the father becomes liable to maintain her once more if she lacks the property necessary to maintain herself. With regard to sons, the father need only maintain them until they attain puberty, unless the son is both indigent and in some way physically or mentally disabled; though there is some doubt as to whether the Indian Majority Act 1875 may have superseded this rule of Muslim law so as to entitle the son to maintenance beyond puberty to the age of majority(13). There is likewise some doubt whether the child is in all cases entitled to past maintenance or only when he has obtained a

310

court order or some express agreement about the level of maintenance his father is to pay(14).

Whatever the applicability of the 1875 Act to the Muslim law of maintenance, it certainly applies to the provisions of the Criminal Procedure Code 1898, s.488 (1973 s.125 in India), whereby a father or mother must maintain a son who is a minor (whether or not married); an unmarried minor daughter; and a married one if her husband cannot maintain her; or an unmarried son or daughter, or married son, if although not minor these are physically or mentally disabled, always assuming that they are unable to maintain themselves.

It has been held that where someone not obliged to maintain a child does so the father is to that extent relieved of his obligation and the stranger cannot claim any reimbursement from the father unless the maintenance has previously been fixed by the court(15).

The Muslim scheme of maintenance imposes on adult children similar obligations in respect of those persons who in normal circumstances were liable to maintain the children until puberty, and who are now poor, the children being in a position to do so. Where a child can only afford to maintain one of its parents, the Hanafi law favours the mother. Such liability for (usually elderly) relatives who cannot maintain themselves extends only to those within the prohibited degrees for the purposes of marriage, and in order of proximity. The Criminal Procedure Code too obliges children to maintain poor parents but unlike the Muslim law does not extend this liability to more remote relatives(16).

Although the obligations of maintenance are supposed to reflect legally the interest the maintainer has in inheriting from the maintained and socially the concept of the extended family, there is in no case any rule such as that in the law of inheritance that both parties must be Muslim for the obligation to arise.

Custody of Children (Hizanat, Hidana)

In the classical Hanafi law the custody of the child is first vested in the mother as the person best fitted to ministering to the child's needs and to release the father for work. The Hanafi law as practised in the Indian subcontinent awards the mother custody until a son reaches seven years or a daughter puberty, whereupon custody is transferred to the father(17). In the classical law the mother's custody can be lost to the father on the occurrence of certain events, in particular where she marries another man not related to the child within the prohibited degrees: merely to have divorced the child's father will not deprive the mother of custody(18). (However, the Indian and more openly the Pakistan Courts have held this not to be an invariable rule, holding it to have no Qur'anic basis)(19). Abandonment of Islam, neglect of the

311

child and taking to an immoral life also have this effect(20). In the absence of the mother at a time when she would prima facie have had custody the other female relations of the child take on custody, preference being given to maternal relations, subject to similar disqualifications. The rationale for depriving the mother of custody in the event of her remarriage is that she is likely to have children by her new husband and in the nature of things the children of the former marriage will be less favourably treated in the new household. The same reasoning does not seem to have been applied where custody is vested in the father and he remarries(21).

The position in the Indian subcontinent today has been complicated by two factors: the enactment of the Guardians and Wards Act 1890 and the emphasis of courts in Pakistan in applying to the Act presumptions as to what is in the interests of the child.

Guardians and Wards Act 1890

s.17 (1) In appointing or declaring the guardian of a minor the Court shall, subject to the provisions of this section, be guided by what, consistently with the law to which the minor is subject, appears in the circumstances to be for the welfare of the minor.

(2) In considering what will be for the welfare of the minor, the Court shall have regard to the age, sex and religion of the minor, the character and capacity of the proposed guardian and his nearness of kin to the minor, the wishes, if any, of a deceased parent, and any existing or previous relations of the proposed guardian with the minor or his property.

(3) If the minor is old enough to form an intelligent preference, the Court may consider that preference.

(4) As between parents who are European British subjects adversely claiming the guardianship of the person, neither parent is entitled to it as of right, but other things being equal, if the minor is a male of tender years or a female, the minor should be given to the mother, and if the minor is a male of an age to require education and preparation for labour and business, then to the father.

(5) The Court shall not appoint or declare any person to be a guardian against his will.

s.25 If a ward leaves or is removed from the custody of a guardian of his person, the Court, if it is of opinion that it will be for the welfare of the ward to return to the custody of his guardian, may make an order for his restoration, and, for the purpose of enforcing the order

may cause the ward to be arrested and to be delivered
into the custody of the guardian.

Of course this Act extends beyond custody to guardianship
over person and property. The person who would under Muslim
law be entitled to custody or guardianship may act
automatically and has no need to apply for appointment under
the Act but may do so(22).

It will be seen that the appointment under the Act must
take into account the welfare of the child consistently with
the law to which the child is subject, but subject to the
provisions of the Act (i.e. s.17 (2), (3)) which prevail.
There seems to be a difference of emphasis in the Indian and
Pakistani courts as to the interpretation of the statute to
the extent that the Pakistani courts seem more willing to
depart from the classical rule that remarriage of the mother
invariably causes her to lose custody of the child to its
father or other relation, on the basis that there is no
Qur´anic support for such a doctrine and that the Courts in
their capacity as successors to the qadis, retain a discretion
in the matter(23). In India the statutory criteria specified
in S.17 (2) and (3) seem to have greater weight, but in
Pakistan there is a very strong presumption that the welfare
of the child is to be identified with the rules of the child´s
personal law(24).

There may be an important difference in the
considerations to be taken into account by the court when
hearing an application for restoration of custody under s.25
as opposed to appointment of a guardian under s.17 in as much
as s.25 does not require a court to make an order consistently
with the law to which the minor is subject(25). This could
have the unfortunate effect of encouraging in some
circumstances abduction of the child to gain the benefit of
s.25.

Guardianship of the Child´s Property and Person

Irrespective of who has custody of the child the father,
being liable to maintain it, has general supervision over its
upbringing. More specifically the classical law recognises
the father as the legal guardian of the child´s property and
person until majority(26), and failing him the father´s
executor (wasi), the grandfather and his executor in that
order of priority. Failing any of these the court must
appoint one. The Muslim law severely restricts the guardian´s
powers over the property of the child. Immoveable property
may be sold only when it is possible to obtain double its
value or when the child has no other property and the sale is
necessary for its maintenance, where the cost of maintaining
the property exceeds its income, where it is falling into

313

decay, and in certain cases of great exigency, such as where the child's title to the property is disputed(27). Moveable property may be sold for necessities of life (28). Under no circumstances can a guardian purchase property from the child: such a sale is wholly void(29). Once again the Guardians and Wards Act 1890 makes provision for the appointment of a person as guardian of the child's property and the criteria for appointment directed by that Act apply here too(30).

A person who without the sanction of Muslim law or the court (under the 1890 Act) takes upon himself control and management of the child's property, sometimes called a de facto guardian, merely has custody of that property in fact and acquires thereby the liabilities of a properly appointed guardian but no rights except to sell moveables for necessities, any other transaction being void(31).

Where a guardian has been appointed by the court no alienation of immoveable property is possible without the sanction of the court and any attempted transaction without such approval is voidable at the instance of the child or anyone else affected by it(32). With respect to moveable property a person appointed under the 1890 Act must deal with it with the same care as if he were an ordinary man of prudence dealing with his own property(33).

Guardianship of the person comprises the right and duty to act as marriage guardian and in this context the Act of 1890 has no application: it is purely a matter of Muslim personal law(34). The right to contract a child's marriage ends when it attains puberty in Hanafi law but until then the child's consent is irrelevant, though the severity of this rule is to some extent mitigated by the option of puberty considered earlier(35). Priority for marriage guardianship falls first to the father, then to the paternal grandfather and then to the brothers and other agnatic relatives and finally to the mother and maternal relatives, failing any of which the qadi may act as such. If a more remote relative in the case where a proximate one exists purports to contract the child in marriage, the marriage is invalid unless the true marriage guardian consents(36). Of course the exercise of the right may now entail penal sanctions, as has already been seen(37).

ABDUL GHANI (Appellant) v. Mst. TALEH BIBI (Respondent).
PLD 1962 (W.P.) Lahore 531. (Masud Ahmed J.)

Judgement:.....11. The only point that remains to be decided is, whether it had been established that Mst. Naziran Bibi is the legitimate daughter of Allah Bakhsh. The decision of this question would depend mainly, if not wholly, on the determination of the question as to whether the provisions of section 112 of the Evidence Act are applicable to this case, or whether, for deciding the question of legitimacy of Mst.

314

Naziran Bibi, the provisions of Muhammadan Law, on this subject, only would be applicable.

12. Section 112 of the Evidence Act, on which reliance was placed by the trial Court for giving a finding in favour of Mst. Naziran Bibi, as being the legitimate daughter of Allah Bakhsh, reads as follows:-

"The fact that any person was born during the continuance of a valid marriage between his mother and any man, or within two hundred and eighty days after its dissolution, the mother remaining unmarried, shall be conclusive proof that he is the legitimate son of that man, unless it can be shown that the parties to the marriage had no access to each other at any time when he could have been begotten."

13. The rule of Muhammadan Law, relied upon by the appellants, to show that Mst. Naziran Bibi is not the legitimate daughter of Allah Bakhsh, is stated in Ameer Ali´s Muhammadan Law, at pages 190 to 193 of the Fifth Edition, in the following words:-

"According to the Sunni Schools, the presumption of legitimacy is so strong, that in cases where a child is born six months from the date of marriage and within two years after dissolution of the marital contract, either by the death of the husband or by divorce, a simple denial of paternity on the part of the husband would not take away the status of legitimacy from the child.
"According to the Sunni Schools, therefore, where a child is born to a woman within the period indicated, viz. six months or more from the date of marriage, and within ten months after dissolution of marital contract either by the death of the husband or divorce such child is affiliated, without an express acknowledgment on the part of the father. Nor will a simple denial of paternity by the husband take away the status of legitimacy from the child.
"If a man committed fornication with a woman and she became pregnant and he then married her, after which she gave birth to a child, if the child was born at six months or more from the date of marriage, its nasab would be established in the father, i.e., it would be regarded as the legitimate offspring of the woman´s husband; but if it was born within less than six months no ascription would take place unless the man acknowledged it to be his issue, but did not say it was his by fornication.
"In other words, it is the right of the man to legitimate a child born within the time by acknowledging expressly or impliedly that the conception took place in wedlock."

14. According to Ameer Ali (page 201) section 112 of the Evidence Act embodies the English rule of law, and cannot be

315

held to vary or supersede, by implication, the rules of Muhammadan Law. This rule of Muhammadan Law was accepted by their Lordships of the Privy Council in <u>Ashrufooddowla's case</u> ((1866) 11 Moo. I A 94-113) and it was held that the presumption of legitimacy from marriage follows the bed and is not ante-dated by relation. Wilson in his Anglo-Muhammadan Law (Fifth Edition, page 161) comparing section 112 of the Evidence Act with the rule of Muhammadan Law, on the question of legitimacy, says as follows:-

> "The rule of the Indian Evidence Act, section 112, that legitimacy is conclusively presumed from birth during the continuance of a valid marriage or within 280 days after its termination, unless it be shown that the married parties had no access to each other at any time when the alleged child could have been begotten, is really, notwithstanding its place in the statute book, a rule of substantive marriage law rather than of evidence, and, as such, has no application to Muhammadans, so far as it conflicts with the Muhammadan rule that a child born within six months after the marriage of its parents is not legitimate."

15. The learned counsel for the appellants also relied on the observations of Mr. Justice Mahmood in <u>Muhammad Allahdad Khan and another v. Muhammad Ismail Khan and others</u> (I L R 10 All. 289),in which after discussing the relevant facts of the case, the learned Judge observed as follows, at page 339:-

> "Such being my view of the facts of the case, it is not necessary to enter into any elaborate discussion as to how far the provisions of section 112 of the Indian Evidence Act (I of 1872), as to birth during wedlock being conclusive proof of legitimacy, would affect a case such as this. That section of course proceeds upon adopting the period of birth, as distinguished from conception, as the turning point of legitimacy. It is a peculiarity of the English law that it does not connect itself with the conception, but cnsiders a child legitimate who is born of parents married before the time of his birth, though they were unmarried when he was begotten.
>
> "That peculiarity of the English law has no doubt been imported into India by section 112 of the Indian Evidence Act, and it may some day be a question of great difficulty to determine how far the provisions of that section are to be taken as trenching upon the Muhammadan law of marriage, parentage, legitimacy, and inheritance, which departments of law, under other statutory provisions, are to be adopted as the rule of decision by the Courts in British India. Fortunately the difficulty does not arise in this case owing to the date of the marriage of Ghulam Ghaus with Moti Begum with reference

to the birth of Allahdad being uncertain, and I need not
therefore refer to the difficulty any further than by saying
that there is enough authority in the texts of the Muhammadan
law to show that, under that system of jurisprudence,
questions of legitimacy are referred to the date of the
conception of the child and not to the period of his birth."

16. In <u>Mazhar Ali and others v. Budh Singh and another</u>
(I L R 7 All. 297), the same learned Judge, dealing with
another rule of Muhammadan Law, regarding missing persons held
that that rule was of evidence and applied to Muhammadans
also. The following observations made at page 310 of the
reported judgment, in which a distinction has been drawn
between Muhammadan rules of substantive law and rules of
evidence are very significant.

"Now, reading these texts carefully, there can, I think,
be no doubt, firstly, that the rule of the Muhammadan
Law as to missing persons has arisen from a maxim
relating to the subject of evidence, and the rule of
<u>istis-hab</u>, which is the outcome of that maxim, cannot be
regarded as a rule of succession, inheritance, or
marriage, secondly, that among the great doctors of the
Muhammadan law itself there is a great difference of
opinion as to the exact manner in which the rule of
<u>istis-hab</u> is to be applied to missing persons; thirdly,
that as to the period necessary to elapse before the
presumption of death can be applied to missing persons,
Muhammadan jurists themselves are far from being
unanimous; fourthly, whilst some of the greatest doctors
of the law would leave the fixation of period to the
discretion of the Judge in each individual case, others
consider the preferable course to be that the matter
should be determined by the Imam, that is, by the ruling
authority, as distinguished from the Kazi or the Judge
presiding in a judicial tribunal. These conclusions are
amply borne out by the texts which I have quoted, and
they convince me that the rule of Muhammadan law as to
missing persons is a rule belonging purely to the domain
of legal presumptions falling under the head of the law
of evidence; and, I may say, with due deference, that in
my opinion the reported cases which have been cited and
which tend to support a contrary opinion are not based
upon a sound view of the Muhammadan Law. It is true
that, in some of the most celebrated treatises of that
law, the rule has been discussed as if it were a part of
the law of inheritance and succession; but, on the other
hand, the Hedaya itself and some other equally
authoritative treatises have dealt with the subject in a
perfectly separate chapter, obviously because the
authors regarded it as too general to be classed under
any particular head, applying, as it does, to all the
branches of law in which the death of a missing person

317

may happen to be the subject of investigation. I think
that in administering a medieval system of law it is
supremely important that the Courts of justice in
British India should draw a clear distinction between
the rules of substantive law and those which belong
purely to the province of procedure, because, whilst
under section 24 of the Civil Courts Act the Courts are
bound to administer the former branch of the law
according to native laws in cases of succession,
inheritance, and marriage,..... The rule as to missing
persons appears to my mind to be purely a rule of
evidential presumption, and though before the passing of
the Evidence Act there might have been perhaps some
justification for the Courts to apply the rule to cases
of Muhammadan succession, inheritance, and marriage, the
provisions of cl.(1), section 2 of the Evidence Act
leave no doubt in my mind that we are now bound, in
connection with all questions of evidence, to administer
the rules contained in that Act, and it follows that the
present case is governed by section 108 of the statute."
It may, at this stage, be pointed out that when both these
decisions were given, section 2 of the Evidence Act was on the
statute-book. This section reads as follows:-
"On and from that day (1st September 1872) the following
laws shall be repealed:-
(1)   all rules of evidence not contained in any
      Statute, Act or Regulation in force in any part of
      British India;
(2)   all such rules, laws and regulations as have
      acquired the force of law under the 25th section
      of the Indian Councils Act, 1861, in so far as
      they relate to any matter herein provided for; and
(3)   the enactments mentioned in the schedule hereto,
      to the extent specified in the third column of the
      said schedule;
But nothing herein contained shall be deemed to affect
any provision of any Statute, Act or Regulation in force
in any part of British India and not hereby expressly
repealed."
This section was repealed by the Repealing Act, 1938, the
preamble of which is in the following words:-
"Whereas it is expedient that the enactments specified
in the schedule which are spent or have otherwise become
unnecessary or have ceased to be in force otherwise than
by expressed specific repeal, should be expressly and
specifically repealed; It is hereby enacted as follows."
It may also be added that the enactments specified in the
Schedule to the Repealing Act, 1938, appear to have been
repealed because of the insertion of section 6-A in the
General Clauses Act by the General Clauses (Amendment) Act,
1936, as according to the newly added section of this Act, in
318

spite of the repeal of a Repealing Act, the amendments made by
it continue to remain in operation. It is how section 6-A of
the Act reads:-

"Where any Central Act or Regulation made after the
commencement of this Act repeals any enactment by which
the text of any Central Act or Regulation was amended by
the express omission, insertion or substitution of any
matter, then, unless a different intention appears, the
repeal shall not affect the continuance of any such
amendment made by the enactment so repealed and in
operation at the time of such repeal."

According to the late Chief Justice of Pakistan Mr. Justice
Muhammad Monir, (Monir´s Principles and Digest of the Law of
Evidence, Fourth Edition, pages 8 and 9), section 2 of the
Evidence Act was repealed because its provisions were spent
and had become unnecessary. The question as to whether by
repeal of section 2 of the Evidence Act, the rules of
evidence, not contained in any Statute, Act or Regulation, as
for instance, rules of Muhammadan Law, had been revived or
not, would be discussed at its proper place.

17. The rule of Muhammadan Law regarding legitimacy,
which was accepted by their Lordships of the Privy Council in
Ashrufooddowla´s case and by the Full Bench of the Allahabad
High Court in Muhammad Allahdad Khan´s case, is stated by
Baillie in his "Digest of Muhammadan Law" (pages 392 and 393)
in the following words:-

"The shortest period of gestation in the human species
is six months. And if a man should marry a woman, and
she is delivered of a child within six months from the
day of marriage, the paternity of the child from him is
not established, because conception must have taken
place before the marriage; but if she is delivered at
six months or more its paternity is established, because
of the subsisting firash, or bed, and the completion of
the term of pregnancy, whether he acknowledges the child
or remains silent; and if he should deny its birth, that
may be established by the testimony of one woman bearing
witness to the fact."

Another learned author, Mulla, in his "Principles of Mahomedan
Law" (Fifteenth Edition, pages 283 and 284), relying on
Baillie, observes as follows:-

"A child born within less than six months after marriage
is illegitimate. A child born after six months from the
date of marriage is presumed to be legitimate, unless
the putative father disclaims the child. A child born
within two years after the termination of the marriage
is presumed to be legitimate, unless disclaimed. This
is the rule of Hanafi law."

18. In a subsequent case the Allahabad High Court took a
different view of the matter and did not follow the line of
reasoning adopted by Mr. Justice Mahmood in Muhammad Allahdad

319

Khan´s case. That Court held in <u>Sibt Muhammad v. Muhammad Hameed and others</u> (I L R 48 Ali. 625) that on the question whether a Muhammadan child born within six months of the marriage of its parents was to be considered legitimate, section 112 of the Evidence Act applied and the child was legitimate. Referring to the views of Mr. Justice Mahmood, as expressed in <u>Muhammad Allahdad Khan´s case</u>, their Lordships observed as follows:

> "Mr. Justice Mahmood did not express his own opinion regarding the solution of this difficulty, since it was unnecessary for him to do so for the decision of that case. Although that judgment was pronounced so long ago as 1888, the question how far section 112 of the Evidence Act is to be taken as overriding the rules of Muhammadan law does not seem to have been determined in any reported decision."

Their Lordships did not accept the view of Sir Roland Wilson in his treatise on Anglo-Muhammadan Law and citing, with approval, the views of two other learned authors, Messrs. Mulla and Tyabji, stated as follows:-

> "Section 112 of the Evidence Act applies by its terms to all classes of persons in British India and no exception is made in favour of Muhammadans. If it had been intended that the provisions of section 112 should not apply to Muhammadans, we should certainly expect to find a clear proviso to this effect. This course has been followed in other enactments, when general provisions of law were not intended to affect the rules of Muhammadan Law..... So if the legislature had intended that the provisions of section 112 of the Evidence Act should not apply to Muhammadans, or should not affect the rules of Muhammadan Law, this intention should have been clearly expressed. Section 112 is perfectly clear in its terms and we are not entitled to refuse to give effect to its provisions merely on the ground that such provisions are out of place in the Evidence Act and should have been included in the department of family law, or on the ground that the effect of these provisions, in that application to Muhammadan law, was unforeseen, or would be undesirable. In our view we are bound to give effect to the clear provisions of section 112, although they conflict with the rules of Muhammadan Law."

19. The Punjab Chief Court also held the view that the provisions of section 112 of the Evidence Act apply to Mussalmans, to the exclusion of the rules of Muhammadan Law on the subject. In <u>Rahmat Ali v. Mst. Allahdi</u> (1 P R 1884), it was held by that Court that the rule of Muhammadan Law regarding legitimacy of a child was a rule of evidence within the meaning of section 2 of the Evidence Act, although it was also a part of the substantive Muhammadan Law and that when reading section 2 of the Evidence Act with section 5 of the

Punjab Laws Act, the Courts are not bound to follow the said rule of Muhammadan Law. It was held further that section 112 of the Evidence Act did not lay down a maximum period of gestation and, therefore, did not bar the proof of the legitimacy of a child born more than 280 days after the dissolution of marriage, the effect of that section being merely that no presumption in favour of legitimacy is raised and the question must be decided simply upon the evidence for and against legitimacy. In a subsequent case Waras Muhammad v. Ali Bakhsh (76 P R 1891) the same Court held that the rule of Muhammadan Law which fixes two years as the period of gestation was a rule of evidence within the meaning of section 2 of the Evidence Act and that the effect of that section, when read with section 5 of the Punjab Laws Act, 1872, was that, under the latter Act, the Courts were not bound by the rule of Muhammadan Law.

20. The Lahore High Court took a slightly different view of the matter and held in Ghulam Mohy-ud-Din Khan v. Khizar Hussain (I L R 10 Lah. 470) that the plaintiff, who was born within 280 days after the death of one Hussain Bakhsh, who had married his mother some fourteen years before his death, was to be presumed to be the legitimate son of Hussain Bakhsh, in accordance with section 112 of the Evidence Act and that this presumption could only be rebutted by showing that Hussain Bakhsh was not his mother's husband at the time when he could have been begotten.

21. In Muhammad Allahdad Khan's case, Mr. Justice Mahmood observed: "It may some day be a question of great difficulty to determine how far the provisions of that section are to be taken as trenching upon the Muhammadan Law of marriage, parentage, legitimacy and inheritance, which departments of law under other statutory provisions are to be adopted as the rule of decision by the Courts in British India." When making these observations the learned Judge had in his mind the provisions of section 24 of the Civil Courts Act, under which in cases of successions, inheritance, marriage, etc., the substantive rules of Muhammadan Law, as distinguished from pure procedural laws, appear to have been made applicable. The position in this part of the country was also similar, because under section 5 of the Punjab Laws Act, before it was first amended by the Muslim Personal Law (Shariat) Application Act, 1937, and, again, by the West Punjab Muslim Personal Law (Shariat) Application Act, 1948, and by the Punjab Muslim Personal Law (Shariat) Application Act, 1951, in matters such as legitimacy, marriage, etc., personal law of the parties was made applicable. There was, thus, an apparent conflict between section 2 of the Evidence Act, which had repealed rules of evidence of Muhammadan Law, and section 5 of the Punjab Laws Act which made applicable all substantive rules of Muhammadan Law relating to certain matters, including marriage, legitimacy, etc.

22. The rule of Muhammadan Law regarding legitimacy is, in my opinion, not a mere rule of evidence, because under it if a child is born six months after the marriage of its parents, or within two years of the dissolution of the marriage, by death or divorce, it is considered to be the legitimate child of its father, unlike the rule of evidence in section 112 of the Evidence Act, under which only a presumption of legitimacy can be raised under certain circumstances. Under this rule of Muhammadan Law there is no question of such a presumption being raised and a child born after six months of the date of marriage of its parents, is considered to be a legitimate child. That rule adopts the period of conception as the turning point of legitimacy, unlike the English Law which does not concern itself with conception but considers a child legitimate who is born of parents married before the time of its birth. This peculiarity of the English Law, as has been remarked by Mr. Justice Mahmood, in Muhammad Allahdad Khan's case, has been imported into this country by section 112 of the Evidence Act, as a rule of evidence only.

23. From what has been stated above, it is apparent that there are two divergent views on this subject. One of the views, which was expressed clearly by Mr. Justice Mahmood in Muhammad Allahdad's case, and which has been supported by such learned authors as Amir Ali and Wilson, is that the rule of Muhammadan Law regarding legitimacy being a part of substantive law, the same could not be varied, or superseded, by the rule of evidence laid down in section 112 of the Evidence Act. The other view, which was expressed by the Allahabad High Court in Sibt Muhammad's case, is that although the provisions of section 112 of the Evidence Act come into conflict with the rule of Muhammadan Law, on this subject, they apply to Mussalmans also. The same view, as stated above, was expressed in two cases by the Punjab Chief Court, while its successor, the Lahore High Court, expressed a slightly different view and held in Ghulam Mohy-ud-Din Khan's case that the presumption of legitimacy could be rebutted by showing that the child's father, Hussain Bakhsh, was not husband of its mother at the time when it could have been begotten, meaning thereby that if the child was begotten before its mother's marriage with Hussain Bakhsh, it could not be considered to be the latter's legitimate child. The reasoning of that eminent Judge, Mr. Justice Mahmood, is unassailable, and although he did not give a final decision in the matter, this being unnecessary for the purpose of that particular case, his view clearly was that by section 2 of the Evidence Act, the rule of Muhammadan Law regarding legitimacy had not been repealed. Their Lordships of the Privy Council, in Ashrufooddowla's case, also held that the rule of Muhammadan Law, on this subject, applied to Mussalmans and that the presumption of legitimacy from marriage followed the

322

bed and that whilst the marriage lasted, the child of the woman was taken to be the husband´s child, but that this presumption was not ante-dated by relation. As at the time of decision of this case section 2 of the Evidence Act was not on the statute-book, in deciding the case, their Lordships were guided only by the rules of Muhammadan Law on the subject. This authority, therefore, is not of much help in deciding the point in issue. Amir Ali and Wilson, however, both expressed the same view, on this subject, as was expressed by Mr. Justice Mahmood, and were of the opinion that the rule of evidence laid down in section 112 of the Evidence Act had no application to Mussalmans.

24. Whether the view expressed by that eminent Judge, Mr. Justice Mahmood, and the two learned authors, Amir Ali and Wilson, is considered to be correct, or whether the view expressed by the Allahabad High Court in Sibt Muhammad´s case is held to be laying down the correct law on this subject, by the repeal of section 2 of the Evidence Act, the position, in my opinion, has materially altered and the arguments advanced by the Allahabad High Court, in Sibt Muhammad´s case, can no longer be advanced in support of that view.

25. Section 2 of the Evidence Act, as stated in an earlier part of this judgment, repealed (1) all rules of evidence not contained in any statute etc, (2) all rules and laws in force under the Indian Councils Act, and (3) all enactments mentioned in the Schedule to the Evidence Act. The rule of Muhammadan Law regarding legitimacy, being part of rules not contained in any statute, it fell within the purview of the first clause of this section, and therefore, was repealed by it. This section was repealed by the Repealing Act, 1938. The question that requires decision now is whether by repeal of section 2 of the Evidence Act the rule of Muhammadan Law, on this subject, has been revived, or whether it continues to stand repealed.

26. Section 6-A of the General Clauses Act, to which reference was made during arguments, was on the statute book when the Repealing Act, 1938, was passed and therefore, the repeal of section 2 did not affect the continuance of any amendments made by that section, so far as it repealed statute law. The repeal of rules of Muhammadan Law by section 2 of the Act, however, stands on a different footing, because those rules of Muhammadan Law were not part of a Central Act or Regulation and hence their repeal by section 2 of the Evidence Act was not saved by section 6-A of the General Clauses Act. What this section lays down is that where any "Central Act or Regulation" made after the commencement of the General Clauses Act, repeals any "enactment", by which the text of any "Central Act or Regulation" was amended, then unless a different intention appears, the repeal shall not affect the continuance of any amendments made by the enactments so repealed. The expression "Central Act or Regulation"

323

occurring in the first part of this section would be the Repealing Act, 1938, the expression "enactment" would be section 2 of the Evidence Act and the expression "Central Act or Regulation" occurring in this section, for the second time, would be the rules, laws, regulations and enactments mentioned in clauses (2)and (3) of section 2 of the Evidence Act, which had been repealed by that section. As a result of repeal of section 2, by virtue of section 6-A of the General Clauses Act, the rules, laws, regulations and enactments mentioned in clauses (2) and (3) of section 2, would not be revived, but the rules of evidence mentioned in clause (1) of section 2 of the Evidence Act, being not part of a Central Act or regulation, the same would not stand repealed after the Repealing Act, namely, section 2 of the Evidence Act, had itself been repealed. On this view of the matter, I am of opinion that, after the repeal of section 2 of the Evidence Act, the rules of Muhammadan Law, which had been repealed by clause (1), have been revived and are now part of the law of Evidence.

27. In coming to this conclusion I am not unmindful of the views expressed by our late Chief Justice in his Principles and Digest of the Law of Evidence (Fourth Edition pages 8 and 9) to the effect that section 2 was repealed, because its provisions had been spent and had become unnecessary. That view was based on the authority of an Allahabad case King v. King (A I R 1945 All. 190) but a reference to that authority would show that the observations made therein were of a general nature and were not in accordance with the provisions of section 6-A of General Clauses Act. The case in question was under the Divorce Act and the learned Single Judge (Allsop, J.), who decided it, relying on an earlier decision of his own Ernest Lionel Doutre v. Anne Ruth Doutre (A I R 1939 All. 522) and an English case Russell v. Russell (1924 A C 687) which was also a divorce case, expressed the opinion that the English rule that the evidence of non-access by husband or wife was inadmissible did not apply to India, because it was a rule of evidence and all proceedings in this country were governed by the rules in the Evidence Act. The alternative argument advanced by the learned Judge, for coming to this conclusion, was that if the English rule of evidence was applicable to such a case, the same had been repealed and the repeal of section 2 of the Evidence Act, by the subsequent Amending and Repealing Act, made no difference, because its repeal did not have the effect of re-enacting the rules so repealed. The relevant rule of evidence, which was sought to be made applicable to that case, was also not contained in a statute, like the rule of Muhammadan Law, which is sought to be made applicable in the present case, and, to this extent, the views expressed in this judgment are applicable to the present case, but as, unfortunately, no reasons were given for holding that the

repeal of section 2, by the subsequent Repealing Act, did not have the effect of re-enacting the repealed rules, this authority is not of much help in deciding the disputed question. Consequently, as the views expressed by our late Chief Justice are based on this very authority and are not supported by the language of section 6-A of the General Clauses Act, the same will have to be overlooked for deciding the disputed question.

28. It was also suggested, during arguments, that as the legislature could not have intended to re-enact the rules of evidence, which had been repealed by section 2 of the Evidence Act, when that section was repealed, effect will have to be given to the intention of the legislature, and, therefore, the rule of Muhammadan Law, on this subject, cannot be considered to have been revived. It is an established rule of interpretation that the intention of the legislature can be gathered only from the language used by it in any statute and that if the language is unambiguous and capable of one meaning only, effect will have to be given to it even if it leads to unreasonable results. The preamble to the Repealing Act, 1938, which has been reproduced in an earlier part of this judgment, indicates that the enactments specified in the Schedule to the Act, which includes section 2 of the Evidence Act, were repealed, because they "had been spent, had otherwise become unnecessary or had ceased to be in force."

29. It appears that the draftsman of this Repealing Act confined his attention only to the effect of amendments made in enactments, such as Acts and Regulations, and did not have in his mind amendments made in other laws, which were not contained in such enactments. Neither from the preamble, nor from the body of the Repealing Act, can it be gathered that the intention was not to revive laws which were not contained in any enactments, such as the rules of evidence of Hindu and Muhammadan Law. The savings clause of this Repealing Act, which is almost a copy of section 6-A of the General Clauses Act and which reads as follows, makes this intention quite clear:-

"Where this Act repeals any enactment by which the text of any other enactment was amended by the express omission, insertion or substitution of any matter, the repeal shall not affect the continuance of any such amendment made by the enactment so repealed and in operation at the commencement of this act."

I am, therefore, of opinion that it was not the intention of the legislature that those rules, which were not contained in any statute and which had been repealed by section 2 of the Evidence Act, were not to be revived after that section itself was repealed.

30. Having held that the rule of Muhammadan Law, regarding legitimacy, was a rule of substantive law and having also held that by the repeal of section 2 of the Evidence Act

this rule of Muhammadan Law had been revived, <u>Mst</u>. Naziran
Bibi cannot be held to be the legitimate daughter of Allah
Bakhsh, because she was born within six months of the marriage
of her mother, Aisha Bibi, with Allah Bakhsh. The finding of
the trial Court on issue No. 1 is, therefore, wrong and is,
hereby, set aside. However, as <u>Mst</u>. Naziran Bibi has been in
possession of the land for more than 12 years, but was not
entitled to it in her own right, she had become owner of it by
reason of adverse possession. On this ground alone the
appellants' suit should have been dismissed, even if the trial
Court had found the first issue in their favour.

31. The learned counsel for the appellants, at the close
of the arguments, contended that as <u>Mst</u>. Aisha Bibi was
pregnant at the time of her marriage with Allah Bakhsh, her
marriage was void and for this reason also <u>Mst</u>. Naziran Bibi
could not be considered to be the legitimate daughter of Allah
Bakhsh. In view of what has been stated above, the decision,
on this question, is not of much importance, but it may be
added that according to Muslim Jurists the marriage of a
pregnant woman is not void, but is invalid and the offsprings
of this marriage are considered to be legitimate. Amir Ali,
in his Muhammadan Law (Fifth Edition page 202), relying on the
opinion of Abu Yusuf and Muhammad, observes as follows:-

> "There is great difference between a marriage which is
> void <u>ab initio (batil)</u> and one which is invalid <u>(fasid)</u>.
> If a man were to contract a marriage with a woman
> related to him within the prohibited degrees, the
> marriage would be void <u>ab initio</u>..... An invalid
> marriage is one where the parties do not labour under an
> inherent inepacity or absolute bar, or where the
> disability is such as can be removed at any time. The
> issue of such unions are legitimate."

The position is stated more clearly in Hedaya (Book 11
Chapter I, page 32) in the following words:-

> "A man may lawfully marry a woman pregnant with whoredom
> but he must not co-habit with her until after her
> delivery. This is the doctrine of Haneefa and Muhammad.
> Abu Yusuf says that a marriage made under such a
> circumstance is invalid."

No contrary authority was cited by the appellants' counsel in
support of his contention. In view of the decision already
given, it is unnecessary to discuss the matter further.....

M. YAQUB ALI, J. - I agree.

———

AMAR ILAHI (Appellant) v. Mst. RASHIDA AKHTAR (Respondent)
PLD 1955 Lahore 412. (Akhlaque Husain J.)

Judgement.....This appeal arises out of an application under
section 25 of the Guardians and Wards Act filed by the
appellant, Sh. Amar Elahi, in the Court of the Guardian Judge,
Lahore, against the respondent Mst. Rashida Akhtar for the
custody of their daughter Kishwar Sultana. The admitted, or
proved, facts relating to the dispute are as follows. The
appellant married the respondent some time in 1936 and Kishwar
Sultana was born to them on the 7th of April, 1937. Soon
afterwards the parents fell out with each other and a
protracted litigation between them ensued. Ghulam Husain, the
father of the respondent, obtained an order against the
appellant under section 488, Cr. P. C., for the payment of a
monthly amount for maintenance of the minor. The appellant
sued the respondent for restitution of conjugal rights and the
latter instituted proceedings for dissolution of her marriage
with the appellant and also demanded the payment of her dower
money. The appellant divorced the respondent and eventually
the parties filed a compromise in the suit for dissolution of
marriage whereby the respondent gave up her claim to dower and
also released the appellant from his liability to pay
maintenance for the minor. On his part the appellant
renounced all rights to the custody of the minor girl and
agreed that the latter should continue to live with her
mother. ("I shall have no right over my daughter named Mst.
Kishwar Sultana and she will live with her mother").
Admittedly, since then the appellant has had nothing whatever
to do with the minor, who stated in the witness box that she
has never seen her father, not even once. Soon after
divorcing the respondent the appellant married another lady
from whom he has five children, the eldest child being a boy
who is now about fifteen years old. In September 1951, the
respondent married one Mirza Hidayat Ullah and the appellant
filed the present application under section 25 of the Guardian
and Wards Act on the 21st of December, 1951. To complete the
picture, it may be mentioned, that the respondent's mother was
a real sister of the appellant's father and that the
respondent's sister, who was examined in this case as R. W. 1,
is married to the real brother of the appellant.

It has been brought out in evidence that the appellant
has an income of only Rs. 150 per month, that the minor has
since some time been living with her maternal aunt whose
husband is a brother of the appellant and is in service as a
D.F.O. and that the minor is being educated and was, at the
time the application was filed in the lower Court, reading in
the 8th standard. After considering all the circumstances of
the case, the learned Guardian Judge was of the opinion that
"it is not in the welfare of the girl that she should be
restored to the custody of her father", and dismissed the

327

application by his order dated the 11th of March, 1954. Against that order the appellant has come up to this Court in appeal.

It was strenuously contended by the learned counsel for the appellant that on account of her remarriage with a person who is not related to the minor within the prohibited degrees the respondent has absolutely disqualified herself from being the custodian of the minor's person and, therefore, there is no alternative to the grant of the appellant's petition. Reliance was placed upon a Single Bench decision of this Court in <u>Mst. Mehraj Begum v. Yar Muhammad</u> (A I R 1932 Lah. 493), and the ruling of a Single Bench Judge of Baghdad-ul-Jadid High Court in <u>Mst. Ghulam Janat v. Bahar Shah and others</u> (P L D 1952 B J 53). In both these cases a ruling of the Oudh Chief Court in <u>Ansar Ahmad v. Samidan</u> (A I R 1928 Oudh 220) was followed without any discussion. In <u>Ansar Ahmad's case</u> Pullan J., without reference to any authority, laid down: "Where the law definitely lays down that an appointment of a certain guardian cannot be made, it is not proper for the Court to disregard the Law even in the interests of the minor." I regret I am unable to agree that these rulings have correctly stated the law on the subject. The abstract proposition stated by Pullan J. is unexceptionable, but the question is, has the Muslim law absolutely prohibited a mother who marries a person not related to the minor within the prohibited degree from being appointed as a guardian under all circumstances? It is true that such a view has been expressed in some reported cases, but there is no warrant for it in the original texts of Muslim law. In the chapter on "<u>Hizanat</u>" in Baillie's Digest of Mahomedan Law it has been stated: "The rights of all the women before mentioned are made void by marriage with strangers." Keeping in view the entire scheme of Muslim law regarding <u>Hizanat</u>, there can be no doubt that "the rights" referred to in this sentence is the preferential rights of certain female relations of the minor to its custody. The females possess this right in the following order:-

    (1)   mother;
    (2)   mother's mother, how high soever;
    (3)   father's mother, how high soever;
    (4)   full sister;
    (5)   uterine sister;
    (6)   consanguine sister;
    (7)   full sister's daughter;
    (8)   uterine sister's daughter;
    (9)   consanguine sister's daughter;
   (10)   maternal aunt, in like order as sisters; and
   (11)   paternal aunt, also in like order as sisters.

The right referred to above can only mean the right of a particular female who, failing those mentioned prior to her, has a right to the custody of the minor, in preference to

328

those whose rights have been subordinated to hers. It is a well accepted maxim of Muslims that, failing any female or male relations possessing the right to the custody of a minor or such relations as there may be having lost their "right" on account of some defect or disqualifications, the care of the person of the minor is a concern of the Judge who may make such an order as he may deem proper and may appoint even a stranger for that purpose. From this it is clear that when it is said that the right of a certain relation has been lost, it can only mean that all things being equal, he or she, as the case may be, must be relegated to a position in the order of priority below those who follow him or her. Thus there can be no room for supposing that the Muslim Law does not permit a disqualified relation to rank even with strangers.

The corresponding rule in Hamilton's Hedaya has been discussed and explained in Mst. Samiunnisa v. Mst. Saida Khatun (A I R 1944 All. 202) by Malik J. in the following passage, with which I respectfully agree:-

> "The whole law on the subject seems to have been developed on a reply by the Prophet to a woman who had separated from her husband that she had a right in the child in preference to that of her husband so long as she did not marry with a stranger. The reason given in the Hedaya is that the stranger to whom the mother may be married will not have the same affection for the child and may ill-treat her and the context in which the whole matter is discussed is the respective merit of the various relations and the central idea is as to who is more likely to look after the welfare of the minor. There seems to be nothing in that chapter to indicate that it is a sort of punishment to the mother when she, by reason of the fact that she has married a stranger, is to be punished by not being allowed to have the custody of the child even though there may not be any other person capable of looking after the minor."

It would thus appear that by marrying a stranger a mother, or a female relation, only loses her preferential right to the custody of a child which means that if there is another relation of the minor who possesses a right under the Muslim law to the custody of the person of the minor and to whom the welfare of the minor can be safely and properly entrusted, such a female relation cannot claim the custody of the child as of right. In this view I am supported by the rulings in the case of Mst. Samiunnissa v. Mst. Saida Khatun Tumina Khatun v. Goharjan Bibi (A I R 1942 Cal. 281), In re Ghulam Muhammad (A I R 1942 Sind 154) and Gunna and another v. Dargahi (A I R 1925 Oudh 623). It would be wholly wrong to suppose that the Muslim law of guardianship creates rights in respect of minors for the benefit of their guardians. On the contrary, that branch of the law was evolved for the benefit and welfare of the minor; and certain relations were given

329

preferential rights to the custody of the minor because normally those persons are more interested in the welfare of the minor and are, therefore, better suited to act as guardians.

Even if the appellant's contention were sound, it would not be decisive in this case because here the Court is not called upon to appoint a guardian at all. This is a case where a guardian is asking for the return of the minor to his custody. The distinction between the two cases is apparent from a bare perusal of section 17 subsection (1) and section 25 subsection (1) of the Guardians and Wards Act.....

.....It will be noticed that the Court is not required, while dealing with an application under section 25 for the return of the minor to the custody of its guardian, to make an order "consistently with the law to which the minor is subject", as in the case of appointment of guardian. All that the Court has to consider is whether ´it will be for the welfare of the ward to return to the custody of his guardian´.

Applying the test laid down in section 25 it cannot be said that in the circumstances of this case it would be for the welfare of the minor, Kishwar Sultana, to return to the custody of her father. The appellant, in order to avoid his liability for the maintenance of the minor, and for the dower debt of her mother, gave up all claim to the custody when the child was of tender age. Since then he has not only taken no interest whatever in her existence but has never cared even to see her; and the girl is now unable to recognise her father and unwilling to go to him. These facts demonstrate the appellant's selfish nature and his utter indifference to the minor. On the other hand the mother and her sister have done creditably by the minor. They have not only brought her up as best as their means permitted but have also given her education. The girl is now of a sufficiently mature age and discretion and her refusal to go to the appellant must, in the absence of special circumstances to the contrary, be respected. The appellant had launched upon the present litigation apparently for the purpose of being able to marry the girl to some one of his choice. He is hardly the right person to select a husband for the girl; and the latter's refusal to go to him also impliedly includes her refusal to accept a husband of his choice. Moreover, she would be eighteen years of age within a few months and there is now no question of any one inflicting upon her a husband contrary to her wishes.

For the foregoing reasons I uphold the order of the lower Court and dismiss this appeal with costs.

———

ZORAH BEGUM (Appellant) v. LATIF AHMED MUNAWWAR (Respondent)
PLD 1965 Lahore 695. (Yaqub Ali J.)

Judgement.....2. The dispute relates to the custody of two
minor children of Sheikh Latif Ahmad Munawwar and Mst. Zohra
Begum (parties to the two appeals), namely, Khalid Latif, who
attained the age of seven years and Robeena Khatoon, who is
yet below the age of puberty. Both the children are in the
custody of the mother, but in pursuance to an application made
by the father under section 25 of the Guardians and Wards Act,
Mr. Ishaq Rahim Bakhsh, Guardian Judge, Lahore, had directed
that the custody of the boy be handed over to the father and
the custody of the girl retained by the mother. It is against
this order that both the parties have preferred the
above-mentioned appeals in this Court.....
.....7. The order of the learned Guardian Judge, dated the
22nd of April 1962, was based on the view expressed by this
Court in Chand Bibi v. Bulbullah (P L D 1958 Pesh. 26) and
Khanamji v. Farman Ali (P L D 1962 Lah. 166). In the first
case Abdul Hamid, J. expressed the view that "the language of
the phrase ´consistently with the law to which the minor is
subject´ clearly means that the appointment should be
consistent and not inconsistent with the personal law of the
minor. If the interests of a minor demand that his person
should be in the care of his mother who has remarried a
stranger, but the rule of minor´s personal law forbids the
appointment of such mother, the appointment of the mother will
be inconsistent with that law." In the second case Jamil
Hussain Rizvi, J. extended the rule still further by laying
down that if a father otherwise neglects the children of the
first wife and fails to maintain them notwithstanding an order
made against him under section 488, Criminal Procedure Code,
the Courts have no authority to refuse to him the custody of
the children under section 25 of the Guardians and Wards Act.
A more exhaustive decision on the subject was delivered by
Kaikaus J. in Muhammad Bakhsh v. Mst. Ghulam Fatima (P L D
1953 Lah. 73). In construing the clause ´consistently with
the law to which the minor is subject´ the learned Judge laid
down that "all rules of Muhammadan Law relating to the
guardianship and custody of the minor are merely application
of the principle of benefit of the minor to diverse
circumstances. Welfare of the minor remains the dominant
consideration and the rules only try to give effect to what is
minor´s welfare from the Muslim point of view." These
observations are confined to the construction of section 17 of
the Guardians and Wards Act, but the same considerations were
applied to section 25, which does not contain the provision
´consistently with the law to which the minor is subject´, on
the following reasoning:-
    "It may be objected that if every rule of Muhammadan Law

331

is subordinate to the interests of the child, how do the rules affect a case under section 25 at all. The answer is simple. We will regard the rules as raising a presumption till exceptional circumstances are proved. The above question from Tyabji´s Muhammadan Law is substantially to the same effect. If I were dealing with an application under section 17, I would have to apply Muhammadan Law because of the words ´consistently with the law to which the minor is subject´ in that section. But the Act recognises the father as natural guardian and the only application he can file is under section 25. If I do not apply Muhammadan Law in this case it would create an anomaly in that if a relative other than the father applies under section 17 he can have all the rights which personal law gives him, whereas the father, because he has to apply under section 25, would not get the benefit."

With utmost respect to the learned Judge, I may venture to say that a father can, in no circumstances, be placed at a disadvantage in comparison to any other relative of the minor, who may apply under section 17 of the Guardians and Wards Act for appointment as a guardian. A father is a natural guardian of his minor children and, as observed by the learned Judge at page 81 of the report even when the minor children are in the custody of the mother, the legal control of the children vests in the father. This cannot be said of any other relative who is appointed as a guardian of the minor. In determining the question whether the custody of a minor shall be given to such a relative under sections 17 and 25 of the Guardians and Wards Act, the Court will be primarily guided by the welfare of the minor and if, on the facts of a given case, a father does not succeed as against the mother in obtaining the custody of the children, no Court would give their custody to a relative, other than the father, who applies under section 17 of the Guardians and Wards Act.

8. The more important question which falls for determination in the case is, "What is the law to which the minor is subject?" Mr. A.R. Sheikh (as he then was), learned counsel, brought to my notice various Text Books on Muslim Law in which there is a divergence of opinion as to the age of a minor son and a daughter at which the mother loses the right of their custody. In view of this conflict, one of the questions referred to the Full Bench was "In case of conflicting views expressed in text books on Muslim Law, such as Hedaya, Fatawai-i-Alamgiri, Radd-ul-Mukhtar, Muhammadan Law by Sayyed Amir Ali, etc., how are the Courts to determine which view is correct?" The answer given by the Full Bench is that where there is no Quranic or Traditional Text or an Ijma´ on a point of law, and if there be a difference of views between A´imma and Faqih, a Court may form its own opinion on a point of law. In support of this view reliance was placed

on the following questions and answers in Al-Risala by
Imam-Al-Shafai."

> "He asked: I have found the scholars in former and
> present times, in disagreement on certain (legal)
> matters. Is it permissible for them to do so?"
> "(Shafei´) replied: Disagreement is of two kinds; one
> of them is prohibited, but I would not say the same
> regarding the other."
> "He asked: What is prohibited disagreement?"
> "(Shafei´) replied: On all matters concerning which God
> provided clear textual evidence. His book or (a Sunna)
> uttered by the Prophet´s tongue, disagreement among
> those to whom these (texts) are known is unlawful. As
> to matters that are liable to different interpretation
> or derived from analogy, so that he who interprets or
> applies analogy arrives at a decision different from
> that arrived at by another, I do not hold that
> (disagreement) of this kind constitutes such strictness
> as that arising from textual (evidence)."

On this view, it would be permissible for Courts to differ
from the Rule of Hizanat stated in the Text Books on Muslim
Law for there is no Quranic or Traditional Text on the point.
Courts which have taken the place of Qazis can, therefore,
come to their own conclusions by process of Ijtihad which,
according to Imam-Al-Shafei´ is included in the doctrine of
Qiyas. It has been mentioned earlier that the rule propounded
in different Text Books on the subject of Hizanat is not
uniform. It would, therefore, be permissible to depart from
the rule stated therein if, on the facts of a given case its
application is against the welfare of the minor. I am
fortified in this view by the instances in which a Qazi
finding hardship in the application of a rule of law to which
the parties belonged sent the case to the Qazi of another
School of Law which took a liberal view of the matter.

9. Turning to the merits of the present case, it is not
difficult to pronounce where the welfare of the minors lies.
It has been found that the mother does not suffer from any
mental ailment and by now has for the last 9 years brought up
the two children without any apparent shortcoming. Both of
them attend school and no complaint was made by Sheikh Latif
Ahmad Munawwar about their physical well-being. It has,
therefore, to be seen whether it would be in the welfare of
the minors to give them in the custody of the father. It is
an admitted fact that uptil now Sheikh Latif Ahmad Munawwar
has not contributed a single penny towards their maintenance.
In fact, he has not even seen them once since 1953. In the
circumstances, if the custody of Khalid Latif and Robeena
Khatoon is given to Sheikh Latif Ahmad Munawwar, they shall
find themselves, more or less, choked in the custody of a
stranger, who has had such a long drawn and bitter litigation
with their mother. In the circumstances, it is likely that if

they are removed from the affection of their mother, their
emotional and mental growth may be retarded. The plea raised
in the written statement that the petition under section 25 of
the Guardians and Wards Act by Sheikh Latif Ahmad Munawwar was
a counterblast to the civil suit and the complaint under
section 488, Criminal Procedure Code, instituted by Mst. Zohra
Begum against him rather than motivated by a sudden outburst
of affection for the welfare of the minors.

    10. In the result, it is found that it is in the welfare
of Khalid Latif and Robeena Khatoon, minors, to remain in the
custody of their mother, Mst. Zohra Begum.....

ATIA WARIS (Appellant) v. SULTAN AHMAD KHAN (Respondent)
P.L.D. 1959 Lah. 205. (Mahmud J.)

[The appellant was seeking the return to her custody under
s.25 of the Guardians and Wards Act 1890 of her daughter, the
mother being a Roman Catholic by faith]

Judgement:.....7. It is not denied that the appellant, under
the Shariat, is a natural guardian of the female minor and that
there is not an iota of evidence on the record that she was in
any was immoral in character. Her character is beyond
reproach. The important question that remains to be
considered is "is it in the welfare of the minor that she
should remain in the custody of the respondents?".....
.....Section 25 of the Act enjoins the return to custody of
the minor 'if it will be for the welfare of the minor'. This
is, therefore, the deciding consideration.

    8. A comparison of this section with section 17 also
goes to indicate that the dominant consideration in an
application under section 25 of the Act is the 'welfare' of
the minor. In section 17 in appointing a guardian the welfare
of the minor has to be considered consistently with the law to
which the minor is subject. Section 25 does not contain the
words "consistently with the law to which the minor is
subject". It thus appears that in an application under
section 25 which can be made by a legal guardian or a natural
guardian, the dominant consideration is the welfare of the
minor. This does not, however, mean that the personal law to
which the minor is subject is of no consequence. If a
guardian has been appointed under section 17 it will be
presumed that the welfare of the minor lies in his or her
restoration to the lawful guardian, until it is proved to the
contrary. Similarly if a person is a natural guardian under
the personal law, it shall be presumed that the interest of
the minor lies in his restoration, to him or her, until the
contrary is proved, for the personal law must be deemed to
enjoin what is for the welfare of the minor. Under the Muslim
Personal Law the mother is entitled to the custody of a girl
334

up to her attaining the age of puberty, and, consequently, if she applies for the restoration of her minor daughter the Court must raise an initial presumption in her favour. In Muhammad Bashir v. Mst. Ghulam Fatiman (P L D 1953 Lah. 73 p. 81) Kaikaus J., has held that "all rules of Muhammadan Law relating to guardianship and custody of the minor are merely the application of the principle of benefit of the minor to diverse circumstances. Welfare of the minor remains the dominant consideration and the rules only try to give effect to what is minor´s welfare from the Muslim point of view". The conclusion is that "we will regard the rules as raising a presumption of welfare till exceptional circumstances are proved". Mr. Jafery the learned counsel for the appellant contends that the minor must be restored to the natural guardian entitled to the custody under the personal law, even if the minor´s welfare lies elsewhere and it may even be against her welfare. His argument is that the welfare of the child can be ignored if it conflicts with the personal law and he relied for this proposition on Ansar Ahmad v. Sameedan (A I R 1928 Oudh 22), Mst. Miraj Begum v. Yar Muhammad (A I R 1932 Lah. 493) and Mst. Kundan Begum v. Aishan Begum (A I R 1939 All. 215). These are cases under section 17 of the Guardians and Wards Act. In the first case, the mother of a minor girl had married a stranger, i.e., outside the prohibited degree. In considering her right to the custody of a female minor and rejecting her claim to her custody it was held as follows:-

> "All the authorities of Muhammadan Law are agreed that the mother is disqualified from guardianship even of her minor daughter if she marries a man who is not related to the minor within the prohibited degrees. Under section 17 of the Act a Court in appointing a guardian must make an appointment ´consistently with the law to which the minor is subject´. Where the law definitely lays down that an appointment cannot be made, it is not proper for the Court to disregard the law even in the interest of the minor."

The other two cases being alike on facts followed the first case, and a direction was given that in place of the mother the other persons eligible for apointment as guardian under the Muhammadan Law be considered for appointment as guardian bearing in mind the welfare of the minor. These three cases illustrate the principle that in face of a positive prohibition in the personal law the mother should not be appointed a guardian of the person of a female minor and other persons eligible should be considered and appointed, bearing in mind the welfare and interests of the minor. These cases do not lay down the principle contended for by the learned counsel, and his contention is also opposed to the weight of authority and large majority of decisions in cases under section 25 of the Guardians and Wards Act. The learned counsel for the respondents relied, on the other hand, on

Mst. Siddiq-un-Nisa v. Nizam-ud Din (I L R 54 All. 128), a
Division Bench Case under section 17 of the Act which holds
that "as to the power to appoint and declare the guardian of a
minor the personal law of the minor is to be taken into
consideration, but that law is not necessarily binding upon
the Court which must look to the welfare of the minor
consistently with that law." Again in Nadir Mirza v. Munir
Begum (A I R 1930 Oudh 471) it was held as follows:-

"Under the Guardians and Wards Act a Court in appointing
or declaring a guardian of the minor is guided first by
the provisions of section 17 of the Act, and secondly by
what appears to be for the welfare of the minor
consistently with the law to which the minor is subject.
If the Court had only got to consider the law, the
mother, even although she is no longer a Muhammadan,
would be able to take this child away from his father's
house and act as his guardian, but the Act allows a
Court much wider discretion than this. By placing the
provisions of the section above the law to which the
minor is subject the Act makes it open to the Court to
consider other matters as well as the personal law even
if they are opposed to that law."

In Winifred MacQuillan v. Winifred Chapman (A I R 1920
Cal. 346) it has been held that in appointing a guardian the
welfare of the child must outweigh all other considerations
even though the effect may be to deprive the mother of custody
of the child. In re Gulbai and Lilbai, Minors, Dhaklibai
widow (I L R 32 Bom. 50) it has been laid down that the entire
well being and happiness of the minors ought to be the main
and paramount consideration of the Court in selecting a
guardian. Mst. Haidri Begum v. Jawed Ali Shah (A I R 1934
All. 722) decides that the main question for consideration is
what would be more conducive to the child's welfare i.e., the
child would be better looked after and the personal law of the
parties should also be taken into consideration. In T.N.
Muthuveerappa Chetti alias T.N. Batcha Chetti and another v.
T.R. Ponnuswami Chetty (13 I C 16) also it was held that the
welfare of the minor was the main consideration though regard
must be had to well recognised right of guardianship.
Saraswatibai Shripad Ved. v. Shripad Vasanji Ved (A I R 1941
Bom. 103) lays down that the paramount consideration is the
interest of the minor rather than the right of the parents.

10. That welfare of the minor is the paramount
consideration; that material, moral and spiritual well being
is the deciding and governing consideration in awarding
custody of the minors is illustrated by the following cases,
which also throw a light on what constitutes their welfare.
In case W. v. W (1926 Law Reports (Pro. Div.) P.111) Lord
Merrivale emphasised that the welfare of the minor was the
first and foremost consideration (on the construction of the
enactment) and that many elements entered into the welfare of

an infant and such matters, which were of immediate
consideration were the comfort, the health and the moral,
intellectual and spiritual welfare of the child. In <u>Mookand
Lal Singh v. Nobodip Chander Singha and another</u> (I L R 25 Cal.
881) the question of money, comfort and moral and religious
welfare are emphasised in the words below:-

> "Then we have to consider what is really for the welfare
> of this minor using the term ´welfare´ in its wider
> sense and looking not only to the question of money and
> comfort but to the moral and religious welfare of the
> child and to the ties of affection."

In <u>Bindo (opposite party) v. Sham Lal (applicant)</u> (I L R
29 All. 210) the consideration was whether the girl would be
as happy in the new home as in previous so that her
´happiness´ was her welfare. <u>In re Gulbai and Lilbai, Minors,
Dhaklibai, widow, petitioner</u>, the welfare is more exhaustively
defined and is the paramount consideration. It was held that:

> "But the mere legal right to be appointed a guardian,
> the preference of the minors and the existing or
> previous relations are very minor considerations as
> compared with the main question – what order would be
> for the welfare of the minor? In making orders
> appointing guardians for the persons of minors the <u>most
> paramount</u> consideration for the Judge ought to be – what
> order under the circumstances of the case would be best
> for securing the welfare and happiness of the minor?
> With whom will they be happy? Who is most likely to
> contribute to their well being and look after their
> health and comfort? Who is likely to bring up and
> educate the minors in the manner in which they would
> have been brought up by the parents if they had been
> alive? In fact the main question for the Court to
> consider in the case of the unfortunate minors who have
> lost their natural guardian is – who amongst the
> relations or for the matter of that, friends of the
> minors can you select who will supply as nearly as
> possible the place of their lost parent or parents? The
> interest, well being and happiness of the minors ought
> as I said before to be the main and paramount
> consideration for the Court in selecting the guardian of
> the person of a minor."

In cases of female minors the consideration of who can provide
a dowry and marry off the minor suitably is also a strong
consideration affecting her welfare as in <u>Muhammad Bashir v.
Mst. Ghulam Fatima</u>. All these cases lead me to the conclusion
that the welfare of the minor is the dominant consideration.
In considering the welfare the Court must presume initially
that the minor´s welfare lies in giving custody according to
the dictates of the rules of personal law, but if
circumstances clearly point that his or her welfare dominantly
lies elsewhere or that it would be against his or her

interest, the Court must act according to the demand of the welfare of the minor, keeping in mind any positive prohibitions of personal law.

11. Under the law, a minor must be presumed to have the father's religion and corresponding civil and social status and it is the duty of a guardian to train and bring up his ward in his father's religion. Helen Skinner v. Sophia Evelina Orde etc. ((1871) 14 M I A 309) and Canon S. S. Alluntt v. Mst. Badamo and another (32 I C 897). This is conceded by the learned counsel for the appellant, and he points out that the appellant has undertaken in her statement to bring up the minor as a Muslim. The learned counsel for the respondents relying on Nadir Mirza v. Munni Begam; Mookand Lal Singh v. Nobodip Chunder Singha and another and Ram Parasad v. District Judge of Gorakhpur and another (57 I C 651) insists that she would not do so and that the minor's faith is not safe in her hands, as she could not bring her up as a Muslim. In Nadir Mirza v. Munni Begam the following observations were made:-

> "Generally speaking a Court of justice is loath to take sides in a case between rival religions, and where a male child has been born and brought up in the faith of his father, he should not be handed over to his mother who left that faith, and has thereby stepped outside the family in which she was married, with certainty that the boy will be induced to leave the religion of his father for the new religion of the mother.
> Where a child is born to a Shia Muhammadan and has been brought up in that faith by the father till his death, and has not lived for two years with his mother after she changed her religion, the mother should not be allowed to come forward on the father's death and take away from the custody of his paternal grandfather the son, whom she had herself left with his father, from the religion and surroundings in which he has so far been brought up."

As the mother had been separated from the child for about two years so that the ties of affection were no longer strong, had left her son with his grand-parents, as she had one child already with her, as she could not even look after the son, who was with her, as she was living in a charitable home due to her poverty and had changed her religion, it was not considered in the minor's interest to hand over the child to the mother, who was entitled under the personal law to his custody.

In Mookand Lal Singh v. Nobodip Chander Singha and another the father who was originally a Hindu had become a Christian and had abandoned his family residence leaving the minor with the paternal and maternal uncles of the boy. It was held that the father though, prima facie, entitled to the custody of the infant child could be deprived of the paternal right if the circumstances justified it, and, in case of a child who had been brought up as a Hindu, had expressed a desire to remain a Hindu, by living with his Hindu relations, who were maintaining him and were looking after his education properly, it was not in the welfare of the child that he should be handed over to the father and brought up in the Christian faith. The restoration of the minor to the father was, therefore, refused. The following observation may be quoted with advantage, as applicable to the present case, for the suspicion that the child's custody was desired to bring him up in a different religion weighed for disentitling the father from the custody of his son:-

> "There are some matters incidental to this question, – and one can scarcely avoid, if not concluding, at any rate suspecting, that the real question in this litigation is as to whether this child is to be brought up as a Christian or as a Hindu, – which to my mind are fairly well established."

Reliance was placed on the observations of Lord Justice Lindley in the case of In re Newton (Law Reports 1896 Chancery Division, Volume I, 740):-

> "But as a legal proposition, it is clear that the Court has jurisdiction in a proper case to deprive a father of the custody of his children, and it also has jurisdiction to decline to change the religion in which the children have been brought up."

It was pointed out that the judiciary administered the law, that the Judge could not say that one religion was better than another, and that under the Guardians and Wards Act the welfare of the child must be looked to. As the child had been allowed by his father to remain with his Hindu relations, who were willing to educate and take care of him, who had in fact maintained and educated him for some years at their own costs, as the child had been permitted to be brought up according to the rights of the Hindu religion, and if the child was handed over to the father it would have resulted in the breaking of the ties of affection and destroying the associations connected with his Hindu relations, the father was regarded as having abdicated his parental rights: this demand of the child's custody was held to be "a capricious, if not a cruel, resumption of his paternal authority" to compel the child to be brought up henceforth as a Christian. In Ram Pershad v. District Judge of Gorakhpur and another which is a case under section 17 of the Guardians and Wards Act, it was held that in considering the question of the custody of a young girl and the appointment of a guardian, regard should be had to the material and spiritual welfare of the child. Having regard to section 17 of the Guardians and Wards Act preference should be given to one who will bring her up in the religion of her people. In this case Mst. Rajeshri was the daughter of Mst. Zagmag, a prostitute, and Ram Prasad, the minor's uncle, in whose custody she was, wanted the child to be taught singing and dancing with a view to adopting the profession of a dancing girl. The Guardian Judge had placed the child in the custody of Miss Booth of the Zenana Bible and Medical Mission, Gorakhpur. Miss Booth was a lady very highly respected and there was no doubt that the work she did was a labour of love and work done well; but all the same it was held by the Allahabad High Court (Sir Grimwood Mears, Chief Justice, and Sir P.C. Benerji) that she was a Christian and unconsciously it must be that the daily teaching in her institution would have a tendency to remove the early traces of the religion, Hindu or Muhammadan, from the minds of children who were in her care and to instil into them the principles of the Christian religion. It was not doubted for a moment that this was done by way of proselytising, but as the mind of the child was very impressionable, even the simple Bible stories which were only taught, told beautifully and with feeling must, it was held, sink into the mind and bear fruit. Therefore, when the child had reached an age when she could make up a decision for herself, it was very likely that the decision would be one to embrace the Christian faith, and that would particularly be the case if, as was stated, Miss Booth treated the children with loving kindness and they were happy with her. The uncle of the minor having been found unsuitable, a Hindu gentleman Avadh Behari Saran, a stranger, was allowed to have the custody of Mst. Rajeshri, so that she could be brought up as a Hindu, and was removed from surroundings in which she was likely to change her religion for Christianity.

12. On the basis of the above decisions the learned counsel for the respondents urges that it was impossible for the minor to be brought up in the faith of her father if she was entrusted to her mother's custody. In this connection it is pointed out that the appellant had been a devout Christian before her marriage, had had no interest in Islam even after conversion and had started attending the Church regularly after the death of her husband on her return to her parents. In these circumstances, it was argued that there could not be the least doubt that the minor would not be brought up according to the faith of her father, and she must inevitably grow up as a Christian especially because the petitioner's parents are so strongly devoted to Christianity as to entertain the feelings which are contained in Exh. D. 1, i.e., the father wanted to poison the appellant rather than that she should marry a Muhammadan. The father is a Protestant and the mother is a Roman Catholic and both are devout Christians, the mother more so. It is argued that no arrangement could be made in the house of her mother for bringing her up as a Muslim for the mother knew nothing at all about Islam. The Guardian Judge has mainly relied upon this consideration in refusing the custody of the minor to the mother. The fear that the minor would not be brought up in the faith of her
340

father, which undoubtedly is the duty of the guardian to do,
is real and substantial, in spite of the finding that it
cannot be held that the appellant has been reconverted to
Christianity. It is clear by her own conduct where her choice
lies and what feelings she entertains towards the Christian
religion and her parents´ feelings are also clear. The minor
has to be brought up in her grand-parents´ house and as such
must depend upon them and was bound to be influenced by their
faith and beliefs. It is thus argued with good reason that
she was bound to grow up as a Christian by being influenced by
them and there could be no possibility of the minor being
brought up as a Muslim even if the mother left her parents,
which was unlikely. I, therefore, agree, on the basis of the
above discussion, with the view of the trial Court that it is
not in the welfare of the minor to entrust her custody to the
mother, for the minor would not be brought up in the faith of
her father. There is really more to this. The aplication
seems to be motivated by an ulterior motive and that appears
to be to obtain the minor so that she grows up as a Christian.
Mr. Matheus though deadly opposed to the marriage and though
he had not cared to meet the children during the life time of
Waris Sultan Khan, suddenly supported his daughter for the
custody of this minor. He has a large family consisting of a
wife, four daughters and a son to feed, clothe and educate.
He was a guard in the N. W. Railways, and is now on leave
preparatory to retirement getting about Rs. 225 p.m., as he
told me. He is due to retire on 13th August 1959 when his
service will cease. His wife has also no income now as they
are now living at Rawalpindi. Mr. and Mrs. Matheus have not
the means, nor affection for the child to show such sudden
anxiety for the care of the child, and the only reason one can
think of is that they are anxious that the minor should grow
up in the fold of Christianity and add to the number. The
view expressed in <u>Mookand Lal Singh v. Nobodip Chander Singh
and another</u> has an important bearing on this application. It
will not be in the interest of the minor to grant such an
application.

13. This is not the only consideration which leads me to
the decision that it is not for the welfare of the minor that
she should be entrusted to her mother. Her welfare in my view
lies in her remaining with her paternal aunt and grand-parents
who admittedly are looking after her and are bringing her up
well. It is established on the evidence on the record that
the child was fed by and brought up by her aunt <u>Mst.</u> Qamar
Sultan, and she used also to sleep with her so that as
admitted by the appellant, the child is intensely devoted to
her and her paternal grand-parents. As the first child as is
not unusual, she was left to be looked after by the
grand-parents, for the appellant and her husband must have
been engrossed in their own love as young people happily
married are, and cared more for their own happiness than the

341

care of the child, whose upbringing was welcomed by her aunt and grand-parents. Ths minor is now devoted to her aunt and grand-parents after four years' association, and it is not in her interest to tear her away from them and break up the ties of affection (which would be a cruel exercise of her maternal right) and hand her over to the mother, whose ties are not so strong and who left the child of her own choice to go to her parents, which shows that her desire to leave for personal comfort was stronger than the affection she had for this child. The child has now been parted from the mother for over a year and a half, has not been seen or visited by her so that the ties of affection are very slender and it is not the motherly love and affection which could have prompted this application.

13. The next and a very important consideration is that the mother is practically penniless and has not the means to support herself or her children. Though at the time of her making the application she was employed as a teacheress at Rs. 75 per mensem in Y.W.C.A., Multan, she is out of a job now. On the evidence it is clear that even at Multan the son, who is with her, was provided for and looked after by the maternal grand-parents. A sum of Rs. 75 could hardly have been sufficient for the needs of the mother and the child for there was an Aya to pay Rs. 20 or Rs. 25 p.m. as salary. They were thus being supported by the appellant's parents. They are now entirely on their mercy, for the appellant is now without a job and has no means even to feed herself or her child, what to speak of providing for their education or their growing needs as time passes. Therefore, she is wholly unsuited, because of her utter lack of resources to have the custody of the minor. It is stated at the Bar on the basis of a letter a copy of which has been placed on the file, that the appellant is likely to get a job in the Bern Hall School in the first week of March 1959. No salary is mentioned and no definite post is offered in the letter. It is, however, mentioned orally that the salary that she is likely to get is going to be about Rs. 150 a month. Even so, her resources will be too meagre to bring up two children besides maintaining herself. The job may be of uncertain duration even if the offer be taken as firm. The minor, if handed to her custody, would be placed in straitened circumstances from a position of security and comfort and her prospects would be jeopardized. The minor is being cared for and well looked after by the respondents on the appellant's own admission and the respondents love her dearly. Another consideration to bear in mind is her happiness. Apart from being taken away from the people to whom she admittedly is devoted she would be extremely unhappy in the new and changed circumstances, where she will be in a home with so many strangers. It is admitted before me that besides the appellant, four daughters and one son are living with Mr. and Mrs. Matheus at Rawalpindi. One of the daughters

is married to Mr. Daniels. They have two children and they are also living jointly with them. In this home she could neither have an equal or same status nor consideratin or affection as she is getting now. Her position amongst them would be that of a stranger and an interloper particularly if she is to be brought up as a Muslim. She will also be among persons, who are not in the prohibited degree and for this reason on grounds of dictates of rules of personal law also this home is not suitable for her.

14. The appellant is still young and may well marry and in such an event she would be disentitled, under the personal law, to have the custody of the minor. It is not in my view for the welfare of the minor, that she should now be removed from the people, who are looking after her, to be handed over to a new family and she may have to be driven out of that house, back again. Frequent breaking of ties of affection is not in the interest of the minor.

15. The Court has also to bear in mind the welfare of the minor with regard to her prospects of marriage and dowry. It is clear that the appellant will be in no position to provide her with a dowry or to marry her suitably. The respondents are in a far better position to do so. To leave her with them, is, therefore, in her larger interests. Mr. Sultan Ahmad respondent No. 1 has had his claim verified to the tune of Rs. 296,000 in respect of property left by him in India. He has offered to make a will giving this minor and her minor brother in the custody of the appellant, the share which their deceased father, Waris Sultan Khan, would have got according to Shariat on his death as if he were alive. He undertakes to execute the will and I propose to bind him by this order and direct that he shall make a will and deposit it in Court within a month of today. This is a very material advantage which the minor gets by remaining with the respondents and she cannot hope to get any property from her mother. The circumstances of the respondents´ family are such that the minor can be brought up suitably according to her social status and position. Mst. Qamar Sultan and her sister run a private K. C. School so that they can look after the education and bringing up of the child even in case anything happens to the grand-parents of the minor.

16. The appellant´s father, who was present during the hearing of the appeal, has stated that he is getting Rs. 225 p.m. as pay preparatory to retirement as a guard and is due to retire on 13th of August 1959 when he will cease to have any income. He claimed that he had received Rs. 20,000 as gratuity and another Rs. 9,000 was due to him. This was pressed before me as income of the family. It cannot be considered as income of the appellant and in any case the gratuity must be treated as a capital saving and not as income which the Matheus will need for themselves and their own children and they are getting on in years. Theirs is not, in

343

my view, a home suitable for the minor and she should not be thrown on the charity of the Matheus.

17. In view of what is contained in Exh. D 1, it is clear that the father of the minor would not have desired the minor to be brought up in the home of her maternal grand-parents. He would undoubtedly have liked her to be brought up by her paternal grand-parents in accordance with Muslim traditions. This circumstance must also be borne in mind. With the mother having no income and considerations of the material, intellectual, moral and spiritual welfare of the minor as stated above outweigh the demands of rules of personal law, and overwhelmingly demand that the minor shall remain with the respondents. The finding on issue No. 5 must, for all these above reasons, be in favour of the resondents. It is not, therefore, for the welfare of the minor that she should be handed over to the appellant. I, therefore, dismiss the appeal but, in the peculiar circumstances of the case, the parties shall bear their own costs.

The respondent shall at all times allow the appellant to see and meet <u>Mst</u>. Samar Waris minor without any hinderance.

MST. GHULAM FATIMA (appellant) v. SH. MUHD BASHIR (respondent) P.L.D. 1958 (W.P.) Lah. 596. (Akhlaque Husain J.)

[After a long battle involving the question of whether the mother of a child was entitled to custody in preference to the father even after she had remarried to a man not within the prohibited degrees to the child, and dealing with the interpretation of the Guardians and Wards Act 1890, the father of the child in question was awarded custody. He had paid no maintenance for the child during the time when the mother had custody after her remarriage. The mother now sought to recover from the father Rs. 900 as the amount spent by her on the maintenance of the child in the three years preceding the commencement of the suit. The sole question which fell to be decided in this case was whether in the circumstances the mother could claim this amount.]

<u>Judgement</u>.....On behalf of the plaintiff-appellant great reliance was placed upon ruling of the learned Single Judge of the Madras High Court in <u>Kachi Muhaidia Tharaganar v. Sainambu Ammal and others</u> (A I R 1941 Mad. 582), wherein Abdul Rahman, J. remarked: "the rules of maintenance, so far as the children are concerned, have got really nothing to do with the father's right of custody. If the father has any right of custody of his children, he is entitled to enforce that right but the fact that he has not done so or that his children are residing elsewhere does not, in my opinion, deprive them of their right to claim or recover maintenance from their father." The learned lower Appellate Court, on the other hand, has based

344

its decision upon a ruling of the Bombay High Court in <u>Dinsab Kasimsab v. Muhammad Hussen Dinsab and another</u> (A I R 1945 Bom. 390) where a Division Bench of that Court remarked: "The maintenance, which the father, whether a Hindu or a Muhammadan, is under an absolute obligation to provide for his minor sons and unmarried daughters, does not necessarily mean a separate allowance in cash or kind, as appears to have been assumed by Abdur Rahman, J. in I L R 1941 Mad. 760"; and the following opinion of Justice Kania in 43 Bom. L R 823 was preferred:-

> In my opinion the Muhammadan Law, like other systems of law, while putting an obligation on the father to maintain his children, gives with it a right to the father to keep the children in his house, unless according to the law governing the parties some other person is the lawful guardian of the person of the child."

A reference to the original text books on Hanafi Law would show that the proposition laid down by Kania, J. is in accordance with that law. A father is not liable to maintain a child separately if the latter keeps away, or is kept away, by someone not entitled to its custody, from his house without his consent. In other words, a father is bound to maintain an indigent child himself; but not through another unless so directed by the Kazi or the Court.

A father's liability to maintain his children, excepting of course those who have not been weaned, extends only to such of them as are really in need of maintenance. It is in the case of a wife alone that her right to maintenance is recognized regardless of her own financial position. A child having means of its own is by common consent not entitled to any maintenance from his father. It follows from these premises that a child, who is being already voluntarily maintained by another and therefore does not stand in need of his food, clothing or lodging, cannot require its father to pay maintenance. Similarly a person maintaining the child of another voluntarily without reference to its father would not be entitled to claim its maintenance from the father.

It also seems clear from the authorities on Hanafi Law that neither the child nor the person who maintains it can claim past maintenance from the father unless the same has been previously fixed either by a decree of the Court or by the father himself. This proposition seems to flow from the propositions mentioned in the preceding paragraph and is supported by the exposition of the law relating to maintenance in the text books. The Hedaya Hamilton's Second Edition, page 149 states:-

> "<u>Arrear not due in a decreed maintenance</u>. - If the Kazee decrees a maintenance to children, or to parents, or to relations within the prohibited degree, and some time should elapse without their receiving any, their right

to maintenance ceases, because it is due only so far as may suffice, according to their necessity (whence it is not so to those who are opulent), and they being able to suffer a considerable portion of time to pass without demanding or receiving it, it is evident that they have a sufficiency, and are under no necessity of seeking a maintenance from others: contrary to where the Kazee decrees a maintenance to a wife, and a space of time elapses without her receiving any, for her right to maintenance does not cease on account of her independence, because it is her due, whether she be rich or poor".

"Unless where it is decreed to be provided upon the absentee´s credit. — What has been observed on this occasion applies to cases only in which the Kazee has not authorized the parties to provide themselves a maintenance upon the absentee´s credit but where he has so authorized them, their right to maintenance does not cease in consequence of a length of time passing without their receiving any, because the authority of the Kazee is universal, and hence his order to provide maintenance upon credit is equal to that of the absentee himself wherefore the proportion of maintenance for the time then elapsed is a debt upon the absentee, and does not cease from that circumstance. — The time here meant is any term beyond a month; and if the time elapsed be short of that term, maintenance does not cease."
These passages clearly lay down that even decreed maintenance is allowed to remain in arrears for some time, cannot be recovered from a non-absentee father, on the grounds that maintenance due only when the claimant, other than a wife, is in actual need of it and the fact that it was not claimed indicates that it was not needed. In the Urdu translation of Durral Mukhtar by M. Khurram Ali (Naval Kishore Press), it is laid down that should there be any dispute between the mother and the father regarding the maintenance of a child the Kazee should fix the amount of maintenance and order the father to pay to the mother until the latter is found guilty of misappropriation. It is further stated that if the father is poor and the mother well off then the latter will be ordered to maintain the child and recover the amount from the father as a debt when he is able to pay it (page 273). At page 460 of Baillie´s Muslim Law (Third Impression, 199 Premier Book House, Lahore) it is stated "when the father is able, but refuses, and the Judge has decreed the maintenance of a child against him, or when, after the decree against him, he abandons the child without having the means of subsistence, and the mother incurs debt under the direction of the Judge, she may have recourse to her husband for it". An examination of the authorities leaves no room for doubt that past maintenance — except, perhaps, for a very short period —

cannot be recovered from the father by the mother who has maintained a child unless it has become due under either the decree of the Kazee or agreement by the father. In view of the state of the Hanafi Law the plaintiff-appellant is not at all entitled to a decree because she had not previously asked a Court to pass a decree for maintenance against the defendant-respondent and the latter himself had not agreed to pay any.

Even if the plaintiff were entitled to recover undecreed maintenance I would hold that in the circumstances of this case she had not maintained the child on behalf of the father. It is an admitted fact that the plaintiff never claimed, and the defendant never paid, any maintenance ever since the plaintiff was divorced by the defendant in 1946. It was only after she had to hand over the custody of the child to the father in pursuance of the Court order that she filed the present suit to recover maintenance for such period as was not, according to her, barred by the Law of Limitation. Indeed in the previous case for the custody of the child it seems to have been contended on behalf of the mother that she was able to maintain the minor out of her own pocket. In the judgment of this Court in Muhammad Bashir v. Mst. Ghulam Fatima (P L D 1953 Lah. 73 at p.82), it was said:-

"The mother gets only about Rs. 60 as pay and this income would be hardly sufficient to meet the expenses of both if the girl is to be properly educated".

It was also urged on her behalf that the father had taken no interest in the child and had not paid any maintenance and to this the Court remarked: "but none was asked for." Be that as it may the circumstances of the case leave no room for doubt that the plaintiff-appellant had, until she lost her case for the custody of the minor in this Court no intention of claiming the maintenance of her daughter from the defendant-respondent.

For the foregoing reasons, the present appeal must fail except as regards costs. In the particular circumstances of the case the parties are ordered to bear their own costs in this Court as well as in the Courts below.

KAISER PARVEZ and another (appellants) v. ABDUL MAJID and other (respondents)
A.I.R. 1982 All. 9. (S.J. Hyder J.)

Judgement.....These are two connected Second Appeals which are directed against the judgment and decree of the Civil and Sessions Judge, Gyanpur, passed in Civil Appeal No. 10 of 1968 and Civil Appeal No. 11 of 1968.

2. It is not in controversy that Aslam Parvez and Kaiser Parvez, one of whom is appellant in Second Appeal No. 855 of 1972 and the other is in the Second Appeal No. 858 of 1972,

are real brothers. The name of their father was Mohammad Yasin. The suits had been filed by both the plaintiffs-appellants under the guardianship of their mother Smt. Roohunnisa. Abdul Razzaq was the grandfather of the plaintiffs-appellants. He gifted the properties in dispute in favour of the two appellants. Mohammad Yasin, acting as natural guardian of the minor plaintiffs, executed two sale deeds in favour of the defendants-respondents. Each of the sale deeds was executed on January 29, 1964.

3. The case of the plaintiffs-appellants was that Mohammad Yasin suffered from some abdominal ailment and he was hospitalised on January 8, 1964. A major operation was performed on Mohammad Yasin in connection with his ailment and he was discharged from the hospital on January 27, 1964. He was very weak and the defendants-respondents cajoled him by means of blandishments to execute the sale deeds of the plaintiffs' property. It was also stated that Mohammad Yasin was also unconscious at the time of the execution of the sale deeds and it was only after some time that he came to know that he had been made to execute the sale deed. It was further stated that the Sub-Registrar of Bhadohi was in collusion with the defendants-respondents and acted as their tool in registering the documents. It was pleaded that the plaintiffs-appellants were Bhumidhars of the land covered by the two sale deeds and their father and natural guardian had no right to transfer their Bhumidhari rights in the land in favour of the defendants-reapondents without obtaining the sanction of the court. Mohammad Yasin, father of the plaintiffs-appellants, was also impleaded as a defendant in the two suits.

4. In his written statement, Mohammad Yasin supported the case of the plaintiffs-appellants. On the other hand the contesting defendants-respondents filed a joint written statement in the two suits. They traversed the allegations made by the plaintiffs in the suit and raised a number of pleas in their defence.

5. The trial court framed a number of issues on the pleadings of the parties. It decided all the material issues against the plaintiffs-appellants and in consequence dismissed their suit. The first court of appeal affirmed the findings recorded by the trial court and refused to grant any relief to the plaintiffs-appellants. It is, in these circumstances, that the plaintiffs-appellants have approached this court by filing two separate second appeals.

6. Suffice it to say that the two courts below have decided against the plaintiffs-appellants on the questions of fraud and undue influence. They have also held that there was no evidence worth the name on the record to sustain the allegation that there was any collusion between the contesting defendants-respondents and the Sub-Registrar, Bhadohi. They have also found it as a fact that Mohammad Yasin was

hospitalised on January 8, 1964 and was discharged from there on January 27, 1964. They have held that he executed the sale-deeds in favour of the contesting defendants-respondents after understanding the nature of the transaction. It has further been held that Mohammad Yasin being the natural guardian of his sons, who are the appellants before this court, was fully competent to execute a sale deed of the property belonging to the appellants and it was not necessary for him to obtain any permission from the Court. As a result of the above findings, the two courts below have come to the conclusion that the sale deed executed by Mohammad Yasin as guardian of plaintiffs-appellants in favour of contesting defendants-respondents on January 29, 1964 was legal and binding and could not be called in question.

7. Learned counsel appearing for the appellants in the connected appeals has strongly contended that Mohammed Yasin had no unrestricted power to alienate immovable properties of minor plaintiffs-appellants. He could dispose of the said property only in certain circumstances recognised under the Mohammedan Law. In that connection, he invited my attention to paragraph 362 of Mulla's Mohammedan Law, 15th Edition and certain other authorities to which I shall presently refer. However, before dealing with the submission of the learned counsel, it is appropriate to refer to certain salient features of Mohammedan Law relating to guardianship which have a bearing on the discussion which shall presently follow.

8. Mohammedan Law makes a distinction between guardians of persons and guardians of property. In the instant case we are not concerned with the guardianship of persons and have to focus our attention only to the law relating to guardianship of property. Anglo-Mohammadan Law recognises two principal kinds of guardianship. In the first category falls the natural guardian and they include (1) father (2) the executor appointed by the father's will (3) the father's father and (4) the executor appointed by the Will of the father's father. The right of legal guardianship accrues in accordance with the order of precedence given above. Another thing to be noted in this connection is that the legal guardians mentioned at items 2 and 4 above can only be appointed in respect of what is known as 'Yatime Saghir' (orphaned minor). The rights of a guardian appointed by a court to alienate the property belonging to a minor are governed by the provisions of Guardians and Wards Act. In so far as the right of a legal guardian to alienate the property the Law is stated by Mulla in paragraph 362 of his book on Mohammadan Law, 15th Edition, in the following words:

"362. Alienation of immovable property by legal guardian – A legal guardian of the property of a minor has no power to sell the immovable property of the minor except in the following cases, namely: (1) Where he can obtain double its value; (2) Where the minor has no other property and the sale is necessary for his maintenance; (3) Where there are debts of the deceased, and no other means of paying them; (4) Where there are legacies to be paid, and no other means of paying them; (5) Where the expenses exceed the income of the property; (6) Where the property is falling into decay, and (7) When the property has been usurped and the guardian has reason to feel that there is no chance of fair restitution."

9. Incidently it may also be pointed out that another category of guardians have also come to be recognised under Anglo-Mohammadan Law and they are euphemistically called as de facto guardians. A de facto guardian is a person who is not a legal guardian nor a guardian appointed by the court but has placed himself voluntarily in charge of the person and property of the minor.

10. Learned counsel for the appellants referred to the cases of Imambandi v. Mutsaddi, (1918) 45 Ind App 73 : (AIR 1918 PC 11), Mahommed Ejaz Hussain v. Mohommed Iftikhar Hussain, (1932) 59 Ind App 92 : (AIR 1932 PC 76), Mt. Anto v. Mt. Reoti Kuer, AIR 1936 All 837 (FB) and Mrs. Eishu Chugani v. Rang Lal Agarwala, AIR 1973 Cal 64 in support of his contention. All these cases are, however, distinguishable. All that has been held in the said cases is that a de facto guardian had no right to alienate the immovable property of a minor or to refer a dispute on behalf of the minors to arbitration.

11. Finally the learned counsel has referred to the case of Asafuddula Beg v. Ram Ratan, AIR 1940 All 74. In this case, Thom. C.J. stated law in the following words:-
    "The legal guardian of a Mohammedan minor is not entitled to alienate the property of the minor except in certain cases. The property may be alienated by the guardian where the minor has no other property and the sale is necessary for his maintenance."

12. In that case the sale deed itself recited that the sale was being effected for the purposes of providing education to the minor. In spite of making the said observation, the Chief Justice did not accept the contention advanced on behalf of the appellants of that case on the ground that the case relating to the minority of the person concerned had not been taken in the written statement filed on his behalf.

13. The result of the foregoing discussion is that we are left only with the authority of Mulla´s Mohammedan Law. The case has to be viewed in the light of the second condition contained in paragraph 362 quoted above. Learned counsel urged that the minors had other agricultural property and as such Mohammad Yasin was incompetent to execute the sale deed in accordance with the second condition of paragraph 362 from Mulla´s Mohammedan Law. Carried to its logical conclusion the argument urged on behalf of the appellants, appears to be that

if a minor possesses more than one property, his legal guardian is incompetent to alienate any of the properties possessed by the minor. It is true that Exts. 5, 6, 7 and 8 go to show that the minors did possess some agricultural property besides the property alienated by Mohammad Yasin as their legal guardian. However, the contention of the learned counsel for the appellants in the form stated by him cannot be accepted. The interpretation placed by him on the second condition enumerated in paragraph 362 of the Mohammedan Law is patently erroneous.

14. On a proper reading of the second condition, the emphasis is on the maintenance of the minor. If the minor possesses even a single item of property, which is sufficient for his maintenance, the legal guardian would not be authorised to transfer the same in accordance with the said condition on the other hand if a minor possesses small items of a number of properties, the total income of which is wholly inadequte to meet his expenses, any one item of the property sale proceeds of which are sufficient for his maintenance can be legitimately transferred by the legal guardian and such transfer would be binding on him.

15. The last court of facts has found that Mohammad Yasin was carrying on cloth business which had stopped on account of his illness. He restarted the said business after alienating the property of his minor sons who are appellants before this court. Mohammad Yasin himself entered the witness box and stated that stock worth about Rs. 12,000/- was present at the shop at the time of his discharge from the hospital. His statement has been disbelieved by the first court of appeal. The court of appeal has, therefore, come to the conclusion that the income earned from the business of the cloth shop was necessary to maintain the minors and that the sale proceeds of the property of the minors were invested in the said business. The findings recorded by the court of appeal on this point are findings of fact which cannot be called in question. I, therefore, find no merit in the two second appeals.

16. The result is that the second appeals are hereby dismissed with costs.

———————

IMAMBANDI (appellant) v. MUTSADDI (respondent)
L.R. 45 I.A. 73 (1919) (Judicial Committee)

[The question before the Privy Council in this appeal was the extent to which a mother´s dealings with her child´s property bound the child, in the face of a conflicting body of case law]

Judgement.....It is perfectly clear that under the Mahomedan law the mother is entitled only to the custody of the person

351

of her minor child up to a certain age according to the sex of the child. But she is not the natural guardian; the father alone, or, if he be dead, his executor (under the Sunni law), is the legal guardian. The mother has no larger powers to deal with her minor child's property than any outsider or non-relative who happens to have charge for the time being of the infant. The term "de facto guardian" that has been applied to these persons is misleading; it connotes the idea that people in charge of a child are by virtue of that fact invested with certain powers over the infant's property. This idea is quite erroneous; and the judgment of the Board in <u>Mata Din v. Ahmed Ali</u> (L.R. 39 I.A. 49) clearly indicated it. There an infant's share was sold by the elder brother in whose charge the child was, along with his own share, to pay a joint ancestral debt. The vendee at the time of the sale was in possession of the whole property under a mortgage executed by the ancestor. On attaining majority the younger brother, ignoring the sale, brought a suit against the vendee-mortgagee for the redemption of his own share. The defence set up was that the sale by the infant's de facto guardian, made for a valid necessity, was binding on the infant. The lower Courts decreed the plaintiff's claim; on appeal to this Board the arguments proceeded on the same lines as in the present case, though in reverse order.

Lord Robson, in delivering the judgment of the Board, observed as follows: "It is urged on behalf of the appellant that the elder brothers were de facto guardians of the respondent, and, as such, were entitled to sell his property, provided that the sale was in order to pay his debts and was therefore necessary in his interest. It is difficult to see how the situation of an unauthorized guardian is bettered by describing him as a 'de facto' guardian. He may, by his de facto guardianship, assume important responsibilities in relation to the minor's property, but he cannot thereby clothe himself with legal power to sell it." And he went on to add: "There has been much argument in this case in the Courts below, and before their Lordships, as to whether, according to Mahomedan law, a sale by a de facto guardian, if made of necessity, or for the payment of an ancestral debt affecting the minor's property, and if beneficial to the minor, is altogether void or merely voidable. It is not necessary to decide that question in this case."

And he then proceeded to state the reasons why that was not considered necessary. This latter passage in Lord Robson's judgment has created the impression that their Lordships' decision was confined to the special facts of that case and left open the general question regarding the validity of alienations by unauthorized guardians of the property of minors.

As already observed, in the absence of the father, under the Sunni law, the guardianship vests in his executor. If the father dies without appointing an executor (wasi) and his father is alive, the guardianship of his minor children devolves on their grandfather. Should he also be dead, and have left an executor, it vests in him. In default of these de jure guardians, the duty of appointing a guardian for the protection and preservation of the infants' property devolves on the judge as the representative of the Sovereign: Baillie's Digest (ed. 1875), p.689; Hamilton's Hedaya, vol. 4, bk. 52, c.7, p.555. No one else has any right or power to intermeddle with the property of a minor, except for certain specified purposes, the nature of which is clearly defined. But the powers of even the de jure guardians are confined within legal limits. For example, whilst an executor-guardian (wasi) may "sell or purchase movables on account of the orphan under his charge either for an equivalent or at such a rate as to occasion an inconsiderable loss," dealings with his immovable property are subjected to strict conditions: Baillie's Digest, p.687. The reason for the restrictions is thus given in the Hedaya, vol. 4, p.553: "The ground of this" (the difference in the power of dealing with the two kinds of property) "is that the sale of movable property is a species of conservation, as articles of that description are liable to decay, and the price is much more easily preserved than the article itself. With respect, on the contrary, to immovable property, it is in a state of conservation in its own nature whence it is unlawful to sell it – unless, however, it be evident that it will otherwise perish or be lost, in which case the sale of it is allowed." In fact, the Mussulman law appears to draw a sharp distinction between movable and immovable property (a'kar) in respect of the powers of guardians, as will be seen from the following passage in Baillie's Digest, bk. 10, c.8, p.689: "With regard to the executor of a mother or a brother, – when a mother has died leaving property and a minor son, and having appointed an executor, or a brother has died leaving property and a minor brother, and having appointed an executor, the executor may lawfully sell anything but a'kar (A'kar is immovable property, and includes houses, groves, orchards, etc. [This and the subsequent footnotes form part of the judgment as delivered. – REPORTER.]) belonging to the estate of the deceased, but can neither sell the a'kar, nor lawfully buy anything for the minor but food and clothing, which are necessary for his preservation. The executor of a mother has no power to sell anything that a minor has inherited from his father, whether movable or immovable, and whether the property be involved in debt or free from it. But what he has inherited from herself when it is free from debts and legacies, the executor may sell what is movable, but he cannot sell a'kar. If the estate is involved in debt or legacies, and the debt is such as to absorb the whole, he may sell the whole, the sale of a'kar coming within his power: and if the debt does not absorb the whole, he may sell as much of it as is necessary to defray the debts, and as to his power to sell the surplus there is the same difference of opinion as has been stated above."

When the mother is the father's executrix, or is appointed by the judge as guardian of the minors, she has all the powers of a de jure guardian. Without such derivative authority, if she assumes charge of their property of whatever description and purports to deal with it, she does so at her own risk, and her acts are like those of any other person who arrogates an authority which he does not legally possess. She may incur responsibilities, but can impose no obligations on the infant. This rule, however, is subject to certain exceptions provided for the protection of a minor child who has no de jure guardian. A fatherless child is designated in the law-books an "infant-orphan" (yeteem saghir). The Hedaya classified the acts that may have to be done for an infant under three heads. It says: "Acts in regard to infant-orphans are of three descriptions, viz: (1) Acts of guardianship, such as contracting an infant in marriage, or selling or buying goods for him, a power which belongs solely to the walee, or natural guardian, whom the law has constituted the infant's substitute in those points; (2) acts arising from the wants of an infant, such as buying or selling for him on occasions of need, or hiring a nurse for him, or the like, which power belongs to the maintainer of the infant, whether he be the brother, uncle, or (in the case of a foundling) the mooltakit (a "mooltakit" is a person who undertakes to bring up a foundling or an orphan-child), or taker-up, or the mother, provided she be the maintainer of the infant; and as these are empowered with respect to such acts, the wallee, or natural guardian, is also empowered with respect to them in a still superior degree; nor is it requisite, with respect to the guardian, that the infant be in his immediate protection; (3) acts which are purely advantageous (in the original the words are "nafa' mahaz" which mean "unmixed benefit") to the infant, such as accepting presents or gifts, and keeping them for him, a power which may be exercised either by a mooltakit, a brother, or an uncle, and also by the infant himself, provided he be possessed of discretion, the intention being only to open a door to the infant's receiving benefactions of an advantageous nature" (vol. 4, bk. 44, p.124).

The examples given under the second head indicate the class of cases in which the acts of an unauthorized person who happens to have charge of a child are held to be binding on the infant's property. They also help to explain and illustrate the extent of such "de facto guardian's" powers. The permissibility of these acts depends on the emergency which gives rise to the imperative necessity for incurring liabilities without which the life of the child or his perishable goods and chattels may run the risk of destruction.

For instance, he may stand in immediate need of aliment, clothing, or nursing; these wants must be supplied forthwith. He may own "slaves" or live-stock; food and fodder must be immediately procured. And these imperative wants may recur from time to time. Under such circumstances power is given to the lawful guardian to incur debts or to raise money on the pledge of the minor's goods and chattels (mata´) (Mr. Hamilton translates "mata´" as meaning "personal chattels") (Majma´-ul-Anhar, vol. 2, p.571). And this power, in the absence of a de jure guardian, the law extends to the person who happens to have charge of the child and of the child's property, though not a constituted or authorized guardian.

There is no reference to the pledge or sale of immovable property (a´kar), as the power of dealing with that class of property is confined to the de jure guardians, and is treated in the Fatawai Alamgiri in a separate chapter: Baillie's Mahomedan Law of Sale, c.xvi.

It is to be observed that under the third "description" of acts that may be needful for an infant, a person in charge of a child, although not a de jure guardian, may validly accept on behalf of his ward an unburdened bounty, it being an act "purely advantageous" to the child, to use the expression of the Hedaya.

The reasoning on which it is sought to give to persons who happen to have charge of the person and property of a child, and are, therefore, called "de facto guardians," the same powers as are possessed by de jure guardians is purely inferential. It proceeds on the analogy of a dealing by an outsider who purports to sell another's property without any authority from the real owner. Such a person in the Hanafi law is called a "fazuli," or, as Mr. Hamilton spells it, "fazoolee," which expression is defined by Richardson to mean a person "busying himself in things not belonging to him, or acting without authority." With the effect of the acts of a fazuli their Lordships will deal presently. Before doing so they wish to refer briefly to the state of the decisions in the Indian Courts.

The Calcutta High Court, in sustaining transactions entered into by de facto guardians, has proceeded mainly on considerations of necessity for and benefit to the infant. The other High Courts, generally speaking, have cut the Gordian knot by holding that all such dealings with a minor's property were void.

Their Lordships do not feel called upon to examine in detail either set of decisions. But the last case on the subject in the Madras High Court requires their careful and respectful consideration: Ayderman Kutti v. Syed Ali (I.L.R. 37, M. 514). In their judgment in this case the learned judges have examined the law at considerable length, and their decision appears to divide itself into three broad propositions: first, that as regards the powers of guardians, de jure as well as de facto, the Mahomedan law recognizes no distinction as to the nature or kind of property, namely, whether it is immovable or movable; secondly, that in substance the powers of an unauthorized person who has charge of an infant are co-extensive with those of a lawfully constituted guardian, except in so far that the acts of the former are subject to considerations of necessity or benefit to the infant; and, thirdly (and this seems to form the essence of the judgment), that dealings by "a de facto guardian" are neither void nor voidable, but are "suspended" until the minor on attaining majority exercises his option of either ratifying the transaction or disavowing it.

With regard to the first of the above propositions, their Lordships have already indicated their views. In their opinion the Mahomedan law, for obvious reasons, makes a distinction, and a sharp distinction, between "goods and chattels" (mata´) and immovable property (a´kar) with regard to the powers of dealing by guardians.

The second proposition, speaking with respect, appears to their Lordships to lose sight of the fact that the acts of de jure guardians also are subject to the conditions of necessity for or benefit to the infant. So that, upon the reasoning of the Madras judgment, the powers of "a de facto guardian" would, to all intents and purposes, be co-extensive with those of a de jure guardian. This conclusion would wipe out one of the most important safeguards provided by the Mahomedan law for the protection of the interests of infants. The learned judges say that "The law as regards the effect of dealings with a minor´s property by a de facto guardian otherwise than in a case of absolute necessity or clear advantage to the minor is but a corollary of the general rule relating to salisly [sic], a person professing to deal with another´s property, but without having legal authority to do so, i.e., by a fazuli, as he is technically called; such sales generally are treated as mauquf, or dependent." Then, after referring to various authorities, they continue as follows: "The result of the above discussion is that, according to Muhammadan jurists, in cases of urgent and imperative necessity, such as those mentioned, the de facto guardian can alienate the property of the minor, no distinction being made between movable and immovable property."

It would have been an advantage to their Lordships if they had been placed in a position to judge for themselves, on the actual texts, the meaning of the Arabian text-writers and commentators. However, the Hedaya and the Fatawai Alamgiri are recognized as standard authorities in India on the Hanafi branch of the Sunni law. Of the Hedaya there is a rendering in English made by Mr. Hamilton under the orders of Warren Hastings; and a large part of the Fatawai Alamgiri, paraphrased into English by Mr. Neil Baillie, forms the words commonly known as Baillie´s Digest (Hanafia Law). Both Mr.

Hamilton and Mr. Neil Baillie in their renderings have, with the object of elucidation, occasionally added phrases which do not exist in the original, but on the whole the English versions of the Hedaya and of the Fatawai Alamgiri are valuable works on Mahomedan law.

The subject of sales by unauthorized persons is treated in the Hedaya in a separate section entitled "of Fazoolee Beea (correctly, Bai´), or the sale of the property of another without his consent" (vol. 2, bk. 16, p.508). It says: "If a person were to sell the property of another without his order the contract is complete, but it remains with the proprietor either to confirm or dissolve the sale as he pleases. Shafei is of opinion that the contract, in this case, is not complete, because it has not issued from a lawful authority, for that is constituted only by property or permission, neither of which exist in this case." It then proceeds to give the arguments of the Hanafi doctors in support of their view that the unauthorized contract is "complete." And then it adds: "If the proprietor should die, then the consent of the heirs is of no efficacy in the confirmation of the fazoolee sale, in either case, that is, whether the price have been stipulated in money or in goods; because the contract rested entirely on the personal assent of the deceased."

In other words, the so-called sale remains wholly ineffective until it receives the "confirmation" of the owner, to whom alone belongs the power of "confirming" it. If he dies before he has "confirmed" it, the transaction falls to the ground, as the right to adopt the fazuli´s act does not pass to his heirs.

In the Fatawai Alamgiri (the "Book on Sale" in the Fatawai Alamgiri has been rendered into English by Mr. Baillie under the name of the "Mahomedan Law of Sale") the subject is treated under the designation of "dependent sales" (vol. 3, p. 245; Baillie´s Mahomedan Law of Sale, pp. 218-219): "When a person sells the property of another, the sale is suspended, according to us (i.e., the Hanafis), for the sanction or ratification of the proprietor; and the existence of both the parties to the contract, and of the subject of sale, is a necessary condition to the validity of his sanction..... If the owner should die before sanctioning the sale, sanction by his heir would not suffice to give it operation. Sanction by an owner himself renders a sale operative."

The word in the above passage translated as "suspended" is derived from the same root as the word that has been translated in the heading as "dependant," and in this connection really means "is dependent upon"; also the words "or ratification" have been introduced by Mr. Baillie by way of explanation. The word ijazat in the original is rightly rendered into "sanction."

The Majma´-ul-Anhar states the rule relating to a sale by a fazuli in similar terms; it says in substance that such a

357

sale is "established" (takes effect) on the sanction of the malik (owner), subject to four conditions, which it specifies. And then it adds significantly that according to Shafei (the founder of the second great Sunni school of law) all dealings by an unauthorized person are absolutely void (batil) (vol. 2, p.88).

In their Lordships' opinion the Hanafi doctrine relating to a sale by an unauthorized person remaining dependent on the sanction of the owner refers to a case where such owner is sui juris, possessed of the capacity to give the necessary sanction and to make the transaction operative. They do not find any reference in these doctrines relating to fazuli sales, so far as they appear in the Hedaya or the Fatawai Alamgiri, to dealings with the property of minors by persons who happen to have charge of the infants and their property – in other words, the "de facto guardians."

The Hanafi doctrine about fazuli sales appears clearly to be based on the analogy of an agent who acts in a particular matter without authority, but whose act is subsequently adopted or ratified by the principal which has the effect of validating it from its inception. The idea of agency in relation to an infant is as foreign, their Lordships conceive, to Mahomedan law as to every other system.

In this connection it should be noted, that whilst chapter 12 deals exclusively with the effect of "dependent sales," in chapter 16 the rules relating to the powers of guardians are discussed at considerable length: Bailie's Mahomedan Law of Sale, p.243; Fatawai Alamgiri, vol. 3, p.229. The following rule lays down the conditions governing the sales by the executor (i.e., the appointed guardian) of the immovable property of an infant: "And, according to modern decisions, the sale of immovable estate by an executor is lawful only in one of the three cases following: that is, where there is a purchaser willing to give double its value, or the sale is necessary to meet the minor's emergencies, or there are debts of the deceased, and no other means of paying them": Baillie's Mahomedan Law of Sale, p. 247; Fatawai Alamgiri, vol.3, p. 233.

Having regard to the object in view, this dictum appears to their Lordships to apply to all forms of property which, like a'kar, combine both security and permanency. But it does not exclude the discretion of the judge to sanction any alteration of investment in the interests of the infant.

The following case affords a further illustration of the limitations on the powers of "de facto guardians": "A woman after the death of her husband sells property that belonged to him, supposing herself to be his executrix, and her husband having left minor children; she after some time declares that she was not the executrix, her assertion, however, is not to be credited as against the purchaser, but the sale remains in suspense till her children arrive at puberty. If they should admit that she was the executrix, the sale by her is lawful; but if they deny the fact, the sale is void; and though the purchaser should have manured the purchased land, he has no recourse for reimbursement against the woman. What has been said is on the supposition that the woman sues for a cancellation of the sale, on the ground that she was not the executrix; but if the minor sue on that ground, his claim is to be heard": Baillie, p. 249; Alamgiri,vol. 3, p.234.

The rest of the passage is immaterial for the purposes of this judgment.

The above case shows that even where the mother believes she is vested with authority as her husband's executrix, and in that belief purports to deal with the minor's property, a purchaser let into possession by her is liable to be ejected at the instance of the minor. Her own subsequent denial of authority does not affect the purchaser's position; but if the transaction is impugned by the rightful owner, namely, the infant, the onus is on the vendee to establish the foundation of his title, that is, that his vendor possessed in fact the authority under which she purported to act.

A further rule, which is given in the "Book on Pledges" (Mortgages) (Kitab-ur-Rahn) of the Fatawai Alamgiri, which does not appear to have been translated by Mr. Baillie, is equally explicit. After stating the principle applicable to the powers of the father to pledge or mortgage his minor child's property, it goes on to say: "the mother: if she pledges (mortgages) the property of her infant child, it is not lawful, unless she be the executrix (of the father) or be authorized therefor by the guardian of the minor; or the judge should grant her permission to pledge the infant's property. Then it is lawful; and the right to possession and user is established in the murtahin (pledgee or mortgagee) without power of sale": Fatawai Alamgiri, vol. 5, p.638.

It seems to their Lordships that the power to sell cannot be wider than the power to mortgage.

For the foregoing considerations their Lordships are of opinion that under the Mahomedan law a person who has charge of the person or property of a minor without being his legal guardian, and who may, therefore, be conveniently called a "de facto guardian," has no power to convey to another any right or interest in immovable property which the transferee can enforce against the infant; nor can such transferee, if let into possession of the property under such unauthorized transfer, resist an action in ejectment on behalf of the infant as a trespasser. It follows that, being himself without title, he cannot seek to recover property in the possession of another equally without title.

West Pakistan Family Courts Act, 1964

Preamble - Whereas it is expedient to make provision for the establishment of Family Courts for the expeditious settlement and disposal of disputes relating to marriage and family affairs and for matters connected therewith;

It is hereby enacted as follows:-

1. Short title, extent and commencement - (1) This Act may be called the West Pakistan Family Courts Act, 1964.

(2) It extends to the whole of the Province of West Pakistan, except the Tribal Areas.

(3) It shall come into force in such area or areas and on such date or dates as Government may, by notification in the official Gazette, specify in this behalf.

2. Definitions - In this Act, unless the context otherwise requires, the following expressions shall have the meanings hereby respectively assigned to them, that is to say:

(a) "Arbitration Council" and "Chairman" shall have the meanings respectively assigned to them in the Muslim Family Laws Ordinance, 1961;

(b) "Family Court" means a Court constituted under this Act;

(c) "Government" means the Government of West Pakistan;

(d) "party" shall include any person whose presence as such is considered necessary for a proper decision of the dispute and whom the Family Court adds as a party to such dispute;

(e) "prescribed" means prescribed by rules made under this Act.

3. Establishment of Family Courts - Government shall establish one or more Family Courts in each District or at such other place as it may deem necessary and appoint a Judge in each of such Courts.

4. Qualifications of Judge - No person shall be appointed as a Judge of a Family Court unless he is or has been a District Judge or is or has been a Senior Civil Judge

or Civil Judge, First Class.

5. <u>Jurisdiction</u> – Subject to the provisions of the Muslim Family Laws Ordinance, 1961, and the Conciliation Courts Ordinance, 1961, the Family Courts shall have exclusive jurisdiction to entertain, hear and adjudicate upon matters specified in the Schedule.

6. <u>Place of sitting</u> – Subject to any general or special orders of Government in this behalf, a Family Court shall hold its sittings at such place or places within the districts as may be specified by the District Judge.

7. <u>Institution of suits</u> – (1) Every suit before a Family Court shall be instituted by the presentation of a plaint or in such other manner and in such Court as may be prescribed.

(2) The plaint shall contain all facts relating to the dispute and shall contain a Schedule giving the number of witnesses intended to be produced in support of the plaint, the names and addresses of the witnesses and a brief summary of the facts to which they would depose:

Provided that the parties may, with the permission of the Court, call any witness at any later stage, if the Court considers such evidence expedient in the interests of justice.

(3) All documents which the plaintiff intends to rely upon in respect of his claim shall be appended to the plaint.

(4) The plaint shall be accompanied by as many duplicate copies thereof [including the Schedule and the lists of documents referred to in subsection (3)], as there are defendants in the suit, for service upon the defendants.

8. <u>Intimation to defendants</u> – (1) Within three days of the presentation of the plaint to a Family Court the plaintiff shall send to each defendant by registered post, a copy of the plaint together with a copy of the Schedule as mentioned in section 7 (2) and copies of all documents mentioned in section 7 (3).

(2) Save as may otherwise be prescribed, the plaintiff shall also, within the time specified in subsection (1), cause notice to be inserted in any two newspapers approved by the Family Court of the fact of his having filed the plaint.

9. <u>Written statement</u> – (1) Within fifteen days of the service of notice upon him by registered post or the appearance of a notice in a newspaper, whichever is earlier, the defendant shall appear in Court and file his written statement.

(2) With the written statement the defendant shall attach:

(a) copies of the entire documentary evidence that he wishes to produce in the case; and

(b) a list of the names and addresses of his witnesses along with a precis of the evidence that each witness is expected to give.

(3) Copies of the written statement and the documents referred to in subsection (2) shall be sent by registered post
362

by defendant to the plaintiff within three days of his filing the written statement:

Provided that if there are several defendants and they file a joint written statement, only one of them shall send a copy of the written statement with the documents mentioned in subsection (2).

(4) If the defendant fails to appear within the time specified in subsection (1), the Family Court may proceed against him ex parte.

10. Pre-trial proceeding – (1) As soon as may be, after the written statement has been filed, the Court shall fix a date for pre-trial hearing of the case and issue notices to the parties for attending the Court on the date so fixed.

(2) On the date so fixed, the Court shall examine the plaint, the written statement (if any) and the precis of evidence and documents filed by the parties and shall also, if it so deems fit, hear the parties and their counsel.

(3) At the pre-trial, the Court shall ascertain the points at issue between the parties and attempt to effect a compromise or reconciliation between the parties, if this be possible.

(4) If no compromise or reconciliation is possible, the Court shall frame the issues in the case and fix a date for evidence.

11. Recording of evidence – (1) On the date fixed for recording of evidence, the Family Court shall examine the witnesses produced by the parties in such order as it deems fit.

(2) The Court shall not issue any summons for the appearance of any witness unless, within three days of the framing of issues, any party intimates to the Court that it desires a witness to be summoned through the Court and the Court is satisfied that it is not possible or practicable for such party to produce the witness.

(3) The witnesses shall give their evidence in their own words and no question shall be put to them by any party or any counsel of a party by way of examination-in-chief, cross-examination or re-examination:

Provided that the Court may, if it so deems fit, put any question to any witness for the purpose of elucidation of any point which it considers material in the case.

(4) The Family Court may permit the evidence of any witness to be given by means of an affidavit:

Provided that if the Court deems fit it may call such witness for the purpose of examination in accordance with subsection (3).

12. Conclusion of trial – (1) After the close of evidence of both sides, the Family Court shall make another effort to effect a compromise or reconciliation between the parties.

(2) If such compromise or reconciliation is not possible, the Family Court shall announce its judgment and give a

363

decree.

13. Enforcement of decrees – (1) The Family Court shall pass a decree in such form and in such manner as may be prescribed, and shall enter its particulars in the prescribed register.

(2) If any money is paid or any property is delivered in the presence of the Family Court, in satisfaction of the decree, it shall enter the fact of payment and the delivery of property, as the case may be, in the aforesaid register.

(3) Where a decree relates to the payment of money and the decretal amount is not paid within the time specified by the Court, the same shall, if the Court so directs, be recovered as arrears of land revenue, and on recovery shall be paid to the decree-holder.

(4) The decree shall be executed by the Court passing it or by such other Civil Court as the District Judge may, by special or general order, direct.

(5) A Family Court may, if it so deems fit, direct that any money to be paid under a decree passed by it be paid in such instalments as it deems fit.

14. Appeals – (1) Notwithstanding anything provided in any other law for the time being in force, a decision or a decree passed by a Family Court shall be appealable to the High Court only.

(2) No appeal shall lie from a decree passed by a Family Court:

(a) for dissolution of marriage, except in the case of dissolution for reasons specified in clause (d) of item (viii) of section 2 of the Dissolution of Muslim Marriages Act, 1939;

(b) for dower not exceeding rupees one thousand;

(c) for maintenance of rupees twenty-five or less per month.

15. Power of Family Court to summon witnesses – (1) A Family Court may issue summons to any person to appear and give evidence, or to produce or cause the production of any document:

Provided that:

(a) no person who is exempt from personal appearance in a Court under subsection (1) of section 133 of the Code of Civil Procedure, 1908, shall be required to appear in person;

(b) a Family Court may refuse to summon a witness or to enforce a summons already issued against a witness when, in the opinion of the Court, the attendance of the witness cannot be procured without such delay, expense or inconvenience as in the circumstances would be unreasonable.

(2) If any person to whom a Family Court has issued summons to appear and give evidence or to cause the production of any document before it, wilfully disobeys such summons, the Family Court may take cognizance of such disobedience, and after giving such person an opportunity to explain, sentence him to a fine not exceeding one hundred rupees.

364

16. Contempt of Family Courts – A person shall be guilty of contempt of the Family Court if he, without lawful excuse:

(a) offers any insult to the Family Court; or

(b) causes an interruption in the work of the Family Court; or

(c) refuses to answer any question put by the Family Court, which he is bound to answer; or

(d) refuses to take oath to state the truth or to sign any statement made by him in the Family Court;

and the Family Court may forthwith try such person for such contempt and sentence him to a fine not exceeding rupees two hundred.

17. Provisions of Evidence Act and Code of Civil Procedure not to apply – (1) Save as otherwise expressly provided by or under this Act, the provisions of the Evidence Act, 1872, and the Code of Civil Procedure, 1908, shall not apply to proceedings before any Family Court.

(2) Sections 8 to 11 of the Oaths Act, 1873, shall apply to all proceedings before the Family Courts.

18. Appearance through agents – If a person required under this Act to appear before a Family Court, otherwise than as a witness, is a pardah nashin lady, the Family Court may permit her to be represented by a duly authorised agent.

19. Court-fees – Notwithstanding anything to the contrary contained in the Court Fees Act, 1872, the court-fees to be paid on any plaint filed before a Family Court shall be rupee one for any kind of suit.

20. Investment of powers of Magistrates on Judges – Government may invest any Judge of a Family Court with powers of Magistrate First Class to hear the case under section 488 of the Code of Criminal Procedure, 1898.

21. Provisions of Muslim Family Laws Ordinance to be applicable – (1) Nothing in this Act shall be deemed to affect any of the provisions of the Muslim Family Laws Ordinance, 1961, or the rules framed thereunder; and the provisions of sections 7, 8, 9 and 10 of the said Ordinance shall be applicable to any decree for the dissolution of marriage solemnized under the Muslim Law, maintenance or dower, by a Family Court.

(2) Where a Family Court passes a decree for the dissolution of a marriage solemnized under the Muslim Law, the Court shall send by registered post, within seven days of passing such decree, a certified copy of the same to the appropriate Chairman referred to in section 7 of the Muslim Family Laws Ordinance, 1961, and upon receipt of such copy, the Chairman shall proceed as if he had received an intimation of Talaq required to be given under the said Ordinance.

(3) Notwithstanding anything to the contrary contained in any other law, a decree for dissolution of a marriage solemnized under the Muslim Law shall:

(a) not be effective until the expiration of ninety days

365

from the day on which a copy thereof has been sent under subsection (2) to the Chairman; and

(b) be of no effect if within the period specified in clause (a) a reconciliation has been effected between the parties in accordance with the provisions of the Muslim Family Laws Ordinance, 1961.

22. <u>Bar on the issue of injunctions by Family Court</u> – A Family Court shall not have the power to issue an injunction to, or stay any proceedings pending before, a Chairman or an Arbitration Council.

23. <u>Validity of marriages registered under the Muslim Family Laws Ordinance, 1961, not to be questioned by Family Courts</u> – A Family Court shall not question the validity of any marriage registered in accordance with the provisions of the Muslim Family Laws Ordinance, 1961, nor shall any evidence in regard thereto be admissible before such Court.

24. <u>Family Courts to inform Union Councils of cases not registered under the Muslim Family Laws Ordinance, 1961</u> – If in any proceedings before a Family Court it is brought to the notice of the Court that a marriage solemnized under the Muslim Law after the coming into force of the Muslim Family Laws Ordinance, 1961, has not been registered in accordance with the provisions of the said Ordinance and the rules framed thereunder, the Court shall communicate such fact in writing to the Union Council for the area where the marriage was solemnized.

25. <u>Family Court deemed to be a District Court for purposes of Guardians and Wards Act, 1890</u> – A Family Court shall be deemed to be a District Court for the purposes of the Guardians and Wards Act, 1890, and notwithstanding anything contained in this Act, shall in dealing with matters specified in that Act, follow the procedure prescribed in that Act.

26. <u>Power to make rules</u> – (1) Government may, by notification in the official Gazette, make rules to carry into effect the provisions of this Act.

(2) Without prejudice to the generality of the provisions contained in subsection (1), the rules so made may, among other matters, provide for the procedure, which shall not be inconsistent with the provisions of this Act, to be followed by the Family Courts.

<u>Schedule</u>
[See section 5]

1. Dissolution of marriage.
2. Dower.
3. Maintenance.
4. Restitution of conjugal rights.
5. Custody of children.
6. Guardianship.

APPENDIX II

Select Bibliography

(1)   Sources, History, Methodology.

Agarwala, K.S. "On the relative weight of the Three Primary
        Authorities in the Hanafi School of Mahomedan Law"
        A.I.R. 1932 Journal 23
Aghnides, N.P. "Mohammedan Theories of Finance" (New York
        1916)
Ahmad, M.B. "Theory and Practice of Law in Islam" (1961) 9
        Journal Pak. Hist. Soc. 8
Anderson, J.N.D. "The Study of Islamic Law" (Ann Arbor)
Badr, G.M. "Islamic Law. Its Relation to other Legal
        Systems" (1978) 26 A.J.C.L. 187
Ba'th, M.H. "Islam Jurisprudence" (Washington 1979)
Coulson, N.J. "A History of Islamic Law" (Edinburgh 1964)
Coulson, N.J. "Conflicts and Tensions in Islamic
        Jurisprudence" (Chicago 1959)
Coulson, N.J. "Doctrine and Practice in Islamic Law: One
        Aspect of the Problem" (1950) 18 B.S.O.A.S. 211
Daura, B. "A Brief Account of the Development of the Four
        Sunni Schools of Law and some Recent Developments"
        (1968) J.I.C.L. 1
Derrett, J.D.M. "An Introduction to Legal Systems" (London
        1968)
Faruki, K. "Islamic Jurisprudence" (Karachi 1962)
Faruki, K. "The Evolution of Islamic Constitutional Theory
        and Practice from 622 to 1926" (Lahore 1971)
Fyzee, A.A.A. "The Relevance of Muhammadan Law in the
        Twentieth Century" 1963 C.L.J. 261
Goldziher, I. "Muslim Studies Vol. II" (Translated by Barber
        C.R. and Stern S.M.) (London 1971)
Haj Nour, A.M. "The Schools of Law: their Emergence and
        Validity Today" (1977) 7 J.I.C.L. 54
Hasan, A. "Al Shafi'i's Role in the Development of Islamic
        Jurisprudence" (1966) 5 Islamic Studies 239

Hasan, A. "Ijma in the Early Schools" (1967) 6 Islamic
    Studies 121
Hasan, A. "Origins of the Early Schools of Law" (1970) 9
    Islamic Studies 255
Hasan, A. "Modern Trends in Ijma" (1973) 12 Islamic Studies
    121)
Hasan, A. "The Principle of Istishan in Islamic
    Jurisprudence" (1977) 16 Islamic Studies 347
Hasan, A. "The Theory of Naskh" (1965) 4 Islamic Studies 181
Hasan, A. "The Classical Definition of Ijma: the Nature of
    Consensus" (1975) 14 Islamic Studies 261
Hasan, A. "The Definition of Qiyas in Islamic Jurisprudence"
    (1980) 19 Islamic Studies 23
Hidayatullah, M. "The Role of the Qur'an in the Development
    of the Shariah" (1975) 6 Islam and the Modern Age 57
Hicks, S.C. "The Fuqaha and Islamic Law" (1978) A.J.C.L.
    Suppl. 1
Hourani, G.F. "The Basis of Authority of Consensus in Sunnite
    Islam" (1964) 21 Studia Islamica 13
Ishaq, M. "Historical Survey of Fiqh and Muslim
    Jurisprudence" (1963) 8 J.A.S. Pakistan 27
Jah, U. "The Importance of Ijtihad in the Development of
    Islamic Law (1977) 7 J.I.C.L. 31
Khaddhuri, M. "Nature and Sources of Islamic Law" (1953) 20
    Geo. W.L.R. 3
Khaddhuri, M. "Islamic Jurisprudence" (Shafi's Risala)
    (Baltimore 1961)
Khalil, S. "Ash-Shafi'i's Risalah: Basic Ideas" (1974
    Pakistan)
Khan, W. "The Sunni Jurists and Principles of Legislation"
    (1960) 7 Justitia 51
Latifi, D. "Rationalism and Muslim Law" (1973) 4 Islam and
    the Modern Age 43
Ling, T.C. "Islam's Alternative to Fundamentalism" Bulletin
    of the John Rylands U.L. of Manchester Vol. 64 No. 1
    (1981) 165
MacDonald, D.B. "Development of Muslim Theology Jurisprudence
    and Constitutional Theory" (Lahore 1964)
Mahmood, T. "Custom as a Source of Law in Islam" (1972) 14
    J.I.L.I. 583
Makdisi, G. "The Significance of the Sunni Schools of Law in
    Islamic Religious History" (1979) 10 I.J.M.E.S. 1
Maududi, M. "Islamic Law and Constitution" (Lahore 1967)
Mujeeb, M. "Orthodoxy and the Orthodox: The Shariah as Law"
    (1964) I.C. 27
Nawaz, M.K. "A Re-examination of some Basic Concepts of
    Islamic Law and Jurisprudence" (1963) 12 I.Y.B.I.A. 205
Nawaz, M.K. "Some Aspects of Interpretation of Islamic Law in
    India in the Past" (1960-1) 10 I.Y.B.I.A. 127
Nour, A.M. "Qias as a Source of Islamic Law" (1974) 5
    J.I.C.L. 18
368

Qadri, A.A. "Islamic Jurisprudence in the Modern World"
(Lahore 1973)
Rabbo, S.A. "Sources of Islamic Law" (1980) The Search 280
Rahman, F. "Concepts Sunnah and Hadith in the Early Period"
(1962) 1 Islamic Studies No. 2, 1
Rahman, F. "Concepts Sunnah Ijtihad and Ijma in the Early
Period" (1962) 1 Islamic Studies No. 1, 1
Rahman, F. "Towards Reformulating the Methodology of Islamic
Law" (1979) 12 N.Y.U.J. of Int. Law and Politics 219
Ramadan, S. "Islamic Law: its Scope and Equity" (London 1970)
Rankin, C. "Custom in the Personal Law of India" (1939) 25
Transactions of the Grotius Society 89
Schacht, J. "An Introduction to Islamic Law" (Oxford 1964)
Schacht, J. "The Origins of Muhammadan Jurisprudence" (Oxford
1950)
Siddiqi, M.Z. "The Importance of Hadith as a Source of
Islamic Law" (1964) Studies in Islam 19
Weiss, B. "Interpretation in Islamic Law" (1978) 26 A.J.C.L.
199
Yusuf, S.M. "The Sunnah - its Transmission, Development and
Revision" (1963) 37 I.C. 271

(2)   General Accounts - Indian Subcontinent

Abdul Halim, Sh. "Muslim Family Laws" (Lahore 1978)
Abdur Rahman, A.F.M. "Institutes of Musulman Law" (Calcutta
1969)
Ali, S.A. "Law of Family Courts" (Karachi 1975)
Ameer Ali, S. "Mohammedan Law" (Lahore 1976) (Vol. I 5th,
Vol. II 7th ed.)
Baillie, N.B.F. "Digest of Moohummudan Law" (London 1875)
Fyzee, A.A.A. "Cases in the Muhammadan Law of India and
Pakistan" (Oxford 1965)
Fyzee, A.A.A. "Outlines of Muhammadan Law" (Oxford 1974) (4th
ed.)
Hamilton, C. (ed. Grady) "The Hedaya" (London 1870)
Jones, W. (ed. Rumsey) "Al Sirajiyyah" (translated) (Calcutta
1890)
Khalid, S.R. "Muslim Law" (Lucknow 2nd ed. 1979)
Khan Bahadur, M.Y. "Mahomedan Law" (Tagore Law Lectures
1891-2) (Calcutta 1895)
Macnaughten, W.H. "Principles and Precedents of Moohummudan
Law" (Calcutta 1825)
Mahmood, S. "Principles and Digest of Muslim Law" (Lahore
1967)
Mahmood, T. "The Muslim Law of India" (New Delhi 1980)
Merchant, M.V. "Qur´anic Laws" (Lahore 1947)
Mulla, D.F. "Principles of Mahomedan Law" (Bombay 1976) (18th
ed.)
Pearl, D.S. "Textbook on Muslim Law" (London 1979)
Pearl, D.S. "Family Law in Pakistan" (1969) 9 Journal of
369

Family Law 165

Pearl, D.S. "The Legal Rights of Muslim Women in India Pakistan and Bangladesh" (1976) 6 New Community 68

Rahim, A. "The Principles of Muhammadan Jurisprudence" (Madras 1911)

Saksena, K.P. "Muslim Law as Administered in India and Pakistan" (Lucknow 1963) (4th ed.)

Sircar, S.C. "The Muhummadan Law" (Tagore Law Lectures 1873) (Calcutta 1873)

Tandon, M.P. "Text-Book of Mahomedan Law" (Allahabad 1977)

Tanzil-ur-Rahman "A Code of Muslim Personal Law" (two Vols.) (Karachi 1978, 1980)

Tyabji, F.B. "Muslim Law, The Personal Law of Muslims in India and Pakistan" (Bombay 1968)

Verma, B.R. "Mohemmadan Law in India and Pakistan" (1978 Delhi)

Vesey Fitzgerald, S. "Muhammadan Law: an Abridgement according to its Various Schools" (London 1931)

Wilson, R. "Anglo-Muhammadan Law" (Calcutta 1930) (6th ed.)

(3) General Accounts - Other Countries

Altman, I. "Islamic Legislation in Egypt in the 1970´s" (1979) 13 Asian and African Studies 199

Anderson, J.N.D. "Family Law in Africa and Asia" (London 1965)

Anderson, J.N.D. "Islamic Law in Africa" (London 1954)

Anderson, J.N.D. "The Significance of Islamic Law in the World Today" (1960) 9 A.J.C.L. 187

Djamour, J. "The Muslim Matrimonial Court in Singapore" (London 1966)

Eisenman, R.H. "Islamic Law in Palestine and Israel" (Leiden 1978)

Hill, E. "Orientalism and Liberal-Legalism: the Study of Islamic Law in the Modern Middle East" (1976) R.M.E.S. 57

Ibrahim, A. "Islamic Law in Malaya" (Singapore 1965)

Khaddhuri, M.K. and Liebesny, H.J. "Law in the Middle East" (Washington 1955)

Layish, A. "Women and Islamic Law in a non-Muslim State" (New York 1975)

Liebesny, H.J. "The Law of the Near and Middle East" (Albany 1975)

Mahmood, T. "Personal Laws in Bangladesh: a Comparative Perspective" (1972) 14 J.I.L.I. 583

(4) History of the Administration of Justice in India and Pakistan

Ahmad, M.B. "The Administration of Justice in Medieval India" (Aligarh 1941)

Archbold, W.A.J. "Outlines of Indian Constitutional History (British Period" (London 1926)

Bhatia, H.S. "Origin and Development of Legal and Political System in India" (Vols. I, II, III) (New Delhi 1976)

Chaudhary, A.C. "Independence of the Judiciary and the Administration of Justice in Pakistan" Lawasia 1972, 158

Coulson, N.J. "Muslim Custom and Case Law" (1959) 6 N.S. Die Welt des Islams 13

Derret, J.D.M. "Religion Law and the State in India" (London 1968)

Dubey, H.P. "A Short History of the Judicial Systems of India and Some Foreign Countries" (Bombay 1968)

Fawcett, C. "The First Century of British Justice in India" (Oxford 1934)

Fyzee, A.A.A. "The Impact of English Law on Shari´at in India" (1964) 66 Bombay L.R. (J) 107, 121

Fyzee, A.A.A. "Development of Islamic Law in India: a Bird´s Eye View" in "Socio Cultural Impact of Islam on India" ed. Attar Singh (Chandighar 1976)

Gledhill, A. "The Reception of English Law in India" in W.B. Hamilton (ed.) "The Transfer of Institutions" (Durham N.C. 1964), p.165

Jain, M.P. "Outlines of Indian Legal History" (Bombay 3rd ed. 1972)

Mahmood, T. "Muslim Personal Law (Role of the State in the Subcontinent)" (New Delhi 1977)

Mannan, M.A. "The Superior Courts of Pakistan" (Lahore 1973)

Misra, B.B. "The Central Administration of the East India Company" (Manchester 1959)

Misra, B.B. "The Judicial Administration of the East India Company in Bengal 1765 - 1782" (Delhi 1961)

Patra, A.C. "The Administration of Justice under the East India Company in Bengal, Bihar and Orissa" (London 1962)

Pearl, D.S. "Historical Background to the Personal Systems of Law" (1974) Studies in Islam 95

Pearl, D.S. "Interpersonal Conflict of Laws between Two Classes (1978) Indian Socio-Legal Journal Vol. IV, No.1 p.15

Pearl, D.S. "Interpersonal Conflict of Laws: India Pakistan and Bangladesh" (Bombay 1981)

Rankin, G.C. "Background to Indian Law" (Cambridge 1946)

Setalvad, M.C. "The Common Law in India" (London 1960)

Setalvad, M.C. "The Role of English Law in India" (Jerusalem 1966)

Srivastava, R.C. "Development of the Judicial System in India under the East India Company 1833 - 1858" (Bombay 1971)

Trevelyan, E.J. "The Constitution and Jurisdiction of Courts of Civil Justice in British India" (Calcutta 1923)

Yaduvansh, U. "The Decline of the Role of the Qadis in India 1793 - 1876" (1969) 6 Studies in Islam 155

(5)   Marriage, Divorce, Parent and Child

Abdel Hamid, I. "Dissolution of Marriage in Islamic Law"
    (1956) 3 Islamic Quarterly 161, 215; 4 Islamic Quarterly
    3, 57, 97
Abdul, K. "Marriage in Islam" 4, 7 (1963) Pakistan
    Philosophical Journal 51
Afzal, M. "Muslim Marriages: Age Mehr and Social Status"
    (1973) 12 Pakistan Development Review 12 48
Ahmed, K.N. "A Commentary on the Dissolution of Muslim
    Marriages Act, (Act No. VIII of 1939)" (Karachi 1955)
Ahmed, K.N. "Muslim Law of Divorce" (Islamabad 1978) (2nd
    ed.)
Al-Faruqi, L. "Women's Rights and the Muslim Women" (1972) 3
    Islam and the Modern Age 3 2 76
Algase, R.C. "Is Dowry Obligatory" (1978) 1 Hamdard Islamicus
    78
Ameer Ali, S. "The Legal Position of Women in Islam" (London
    1912)
Anderson, J.N.D. "Irregular and Void Marriages in Hanafi Law"
    (1950) 13 B.S.O.A.S. 357
Anderson, J.N.D. "Reforms in the Law of Divorce in the Muslim
    World" (1970) XXXI Studia Islamica 31 41
Anderson, J.N.D. "The Problem of Divorce in the Shari'a of
    Islam" J.R.C.A.S. (April 1950) 169
Arousi, M.El. "Judicial Dissolution of Marriage" (1977) 7
    J.I.C.L. 13
Banerjee, P.C. "The Law of Maintenance" (West Bengal 1981)
Basu, K.K. "Hindu Muslim Marriages" Indian Law Review (1948,
    1949) 2 249
Daura, B. "The Limit of Polygamy in Islam" (1969) 3 J.I.C.L.
    21
Desai, K. "Indian Law of Marriage and Divorce" (3rd. ed.
    Bombay 1978)
Diiran, P. "Who is a Muslim?" (1978) Indian Socio-Legal
    Journal IV p.75
Donaldson, D.M. "Temporary Marriage in Islam" Muslim World 26
    (1936) 358
El-Sayed, D.H. "The Institution of Marriage in Islam" Journal
    of Islamic Studies 1 (1968) 45
Esposito, J. "Women's Rights in Islam" (1975) 14 Islamic
    Studies 99
Fyzee, A.A.A. "The Muslim Wife's Rights of Dissolving her
    Marriage" (1936) 38 Bombay L.R. (J) 113
Hinchcliffe, D. "Divorce in Pakistan: Judicial Reform" (1968)
    J.I.C.L. 13
Hinchcliffe, D. "Polygamy in Traditional and Contemporary
    Islamic Law" Islam and the Modern Age Vol. 1 No. 3
    (1970) p. 13
Hinchcliffe, D. "The Widow's Dower Debt in India" Islam and
    the Modern Age 4 (1973) 5

Howard, I. "Muta Marriage Reconsidered in the Context of Formal Procedures for Islamic Marriage" 20 (1975) Journal of Semitic Studies 82

Hussain, M.A. "Marriage and Khula in Islam" Islam and the Modern Age 9 (1978) 86

Hussain, S.A. "Marriage Customs among the Muslims in India" (1976)

Hussain, S.J. "Legal Modernism in Islam: Polygamy and Repudiation" (1965) 7 J.I.L.I. 384

Jain, P.C. "Polygamy Among Muslims" (1969) A.I.R. Journal

Kazi, A.I. "Muslim Family Laws Ordinance" (1964) 1 Karachi Law Journal 57

Khaddhuri, M. "Marriage in Islamic Law: the Modernist Viewpoint" (1978) 26 A.J.C.L. 213

Khambatba, K.J. "Dissolution of Mohammadan Marriage at the Instance of the Wife" (1934) 2 B.L.R.

Latifi, D. "Adoption and the Muslim Law" (1974) 16 J.I.L.I. 118

Mahmood, T. "Presumption of Legitimacy under the Evidence Act: A Century of Action and Reaction" (1972) J.I.L.I.

Mannan, M.A. "The Development of the Islamic Law of Divorce in Pakistan" (1974) 5 J.I.C.L. 89

Mitra, B.B. "The Guardians and Wards Act 1890" (12th ed. Calcutta 1980)

Mokal, S.M. "The Guardians and Wards Act (VII of 1890) and the Majority Act (IX of 1875) With Commentary" (Lahore 1979)

Niazi, K. "Marriage with the People of the Book" Islamic Literature 17 (7) (1971) 13

Pearl, D.S. "Internal Conflict of Laws in Pakistan" (1968) 2 J.I.L.I. 362

Pearl, D.S. "The Impact of the Muslim Family Laws Ordinance in Quetta (Baluchistan) 1966-1968" (1971) 13 J.I.L.I. 561

Pearl, D.S. "Internal Conflict of Laws in Pakistan" (1968) 2 J.I.L.I. 362

Qadri, M.S.A. "Polygamy" 14 Islamic Thought 1 (1970) 1

Rao, P.K. "Muslim Polygamy and Divorce in India" (1969) 3 J.C.P.S.

Reza-ur-Rahim, "A Reconstruction of the Procedure of Divorce according to the Holy Qur'an" Islam and the Modern Age 74 (1975) 40

Schacht, J. "Adultery as an Impediment to Marriage in Islamic and in Canon Law" Archives d'Histoire du Droit Oriental 1 (1952) 105

Shehab, R. "Dowry in Islam" (1979) 2 Hamdard Islamicus 96

Singh, S. "Development of the Concept of Divorce in Muslim Law" (1973) Allahabad L.R. 117

Siraj, "The Legal Effect of Conversion to Islam" (1965, 1966) 7 Mal. L.R. 95

Stern, G. "Marriage in Early Islam" (London 1939)

Stout, L.C. "The Muslim Family Laws Ordinance" (Contributions to Indian Sociology 1979 p.13

The Control of Divorce, World Muslim League Magazine 311 (1967) 57

Ziadeh, F.J. "Equality (Kafa'ah) in the Muslim Law of Marriage" (1957) 6 A.J.C.L. 503

Zwemer, S.M. "The Law of Apostasy in Islam" (London 1924)

Zwemer, S.M. "The Law of Apostasy" (1924) 14 Muslim World 373

(6)   Reform (General Works)

Ahmad, K. "Studies in the Family Law of Islam" (Karachi 1961) [revised edition of "Marriage Commission X-Rayed"]

Ali, M. "Changes in Muslim Personal Law: Scope and Procedure" 14 Islamic Thought 2, 1 (1970)

Ali, S.A. "Impact of Technology and Western Values on Islamic Law in India 1947-65" in "India and Contemporary Islam" ed. S.T. Lockhandwalla (1971)

Anderson, J.N.D. "A Law of Personal Status for Iraq" (1960) 9 I.C.L.Q. 542

Anderson, J.N.D. "Changing Law in Developing Countries" (London 1963)

Anderson, J.N.D. and Coulson, N.J. "Islamic Law in Contemporary Cultural Change" (1967) 18 Saeculum 13

Anderson, J.N.D. "Islamic Law in the Modern World" (New York 1959)

Anderson, J.N.D. "Law Reform in the Muslim World" (London 1976)

Anderson, J.N.D. "Reforms of Family Law in Morocco" (1958) 2 Journal of African Law 140

Anderson, J.N.D. "The Role of Personal Statutes in Social Development in Islamic Countries" (1970) 13 Comparative Studies in Society and History 1, 16

Anderson, J.N.D. "The Tunisian Law of Personal Status" (1958) 7 I.C.L.Q. 262

Anderson, J.N.D. "Is the Sharia Doomed to Immutability?" (1966) 56 Muslim World 10

Bonderman, D. Modernization and Changing Perceptions of Islamic Law" (1968) 81 Harvard Law Review 1169

Coulson, N.J. "Law and Religion in Contemporary Islam" (1978) 29 Hast. L.J. 247

Coulson, N.J. "Reform of Family Law in Pakistan" (1957) VII Studia Islamica Fasc.

Esposito, J.L. "Muslim Family Law Reform: Toward an Islamic Methodology" (1979) 15 Islamic Studies 19

Esposito, J.L. "Women in Muslim Family Law" (New York 1982)

Esposito, J.L. "Perspectives on Islamic Law Reform: the Case of Pakistan" (1980) 13 J.I.L.P. 217

Fyzee, A.A.A. "A Modern Approach to Islam" (Bombay 1963)

Fyzee, A.A.A. "The Reform of Muslim Personal Law in India" (Bombay 1971)

374

Fyzee, A.A.A. "Islamic Law and Theology in India: Proposals
    for a Fresh Approach" (1954) M.E.J. 163
Geijbels, M. "The Sharia and Modernization of the Legal
    System in Islam" (1977) 19 al-Mushir 95
Government of Pakistan, "Report of the Commission on Marriage
    and Family Law" The Gazette Extraordinary, June 20 1956
    p. 1197
Hassan, S.R. "The Reconstruction of Legal Thought in Islam"
    (Lahore 1974)
Hinchcliffe, D. "The Iranian Family Protection Act" (1968) 17
    I.C.L.Q. 516
Imam, M. "Muslim Law Reforms in India and Uniform Civil Code"
    in "Minorities and the Law" ed. M. Imam, (Bombay 1972)
Jafar, M.M. "Future of Islamic Law in Pakistan" (1968) 17
    Iqbal 16
Jafar, M.M. "Future of Islamic Law in Pakistan - Judicial
    Process" (1968) 16 Iqbal 3
Kerr, M. "Islamic Reform" (Berkeley 1966)
Latafi, D. "Muslim Personal Law Reform" (1970) J.C.P.S. 111
Layish, A. "The Contribution of the Modernists to the
    Secularisation of Islamic Law" (1978) 14 M.E.S. 263
Liebesny, H. "Religious Law and Modernisation in the Moslem
    Near East" (1953) 2 A.J.C.L. 492
Mahmassani, S. "Muslims: Decadence and Renaissance -
    Adaptation of Islamic Jurisprudence to Modern Social
    Needs" (1954) 44 Muslim World 186
Mahmood, T. "An Indian Civil Code and Islamic Law" (
    1976)
Mahmood, T. "Family Law and Social Change" (Bombay 1975)
Mahmood, T. "Family Law Reform in the Muslim World" (New
    Delhi 1972) (ed.)
Mahmood, T. "Islamic Law in Modern India" (1972)
Mahmood, T. Civil Marriage Law: Perspectives and Prospects"
    (Bombay 1978)
Maududi, A. "Islamic Law and its Introduction in Pakistan"
    (Karachi 1955)
Muslehuddin, M. "Islamic Law and Social Change" (1982) 21
    Islamic Studies 23
Naqvi, S.A.R. "Modern Reforms in Muslim Family Laws - a
    General Study" (1974) 13 Islamic Studies 235
Naqvi, S.A.R. "Problems in the Codification of Islamic Law"
    International Islamic Conference 1968 40
Narmadakhodie (ed.) "Readings in Uniform Civil Code" (Bombay
    1975)
Pearl, D.S. "Codification in Islamic Law" (1979) 2 Jewish Law
    Annual
Pearl, D.S. "Within the Limits Prescribed by Allah" (1970) 3
    South Asian Review 313
Rahman, F. "A Survey of Modernisation of Muslim Family Law"
    (1980) 11 I J.M.E.S. 451)
Rahman, A. "Shariah in the 1500 Century of Hijra: Problems

and Prospects" (London 1981)

Schacht, J. "Islamic Law in Contemporary States" (1959) 8 A.J.C.L. 133

Schacht, J. "Problems of Modern Islamic Legislation" (1960) XII Studia Islamica 99

Tanzil-ur-Rahman "Islamization of Pakistan Law" (Karachi 1978)

Zayid, M. "The Radicals and the Fundamentalists and Muslim Personal Law" (1974) 5 Islam and the Modern Age 74

(7)   Social and Political Background

Abbot, F. "Islam and Pakistan" (New York 1968)

Ahmad, A. "An Intellectual History of Islam in India" (Edinburgh 1969)

Ahmad, A. "Islamic Modernism in India and Pakistan 1857 - 1964" (London 1967)

Ali, P.S. "Status of Women in the Muslim World" (Lahore 1975)

Awad, B.A. "The Status of Women in Islam" (1964) 8 Islamic Quarterly 17

Ayoob, M. (ed.) "The Politics of Islamic Reassertion" (London 1981)

Bahadur, K. "The Jama´at i Islami of Pakistan: Political Thought and Political Action" (New Delhi 1978)

Baig, M.R.A. "The Muslim Dilemma in India" (Vikas 1974)

Beck, L., Keddi, N. "Women in the Muslim World" (Cambridge, Mass. 1978)

Brijbhushan, J. "Muslim Women in Purdah and Out of It" (New Delhi 1980)

Cantwell Smith, W. "Modern Islam in India" (London 1946)

Donoohue, J.J. and Esposito, J.L. (eds.) "Islam in Transition: Muslim Perspectives" (New York 1982)

Esposito, J.L. "The Changing Role of Muslim Women" (1976) 7, 1 Islam and the Modern Age 29

Ghouse, M. "Secularism, Society and Law in India" (Delhi 1973)

Gledhill, A. "The Islamic Republic of Pakistan" (London 1967)

Gledhill, A. "The Republic of India" (London 1964)

Grunebaum, G.F. (ed.) "Unity and Variety in Islam" (Chicago 1955)

Harmen, S. "Plight of Muslims in India" (London 1977)

Hassan, F. "The Concept of State and Law in Islam" (Washington 1981)

Imam, Z. (ed.) "Muslims in India" (London 1975)

Khalid, D. "The Final Replacement of Parliamentary Democracy by the "Islamic System"" (1979) 20 Pakistan Orient 16

Levy, R. "The Social Structure of Islam" (Cambridge 1971)

Niazi, K. "Modern Challenges Faced by Muslim Families" (Islamabad 1975)

Qureshi, I.H. "The Muslim Community of the Indo-Pakistan Subcontinent 610 - 1947" (The Hague 1961)

Rothermund, D.   (ed.) "Islam in South Asia" (Wiesbaden 1975)

Sadar, Z.   "The Future of Muslim Civilisation" (London 1979)

Said, H.M.   "Enforcement of Islamic Laws in Pakistan" (1979) 2
     Hamdard Islamicus 61

Schimmel, A.   "Islam in the Indian Subcontinent" (Leiden 1980)

Sharma, G.S.   "Secularism: its Implications for Law and Life
     in India" (ed.) (Bombay 1966)

Smith, D.E.   "India as a Secular State" (Princeton 1963)

Smith, J.I.   (ed.) "Women in Contemporary Muslim Societies"
     (London 1980)

Titus, M.T.   "Indian Islam" (Oxford 1930, 1979)

NOTES

Chapter 1

1.   Matthew 22:21.
2.   See below, p.85
3.   See the Hanafi law of talaq, below, Chapter 4.
4.   Though the process had begun before Shafi'i, his work ensured its triumph.
5.   This is a matter of acute controversy, beyond the scope of this work: readers are referred to the bibliography and in particular the works of I. Goldziher, J. Schacht and N. Coulson.
6.   See the review of this material in Mst. Khurshid Jan v. Fazal Dad, PLD 1964 (W.P.) Lah. 558, below, p.27
7.   The so-called closing of the gate of ijtihad: see Mst. Khurshid Jan v. Fazal Dad, below, p.27
8.   Though more modern studies suggest that the traditional view of the dominance of procedure over substantive law in early western legal systems is exaggerated.
9.   e.g. the links between the Hanbali school of law and the Wahhabi movement.
10.   The Hanafi school of law predominates in the Indian subcontinent and is the subject of this book: the Hanafis are also to be found in Turkey, Syria, Afghanistan and Iraq, whilst the Malikis primarily live in Egypt, Somalia, Sudan, North, West and Central Africa. The Hanbalis are now only found in numbers in Saudi Arabia, the Shafi'is in Egypt, Arabia, Kenya and Tanzania.
11.   See note 7.
12.   Detailed discussion of this is outside the scope of this volume.
13.   See below, p.220.
14.   See Schacht's Introduction to Islamic Law, p. 21, (Oxford 1964).
15.   See Bousquet's Le Droit Musulman (Paris 1963).
16.   See T. Mahmood's The Muslim Law of India, p. 4, (New Delhi 1981).

17.   See the bibliography for detailed references to this matter.

18.   ibid.

19.   It was only in 1937 that legislation was enacted whereby the legal authority of custom was substantially abolished and the Shari´a reintroduced in many matters in the subcontinent.

20.   See Jafri Begam´s case, (1885) I.L.R. 7 All. 822.

21.   In Waghela Rajsanji v. Sheikh Masludin (1887) 14 I.A. 89,96.

22.   See Derrett´s <u>Religion Law and the State in India</u>, (London 1968).

23.   e.g. Caste Disabilities (Removal) Act 1850; Abolition of Slavery Act 1843; Child Marriage Restraint Act 1929; Dissolution of Muslim Marriages Act 1939.

24.   In certain areas the Muslim law was almost completely superseded by English inspired codes: Indian Contract Act 1872; Indian Evidence Act 1872; Indian Penal Code 1860.

25.   <u>Introduction to Islamic Law</u>, p. 98, (supra).

26.   Mst. Khurshid Bibi v. Mohd. Amin, PLD 1967 SC 97, below, p.228, 271.

27.   See <u>The Politics of Islamic Reassertion</u>, Chapter 8 (W. Richter), (London 1981).

28.   e.g. Offence of Zina (Enforcement of Hudood) Ordinance 1979, Offence of Qazf (Enforcement of Hudood) Ordinance 1979, etc., see below, p.240.

29.   PLD 1980 FSC 1.

30.   See p.82.

31.   PLD 1980 SC 160.

32.   See p.67.

33.   Chief Martial Law Administrator´s Order No. 1 of 1981, s.4.

34.   i.e. The Indian Independence Act 1947 and the Government of India Act 1935 together with all enactments amending or supplementing the latter Act but not including the Abolition of Privy Council Jurisdiction Act 1949.

35.   United Provinces v. Atiqa, AIR 1941 F.C.16.

36.   State of Bombay v. Narasu Appa Mali, AIR 1952 Bom. 85.

37.   See T. Mahmood´s <u>Muslim Personal Law: Role of the State in the Subcontinent</u>, pp. 106-109.

38.   See Chapter 2.

39.   Quite apart from the forces of tradition and of religious adherence!

40.   Which mitigates the consequences of apostasy.

41.   See T. Mahmood´s <u>The Muslim Law of India</u>, Chapter 2, (supra).

42.   ibid.

43.   See text to notes 21, 22, above.

44.   See Chapter 2.

45. Skinner v. Orde (1871) 14 M.I.A. 309.

46. See Resham Bibi v. Khuda Bakhsh (1938) I.L.R. 19 Lah. 277.

47. See Batholemew (1952) 1 I.C.L.Q. 325, Pearl (1975) 17 J.I.L.I. 272.

48. See Chapter 5.

49. See D. Pearl's _Interpersonal Conflict of Laws: India Pakistan and Bangladesh_.

50. Aga Mahomed Jafar v. Koolsum Bee Bee (1897) 24 I.A. 196.

51. ibid.

52. Bagar Ali v. Anjuman Ara (1903) 30 I.A. 94.

53. ibid.

54. Veerankutty v. Kutti Umma, AIR 1956 Mad. 1004: Mohd. Ismail v. Adul Rashid (1956) ILR 1 All. 143.

Chapter 2

1. Mst. Khurshid Bibi v. Mohd. Amin, PLD 1967 S.C. 97.

2. See p.114.

3. Mt. Atiqa Begum v. Mohd. Ibrahim, AIR 1916 PC 250.

4. Nawab Sadiq Ali v. Jai Kishori, (1928) 30 Bomb. L.R. 1346.

5. ibid.

6. Joygun Nessa Bibi v. Mohd. Ali, AIR 1938 Cal. 71, but see the case of Allah Diwaya v. Kammon Mai, PLD 1957 651, which holds it void.

7. Habibur Rahman Chowdhury v. Altaf Ali Chowdhury, (1921) 48 I.A. 114, in the matter of Ram Kumari, (1891) ILR 18 Cal. 264.

8. Quran Sura 4 Verse 3.

9. See Chapter 1.

10. Tunisian Law of Personal Status 1956 Art.18.

11. It is understood that additional practical difficulties exist for state employees in India: it is a condition of employment that permission be obtained from the employer before contracting a second marriage, which permission is never given.

12. Abdool Razack v. Aga Mahomed Jaffer Bindaneem, (1894) 21 I.A. 56.

13. PLD 1967 S.C. 580.

14. A marriage between a Muslim woman and a Christian man under Muslim law being, of course, impossible under Muslim law.

15. cp. Skinner v. Orde (1871) 14 MIA 309 with John Jiban Chandra v. Abinash, ILR (1939) 2 Cal. 13.

16. Muhd. Mustafizur Rahman Khan v. Rina Khan, PLD 1967 Dacca 652.

17. Mohan v. Mohan, AIR 1943 Sind. 311.

18. See the standard practitioner texts for exhaustive lists.

19. Tajbi v. Mowla Khan, ILR 1917 Bom. 845.

20. ibid, see p.122.

21. Kummali Abubukker v. Vengatt Marakkar, AIR 1970 Ker. 277.

22. Abdul Latif Khan v. Niyaz Ahmad Khan, ILR 1909 All. 343.

23. Shahzada Begum v. Abdul Hamid, PLD 1950 Lah. 504.

24. Abdool Razack v. Aga Mahomed Jaffer Bindaneem, (1894) 21 I.A. 56.

25. Nasim Akhtar v. State, PLD 1968 Lah. 841: cp. Habib v. State, PLD 1980 Lah. 791.

26. See e.g. Assam Moslem Marriage and Divorce Registration Act 1935; Orissa Mohammedan Marriage and Divorce Registration Act 1949; Bengal Mohammedan Marriage and Divorce Registration Act 1876.

27. T. Mahmood's Muslim Personal Law. Role of the State in the Subcontinent p. 71.

28. See J.N.D. Anderson B.S.O.A.S. XIII (1950) 357.

29. Shahzada Begum v. Abdul Hamid, PLD 1950 Lah. 504.

30. Muhd. Hayat v. Muhd. Nawaz, ILR 1935 Lah. 18.

31. Syed Saib v. Meeram Bee, 20 M.L.J. 12.

32. Tajbi v. Mowla Khan, ILR 1917 Bom. 845.

33. Whether through lack of capacity or form: there is simply no marriage.

34. Such women are called mooharim.

35. Rashid Amhad v. Anisa Khatum, (1931) 59 I.A. 21.

36. But see Chapter 5 and Abdul Ghani v. Taleh Bibi, PLD 1962 Lah. 531.

37. Habibur Rahman Chowdhury v. Altaf Ali Chowdhury, (1921) 48 I.A. 114.

38. See Ameer Ali, Vol II, 282.

39. See e.g. Abdool Razack v. Aga Mahomed Jaffer Bindaneem, (1893) 21 I.A. 56.

40. See Seyyed Hossein Nasr (ed.): Shi'ite Islam, p. 227.

41. See S.A. Hussain: Marriage Customs among Muslims in India.

Chapter 3

1. See below, p.150.

2. Traite de Droit Musulman Compare, II, 196.

3. Nasra Begum v. Rijwan Ali, AIR 1980 All. 118.

4. Hamira Bibi v. Zubaida Bibi, AIR 1916 PC 46.

5. but cp. Abdur Rashid v. Mst. Shaheen Bibi, PLD 1980 Pesh. 37.

6. Baillie, Digest of Moohummadan Law Book I, 2nd ed. 95.

7. Mussumat Bebee Bachun v. Sheikh Hamid Hossein, (1871-2) 14 M.I.A. 377,86.

8. Baillie, op. cit. I, 96.

9. ibid, I, 94.
10. Hamira Bibi v. Zubaida Bibi, AIR 1916 PC 46.
11. Jatoi v. Jatoi, PLD 1967 SC 580.
12. Hamira Bibi v. Zubaida Bibi, AIR 1916 PC 46.
13. Eidan v. Mazhar Husain, (1877) ILR 1 All. 483.
14. Nasir ud din Shah v. Amatul Mughni, AIR 1948 Lah. 135.
15. Husseinkhan v. Ghulab Khatum, (1911) ILR 35 Bom. 386.
16. Baillie, op. cit. I, 130.
17. Mt. Razina Khatun v. Mt. Abeda Khatun, AIR 1937 All. 39.
18. Mohd. Sadiq Ali Khan v. Fakhr Jahan Begam, (1931) 59 I.A. 1.
19. Iftikarunissa Begum v. Nawab Amjad Ali Khan, (1871) 7 Beng. L.R. 643.
20. Qasim Husain v. Kaniz Sakina, (1932) ILR 54 All. 806.
21. Shah Bano v. Iftikhar Mohd. Khan, PLD 1956 Kar. 363.
22. Tajbi v. Nattar Sheriff, AIR 1940 Mad. 888.
23. Fatawa Alamgirriyya Vol. I, p. 124.
24. per Abu Hanifa and Muhammad: Abu Yusuf would grant half dower.
25. Baillie, op. cit. I, 97.
26. Baillie, op. cit. I, 98.
27. Abdul Latif v. Niyaz Ahmad, (1909) ILR 31 All. 343.
28. Baillie, op. cit. I, 98.
29. Malik Iftikhar Wali v. Sarwari Begum, AIR 1929 All. 369.
30. See note 26.
31. Bismillah Begam v. Shahr Bano Begam, (1914) 1 O.L.J. 1.
32. Refusal may be inferred from conduct: Nur-ud-din Ahmad v. Masuda Khanam, PLD 1957 Dacca 242.
33. Husseinkhan v. Ghulab Khatum, (1911) ILR 35 Bom. 386.
34. Anis Begam v. Muhammad Istafa Wali Khan, (1933) ILR 55 All. 743.
35. Mst. Rahilan v. Sana Ullah, PLD 1959 Lah. 470.
36. Muniram v. Mukhtar Begam, AIR 1940 All. 521.
37. Kapore Chand v. Kidar Nissa Begum, AIR 1953 SC 413.
38. Muniram v. Mukhtar Begam, AIR 1940 All. 521.
39. Maina Bibi v. Chaudhri Vakil, (1925) 52 I.A. 145.
40. AIR 1916 PC 46.
41. Majidmian v. Bibi Saheb Jan, (1916) ILR 40 Bom. 34.
42. Ali Bakhsh v. Allahad Khan, (1910) 32 All. 551.
43. Tahir-un-Nissa Bibi v. Nawab Hassan, (1914) ILR 36 All. 558.
44. Abdul Wahab v. Mushtaq Ahmad, AIR 1944 All. 36.
45. Shaikh Mohd. Zobair v. Mst. Bibi Sahidan, AIR 1942 Pat. 210.

46. Muzaffar Ali Khan v. Parbati (1907) ILR 29 All. 640.
47. Cooverbai Nasarwanji Bulsara v. Hayatbi Budhanbhar, AIR 1943 Bom. 372.
48. Muhammad Hussain v. Bashiran (1914) 12 All. L.J. 1114.
49. Abdulla v. Shams-ul-Haq, AIR 1921 All. 262.
50. Beebee Bachun v. Sheikh Hamid Hossein (1871) 14 M.I.A. 377.
51. ibid.
52. Mst. Nawasi Begum v. Mst. Dilafroz Begam, AIR 1927 All. 39.
53. Ghulam Ali v. Sagir ul Nissa, (1901) ILR 23 All. 432, but cp. Mohitan v. Zubera, AIR 1954 Pat. 47.
54. The so-called as-sumat: see note 55.
55. Nasir Ahmed Khan v. Asmat Jehan Begum, PLD 1967 Pesh. 328.
56. s.91. When the terms of a contract, or of a grant, or of any other disposition of property, have been reduced to the form of a document..... no evidence shall be given in proof of the terms of such contract, grant or other disposition of property, or of such matter, except the document itself, or secondary evidence of its contents in cases in which secondary evidence is admissible under the provisions hereinbefore contained.
  s.92. When the terms of any such contract, grant or other disposition of property, or any other matter required by law to be reduced to the form of a document, have been proved according to the last section, no evidence of any oral agreement or statement shall be admitted, as between the parties to any such instrument or their representatives in interest, for the purpose of contradicting, varying, adding to or subtracting from, its terms.
57. Abdul Rahiman, v. Aminbai, (1935) 59 Bom. 426.
58. Moonshee Buzloor v. Shumsoonissa Begum, (1867) 11 M.I.A. 551.
59. Mohd. Zaman v. Irshad Begum, PLD 1967 Lah. 1104.
60. See note 32 and text thereto.
61. Itwari v. Asghari, AIR 1960 All. 686.
62. Resham Bibi v. Muhd. Shafi, PLD 1967 AJK 32.
63. Mulkhan Bibi v. Muhd. Wazir, PLD 1959 Lah. 710.
64. See below, p.157.
65. It did not do so in classical law, but does by custom.
66. Ahmed Ali v. Sabha Khatun Bibi, PLD 1952 Dacca 385.
67. Agha Mohd. Jaffer v. Kolsoom Bibi, (1897) ILR 25 Cal. 9.
68. Azmatullah v. Imtiaz Begum, PLD 1959 Lah. 167.
69. Traite de Droit Musulman Compare, Vol. II, 271.
70. Rashid Ahmad v. Anisa Khatun, AIR 1932 PC 23.
71. Ghulam Rasul v. Collector, Lahore PLD 1974 Lah. 495.
72. Mohd. Haneefa v. Pathummal Beevi, 1972 K.L.T. 512.

73. See T. Mahmood's The Muslim Law of India, p. 133.

74. AIR 1979 S.C. 362.

75. Rashid Ahmad Khan v. Nasim Ara, PLD 1968 Lah. 93: Mst. Hajiran Bibi v. Abdul Khaliq, PLD 1981 Lah. 761.

76. Mohd. Ali v. Fareedunnissa Begam, AIR 1970 AP 298.

77. Badarannissa Bibi v. Mafiatalla (1871) 7 Beng. I.R. 442.

78. Yoosuf Ali v. Fyzoonissa, 15 W.R. 296.

79. per Ameer Ali, Vol. II, 321-322.

80. per Ameer Ali, Vol. II, 321, sed quaere.

81. Sabir Khan v. Bilatunnissa, (1919) C.W.N. 888.

82. Hamidoollah v. Faizunnissa, (1882) 8 Cal. 327.

83. Meherally Mooraj v. Sakerbhanoon Bai, (1905) 7 B.L.R. 602, but see Safiuddin v. Soneka, AIR 1955 Assam 153: Ameer Ali, Vol. II, 321.

84. Though note Khwala Mohd. Khan v. Nawab Husaini Begum, (1910) 37 I.A. 152.

85. Khatun Bibi v. Rajjab, AIR 1926 All. 615.

86. Ayatunnessa Bebee v. Karam Ali, (1909) ILR 36 Cal. 23.

87. s.2 (vii) (f): see Chapter 4.

Chapter 4

1. Azizul Husan v. Mohammad Faruq, (1934) ILR 9 Luck. 401.

2. Ma Mi v. Kallandar Ammal, (1927) 54 I.A. 61.

3. ibid.

4. Ahmed Kasim Molla v. Khatun Bibi, (1932) ILR 59 Cal. 833.

5. Ma Mi v. Kallandar Ammal, (1927) 54 I.A. 61.

6. Muhd. Azam Khan v. Akhtar un Nissa Begum, PLD 1957 Lah. 195.

7. Ahmed Kasom Molla v. Khatun Bibi, (1932) ILR 59 Cal. 833.

8. Aklima Khatun v. Mahibur Rahman, PLD 1963 Dacca 602.

9. Ali Nawaz Gardezi v. Lt.Col. Muhd. Yusuf, PLD 1963 SC 51.

10. Inamul Islam v. Hussain Bano, PLD 1976 Lah. 1466 cp. Parveen Chaudhry v. VIth Senior Judge, Karachi PLD 1976 Kar. 416.

11. Fahmida Bibi v. Mukhtar Ahmad, PLD 1972 Lah. 694.

12. Noor Bibi v. Pir Bux, AIR 1950 Sind. 8: Aboobacker Haji v. Mamu Koya, 1971 K.L.T. 663.

13. Mst. Resham Bibi v. Mohd. Shafi, PLD 1967 AJK 32: Majida Khatun Bibi v. Paghalu Muhd., PLD 1963 Dacca 583.

14. s.125 (3) (India) but see s.488 (Pakistan).

15. PLD 1967 SC 97.

16. Mohd. Ishaque v. Ahsan Ahmad, PLD 1975 Lah. 1118.

17. Parveen Begum v. Muhammad Ali, PLD 1981 Lah. 116.

18. Shamshad Begum v. Abdul Haque, PLD 1975 Kar. 855.

19. In Siddiq v. Sharfan 1968 PLD 411 culpability was made a criterion for grant of khul´ itself.

20. Hakim Zadi v. Nawaz Ali 1972 PLD Kar. 540 states the correct position on grant and payment.

21. Mukhtar Ahmed v. Ume Kasoom, PLD 1975 Lah. 805: cp. Mumtaz Mai v. Ghulam Nabi, PLD 1969 BJ 5, Muhd. Ishaque v. Ahsan Ahmad, PLD 1975 Lah. 1118.

22. D. Hinchcliffe, 1968, 2 JILI 13.

23. Zubeda Begum v. Vazir Mahomed Rahimbux, AIR 1940 Sind. 145.

24. Abdul Karim v. Aminabai, AIR 1935 Bom. 308.

25. Ahmad Husain v. Mst. Amir Bano, AIR 1940 All. 63.

26. Mst. Ghulan Sakina v. Falak Sher Allah Bakhsh, AIR 1950 Lah. 45.

27. Ghulam Mohd. v. Emperor, AIR 1933 Lah. 88.

28. Ala ud Din v. Mst. Farkhanda Akhtar, PLD 1953 Lah. 131.

29. Daulan v. Dosa, PLD 1956 Lah. 712.

30. Muni v. Habib Khan, PLD 1956 Lah. 403: Sarwar Jan v. Abdul Majid, PLD 1965 Pesh. 5.

31. Abdul Karim v. Mst. Amina Bibi, AIR 1935 Bom. 308: Abdul Sattar v. Wakila Bibi, PLD 1965 Psh. 1: see note 30.

34. Ghulam Bhik v. Hussain Begum, PLD 1957 Lah. 998.

35. At least in India: for Pakistan see note 41. See also Zafar Husain v. Ummat ur Rahman, AIR 1919 All. 182.

36. Ahmed Suleman Vohra v. Mst. Bai Fatma, AIR 1931 Bom. 76.

37. Mst. Lelan v. Rahim Bakhsh, PLD 1951 BJ 91.

38. Ghulam Bhik v. Hussain Begum, PLD 1957 Lah. 998.

39. Thereby requiring the wife to prove a negative!

40. Abdul Aziz v. Mst. Bashiran Bibi, PLD 1958 Lah. 59.

41. Because of the Offence of Qazf (Enforcement of Hudood) Ordinance 1979, which reintroduces the Muslim offence and liability to Muslim penalties for false allegations of unchastity and specifies the procedure to be adopted, which does not in all respects conform to the earlier case law.

Chapter 5

1. See text to note 11.
2. See Chapter 2.
3. See Chapter 2.
4. See Chapter 1.
5. Sibt Muhd. v. Muhd. Hameed, (1926) ILR 48 All. 625.
6. Abdul Ghani v. Taleh Bibi, PLD 1962 Lah. 531.
7. Habibur Rahman v. Altaf Ali, (1921) 48 I.A. 114.
8. Offence of Zina (Enforcement of Hudood) Ordinance 1979 (Pakistan).
9. Sukha v. Ninni, AIR 1966 Raj. 163.
10. See T. Mahmood´s The Muslim Law of India, pp. 150-1.
11. The Adoption of Children Bill 1972.

12. The precise order is a matter of dispute: see the standard practitioner works.

13. See Mulla, 18th ed., p. 384, rejecting R. Wilson, ss.140-2.

14. Moosa Seethi v. Mariyakutty, (1954) ILR 1 T.C. 690 cp. note 15.

15. Ghulam Fatima v. Mohd. Bashir, PLD 1958 Lah. 596.

16. The obligation extends in Muslim law to those within the bar of consanguinity prohibiting marriage.

17. Idu v. Amiran, (1886) ILR 8 All. 322.

18. Mt. Haidri v. Jawwad Ali Shah, AIR 1934 All. 722.

19. Mohd. Bashir v. Ghulam Fatima, PLD 1953 Lah. 73: Amar Ilahi v. Rashida Akhtar, PLD 1955 Lah. 412.

20. Abasi v. Dunne, (1878) ILR 1 All. 598.

21. Khatija Begum v. Ghulam Dastgir, (1975) 2 An. W.R. 194,197. See also note 24.

22. Guardians and Wards Act 1890, s.7 (1) (b).

23. Zohra Begum v. Sh. Latif Ahmad Munawwar, PLD 1965 Lah. 695.

24. Munawar Jan v. Mohd. Afsar Khan, PLD 1962 (W.P.) Lah. 142.

25. Amar Ilahi v. Mst. Rashida Akhtar, PLD 1955 Lah. 412.

26. Imambandi v. Mutsaddi, (1918) 45 I.A. 73.

27. Eishu Chughani v. Ranglal Agarwala, AIR 1975 Cal. 627: Rahimuddin v. Abdul Malik Bhuyia, PLD 1968 Dacca 801.

28. Zaitoon Begum v. Central Bank Ltd., PLD 1961 Lah. 888 states this more widely.

29. Mir Sarwarjan v. Fakhruddin Mahomed Chowdhuri, (1912) 39 I.A. 1.

30. See s. 17.

31. Imambandi v. Mutsaddi, (1918) 45 I.A. 73.

32. Solema Bibi v. Hafez Mahamad Hossein, (1927) ILR 54 Cal. 687.

33. Guardians and Wards Act 1890 s. 27.

34. Hadish Bepari v. Bogmulla Sheikh, (1898) ILR 25 Cal. 551.

35. See Chapter 4.

36. Ayub Hasan v. Akhtari, AIR 1963 All. 525.

37. Under the Child Marriage Restraint Act 1929. See Chapter 2.

TABLE OF LEGISLATION REPRODUCED

Constitutional Provisions

TABLE OF CASES REPRODUCED

TABLE OF ABBREVIATIONS

A.I.R.	All India Reporter
A.J.C.L.	American Journal of Comparative Law
All. L.J.(R)	Allahabad Law Journal (Review)
Andh. P.L.J.	Andhra Pradesh Law Journal
Bengal L.R. (BLR)	Bengal Law Reports
Bom. L.R.	Bombay Law Reports
B.S.O.A.S.	Bulletin of the School of Oriental and African Studies
Cal. L.J. (C.L.J.)	Calcutta Law Journal
Cal. W.N.	Calcutta Weekly Notes
Camb. L.J.	Cambridge Law Journal
Dacca L.R.	Dacca Law Reports
Geo. W.L.R.	George Washington Law Review
Hast. L.J.	Hastings Law Journal
I.A.	Law Reports, Indian Appeals Series
I.C.	Indian Cases
I.C.	Islamic Culture
I.C.L.Q.	International and Comparative Law Quarterly
I.J.M.E.S.	International Journal of Middle East Studies
I.L.R.	Indian Law Reports
I.Y.B.I.A.	Indian Yearbook of International Affairs
J.A.S. Pakistan	Journal of the Asiatic Society of Pakistan
J.I.C.L.	Journal of Islamic and Comparative Law
J.I.L.I.	Journal of the Indian Law Institute
J.I.L.P.	Journal of International Law and Politics
J. Pak. Hist. Soc.	Journal of the Pakistan Historical Society

J.R.C.A.S.	Journal of the Royal Central Asia Society
Ker. L.J.	Kerela Law Journal
K.L.T.	Kerela Law Times
Madras L.J. (MLJ)	Madras Law Journal
Mal. L.R.	Malaysia Law Review
M.I.A.	Moore´s Indian Appeals
N.Y.U.J. of Int. Law and Politics	New York University Journal of International Law and Politics
O.L.J.	Oudh Law Journal
P.L.D.	All Pakistan Legal Decisions
R.M.E.S.	Review of Middle East Studies
W.R.	Weekly Reporter

GLOSSARY OF COMMON ARABIC TERMS

ahsan	the best
´ariya	gift of usufruct of property
´asaba	agnatic relations
as-su´at	public announcement of dower in excess of private agreement
´awl	reduction
´ayn	corpus
bain	irrevocable
baligh	major, adult
batil	void
bulugh	puberty
dhimmi	non-Muslim person protected by Islamic state
fasid	irregular
faskh	judicial dissolution
fiqh	jurisprudence, study of the Sharia
hadd(hadood)	Quranic penalty(ies)
hadith	tradition
haj	pilgrimage
hasan	approved
haram	forbidden
harbi	infidel, enemy
hiba	gift
hidana	custody
´idda	wife´s period of waiting after divorce/death of husband
ijab	offer
ijma	consensus
ijtihad	personal reasoning
ila	oath of abstinence
imam	leader
isnad	chain, link
istidlal	inference
istihsan	reasoning on the basis of juristic preference

395

istislah	reasoning on the basis of public policy
iqrar	acknowledgment (of relationship)
iwad	return
´jam	unlawful conjunction
kafa´a	equality of the spouses
kalima	profession of tenets of Islam
khul´	dissolution of marriage at wife's request
kitabi	man of a revealed religion
kitabiyya	woman of a revealed religion
li´an	mutual imprecation
madhab	school of law
mahr/mehr	dower
mal	property
manafi	usufruct
mard-al-maut	death sickness
mazalim	administrative court
mubara´at	dissolution of marriage by mutual consent
mujtahid	jurist who exercises ijtihad
muqallid	jurist who follows, imitates (see taqlid)
musha´a	undivided share of property
mut´a	temporary marriage
mutawalli	one who manages a waqf
nafaqa	maintenance
nasab	consanguinity
nashiza	disobedient woman
nashuz	disobedience
nikah	marriage
nikahnama	marriage deed
parda	veiling of women
pardanashin	veiled woman
qabul	acceptance
qadi/qazi	judge
qanun	order, law, regulation
qiyas	reasoning by analogy
radd	return, proportionate increase
raj´i	revocable
ra´y	independent personal reasoning, discretion
riba	interest on a loan, usury
rukhsati	taking of bride to the matrimonial home for cohabitation
sadaqa	present, gift with motive of religious merit
sahih	valid
shari´a	the recommended path of Islam: Islamic Law

shart/shurut	condition(s)
shufa´a	right of pre-emption
siyassa shari´a	government in accordance with the Law
sunna	practice (of the Prophet)
talab	demand
talaq	repudiation
talaq as-sunna ahsan	most approved form of talaq
talaq as-sunna hasan	approved form of talaq
talaq al bid´a	disapproved form of talaq
talaq-i-tafwid	delegated talaq
talaq kubra	third talaq
talaq sughra	talaq pronounced once
talaqnama	divorce deed
tafliq	piecing together of laws from different schools/jurists
taqlid	imitation, following of ijma, precedent
ta´sib	agnatic link
tazir´	discretionary punishment
tuhr	period of "purity" between menstruations
ulama	theologians
umma	community
´umra	life interest
vakil	agent
wali	guardian
waqf	settlement
waqf ala´ l aulad	family waqf
waqf khayri	public waqf
waqfnama	settlement deed
waqif	waqf settlor/donor
wasi	executor
zakat	alms, religious tax
zihar	impious declaration
zina	illicit sexual intercourse/ relations

INDEX